# pathologies of modern space

Empty Space,

Urban Anxiety, and

the Recovery of

the Public Self

kathryn milun

Routledge
Taylor & Francis Group
NEW YORK AND LONDON

First published 2007 by Routledge
605 Third Avenue, New York, NY 10017
4 Park Square, Milton Park, Abingdon, Oxon OX14 4RN

*Routledge is an imprint of the Taylor & Francis Group, an informa business*



**Library of Congress Cataloging-in-Publication Data**

Milun, Kathryn.
Pathologies of modern space : empty space, urban anxiety, and the recovery of the public self / Kathryn Milun.
p. cm.
Includes bibliographical references and index.

ISBN 0-415-95273-5 (hb) -- ISBN 0-415-95274-3 (pb) 1. Agoraphobia--Social aspects. 2. Agoraphobia--Environmental aspects. 3. Public spaces. I. Title.
RC552.A44M55 2006 362.196'85225--dc22
2006028460

ISBN 13: 978-0-415-95273-6 (hbk)
ISBN 13: 978-0-415-95274-3 (pbk)

# Contents

Yodaville: U.S. First urban bombing range. This photograph appeared on the front page of the *Arizona Republic* on August 23, 1999. Marine Corps photographer unknown.

# Preface

## *Empty Space as a Structure of Feeling in the Urban Commons*

I saw the above photo of the U.S. military's first urban bombing range on the front page of the local newspaper when I first moved to Phoenix in August 1999. The ironic heading, "Arizona's Newest Town Inviting Target," referred to the newly completed two-million-dollar structure only seven miles from the U.S. border with Mexico, a potential first stop for illegal immigrants who see its distant street lights, not far from a popular border crossing.[1] It seems outlandish to say that this image of a replica urban war zone appeared emblematic to me of the massively air-conditioned modern American city I was making my home. After all, according to the reporter who covered the site's opening, "there [was] a decidedly Third World feel to the place." It had narrow streets, a shantytown area, and a mock soccer field painted green. No one could mistake it for the U.S.'s sixth largest city, with its signature urban freeway system and sprawling suburbs. "It's a bleak, nightmarish Legoland," wrote the reporter. But to me, working on this book about the feel of public space in modern cities, the idea of a civil space that overlaps with a military one, of civilians who unwittingly inhabit a place that is often at odds with civil habitation, was both a far cry from my situation and an eerie echo of what I was finding in my research.

I was investigating how we come to feel comfortable in cities like Phoenix that are out of sync with their environments, how we create public selves at ease in such gigantic forms of civil space. I was asking a specific set of questions about the relation between the modern Euro-American city's most public forms of space and the psychosomatic public self that these spaces support: What kinds of public space provoke the most anxiety in the modern urbanite? What psychological treatments have we created to help those whose discomfort in public space is so great that they are deemed pathological and seek medical help to recover a sense of their public selves? And finally, what do these treatments tell us more generally about the relations among public space, embodied personhood, and the normative expectations of a public self? The public spaces that provoked the most phobic and pathologized reactions, I was finding, arose from urban areas that were opened up into vast, expansive domains. They were forms of urban emptiness that had become core features of the modern city: in the nineteenth century they were the monumentally broad national squares and wide boulevards that tunneled through razed neighborhoods opening up European capitals; in the twentieth and twenty-first centuries they are mammoth shopping malls surrounded by vast parking terrains and urban freeway systems that stretch and speed ever farther out from city centers. Thus, the image of the U.S. Air Force's new urban bombing range, set in the vast expanses of the Sonoran Desert, reminded me of a spatial imaginary that underlies modern urban design. It evoked the dangerous and very modern idea that, to function with ever greater efficiency, our cities be built out of ever more vast tracks of empty space.

As I pursued my study of empty space as a structure of feeling in the modern city, my research pointed to a startling overlap between psychiatric treatments for soldiers suffering battlefield trauma and treatments for civilians suffering phobic reactions to these vast forms of urban emptiness. For example, in 2004 a drug called propranolol was the object of a clinical study by a Harvard University psychiatrist in the emergency room of a Boston hospital. The drug was initially used to treat the phobic states of Vietnam War veterans who experienced recurring memories of battlefield horrors. In the urban trials, however, the beta-blocking drug was used for the civilian population at large, aiming to help those whose strong visceral memories of a car accident, one of the most common urban traumas, would still prevent them years later from driving on the freeways. By acting preemptively, the drug was found to block the body's capacity to viscerally register the memory of a traumatic experience. Psychologists have long believed that strong, traumatic memories register in the body in visceral ways that often bypass the symbolic systems that make them accessible for conscious recall. Instead, the nervous system holds them in nonsymbolic ways, making the person subject to inexplicable surges of unmarked, objectless anxiety triggered by specific, but apparently meaningless, details. The Boston study found that propranolol effectively interrupts the chemical processes involved in the initial, visceral traumatic imprint. Compared to a control group which did not receive the drug, a person given propranolol immediately following a car accident did not respond with the same heightened reaction three months later when listening to a tape recording that recounted details of the accident: there was no significantly quickened heartbeat or change in breathing rhythms. The drug, taken shortly after the traumatic incident, could dull an initial imprint on the body's autonomic system and thus contribute to a dulling of the future memory of the event. Not only a car accident, but rape—another traumatic event commonly treated in hospital emergency rooms—is a candidate for this drug.

Propranolol may become the potentially overanxious urbanite's drug of choice, but those studying and marketing the drug have not lost sight of its value for the soldier suffering from what is now called post-traumatic stress disorder. There is talk of making the drug available to U.S. soldiers in Iraq, as well as those who still suffer traumas from the first Gulf War, the Vietnam War, and so on. In the past two years, since news of the propranolol studies (also taking place in France and Sweden) have hit the press, journalists and ethicists have warned of the ethical consequences of tampering with memories of the terrible events that happen in war zones. Soldiers fighting insurgents in urban neighborhoods where the enemy is often indistinguishable from civilians might call on the drug to console themselves, it is feared, when making the difficult decision about whether or not to blow up a residence if a pill in their knapsack could assure them that remorse for a mistake would not weigh so heavily on them in the future.[2]

In my research I found considerable historical evidence of this overlap of military and civilian treatments for phobic conditions arising in conjunction with the built emptiness of modern urban space. This was a surprise. I knew that other scholars had found connections between the rise of modern psychiatry and the treatment of battlefield trauma after World War I.[3] I also knew that cultural historians had remarked on the relation between urban emptiness and the construction of the modern public self. But I had never encountered this triangulated connection among the treatment of soldiers, the spatial layout of the modern city's most public sites, and the recovery of a civilian public self. Unlike these previous cultural analysts, I was also noticing that modern urban anxiety presented a conundrum that went beyond social constructivist theories of the self. The clinical literature showed that acute anxiety, triggered by the materiality of specific forms of modern public space, could not be effectively treated as simply a symbolic problem in an individual psyche. Therefore, for me to consider the larger social questions posed by such anxiety only in terms of the inadequate symbolic constructions our culture offers to a highly sensitized self appeared similarly wanting.

Without lapsing into biological reductionism, how could I account for the successes and failures of the various treatments our society has offered those who fit into a broad and increasingly gendered pattern of nervous reaction to public space, where the most common feature is a highly charged kind of emptiness? Why does this emptiness speak, as it were, so directly to the nervous system? What can the more successful treatments, like propanolol, tell us more generally about the normative demands urban space makes on an embodied public self?

In some ways my findings recalled what the esteemed urbanist Richard Sennett had described in the mid-1970s when he noted that the emptiness of public space in modernist urban design, what he called "dead public space," encouraged a specific kind of public self. In his seminal work *The Fall of Public Man: On the Social Psychology of Capitalism*, Sennett argued that so-called International Style, with its skyscrapers and other large-scale, high density buildings, created surrounding street-level areas of "dead space." Planners refer to such public space as the efficient, "traffic-flow-support-nexus for the vertical whole." But the psychological effects of this space, Sennett found, merited closer scrutiny. "The city street acquires, then, a peculiar function," wrote Sennett, "to permit motion—if it regulates motion too much, by lights, one-ways, and the like, motorists become nervous or angry. . . . Today, we experience an ease of motion unknown to any prior civilization, and yet motion has become the most anxiety-laden of daily activities."[4]

Sennett claimed that empty or dead public space only intensified a transformation of the Western urban dweller's public self ongoing since the massive urban population increases brought on by the industrial revolution. In the preindustrial cities of the ancien régime, Sennett argued that the bourgeois citizen understood that clothes, manners, and gestures were modes of civility that were worn like masks in public space. The public self, then, was a matter of playacting with a variety of roles when encountering friends and, increasingly, strangers in the relatively open spaces of the city's streets. As capitalist modes of production brought ever more citizens into the city for jobs, Sennett found that the increased encounter with strangers transformed the playful experience of the citizen's public self, which began to take on characteristics of the proliferating commodities around him. Just as new mass-produced items attracted buyers by advertising the boundlessly mysterious power of their distinctiveness (what Karl Marx called the fetish power of the commodity), people, too, Sennett claimed, began to display their public selves as a form of uniqueness. In a manner well studied by critical theorists of the Frankfurt school, the public self became a way for the masses to express their individual uniqueness in the form of a boundless "authenticity." Under these new circumstances, the role play associated with social masks was eventually no longer seen positively, as playful, but instead as inauthentic. Sennett, and later Christopher Lasch, claimed that the post–World War II project of the Western public self to express its "authenticity" was at bottom an impossibly narcissistic project. As postwar public space was redesigned by International Style and the automobile, the few opportunities to encounter strangers in ways that lead to "authentic" exchange were doomed by the impossibly boundless (and therefore anxious) expectations of what Sennett called public "intimacy."[5] For Sennett, "public man" was lost in this set of circumstances. The only way to re-create a viable public self, he suggested, was to foreclose the narcissistic project and update the importance of socially constructed role play among strangers in the public sphere.

Sennett's erudite study of the *Fall of Public Man* was marked by prefeminist thinking that took the experience of "man" as a neutral placeholder for the public consciousness of all citizens. Nevertheless, his solution to the crisis of the public self resonates with that of feminist thinkers like Judith Butler who argue that subjectivity is a performance in which persons publicly experiment, through parody and subversion, with the limitations of normative roles of selfhood and thus expand the democratic potential of public space.[6] More recently, critics of performance-based theories note that such attention to symbolic role play has neglected the role of the material body and the role of nonsymbolic yet communicative and even collective aspects of a person's affective states.[7] This critique holds true for Sennett's study as well. If the urban emptiness of so much of today's public space increases anxiety and, in the acutely anxious, gives way to historically increasing nervous disorders of the sort that can be "successfully" treated by propanolol—that is to say, can be treated directly at the level of the nervous system—then perhaps we need to come up with a more complex way of listening to a civic body whose speechlessness has not stopped it from communicating how our cities are indeed structures of feeling. Here it is important to note that while pharmacology may be the dominant mode, it is certainly not the only successful mode of treatment that works in such unmediated fashion on the nervous system to relieve the sort of urban anxiety described here. So-called alternative modalities like biofeedback and bioenergetic (body-oriented) psychotherapies that also work on a presymbolic, material body (as we shall see in chapter 7) have also proven to be effective treatments for acute anxiety. The challenge I faced in this book was how to think about urban space, gender, race, and political economy in this differently materialist picture of the public self.

In later works Sennett himself tried to address issues of the city's embodied citizenry. He turned his historical focus on the way women and others relegated to subordinate positions in Western city design made use of collective forms of self-presentation. Sennett focused on the way the urban oppressed could inhabit certain ritual spaces in the city and act out an underside of civic consciousness, sometimes to their benefit. Citing the more somber Sigmund Freud of *Beyond the Pleasure Principle*, Sennett's last work argued that a less conscious, less optimistic historical relation between the body and the city in Western civilization is dramatized in the ritual modes/spaces where "public man's" gendered, mortal, and incomplete body have long been acted out in ways that are little recognized in the rational, secular public sphere.[8] One historical example he offers of this split, spatialized civic (un)consciousness is the open space of the ancient Greek agora.

In fourth-century Athens, the agora was the central marketplace or public square. It was the city's most inclusive, diverse, and unsynchronized form of public space where politics, commerce, religious ceremony, gossip, and entertainment took place side by side. But the agora also had its complimentary public sites on the nearby Pnyx Hill. Terraced into the hill's front side were the seats of the political theater where the *Ekklesia*, the assembly of all citizens, would sit in their prescribed seats forty times a year to listen to the fiery political rhetoric of the orators whose well-orchestrated speeches sought to sway the city's voters on civic matters. The Ekklesia, like other forms of civic life, was only open to Athenian citizens—which meant no women, slaves, or foreigners. Women were excluded from civic engagement in both the agora and the Pnyx, but once a year, in a three-day ritual enacting the body's mysteries of death and birth as narrated in the Demeter myth, women occupied space on the backside of the Pnyx Hill, behind the Ekklesia's seats, leaving their husbands and families for several days in order to act out this underside of their social and material existence close to the earth in small huts dug into the hill.

If the agora was the democratically inspired spatial design for nonsynchronized mixed use in the public space of the city, and the Pnyx's political theater the design for the highly synchronized creation of a common urban voice, for Sennett, the women's ritual demonstrated that those who were not granted civic voice in the agora or the Ekklesia used a different kind of collective, public space—the space of ritual mythos—to act out what was otherwise unrepresentable in civic life. Here is where the body that did not conform to the dominant order—to rational discourse or to the tropes of political rhetoric—repeated a storied truth of its existence. In this study Sennett offered a more complex idea of social role play, a more complex notion of the public self in which the body finds a way to make known the truths of its existence and, in doing so, to still stay hidden from the clarity of the society's symbolic systems. What Sennett was describing as a spatialized, precarious form of political voice for the city's underrecognized and oppressed is not unlike what Freud and other twentieth-century social observers described in the neurotic acting out of the shell-shocked soldier or the Victorian hysteric. Modern psychology, with its various schools of thought, also gives storied forms to what civic bodies can only act out symptomatically.

Similarly, my research on the treatment of acute anxiety showed that modern city design has a civic space where what cannot be spoken, what cannot be represented can nevertheless be publicly acted out in the form of what are now often called "panic attacks." Historically, the public place for this modern affective acting out has been the city's highly abstract, most anxiety-triggering forms of urban space, the empty space built into the monumental squares of nineteenth century European capitols; today, the "stage" for this inscrutable display is the blank expanses of urban freeways that circle through the center of our cities and the big-box architecture of the suburban shopping mall so saturated with commodities that its emptiness is only experienced viscerally. These sites are what the anthropologist Marc Augé has called the "non-places of supermodernity" and they are the most common spatial triggers of a modern anxiety disorder called "agoraphobia."

The psychiatric treatments for urban anxiety I studied in writing this book recovered a public self that featured elements of Sennett's "public man," in many cases fallen in the later twentieth century into the narcissistic project of expressing an authentic self through shopping. But these treatments to attain the normative public self, I found, were also training patients in more complex forms of embodied, nonsymbolic display. Modern psychology trained the overly anxious person for reentry into an agora whose chief characteristic has been a secular, rationally efficient "empty" urban space that is now intensifying into irrational and virtual forms of public space. And, apart from certain feminist psychologies of the 1970s, the dominant treatment modalities I studied did not reveal that those who suffered from acute anxiety in such space had a common story to explain their fear, a ritual mythos with the authority to legitimate alternative, narrativized truths of the body's gendered social existence.[9] Behavioral, cognitive, and now biomedical solutions to the problem of anxiety in the emptiness of contemporary public space remain overwhelmingly uninterested, it must be said, in the social, political, existential, and ontological problems that embodied consciousness raises for the urban patient whose anxiety brings them face to face with the mysteries of life and death. This is why, I will argue, so many of these treatments encourage an introjection of the city's emptiness into the public self of individual citizens. It is as if empty space were itself the mythos behind modern civic life, as if a boundless "universe of nonrecognition" is what increasingly holds the modern urban commons together as a shared structure of feeling.

In this book, my aim is to take up, as Sennett did, the connection between the public self and public space in cities—more specifically, the emptiness that characterizes so much of public space. Overall, I am interested in the relations among empty space, modern subjectivity, and acute anxiety as an embodied form of civic knowing. Keeping empty space in the foreground means, as Sennett showed, focusing on the role of anxiety in the production of the modern urban self. In these pages I follow the last 130 years of clinical literature describing how modern psychiatry and psychology has treated anxiety triggered by vast forms of modern urban space. One consistent feature in this cultural history is the soldier who became a sort of placeholder for a culturally masculine public self that is passed off in psychiatry as the normative self to be achieved in the recovery of all citizens—men and women—from states of intense urban anxiety. In these pages I will examine what this means for those who are trained to "perform" the role of the embattled and traumatized soldier as they recover a self desensitized from the intense anxiety that disables them when they enter the most intensely empty forms of the modern agora.

The following chapters take an interdisciplinary, cultural approach to the emotional life of the public self in urban modernity. They are therefore aligned with recent work in the geography and anthropology of emotions, but likewise take up the concern for a more theoretically sophisticated model of an embodied public self.[10] Anthropologists have traditionally studied emotions in relatively small-scale, homogeneous cultures.[11] My study of the treatments for anxiety in the last 130 years of Euro-American urban life, however, takes a broader view of culture tied to complex processes of nationalism and globalization. I also veer from the traditional culturalist approach by interrogating those dimensions of embodied social life that resist symbolization even as they "communicate" psychosomatically with the material and technological forms of public space around them. Given this complexity, my examination of the modern era's psychological treatments for urban anxiety pries open the individual/social binarism that continues to impede social inquiry and demands that the problem of acute anxiety be viewed beyond the usual dichotomies of "intimate" versus "public," "embodied" versus "symbolic." To this end I cross-reference clinical psychiatric literature with texts by urban planners and cultural geographers, set conversations with therapists and patients next to the reflections of philosophers and literary critics of modernity, and examine dominant and alternative treatment modalities in the context of changes in the large-scale urbanization projects of the last century and a half. All of these efforts to build the modern city and relieve the attendant anxiety it triggers, I argue, go into the making of the modern public self. The built emptiness of the urban commons is inseparable, I show, from our embodied civic (un)consciousness.

# ACKNOWLEDGMENTS

Books like this one are produced in a gift economy, a kind of commons where, over the years, the generosity of teachers, the intellectual curiosity and passion of students and the caring support of colleagues, friends and family create and sustain a public world.

I have been gifted with teachers who modeled critical and responsible thinking, who emphasized historical, philosophical and poetic methods of study, and who held a healthy disregard for the way academics have traditionally divided the world into territorial disciplines. Wlad Godzich created a Department of Comparative Literature at the University of Minnesota during the 1980s which seized that era's theoretical movements and turned them into an intellectual approach that made the broad cultural field in which disciplinary objects arose the object of our study. I am most grateful to have been in graduate school during Wlad's tenure and to have had him as my dissertation director. George Lipsitz, Maria Paganini, Tom Conley, and Reda Bensmaia were teachers who changed the course of my thinking in various ways during this time. Most importantly, I must thank Nancy Armstrong whom I was lucky enough to find at the end of my graduate days and whose wide-ranging intellect, political savvy and generous mentorship have meant more than she will ever know. I succeeded at this public university because I also enjoyed the companionship of fellow graduate students Kate Brady and Julia Van Cleve and the bikeways, public transit system, food cooperatives, parks and lakes of the twin cities, Minneapolis and St. Paul, with their enduring traditions of democratic governance.

My first academic position was in the Department of Anthropology at Rice University. That first year, every Tuesday morning at 9:00 am, my colleagues George Marcus and Michael Fischer, intellectual pioneers in the anthropology of modernity, would meet with me at a strip-mall French café in Houston and educate me with their versions of the history (and future) of cultural anthropology. Beyond their intellectual and personal generosity, George and Michael have contributed, each in his own way, to how I will forever imagine the ideal academic community: rigorous, theoretically astute and open-minded, inventive and, above all, collaborative. Likewise, Steven Tyler, Sharon Traweek, Nia Georges, James Faubion and many of my graduate students at Rice have been at once colleagues, teachers and peers in my becoming an anthropologist. Not even Houston, enclosed by petroleum refineries and sealed up in air-conditioned interiors, with its inescapable freeways, endless suburbs and airports dedicated to the Bush dynasty, not even Houston thwarted the creation of the imaginary academic community in the Anthropology Department at Rice.

My fieldwork in Hungary gave me an altogether different sense of how academic intellectuals can be political thinkers, public servants and gracious hosts. For this I thank Horváth Ivan, Keserű Katalin, Faludy Anikó and Dan Liechty. And to learn this in a city like Budapest where public space—even when dictated by the monumentalism of socialist realism or succumbed to the billboards of advanced capitalism—made urban life a pleasure was an additional gift.

At Arizona State University where I presently teach, the gift economy of public education and public life has severely eroded. Thanks to President Michael Crow's for-profit experiment in higher education, ASU has been corporatized to the extent that the production of knowledge in the public domain has suffered. I wish to acknowledge the struggle of my colleagues and me in this "uncommons" environment where faculty governance has become a thing of the past. The academic freedom and security that enables scholars to teach and research what is in the public interest is now only protected if it makes money. Many of those who disagree with these changes have left or been dismissed. I wish to thank David Theo Goldberg who, before leaving for the University of California at Irvine, helped secure my spousal hire in what was then called the School of Justice Studies; Anne Schneider, dean of the now disassembled College of Public Programs, was also helpful and I am grateful for the grants I received from the Dean's Office that supported research for this book. Jack Kugelmass and Esther Romeyn, who before leaving for the University of Florida at Gainsville, were my close comrades from the (now defunct) interdisciplinary Humanities Program. (How would we have first survived here without your poolside dinners and late-night talks, our diapered toddlers fast asleep on the floor?) Many other colleagues have heard versions of the work in these pages and offered insightful comments: Nan Ellin, David Altheide, Torin Monahan, Elizabeth Horan, and Beth Tobin. Mary Romero, Pat Lauderdale, Helen Quan, Angela Waziyatwin Cavender Wilson, Sharon Crowley, Rhonda Steele, Philip Bernick, Montye Fuse and Eugenia DeLamotte are all colleagues whose intelligence and ethical voices have stood out in these times. And a special thanks to the graduate students in my Comparative Literature/Cultural Studies and Critical Theory courses—in particular, Kaysi Holman, Justin DeSenso, Nadia Fischer, Daniel Crumbo, Jennifer Mensink, and Frankie Cerne—whose intellectual passion and gift for creating community where there was none transformed the classroom and the experience of teaching. Geoffrey Clark, Regents professor of what used to be the Anthropology Department (now renamed by the president a faddish but forgettable moniker) merits special appreciation for fearlessly pointing out how the current state of our public university is better understood by reflecting on the nature of this desert city. Metropolitan Phoenix, whose thriving economy is based on gluttonous use of stolen water and hyperindividuated, unsustainable suburban sprawl, encourages voters and state legislators with little experience of or care for a public domain to turn the people's power over to a King of ice-cream.

Special thanks are due to my editor at Routledge, David McBride, whose wise suggestions helped shape the final manuscript, and to Marsha Hecht, who brought me successfully through the daunting deadlines of the production process. Two anonymous reviewers provided important, well-heeded comments, and I thank you both.

Lastly, during the time I was working on this book (and my forthcoming book: *The Political Uncommons: The Cultural Logic of the Global Commons,* Ashgate 2007), I had three children. While the labor demands of these three gifts are well known by academic men and women in my situation, they remain institutionally invisible and therefore need to be acknowledged. (How many times have I been asked to remove mention of my children or maternity leaves from official reviews, only to have reviewers remark on the mysterious "barren" period in my scholarly production?) I could never have continued my work as a teacher and scholar without the support of my partner, Randel Hanson (who created a garden and a home wherever we moved), my parents Albert and Virginia Milun (who created the home I carry in my heart), and the phone line to my far-flung sisters and brother—Mary Milun Werft, Anne Milun Litecky, Patricia Milun and Dick Milun. Over long distances I have also been sustained by my decades-long friendship with Lynn Skupeko and Kathleen Fluegel. All of these dear ones have given so much to me, and I am grateful that in this gift economy they have allowed me to turn my back on them many times when publication deadlines arose, trusting that I would return when I could. As my son Tobias said after I completed the revisions to this volume, "Mom, even when you're not sitting at your desk, I look at that corner and I still see you there." So, I dedicate this book to my children: Gabriel, Tobias and Francesco. You are growing up in a place far different than the poor villages of your European great-grandparents, different than the small farms and inner-city ethnic neighborhoods of your grandparents, and shockingly different than the cosmopolitan and bohemian aspirations of your parents. The great adventure of this place nevertheless remains how you create and sustain public space beginning from what we all, by right, own in common.

# Introduction

## *Agoraphobia: A Discovery Mode for the Study of Empty Space as a Structure of Feeling in the Urban Commons*

"Emptiness gives me an undefinable anxiety [notes an agoraphobic patient who also has fears of looking down from Alpine summits]. I feel oppressed, my legs become weak in exactly the same way as when I cross wide open spaces. The phenomena are rather similar but in addition I have a peculiar feeling of being attracted by the emptiness, by an irresistible force. I feel an emotion that may appear ridiculous but becomes increasingly exaggerated the more I react." [His doctors Bernard and Jung comment:] The idea of the [Alpine] abyss makes him fearful, but not as much as the idea of the *Place de la Concorde* [the largest public square in Paris].

**—A. Bernard and Ch. Jung,**
"Contribution à l'étude de la cremnophobie"

The agoraphobic syndrome is the commonest and the most distressing phobic-anxiety disorder encountered in adult patients.

**—J. J. Hawkrigg,** "Agoraphobia—1"

*Horror vacui*—fear of emptiness, is the driving force in contemporary American taste. Along with the commercial interests that exploit this fear, it is the major factor now shaping attitudes toward

> public spaces, urban centers and even suburban sprawl. ... Every public space must [now] be packed with distractions.
>
> **—Herbert Muschamp,**
> "Public Space or Private, A Compulsion to Fill It"

When I asked myself how I could empirically study empty space as a structure of feeling in the modern city, I thought of agoraphobia. Agoraphobia is a spatial disorder characterized by a phobic inability to walk across wide open urban spaces, or through streets, empty or crowded. Psychiatric journals in the 1870s were the first to mention the syndrome. A German doctor in Berlin coined the phrase *agoraphobia*, after the ancient Greek *agora*, also calling it *Platzfurcht* (plaza fright). Not long afterward, it was recognized in metropolitan centers throughout Europe and the United States and alternately named *Platzangst*, *peur des espaces* (fear of spaces), *horreur du vide* (horror of emptiness), topophobia, or street fear. Agoraphobia appeared in Europe during a period of massive migrations from countryside to city, together with the construction of monumental architectural forms that accompanied both metropolitan growth and the rise of the modern nation-state. Nineteenth-century agoraphobics experienced the gigantic squares and boulevards introduced into their cities as hostile environments. They perceived these monumental spaces as "empty" and experienced intense anxiety that caused them to retreat to the curb, to their homes, and even to their beds. Today, similar symptoms prevail when the agoraphobic faces a trip to the shopping mall or a drive on the urban freeway.

Various studies show that a significant percentage of the population of industrialized countries suffers from agoraphobia. A recent epidemiological study of psychiatric disorders in the United States that interviewed 15,490 individuals in five metropolitan areas—Baltimore; Durham, North Carolina; Los Angeles; New Haven, Connecticut; and St. Louis—found that over 4 percent of the surveyed population reported having suffered from agoraphobia during the previous year.[1] In all places, the majority of those who suffer from the disorder are now women.[2] Other studies report that anxiety disorders in the United States account for 24.9 percent of all psychological disorders over a lifetime. In the United States since the 1980s and the increasing power of the pharmaceutical industry in psychiatric care, agoraphobia has become a subset of a more general category called *panic disorder*.[3] The new terminology, which has not caught on well in Europe, is one that should be suspect for reasons I will address later in this book.[4] Studies that refer to persons with panic disorder nevertheless show that those with fewer than twelve years of education were ten times more likely to have the disorder than those belonging to a comparison group with a college education.[5] The statistical finding that gender and education play a significant role in these anxiety disorders points to cultural factors, specifically factors related to public space, that are rarely taken into account in the dominant treatment modalities.

In psychology, the statistical and historical material on agoraphobia also demonstrates that it is one of the most intractable of the so-called neurotic disorders. Using standard psychiatric treatments, the prognosis has remained bleak, and agoraphobic patients continue to be disabled for decades. Agoraphobics have been treated by a host of schemas: from the bromides and rest cures prescribed for traversing the squares and boulevards of late-nineteenth-century European capitals, to the surgical lobotomies performed during the 1950s and '60s, when postwar cities constructed ultrarational urban freeway systems, large-scale public housing projects, and (predominantly in the United States) white, middle-class suburbs; and from the chemical remedies that medicate anxiety today in megamalls, traffic jams, and concrete high-rises to the paradoxical self-talk models and labyrinth-walking therapies that abandon the rational and immaterial mind in order to treat the metaphorical and material mind/body. In the chapters that follow, I take a critical, cultural approach to the psychoanalytic, cognitive, behavioral, biomedical, and alternative treatments that have been devised to reinsert the agoraphobic back into public space. I ask how these treatments are informed by cultural assumptions and practices associated with Western urban modernity, its architecture and city planning, its favored philosophical ideas, its dominant economic systems, and the social roles it has historically assigned to women and people of color. The psychological treatments for agoraphobia generally assume that such fearful public behavior is pathological. And certainly agoraphobics themselves have struggled and sought medical help for their disabling behavior in public space. But a broader cultural look at the illness and its treatments shows that this behavior is closer than generally thought to normative, especially for women and people of color whose different experiential being in Euro-American cities is less readily recognized in our most public sites. The cultural study undertaken in this book also notes that these large-scale public sites that have become modernity's crucible for the public self are themselves under general attack today. That is to say, many architects and urban critics have joined the agoraphobic, as it were, in condemning what I will be calling the built environment of empty space—the megamalls and urban freeway systems—as broadly ill-suited to community life.

In the 1990s, for example, trends in urban design such as new urbanism have lead many shopping centers to be retrofitted with pre–World War II designs that simulate small-scale town squares. New urbanism is an anti-sprawl movement that has gained popularity in the United States and has several counterparts with differing strategies in European cities. For the past decade, new urbanist design has been filling in the empty spaces of modernist city planning: the wide minimalist plazas below downtown skyscrapers, the asphalt oceans for parking at midtown and suburban shopping centers—all those vacant expanses that were once monuments to the industrial nature of postwar urban life and epigones of modernist style. Their gaping emptiness inspires a kind of horror vacui in the new urbanist architect for whom they are generally recognized as pathologies of modern space, structures of feeling that are physically difficult for humans to navigate and hostile to face to face encounters.[6] Indeed, new urbanism is a broad movement among architects and planners that has come to reflect what the agoraphobic citizen has long been expressing in modernity through dread and avoidance. In this book, I argue that much of what new urbanism, as well as urban geographers, cultural historians, feminists, and others now readily acknowledge about modern city life, our most sensitive urban citizen, the agoraphobic, has been telling us for decades.

One cautionary note: the kinds of urban sites historically connected to agoraphobia should not by any means be considered causes of the illness. Monumentally empty public space is a trigger, not a cause, of agoraphobia. There are many reasons why a person's spatial sensibility may be more finely tuned to her surroundings during a given period of life—reasons that concern emotional and/or physical trauma, racism, the keenness of a poetic sensibility, or other forms of culturally trained discernment, for example. For the agoraphobic, however, it is clear that certain forms of public space trigger a strong visceral reaction over which she appears to have no skills to gain control. Over the last century, psychology and biomedicine have stepped in to provide those skills, and in this book we can consider the wider meaning of such techniques. But the power of urban space to trigger the phobic reaction is, for me, an invitation to consider the interrelations between space, social skills, medical institutions, and the broader communicative capacity of the nervous system.

## Agoraphobia: The Public Self and the Person of Surplus Sensibility

The agoraphobic is indeed a person of heightened sensibility. A cultural analysis that follows her reluctant tracks in the city and the various forms of her recovery, however, allows us to see beyond the individual's story of disease and cure. Because agoraphobia is arguably inseparable from specific kinds of urban space characterized by their vastness and emptiness, our study can reveal something that is otherwise unrepresentable in urban space: empty space as a structure of urban feeling. Agoraphobia and the history of medical treatments for this disorder, I argue, allow us to understand how empty space has not only become a dominant feature of the built environment but also how it has been introjected into the psychology of the self in modernity. By reviewing the last 130 years of European and American psychiatric treatments for agoraphobia against the history of modern Euro-American cities' large-scale urban renewal projects, this cultural analysis of the mode of recovery of the agoraphobic's public self both describes how such treatments produce the normative urban person and reveals the demands that our most public forms of common space make on all urban citizens. Notably, one century of clinical literature on agoraphobia also shows that the larger social meaning of the disease and the significance of urban spatial triggers have been systematically ignored and eventually suppressed, both in the medical literature and in the general public's understanding. Making these texts available to critical cultural scrutiny reveals that the public self is a spatially sensitive cultural creation.

With his spatial sensibility ignored, the agoraphobic is treated as a person of mere surplus sensibility. In this respect he is not far from the normal population of modern city dwellers whose full sensorium is challenged by the changing shape and scale of urban life in modernity. The urban sociologist Georg Simmel, in his well-known essay "The Metropolis and Mental Life," predicted a century ago that the modern metropolitan type would develop desensitization strategies of heightened rationality to deal with the strangers, confusion, and unknowns encountered everyday on the big city's teeming streets. At the beginning of the twenty-first century, the various treatments meant to bring the withdrawn agoraphobic back into a normative relation with public space suggest that Simmel's predictions were for the most part correct. The modern person's sensibility is at a loss: facing the normative expectations of public space, which is both saturated by the lure of commodities and drained by the "dead space" of the "traffic-support-nexus," the self appears challenged by the overvaluing of abstract, bureaucratic reason in so many domains of modern life. But equally important, the modern self has been deskilled by the undervaluing of knowledge gained from emotional and tactile sensibilities honed in social roles that, for dubious and gendered reasons, are not guaranteed a place in public space.

The fact that women make up the vast majority of agoraphobics today, and that the dominant skills that retrain them to venture back into public space reflect conduct associated with culturally masculine behavior, is, I argue, an indication that the built environment privileges a public self with particular gendered skills of being in the world. For women, agoraphobia often begins after marriage. It is also linked with childbirth and early child care. Just when she needs people most, she is subjected to a kind of programmatic quarantine on the part of the dominant institutions of society. (To this day, medical forms in English label the date she gives birth as D.O.C.—date of confinement. And as I write, the city council of a nearby suburb is voting to ban breastfeeding in public places.) The skills traditionally learned through caring for children and other dependent persons, however, are strikingly dissimilar to the skills the agoraphobic learns as a patient of the dominant treatments that retrain her to reenter public space. Certain behavioral treatments that have succeeded at restoring a limited level of function to the agoraphobic (ones that we will study in great detail in this book), do so with desensitization and cathartic techniques often created for the needs of soldiers whose selves were broken on the twentieth century's European battlefields, in the jungles of Vietnam, and now in the urban guerilla warfare zones of Iraq. These techniques to restore the broken soldier's sense of self and rid him of the anxiety of memories that now provoke so much surplus sensibility are often techniques that ignore the needs of the human personality for community.[7] Spatially speaking, in civilian life the use of such techniques for agoraphobia have served the function of protecting the built environment of monumental, homogeneous, modernist space.

Desensitized to achieve a normal public self or pathologized as the person of surplus sensibility, the agoraphobic looks more and more like the miner's canary in this scenario: the first to register the pathological effects of the demands that this historically recent form of massive homogeneous space makes on our public sense of self. Furthermore, these modes of resituating the person of surplus sensibility back into public space have by all means avoided any serious questioning of the phenomenon or instrumental function of empty space in public life.

## Empty Space as an Existential Feature of the Built Environment

In spite of the obvious relationship between architectural emptiness and the triggers of agoraphobia, throughout the last century agoraphobia has increasingly been treated not as a psychological but as a biological problem, a problem with an individual's biological functioning. Spurred (in part) by the growing power of the pharmaceutical industry, doctors often argue that agoraphobia stems from maladaptive brain chemistry in humans. This presumes that it is ontologically natural as well as culturally normative to exist in daily contact with the urban freeways and shopping malls that agoraphobics find so appalling. Agoraphobia is not to be regarded as a neurotic ailment any more, but is to be understood as a chronic dysfunction with biological origins, like epilepsy. As such, it is often labeled as a disability and, not surprisingly, lifelong medication is presumed necessary to treat it. Thus medical understanding of agoraphobia has suppressed the link between the disorder and the pattern of trigger sites in public urban space in order to medicalize a problem originally considered neurotic rather than permanently disabling. If healthy, nonphobic human beings have accepted vast tracks of homogeneous space as part of their built environment, the medical treatments seem to say, then monumental emptiness has become simply a fact of life, part of our urban condition. Whatever problems it presents for the public self can be handled either as ontological, existential problems of our being in the modern urban world, or as biological problems in persons of surplus sensibility who suffer side effects in relation to the dominant forms of urban space, effects that modern medicine can help them live with.

The existential approach to the built environment of urban modernity is also reflected in architectural thinking. When urban critics who disapprove of the hypercommercial results of many new urbanist remodeling projects suggest that perhaps empty urban space should be accepted and valued as an ontological experience for the public self, they foreground the lack of alternative thinking on the spatial dilemmas we are discussing here. Their solution remains in sync with the medical model we saw above. *New York Times* architecture critic Herbert Muschamp, for example, is critical of how the original intent of new urbanist design—to create pedestrian-oriented main streets and town centers in American suburbs, edge cities, and low-density urban areas—has been corrupted by formulaic, overcommercialized developments; he asks whether Americans are not better off by simply learning to appreciate the emptiness of modernist city design.[8] The urban diversity that was supposed to flock to the new habitats, Muschamp laments, now arrives to "a homogenized atmosphere of chain stores, coordinated street furniture, banners and signs." "Every [empty] public space," he observes, "must [now] be packed with distractions. Food and flower vendors, musicians, banners, fountains, benches and plants must fill every mid-block plaza. They must be packed with young urban professionals, picturesquely enjoying wrap sandwiches and bottles of Evian water."[9] The hyped commercialism that seeks to bring community back together in these sites has left urban critics like Muschamp nostalgic even for the failed public spaces that are now disappearing. Sterile, "dead spaces" like Chase Manhattan Plaza in lower Manhattan should be treated more like Zen gardens, writes Muschamp: "you're in the heart of a huge bank, but there are no commercial interruptions. The emptiness is ideal for sorting out inner and outer worlds … [and] there's no pressure to spend $2 for a cookie."[10]

For Muschamp a kind of noir aesthetic is required to fully appreciate this urban emptiness, as in the classic 1960s films of Italian filmmaker Michelangelo Antonioni, where a noir sensibility was used to portray city

**Figure 1** Still from Michaelangelo Antonioni's "*La Notte*" (1961).

dwellers living among the concrete slabs of modernist suburbs going up on the outskirts of Rome, communicating through the "passive aggression of phone calls" and meeting at highway intersections in "the abstract geometry of the postwar utopia" (see figure 1).[11] When Antonioni's films first came out they were hailed for depicting the malaise of the modern world. With their fragmented cityscapes and industrial wastelands they "were even seen as the causes of the sickness." But after living amidst the glut of the most commercialized products of New Urbanist's revamping of public space, Muschamp thinks we should reconsider the disaffection of Antonioni's characters. Perhaps, he muses, the Italian filmmaker was showing us "a human condition, not merely a modern one." Perhaps "there is no malaise, no need for a cure. There is only an emotional reality to be confronted. … Emptiness may not be a quality to be feared."[12] Cynical or not, critics like Muschamp seem to be saying that living with urban bleakness and appreciating the existential quality of intensely homogeneous public spaces is a legitimate demand that public space makes on the modern self.

According to the biological view of agoraphobia, the existential anxiety experienced by the oversensitive city dweller in certain public spaces can be similarly accepted if it is managed with beta-blockers. As we saw in the preface in the case of propranolol, this class of drugs can even preemptively handle urban anxiety that may potentially be triggered by traumatic memory associations with public space. Regardless of the reasons for the phobic reaction to public space, dominant remedies today involve various forms of desensitization to enable people not only to return to dreaded city sites, but to endure and even accept their lives in these spaces. In this respect they recommend, as do apologists for the vast expanses of modernist design, a public self well-accommodated to the status quo in the built environment.

Such existential acquiescence is also found in the other most common treatment for agoraphobia today, a behavioral form of exposure therapy known as "flooding." During the treatment the patient is most commonly taken to a shopping center (that big-box structure most cited among contemporary agoraphobics as the public location that triggers the most extreme anxiety) and kept there until she has abreacted the full psychosomatic range of anxiety effects. After numerous repetitions, the result can sometimes be cathartic (although it can also fail and simply function to reinforce the agoraphobic habit). As a method of catharsis, flooding allows the patient to release the neurotic symptom and shop normally like any of her neighbors. The technique of flooding was originally developed by British behaviorists for soldiers suffering battlefield trauma during the Second World War. Today, its use for agoraphobics is bordering on a cultural ritual designed to reinsert deeply ambivalent pedestrians, who are now mostly women, into commercial shopping zones.

These treatments compel us to pose the existential question: Why shouldn't the modern self come to embrace a built environment whose most public of sites are marked by the kind of empty space we are describing here? Are modern psychiatrists and urban critics like Muschamp right? Should the agoraphobic urbanite who panics in shopping centers and urban freeways make peace with the felt emptiness of modernist public space? Should he do as so many other nonphobic individuals who feel uneasy with the experience of modern shopping and freeway driving have done—accept this form of urban space as a given social structure to which they must adapt? After all, these vast forms of urban space appear to be expanding on the planet at an unprecedented pace. Many sociologists argue that the modern city that grew out of the European Enlightenment's secular rationality, the city whose public spaces form the core of the agoraphobic's dread, is now the world's dominant social structure. At the turn of the nineteenth century only 14 percent of the global population lived in cities. Only eleven of those cities had a population of a million inhabitants. There are now four hundred cities whose population approaches one million. Twenty of these have over ten million inhabitants. Whether these cities developed after the European model with remnants of their medieval core still at the center and industry at the peripheries, or whether they followed the American model where industry grew up in the central city and the intensity of new growth sent the population sprawling farther and farther out to the margins, modernist city planning is what allows these metropolitan expanses to communicate and function as an ever expanding whole. By the year 2006, according to a report issued by the United Nations Population Fund, half of the world's 6.6 billion people will be living in urban areas.[13] As we shall see in the chapters to come, there are good reasons to believe that the treatments we see for the Euro-American agoraphobic may be exported abroad hard on the heels of an increasing incidence of the disorder that follows the global expansion of modernist city design. In this book we take up the existential question agoraphobia poses for the public self as a discovery procedure to ask the more general question: What kind of public self has been created to live in everyday relation to the built emptiness of modern urban space?

## Empty Space as an Imaginal Structure to Communicate and Mediate the Insertion of the Public Self into the Modern City

Empty space in modernity is not only a feature of the built environment but also an imaginal structure that appears in cultural depictions that seek to capture and make sense of the large scale transformations of the urban world. Modern literature provides a good example of how empty space has become a key mental structure with which to "think" the modern urban experience. Literary critics have recently noted that the expansive growth of the Euro-American city is reflected in the changing way cities are being narrated in the Euro-American literature of the twentieth and twenty-first centuries. Indeed a "central vacuity" appears to be emerging as a characteristic, organizing feature of the narration of the modern city. Historically, the modern novel's attempts to describe an urban life-world increasingly structured by the disruptive demands of capitalism led to a new style of literary representation that could capture an author's reflections in the more volatile dimension of everyday speech.[14] In the novel, everyday speech was elevated to a literary form. It presented itself as a "natural form," one that could best capture or represent the new nature of urban life. Literary historian Klaus Scherpe has argued that these stylistic and linguistic changes we recognize in relation to the rise of the novel can also be used to think about the change that is now occurring in the way the modern city is thematized and represented in Euro-American literature. He writes, "One no longer speaks of the city but of urban in the widest sense possible. The discipline of urban studies not only provides us with terminology based on architectural history such as the Radiant City or the Garden City, but speaks in one breath, inspired by aesthetics, of megalopolis and futureopolis, of collage city and suburbia, of the global village, *ville panique* or even necropolis."[15]

In everyday speech the novel has struggled to narrate our experience of the changing nature of the modern city. And there is no doubt that as visual media take up the aesthetic task of describing urban experience, we are seeing a further struggle to narrate a city increasingly experienced through technologically mediated images. For city dwellers who spend hours of their workdays in their cars, the visceral experience of walking in the city is more likely to come through a traveling shot they see on television than from their shoes actually stepping on the pavement.[16] Through airplane windows and satellite observation we see another long-shot view of the city: terrestrial areas of unbroken, electrically lit vastness in the night sky, an "urban corridor." Literature shows that as a culture, we are coming to represent the unrepresentable complexity of this urban world through a thematics of empty space. In Euro-American literature and literary theory, the modern city is often narrated as a central emptiness (Roland Barthes, 1964) where urban events function in a void (Ernst Bloch, 1991) and the increasing homogenization of metropolitan street life leads to such a level of abstraction (Georg Simmel, 1971) and speed (Paul Virilio, 1991) that the modern narrator tends to refract his or her vision of the city by slowing down, as in the case of Walter Benjamin's flaneur, and giving us a city of details or speeding up and offering a concatenation of urban events passing through a technologically inspired optic, a ride on the underground.[17]

What is lost in the way everyday and literary language now describes the contemporary city is something that an urban critic like Jane Jacobs could still, in the late 1950s, call "the organized complexity" of the modern city. Although we may not yet be able to name it, we can sense what is being lost because it is nonrepresentationally creating a new space for itself. In other words, the new terms we see arising in Euro-American literary descriptions of the modern city suggest that this "organized complexity" is disintegrating without our being able to establish or represent a new "inherent nature" of the urban. Empty space, then, is the nonconceptual, paradoxical, nonrepresentational figure through which we communicate our sense that an unknown but emergent schema is increasingly shaping our cities and our selves. The person of surplus sensibility may in fact be the one who, for various reasons of personal history, is most sensitive to the disintegration of the city's organized complexity. The agoraphobic, like the nonpathologized metropolitan person and the literary narrators of urban modernity, would not have the words to describe what is happening in our cities. To communicate the sense of change, he would only have the figure of empty space.

For the literary critic, patterns in the way authors narrate the modern city provide insight into the way we as individuals narrate our modern urban selves. These imaginary constructs of the city form an aesthetic pattern whose narrative components also have a structuring function: the modern imaginary cityscape as a centrally vacated place provides readers with an imaginal structure through which they can insert themselves into the dominant social conditions of urban life. The literary imagination shows us that the way we as a culture imagine the structure of the modern city is intimately related to the way we orient ourselves in that place. A main argument of this book is that as this "central emptiness" becomes a main thematic of metropolitan space, our ability to imagine our interactions with our surrounding social relations is significantly impaired.[18]

What is the instrumental function of this dominant theme of empty urban space? Just as modernist architecture and commercial advertising use empty space as a background to insert themselves in public space, so does the modern self. The emptiness of public urban space functions as an imaginal backdrop for the commercial structuring of our self identity in modernity. As a structuring metaphor for the modern city, however, this emptiness appears to leave us without an adequate imaginal structure with which to assert ourselves in alternative ways in the city. Just as Richard Sennett argued that the boundaryless dilemma of both the city's "dead space" and of the narcissistic personality type lead to, per his title, *The Fall of Public Man* (see the preface to the present volume), the agoraphobic's dilemma allows us to argue that the boundlessness of the spatial imaginary that helps us insert ourselves into modern city life will fail to help us assert ourselves as urban citizens. Just as literary critics like Scherpe can warn us that privileging the existential aesthetic of urban emptiness is exactly what is wrong with contemporary literature, and just as the new urbanist architect can alert us to the dangers that modernist city design present to the health of urban communities, so too can the treatments for agoraphobia caution us against the desensitization skills we learn to adapt to the built emptiness of public space. If architectural critics like Muschamp actually come to lament the waning aesthetic of urban emptiness as modernist plazas are retrofitted to the expensive cheerfulness of a new urbanist festive marketplace, it is only a sign that we lack aesthetic alternatives to the commercial saturation of empty urban space. All these warnings and lamentations are a good example of how empty space remains not only a dominant feature of our urban spatial imaginary today but also a dominant orienting device for the public self. What alternatives exist to the dominance of empty space as a figure through which to understand our relation to the modern city? "Doesn't the labyrinth at least have straight lines and exact contours?" Scherpe asks, in his study of the trope of emptiness in modern fiction.[19] In chapter 7, on alternative treatments for agoraphobia, we will look at the recent popularity of therapeutic labyrinth walking in American cities. The treatment is suggestive in its own right as a response to pathologies of urban space, but as a heuristic device, the labyrinth reminds me of how the kind of critical spatial thinking in which we are engaging in this book creates contours in what is otherwise simply figural empty space.[20] Is the labyrinth merely a device that allows a person to publicly act out the problem of the fallen, narcissistic public self described by Sennett? Or is it a small, semiutopian, but hopeful step toward moving us away from an urban condition that would imprison the public self in only two possible modes of being—a desensitized person or a person of surplus sensibility?[21] This is a question that can be asked from a different angle at the end of our study of the treatments for agoraphobia.

## Creating the Conceptual Labyrinth and the Interdisciplinary Method for the Study of Empty Space as a Structure of Feeling

To bring clarity to the situation of the public self in empty space we need to create conceptual contours, as it were, in places where our culture has not yet provided us with a mental map. Since agoraphobia represents the predominant expression of the individual's reactive relation to the built emptiness of public space, to better understand empty space as a structure of even normative feeling, as a physical reality emotionally experienced in our everyday lives and embodied in our sense of self, the present volume brings an anthropological outlook to the last century of treatments for agoraphobia.

What do I mean by *anthropological outlook*? Space has traditionally been an important concept in anthropology. Spatial and temporal grammars were key areas of study for ethnographers looking for the generative forms behind the world-making ways of preindustrial cultures.[22] Thus, the layout of a village was a reflection of the villagers' larger cosmological worldview. As a cultural concept in postindustrial societies, space has in the last decade become an object of transdisciplinary study by urban geographers, literary theorists, sociologists, historians, and anthropologists.[23] The modern Western citizen has been subject to enormous changes, transformations, and forced adaptations as space is extended, accelerated, and shrunk by communication, travel, and market technologies. The role of empty space in this process, however, is largely unrecognizable to us. It is "sometimes carelessly reduced and summarized in expressions like 'homogenization of culture' or 'world culture,'" notes French anthropologist Marc Augé.[24] However, it merits close ethnographic scrutiny. The study of empty space undertaken herein should be understood in this broad-based, ethnographically inflected context. For this reason this volume approaches agoraphobia treatments and modern urban space as inseparable field sites that allow us to study a broader phenomena of empty space and the role it plays in the creation of the modern public self. An anthropological outlook in interdisciplinary social research borrows these key concepts of cultural anthropology—*space* and *field site*—as they are being expanded in the ethnography of modernity broadly speaking.[25] While the present volume is not grounded in the usual long-term fieldwork common to ethnographic studies, it does aim for what the anthropologist Michael M. J. Fischer calls "anthropological voice":

> The challenge in renewing the ethnographic and anthropological voice in the twenty-first century is not the disappearance of difference, of different cultures, or of ways of organizing society any more than it is not the disappearance of class, capital, unequal exchange, power, or gender relations. On the contrary, the challenge is that the interactions of various kinds of cultures are becoming more complex and differentiated at the same time as new forms of globalization and modernization are bringing all parts of the earth into greater, uneven, polycentric interaction. The distinctive anthropological voice—the aspiration for cross-culturally comparative, socially grounded, linguistically and culturally attentive perspectives—continues to be valuable amid the pressures to simply turn to statistical indices for all policies and judgments.[26]

Thus, I approach the role of empty space in the constitution of the modern public self in a cross-cultural, comparative manner with attention to linguistic, social and cultural factors that shape the psychiatric treatments of agoraphobia in the U.S. and Europe.[27]

An anthropologically sensitive approach to empty space can also build on work done in other disciplines. Various disciplines have attempted to outline the social dimensions of empty space in modernity and to discuss its implications for the individual person and the public self. As we have seen, literary scholars have suggested that empty space is a metaphor for the problematic relationship of the contemporary urban citizen to the modernist and commercial transformation of public space. Architectural critics have described how emptiness is built into our urban environment and how it serves as an orienting strategy to move people around with greater efficiency at the expense of community life. Sociologists have pointed to the "emptying" of time and space that took place when the universal global map and world-standard time introduced a new homogeneity into everyday life, systematically integrating it into each person's day-to-day activities and creating selves disembedded from their social relations.[28] Recently, one sociologist has described the construction of globalized cosmopolitan public spaces like the Internet or information highway of the 1990s as an agoraphobic complex.[29] Here the agoraphobic is used as a metaphor to describe public spaces of virtual cosmopolitan life which, as they become increasingly boundless, create citizens who are increasingly less able to enter public life in ways that are meaningful. Linking empty space to abstract, homogeneous space, these critics have shown the negative impacts of empty space as a structural dimension that brings abstraction further and further into the individual's everyday experience of modern life.[30]

While sociologists have emphasized the negative impact of empty space, more recently poststructuralist political theory has used empty space as a trope to describe a positive orientation for the public self. In her discussion of spatial politics, Roselyn Deutsche has used the work of political theorist Claude Lefort, for example, who associates empty space with an emergent feature of democracy in a postmodern era. For Lefort, Deutsche points out, along with the radical change in society that accompanied the late-eighteenth-century French Revolution—what Alexis de Tocqueville had called "the democratic invention," when power was suddenly said to emanate from inside the social, from the people, rather than from an external source (namely, the king)—suddenly the place from which power derived its new legitimacy could no longer be represented as an organic totality. Lefort refers to our new, unrepresentable social site of democratic legitimacy as "'the image of an empty place.'"[31] "'In my view,'" he writes, "'the important point is that democracy is instituted and sustained by the *dissolution of the markers of certainty*. It inaugurates a history in which people experience a fundamental indeterminacy as to the basis of power, law and knowledge, and as to the basis of relations between *self* and *other*.'"[32] In this formulation, empty space is no longer associated with homogeneous and abstract space. Rather it is an indication of virtual space whose unbounded complexity promises diversity, potentiality, and possibility, a new basis for social democracy and boundless orientations for the normative public self. Here is an argument, useful to poststructuralist critics like Deutsche but striking from the perspective of either the agoraphobic or social critics like Sennett, that the kind of virtual public space we globally encounter on the small screens in our homes, airports, offices is forming us as a particular, democratic public self best understood as arising in "an empty place," inextricably and productively related to "dissolved markers of certainty" with respect to law, power, and knowledge.[33]

The anthropologically inflected cultural-studies approach to treatments for agoraphobia offered in this book interrogates the above discussions of the function of empty space in modernity and postmodernity and goes beyond their theoretical observations. By focusing on Western culture's clinical experiments and proposed cures for the moment when the problematic of empty space is made manifest for the individual and given personal expression, we have a particular empirical angle from which to consider these discussions. Specifically, we can ask: What do contemporary treatments for the disorder demand of the individual citizen's public, embodied self? How is public space related to the affliction and how is it used in treatments judged successful in reestablishing a person's public effectiveness? How is this effectiveness defined, and what is its relation to public space? What is the nature of the modern subject whose problematic relationship with empty space has been resolved? The present volume hopes to answer these questions with emphasis on differences in the historical treatment of agoraphobic anxiety in men and women. Two gender-specific contexts, the military and the shopping center, emerge as central forms of public orientation for agoraphobic patients. They stand next to the urban freeway as exemplary domains to recover the agoraphobic's lost public self. Behaviorist and pharmaceutical treatments used to establish reintegration of the individual into contemporary public space are especially the focus of interest in this book because they demonstrate the dominant modes of our culture for reestablishing effective personal function in adapting the individual to empty space. The empirical specificity of the clinical literature on agoraphobia allows us to enter the debates on empty space and the self put forth in the sociological, psychological, and philosophical literature from a new angle, one that offers a better understanding of empty space as an embodied cultural logic and as a dominant structure of feeling in modernity.

Previous studies of agoraphobia as a psychosocial pathology come from the fields of cultural geography, cultural anthropology, sociology, and urban studies/architecture. They generally fall into two groups: phenomenological studies of the spatial experience of the agoraphobic and its relation to the nonpathologized experience of women in urban modernity (Susan Bordo, Ruth Bankey, Joyce Davidson, Carol Brooks Gardner) and historical studies of the relation between modern city planning/architecture and the agoraphobic's perception of public space (Esther da Costa Meyer, Anthony Vidler). To my knowledge there have been no critical social studies on the history of treatments for agoraphobia.[34] The present work thus fills a gap in the existing literature. Because this volume focuses on the medical treatments for agoraphobia rather than on the nature of the illness, it can cross-culturally compare how changes in treatments over the last century are also changes in how we as urban citizens broadly speaking are inserted, or normalized, into everyday life in the contours of empty space. Agoraphobia is thus situated within a broader problem concerning the modern legacy of empty space and our emotional relationship to this historically recent form of common space.

In the psychiatric literature one finds scattered mention, in the early case histories, of the newly built monumental city squares that make up the common trigger of patients' first anxiety attacks. As time goes on, however, mention of the object of agoraphobic fear disappears altogether from these psychiatric texts. Instead, the focus is reduced to the subject's inner state in terms of a behaviorist, biomechanistic explanation of the mind. The history of treatments for agoraphobia reflects this dissociation of inner and outer space such that today the dominant therapy aims to chemically alter the structure of the patient's mind with no consideration for the triggers of the disorder, as if agoraphobia reflects a complete inability to see reality. When we study the treatments for agoraphobia embedded in the history of the modern city, however, we can see that the schematic power of empty space operates symbiotically in both the built environment and the psychological models of the normative self. Tracking agoraphobia through its various treatment modalities, I follow what Michel Foucault has called the "biopolitical" aspect of modern life.[35] To the extent that the treatments for agoraphobia help us discern changes in a "naturalized" notion of self expected of urban citizens living in daily relation to an increasing boundlessness of public space, these treatments also give us the proper background to ask about our spatial sensibility as both a biological and a social terrain on which modern power operates. What power arrangements, we can ask, are best served by the various notions of self implied in these treatments?

Normative treatments for agoraphobia reveal a crucial dimension of the role of empty space in modernity, allowing us to see the role played by emptiness, that most unrepresentable of spatial forms, in the formation of the modern Western urban self. Just as the spider's web gives us a gossamer image of how space and time have been transformed into a habitat, the treatments of the agoraphobic, our era's most spatially sensitive citizen, will show us the lived pattern of empty space as a deeply felt, embodied cultural schema of our massive transformation into modern urban citizens.

## The Outline of the Book

Chapter 1 of this volume looks at how material space has fallen out of the psychiatric description as agoraphobia went from being defined as a "fear of public space" to a "fear of fear itself" over the course of the last century. When treatments began to look at agoraphobia as an objectless fear instead of a fear of specific public places, they turned to the treatment of anxiety as such. Since Søren Kierkegaard and the existentialist philosophies of the early twentieth century, anxiety (as objectless fear) has had a particular value in European psychiatry. From this period onward anxiety was often positively associated with authenticity in the person who could philosophically face the nothingness of being. Later it was the European soldier's practical experience with death in the two world wars that would eventually change the way anxiety was treated by modern psychiatry. Both the heroic urban existentialist and the battle-weary soldier have dominated the treatment of anxiety in modernity. The anxious experiences of women who faced equally existential crises generally related to their new urban roles through marriage and motherhood (experiences associated not with the vulnerabilities of death, but with those of new life and child care) are not well recognized by the dominant anxiety treatments. As we see most explicitly in the later chapters, the growing population of agoraphobic women are reinserted into public urban space through treatments that retrain them in culturally masculine behavior. To rediscover the long history of agoraphobia as a gendered response to urban space, I propose that we go back through the clinical literature and bring the anxiety and the treatments of agoraphobia back in line with the specific objects of fear: particular sites of public space associated with emptiness. This first chapter, then, sets forth the need to recover the suppressed spatial triggers and gender-specific responses of the disorder and to interrogate them in conjunction with a history of the dominant and later alternative treatments.

Chapters 2 and 3 then go back through the psychiatric literature of the nineteenth century, focusing on spatial triggers of agoraphobia and the gendered patterns of its occurrence and treatments. This is the era in which we moderns were first imagined in constant, everyday relation to vast, empty urban space. Here, too, I note the gendered options employed by the agoraphobic soldier and the agoraphobic woman to handle the surplus sensibility of the self in the monumental new habitat of imperial, industrial Europe. I consider how different interpretive frameworks—psychoanalytic (object relations) and anti-Oedipal (Deleuze and Guattari)—explain the puzzling historical relation between this nineteenth-century public self and empty space.

Chapters 4, 5, and 6 focus on twentieth-century treatments for agoraphobia in Europe and the United States and their relation to the evolution of the agoraphobic's main urban triggers, the urban freeway and the modern shopping center. As agoraphobia becomes predominantly a women's disease, we move from the psychoanalytic therapies that treat the symptomatic value of agoraphobic fear to those that remove the symptom without mediation of psychological analysis—lobotomy in the 1950s and '60s; abreactive behavioral exposure in vivo (the "flooding" mentioned above) and pharmacology in the 1980s and '90s. These treatments open a new chapter on the role of desensitization in modern urban space and call for us to focus attention on the dominance of behavioral treatments today. Most important, the experience of the soldier's war neurosis remains crucial for our understanding of how women come to be treated and reinserted into those dreaded public spaces of late modernity. With the twentieth-century material I further develop the interpretive framework introduced previously to describe the cultural dimensions of subjectivity and public space.

Chapter 7 considers alternative treatments and discusses how the agoraphobic's surplus spatial sensibility is differently configured when the split mind/body paradigm of Western biomedicine and psychiatry shifts to a nondualist, psychosomatic approach. Recent work on agoraphobia involving neuroscience and effective bioenergetic therapies suggests that the embodied self communicates with its environment in ways that are little understood by traditional Western notions of consciousness. Using these findings to think about public space in urban design, I look first at the alternative therapeutic practice of labyrinth walking, and finally at a recent Dutch strategy for reclaiming urban neighborhoods from the dominance of car culture and its normative demands for a public self grounded in empty space. New spatial designs that create urban commons without creating empty space, I argue, suggest new expectations for twenty-first century public selves, especially for those acutely anxious and marginalized social actors whose grounding in civic life modernity had least prepared. In the conclusion, I reflect on specific questions posed in this introduction concerning the embodied public self and civic space. I emphasize how empty space has acted as a founding myth to explain what modern selves and modern cities have in common and I draw attention to the ways in which city design and psychology currently struggle to disengage themselves from the material and rhetorical force of empty space.

It bears repeating in this introduction that agoraphobia is a complex disorder whose causes are various and tied to individual histories. In no way should the actual urban trigger sites we recover in the clinical literature on agoraphobia be taken as causes of the disorder. Empty space does not cause agoraphobia. On the other hand, agoraphobia emerges historically in relation to certain forms of public space—forms that are, as we shall see, related to empty space. The treatments for the disorder also aim at the reinsertion of the individual back into those very sites. In this book our interest lies in the relation between those sites and the modern urban citizen who has been diagnosed with agoraphobia. The sites are triggers for (not causes of) the main symptoms of the disorder, which are extreme fear in and avoidance of the most common forms of public space in the modern city.

## Agoraphobia and Race: A Final Comment on What Cannot Yet Be Fully Addressed in this Book

The most important distinction I would like to make between the present study and the recent literature on agoraphobia as a psychopathology of modern society concerns the issue of race. Several recent commentators view agoraphobia as a pathology of white suburban women.[36] They note that with its characteristic symptom of withdrawal from public space, agoraphobia is a heightened acting out of the kind of domesticity prevalent among middle and upper middle-class white women for whom the anxieties of *possibility* have arisen, women who have the social and material resources to carry the language of femininity to symbolic excess.[37] Agoraphobia becomes a predominantly female disorder especially in the United States after the Second World War, they argue, when the symptom could only be acted out by affluent white housewives who could afford to live secluded in their suburban homes. For these urban critics the isolation and suburbanization of the agoraphobic individual in the United States is what accounts for the class and race fears that seem to nourish the agoraphobic symptom in white suburban women.[38] In many ways, agoraphobia does resemble a parody of twentieth-century constructions of white, middle-class femininity as a separate, domestic domain. We know that the industrial revolution required a sexual division of labor and a separation of dwelling from workplace. This certainly had an impact on the social identities of men and women even if it was not the origin of the notion that there existed a male public sphere and a female private sphere. However, as many historians have emphasized, despite local laws that would limit their movement, Euro-American women have had a continued presence in the public domain throughout the centuries. Apparently, it was only to men that their various public roles had been invisible.[39]

The strengths of these arguments notwithstanding, the clinical literature I studied shows that it is not so clear that the spatial disorientation of agoraphobia is a disease of white, middle-class, suburban women. While more ethnographic research would be needed to follow up on these findings, I can offer two reasons based on my archival research why it may not be the case that middle-class white women are the main victims of agoraphobia. The first is found by looking at the first clinical study on African Americans with agoraphobia, published in 1991.[40] There are forty patients in the study, all women, with a control group made up of white women of a "similarly low socio-economic background." Notably, only race—not gender or class—is given analytical attention in the study.[41] Both the African American and white women were treated at a large, inner-city clinic with the standard treatment: "behaviorally oriented psychotherapy with in-vivo exposure and tricyclic antidepressants."[42] The researchers found that the black women had a significantly lower rate of improvement with this treatment than did the white women, something they connect to the higher incidence of early childhood trauma and the history of misdiagnosis (and consequent unnecessary hospitalization) suffered by African Americans. This suggests that the scholarly expectation that agoraphobia is a white, suburban women's illness is a misplaced cultural expectation as well. The authors of the psychiatric study note that in addition to the absence of race as a factor in previous studies on agoraphobia, "it appears that treatment studies found in the literature are primarily of white middle-class patients."[43]

In addition to the racial bias informing the scholarship on agoraphobia, there is a second reason to doubt that agoraphobia is so characteristically a disorder of white suburban women. We know that suburban space is not the only product of the transformation of postwar American cities. The new urban freeways that enabled "white flight" from older cities cut through and destroyed the fabric of many inner-city ethnic neighborhoods, much as the restructuring of European capitals had done in the previous century. However, in the second part of the twentieth century the now instrumentally bureaucratized state had the means to relocate the displaced poor to vast, massive, serialized housing projects. While I could not find any studies of agoraphobia per se developing in these new conditions of segregated, monumentally abstract space, my sense is that this is largely because of the sorts of cultural assumptions that inform both medical and sociological research with the idea that agoraphobia is chiefly a disorder of white suburban women.[44]

Let me begin to correct this misperception by focusing attention on one study I came across, published in the *American Journal of Psychiatry* in 1966. The author is a psychiatric consultant hired by New York City to assess what was happening to residents of several brownstone houses relocated to the new housing projects after the city's 1960 directive "to rehous[e] all families living in single-rooms in New York City," a directive that went out shortly after the city's 1958 housing desegregation act—and around the same time that Robert Moses, the civil engineer who transformed (many would say "deformed") New York City declared many older, heterogeneous African American and Puerto Rican neighborhoods eminent domain for the Cross Bronx Expressway. The 1966 study is of the Bloomingdale Neighborhood Conservation Area, where 155 families were relocated, comprising 712 children and adults with single mothers as heads of *all* the households. The study points out that 80 percent of the families who "did not of their own accord ask" to be moved were "Negro," 19 percent "Puerto Rican," and 1 percent "mixed or white." The study has only one thing to say about the monumental chain of identical buildings to which these residents will be moved, describing them as "their new and spacious quarters." It has many things to say, however, about the old neighborhood from which they are moving: it is described as having "deteriorated buildings" with beds "usually shared by as many adults and children as could fit into them. Drug addicts and alcoholics roamed the halls, used the toilets, and were sometimes found sleeping in the kitchen. Sanitary conditions were appalling, with infestation of rats and vermin. There had been incidents of murder, attempted rape, and robberies in these buildings."[45]

Five years after the relocation, the author found that "phobias, or more accurately pan-phobias, became apparent as soon as these clients moved into new homes in new neighborhoods." He adds, "Some of the mothers who could not sleep without close contact with their children or another adult endeavored to return to their old sleeping arrangements. They would invite a sister or a previous paramour to come and stay with them. Although the new apartments had several rooms, only a single room would be used. Travel phobias became apparent and explained why they unconsciously chose their extreme isolation in one neighborhood, regardless of its condition. We could now understand their difficulty in keeping appointments with clinics or schools unless they were accompanied. These clients were not uncooperative but phobic, that is, fearful of doing anything alone. These phobic individuals *returned to their old neighborhoods for shopping.* School phobias developed in some of the children."[46]

Besides its obvious cultural bias assuming that the middle-class, Western individual with his well-bounded, indeed isolated, sense of self forms the "natural" standard of psychic health (even when that self is the primary caregiver of small children), the spatial phobia described in this study has overtones of other misdiagnoses in American history. Why couldn't, for instance, the American Indians of the Great Plains be assimilated to the spatial demands of the General Allotment Act of 1887, which aimed to relocate them out of their collective forms of social organization and give them individual plots, widely separated on the surveyor's grid in the hopes of making them proper farmers raising nuclear families?

There have been many assessments of the failures of the large-scale housing projects that transformed so many large cities in the United States and abroad in this era of modern city planning. Most recently, journalists watching the rioting across France in the fall of 2005 among disaffected third-generation youths who are descendents of the country's first wave of immigrants from former colonies in North Africa note that the unrest exploded from the serial concrete high-rises (the *cités*) that gave structural support to the racial segregation and high unemployment that mounted among these citizens over the years.[47] Thirty-some years ago, it was the demolition of the similarly structured Pruitt-Igoe housing project in St. Louis, Missouri, that spelled out the failures of such urban environments; indeed, the implosion of Pruitt-Igoo has been noted as the signature event of the failure of modernist architecture.[48] Thus, in both the United States and Europe, the vastness of suburban development and the failed efficiency of large-scale, modernist housing projects are linked by a foundational principle of tabula rasa, empty space: in both the modern, settler nation-state and the centrally bureaucratized European state, legitimizing and building for the relocation of people of color who were formerly colonized or enslaved involves the invocation of a tabula rasa or ground zero.[49] This zero, I argue, is related to the pervasive, unrepresentable, "central vacuity" of modern urban space.

The clinical literature I found for my study on treatments for agoraphobia focus almost exclusively on white, European, and Euro-American agoraphobics. While it can provide us with the evidence we need to understand many facets of the spatial pathologies that arise within the modern urban commons, without a more thorough look at issues of race and class it seems premature to generalize that agoraphobia is mainly a disease of white, suburban women. We can say, however, that the treatments that have been designed based on the clinical experiences of white, middle-class women are the ones that are recommended across the board to all women that would be treated with standard psychological approaches to phobias of public urban space.

CHAPTER 1

# The Disappearance of Public Space in Psychiatric Descriptions of Agoraphobia

## *Dr. Westphal (1871) and Dr. Boyd (1991)*

To diagnose agoraphobia, some fear of and tendency to avoid public places is a *sine qua non*: the fear of fear or of harmful consequences to oneself are frequent concomitants but not essential features.

—**Dr. Isaac M. Marks,** *Fears, Phobias and Rituals*

### Introduction

The term *agoraphobia* was first coined by Dr. Carl Friedrich Otto Westphal (1833–1890), a professor at Berlin University. Westphal was an innovator, one of the leaders of the movement for nonrestraint in the treatment of the insane and one of the first to lecture on mental disorders at the University. It was in 1871, shortly after the unification of the German nation-state and the emergence of Berlin as the nation's capital, that Westphal's paper "Die Agoraphobie: Eine Neuropathische Erscheinung" (Agoraphobia: A Neuropathic Phenomenon) first appeared. It provided the case histories of three young men who all presented the same complaint: a fear of crossing certain large, open public squares (*freie Plätze*) in Berlin. On approaching these squares, the men would be overcome with the physical signs of anxiety (heart palpitations, trembling, dizziness, and an immobilizing fear of dying).[1] Westphal had never before seen such symptoms triggered by this type of public space and thus gave the phenomenon a Greek name, *Agoraphobie* (a neologism that literally meant, "fear of the marketplace") and a German name, *Platzfurcht* ("plaza/square fright").

Westphal's article led to a flurry of responses in other European psychiatric journals where doctors wrote of similar patients, mostly male, whose anxiety also made them falter at the curb of their cities' most immense plazas. The articles published on agoraphobia in this period all adopt more or less the same form. Case histories of the afflicted city dwellers, often using the patients' own words to describe feelings of anxiety and the sites of its occurrence, would be followed by an abstract description of the disorder tracing its etiology in terms of various contemporary theories of nervous pathologies. Thus agoraphobia was thought to be a problem of the liver (Cherchevsky) or the ear (M. Lannois and C. Tournier). Insufficient will (Paul Emil Lévy) was also thought to be a cause as was excessive sex and alcohol (Henry Sutherland) or coffee (Legrand du Salle). Others argued that fatigue (Emil Cordes), and childbearing (C.W. Suckling) were central factors.. In the German texts agoraphobia tends to be linked to a species of epilepsy or to an unknown optical malfunction (M. Benedikt). Later, in the 1920s and '30s, it is common to find agoraphobia labeled as a displaced mental symbol (Helene Deutsche, Sigmund Freud) or a degenerative nerve disease linked to syphilis (J. de Busscher, Th. Henusse). More recently, since the late 1950s, it is seen variously as a nervous habit to be broken (behaviorism), a misinterpretation of normal body sensations (cognitive theory), an imbalance of certain hormones, or a mechanical malfunction of "the suffocation centers in the brain" (psychopharmacology and biological psychiatry). The prescribed treatments always correspond to the description of the disorder. Thus, today we find agoraphobia most often described as a chemical imbalance and treated most commonly with a combination of drugs and cognitive-behaviorist techniques.

Given our interest in agoraphobia as a cultural pathology of modern space, we must wonder what has become of social space in the descriptions and treatments of this disorder. Where is the spatial component of agoraphobia in the above-mentioned treatments, and what is being done to reinsert the fearful citizen once again into public space? The past 130 years of clinical literature on the topic of agoraphobia manifest a gradual and eventually complete disappearance of any concern with the social space that originally gave rise to the psychic problem. Today the dominant treatments for agoraphobia show no regard for the common features of the most often reported urban trigger sites. In this chapter I examine how and why social space has been deleted from the description and treatment of agoraphobia by looking closely at how current psychology has translated and interpreted Dr. Westphal's original case studies.

## From Dr. Westphal to Dr. Boyd: The Disappearance of Public Space

In 1991 the *Journal of Anxiety Disorders* published what the author and translator claimed was the first English translation of Dr. Westphal's 1871 case. The article includes translated excerpts of the original German by Ted Crump of the National Institute of Health Library Translation Unit and commentary by Dr. Jeffrey Boyd (M.D., M.P.H.) of Grand View Psychiatric Resource Center and Yale University. Let us follow the translation and commentary carefully in order to see how the public space that was so integral to the first descriptions of agoraphobia—and to subsequent descriptions up until the 1950s when randomized, controlled studies of behaviorists and biopsychiatrists took over—comes to be completely evacuated in our own day. Here then is an excerpt from Crump's translation of Westphal's 1871 text concerning a thirty-two-year-old traveling salesman. At certain points I have inserted the original German text in brackets for comparison. In places where the German text was not translated I have inserted the original German and a translation in brackets.

> He is a thirty-two year old, of medium height, slender build, healthy appearance and is lively in speech and movements. He complains that it is impossible for him to cross an open space [*freie Plätzen*]. If he attempts to do so, he is immediately seized with a feeling of anxiety [*Angstgefühl*], whose location upon questioning he reveals to be more in the head than in the heart region. However, there are often heart palpitations accompanying it. In Berlin the Donhofplatz is the most unpleasant for him; if he tries to cross it, he is struck by the feeling that the distance is very great, miles wide, that he will never get to the other side, and connected to this is the referred-to feeling of anxiety, often accompanied by a general tremor. Turning toward the sides of the square [the Begrenzungen des Plätzes] the closer he comes to the buildings, the more his feeling of anxiety disappears. If he goes arm-in-arm with someone else or involved in conversation across the square [*Platz*], the feeling of anxiety is much less. A staff or an umbrella in his hand gives him no security. On the other hand it has often occurred that, occupied with his thoughts, he crossed a square [*Platz*] without noticing that he had done so. If a wagon is crossing the square [*Platz*], then he can cross with ease if he stays close to it; otherwise he would be entirely unable to, and would go around. He cannot go to Charlottenburg, through the zoological garden, because there are no buildings in the garden.
>
> He is seized by the same feeling of anxiety when he is obliged to pass by walls or long buildings [*Exerciserhaus in der Carlsstrausse, Artillerieschule unter den Linden*; the gymnasium in Carlsstrasse, the artillery

> school in Unter den Linden] or along streets when the shops are closed (as on Sundays or Fridays or later in the evening and late night hours). In the evenings—he usually goes to restaurants in the evenings—he helps himself in Berlin in a singular fashion; either he waits until he sees someone start off in the direction of his home and follows closely behind that person, or he takes up with a lady of the night, engages in conversation with her and thus goes some distance until he finds another similar opportunity and so gradually reaches home.[2]

One of the first things to note in this English version is the translation of the term *angst*. The term has a very different semantic field in German than the term *anxiety* has in English. This is in part due to the interpretation of angst in nineteenth-century German philosophy and theology and its reverberations in German culture. Søren Kierkegaard (1813–1855), the Danish theologian, gave the term *angst* an ontological status, making it "the unavoidable companion of reflective consciousness in man." Angst, for Kierkegaard, arises from the recognition that a state of nothingness is both thinkable and possible: "With every increase in the degree of consciousness," Kierkegaard writes, "and in proportion to the increase, the intensity of despair increases: the more conscious, the more intense the despair."[3] Thus, the experience of angst, which would need to be rendered in English as some combination of anxiety and dread, is associated in various areas of German culture with a fundamental feature of the human condition, one that the twentieth century German philosopher Martin Heidegger—and other thinkers in what became known as existentialism—would privilege as an authentic mode of being in the world. Karl Jaspers, who developed a school of existential psychotherapy around the experience of angst (*Daseinsanalyse*, or "analysis of one's there being"), articulated anxiety's positive aspects and showed great suspicion toward psychiatry's attempts to remove it from everyday life. "Large numbers, particularly of modern people, seem to live fearlessly because they lack imagination," Jaspers writes. "The freedom from *angst* is but the other side of a deeper loss of freedom."[4] Jaspers's work was particularly important in elaborating what came to be an important distinction in the phenomenology of anxiety that has had special meaning for the description of agoraphobia: the distinction between "free-floating" (*freiflottierende*) and "object-related" (*objektbezogene*) anxiety—a distinction between contextless (unsituated) and contextual (situated) anxiety. I will come back to the significance of these important cultural inflections in the vocabulary of anxiety in subsequent chapters. For now it is enough to note that angst is not the same as anxiety, if by that we mean the neurotic symptom. European languages have many terms to describe the experiences associated with the English word *anxiety*. In French, for example, there is *anxiété*, but this word does not cover the same semantic space as *anxiety*. Sometimes the word *angoisse* is proposed as a near synonym (likewise *ansiedad* and *angustia* in Spanish), but *angoisse* better describes the English *anguish* with emphasis on the bodily sensations of the emotion. So here we have the first obstacle to the translation of the nineteenth-century German experience of agoraphobia's Platzangst.

A second question we might ask about the 1991 edition of Westphal's classic nineteenth-century study concerns why this urtext on agoraphobia should resurface in an American psychiatric journal specializing in anxiety disorders at the end of the twentieth century. In the theoretical and review article titled "Westphal's Agoraphobia" that follows the 1991 translation, author Boyd answers our question, noting, "Professor Westphal, [in his] … classic clinical description of agoraphobia … is often said [to have] defined agoraphobia as a fear of public places … whereas for Westphal it was [in fact] a fear of open spaces, some of which were public places, some of which were not. … Westphal emphasizes large open spaces rather than public places, for example: a deserted town plaza, a broad empty boulevard, a theater, a church, the seashore, a small boat in open water."[5]

Immediately we see that Boyd wishes to correct a misreading of Westphal. According to Boyd, it is not "public" space that the agoraphobics in Westphal's study fear; rather, it is a sort of asocial, abstract space: "wide open spaces" as such. Thus, Boyd appears to be uninterested in the preponderance of public urban sites mentioned in Westphal's text where the public spaces outnumber the nonurban sites by far. The preponderance of dreaded public sites in Westphal's text would also elude the general English reader because many of these sites are actually removed from the text in the English translation. (I reinserted, for example, *Exerciserhaus in der Carlsstrausse, Artillerieschule unter den Linden* (the gymnasium in Carlsstrasse, the artillery school in Unter den Linden). By suggesting that the space feared by Westphal's patients is not related to a historical, built environment, Boyd reduces the spatial complexity of the agoraphobic disorder. The geometric common denominator of angst-provoking space thus becomes a generic sort of large, open, or empty space. By reducing what Westphal calls *freie Plätze* (large open squares) to "open space," a space emptied of its public, historical, and social coordinates, Boyd abstracts the agoraphobic's experience of everyday life. This move is partially due to the mistranslation of the opening sentence of Westphal's original essay:

> Seit mehreren Jahren haben sich wiederholt Kranke mit der eigenthümlichen Klage an mich gewandt, dass es ihnen nicht möglich sei, über freie Plätze und durch gewisse Strassen zu gehen und sie aus Furcht vor sochen Wegen in der Freiheit ihrer Bewegungen genirt würden.[6]

> For several years patients have repeatedly come to me with the peculiar complaint that it is impossible for them to go into open spaces [*freie Plätze*] and down certain streets, and because of this fear their freedom of movement is disturbed.[7]

*Freie Plätze* are specifically open spaces in a city (the closest English equivalent to *Plätze* would be "squares" or "plazas"). In English, as in German, the words *square* or *plaza* would not be used to refer to an open space in the countryside. Thus the English translation is conveniently misleading and does not correspond to the overwhelming number of agoraphobic case histories from this period wherein the onset of the disorder is linked to specific metropolitan sites characterized interchangeably by their vastness, their crowdedness, and their emptiness. One might say that the translation Boyd uses to bring nineteenth-century agoraphobia into the purview of late-twentieth-century psychiatry involves a "retroactive homogenization" (or a retroactive abstraction) of the historic agoraphobic's fear-provoking site. City space, public space thus becomes mere space.

## Recovering Public Space in the Urban World of Late-Nineteenth-Century Agoraphobia

The current trend among psychiatrists to retroactively homogenize or abstract the city space of the nineteenth-century agoraphobic is striking when one considers the enormous efforts of our contemporary new urbanists to undo the abstract openness of modernist public space in Euro-American city design. It is as if, on the one hand, urban planners had noticed that the abstract space of modernist design mattered negatively in the mental life of city dwellers while, on the other hand, urban psychologists were proclaiming that the specifics of public space do not matter in the metropolitan person's psychic state. So, what if we were to keep the historical landmarks of the nineteenth century urban trigger sites in our view as we probe into the complexity of the rise of agoraphobia in European cities? What would we see? We would see that these sites provide essential information for a consideration of agoraphobia as a disorder of modernity broadly speaking. This is precisely the period in which European capitals are dismantling their feudal cityscapes in exchange for the huge public squares and wide boulevards that befit great empires. The architectural gigantomania of this period, in fact, corresponds to the second wave of European imperialism that saw Germany (as well as other European nation-states) increase their colonial holdings manifold. The expansive monumentalism of the architecture going up at home corresponds to the extension of empire abroad.

Attention to the specificity of these sites allows us to further reconnect the discipline of psychology to other spheres of social commentary. We understand, then, for example, why the "new" disease of agoraphobia could be used by contemporary critics of nineteenth-century urbanism to point to the dehumanizing effects of modern architecture. The well-known Viennese architect Camille Sitte, in his book *City Planning According to Artistic Principles* (1898), laid out his opposition to the construction of Vienna's Ringstrasse by way of a comparison with the agoraphobic's withdrawal from monumental urban space. We read, "Recently a unique nervous disorder has been diagnosed—'agoraphobia.' Numerous people are said to suffer from it, always experiencing a certain anxiety or discomfort whenever they have to walk across a vast empty space. Agoraphobia is a very new and modern ailment. One naturally feels very cozy in small, old plazas. … On our modern gigantic plazas, with their yawning emptiness and oppressive ennui, the inhabitants of snug old towns suffer attacks of this fashionable agoraphobia."[8]

The Ringstrasse was a vast boulevard 190 feet wide and monumentally out of scale with the historic fabric of the city. It was built on the site of Vienna's ancient ramparts, which had served for centuries as an architectural (and psychological) boundary, protecting the city's historic center where the aristocracy and the wealthy bourgeoisie and their servants lived. The proletariat lived on the other side of the wall in a featureless urban sprawl. Unconscious class fears may well have motivated the critiques of the Ringstrasse since the walls that came down had long separated the city's wealthy from its poor and minorities.[9] The large new spaces in Europe's capital cities might also be sites of intermingling for the many who migrated to the city from rural areas at this time. Here, too, a fear of "the masses" who now had the vast new squares and boulevards as sites for congregation may have provoked anxiety in the bourgeois agoraphobic. (It was most certainly not the working poor who could pay for private sessions with a psychiatrist and thus show up in the clinical literature at this time.)

Besides class fears, the political critique of urban redevelopment during this period also focuses on the alienation experienced by urban citizens. From Charles-Pierre Baudelaire's lament over the restructuring of Paris to Friedrich Engels's critique of "Haussmannization" and later in Georg Simmel's attack on the urban estrangement caused by the abstraction of money as the common denominator in metropolitan life, the concern over social anomie is present.

Perhaps the most famous expression of the feel of modern urban alienation during the period surrounding Westphal's original study comes from the 1895 painting "The Scream," by Norwegian artist Edvard Munch, who had lived in the recently Haussmannized Paris in 1885 (see figure 2).

**Figure 2** "The Scream" by Edvard Munch. 1985 lithograph of the artist's original 1893 painting in Nasjonal galleriet (National Gallery), Oslo.

Munch was by all measures an agoraphobic whose public anxiety attacks—depicted in his artwork and described in his diaries—have been compared to Westphal's description of the agoraphobic's fear of open city space.[10] As art historians have often noted, Munch used his sensibility to describe the speed and alienation of modern urban life, borrowing from the vertiginous balcony view of the French artist Gustave Caillebotte. According to art historian Robert Rosenbaum, Munch, in his

> new pictorial image of modern, Haussmannized Paris, in which regimented city boulevards, stretching infinitely from near to far, tilt up and down at angles of breathtaking velocity ... used the human and spatial premises of Parisian urban images of the 1870s as the founda-

> tion for his rapid shift from the external to the internal world of the modern city-dweller. The funneling perspective of lines of an urban axis suddenly move, as they threaten to do in Caillebotte's painting, from reason to feeling; from the measurement of city spaces to a suicidal plunge; and the anonymous pedestrians constantly encountered singly, in pairs, or in crowds in the city streets are swiftly transformed into the immediate terror of a confrontation with skull-like, menacing faces in the foreground or the potential terror on an encounter with tiny, shadowy figures lurking in the remote distance, Pressing further Caillebotte's images of the new rectilinear facts of Paris city-planning and the new human facts of crowds of strolling, middle-class strangers, Munch turned these urban truths of the late nineteenth century into a private nightmare that accelerated dizzyingly in *The Scream* … inaugurat[ing] a new world of psychological responses to the city. … [11]

Similarly, when the mid-twentieth century German literary critic Walter Benjamin researched the urban space of late-nineteenth-century European empire from his pre–World War II perspective, he found the bourgeois figure of the flaneur, the comfortable man-about-town, as the citizen most able to transform the alienation brought on by the massification of urban life into an aesthetic principle—dandyism.[12] Social critics, artists, and agoraphobics all refer to the same large open urban spaces whether they are describing a metaphorical or sociological ill of modern city life or whether they are simply describing the places they dread to cross. The connection between agoraphobia and expansive changes in the modern city is impossible to deny. For example, in an autobiographical description from an American agoraphobic who, in 1919, makes the case between the "so-called improvements in some of our cities" and his fear of urban space he writes, "I have outgrown the fear of crowds largely, but an immense building or a high rocky bluff fills me with dread. However[,] the architecture of the building has much to do with the sort of sensation produced. Ugly architecture greatly intensifies the fear. In this connection I would remark that I have come to wonder if there is real art in many of the so-called "improvements" in some of our cities, for, judging from the effect they produce on me, they constitute bad art. … "[13]

We can now summarize our discussion of Boyd's commentary by posing two problems with the translation and interpretation of Westphal's original text: first, angst is removed from the semantic field of existential experience, and second, specific places are no longer offered as clues to the etiology of the disorder. Far from giving the illness of agoraphobia some historical depth, the 1991 rendition of Westphal's text encourages late-twentieth-century psychiatrists and psychologists to interpret agoraphobia as an ahistorical, nonsymbolic, physical ailment with no regard to its value as an individual manifestation of a broader cultural pathology that is historically specific and tenaciously related to changes in public urban space.

## The New Symptom: Fear of Fear; The New Disease: Panic Disorder; The New Treatment: Pharmacological Cognitive Behaviorism

The reductive reading of agoraphobia as a mere reaction to abstract, open space not only erases the sociohistorical nature of the illness. The text's achievement of homogeneous over specific urban space is furthermore used to raise one symptom of the pathology—panic—to a new level of recognition, of interpretation and eventually of treatment. In this respect Boyd's interpretation of the nineteenth-century case provides us with an excellent example of what has happened to agoraphobia in modern psychiatry as social space was removed from the medical picture. We see this most clearly in the passage in which Boyd offers an explanation for Westphal's inability to account for the etiology of agoraphobia:

> [Westphal] is unable to account for the etiology of the disorder.... [He] goes to some trouble in the article to discount three theories that had been proposed to explain this phobia of open spaces: epilepsy, dizziness, or an optical distortion of the visual image of large spaces. In the end he is unable to account for the etiology of the disorder. He does not focus on *panic attacks*, and it is therefore all the more striking that symptoms suggestive of panic attacks are evident in the second and third case histories, and probably in the first and last cases also. Westphal describes the first patient's agoraphobia as a "*fear of fear*." As we re-read the article 119 years later, the possibility of panic attacks as the etiology of the agoraphobia springs to mind.[14]

Boyd notes that while Westphal was wrong about the cause of agoraphobia, he did mention the one trait of the illness around which the dominant theory and treatment of agoraphobia in the United States has been built. That symptomatic trait is the "fear of fear." Its new etiology is called "panic disorder," and the new (and currently dominant) treatments come from pharmacological cognitive behaviorism. Let us go over each of these developments more carefully in order to see how the erasure of social space has come to support a particular etiology and treatment for agoraphobia.

*Fear of Fear: A Zero Sign Becomes the New Description of Agoraphobia*

Today, the literature on agoraphobia is dominated by the notion that, unlike other phobic disorders that have specific objects of fear (arachnophobia, hydrophobia, and the like) agoraphobia is characterized by its lack of a specific object. Agoraphobia, in our time, is described merely as an intense and abnormal fear of the experience of fear. Recall that psychiatrists had in the past generally agreed on the distinction between free-floating anxiety (generalized fears) and situational anxiety (phobic anxiety). Agoraphobia had in Westphal's day been viewed as a (place-) specific phobia—thus its name *agora*-phobia. After World War II and the psychiatric research undertaken by behaviorists in Britain, agoraphobia was increasingly described as nonsituational, as "staying-at-home behavior rather than as avoidance of a particular situation."[15] Biological psychiatry takes the description of agoraphobia even farther away from its relation to urban space by locating the problem entirely in the physical brain or hormonal system of the patient. Thus in the United States in the late 1970s and early 1980s, research that was largely sponsored by the pharmaceutical industry focused on one symptom of the disorder—the patient's fear of his own behavior in public space—to the exclusion of all other symptoms (such as avoidance behavior, spousal issues, separation anxiety, and so on). The gradual loss of objectival specificity can be clearly noted in current descriptions of agoraphobia from both medical texts and the popular press.[16]

The "fear of fear" thesis betrays a dramatic collapse of the subject/object relations of the experiential world into a purely phenomenological, subject-based sense of the illness. From a broader anthropological perspective the "fear of fear" thesis can be read as a "zero sign" in our culture at large and it is worth our taking a short detour to better understand the significance of this kind of social sign. In semiotics (the study of sign systems) zero signs are signs that refer only to themselves. Consider, for example, one of the more obvious zero signs, the number *0*. Zero, which entered Western mathematics as Arabic numerals displaced the Roman system of counting, does not point to something else—as do the integers "one," "two," "three," and so forth. It refers only to itself—that is, to itself as "nothing."[17] Zero signs act as rhetorical devices and their appearance on the cultural horizon is an interesting phenomena, a call to arms for the cultural critic. The emergence of a fear-of-fear thesis in late-twentieth-century descriptions of agoraphobia in fact signals several important things about the cultural assumptions of personhood in our day and about how we, as cultural critics, can analyze these assumptions.

Critics note three rhetorical functions in a zero sign. First is the tendency to make complex social contexts disappear. Agoraphobia, understood

**Figure 3** The artist's grid to create one-point perspective: Albrecht Dürer, illustrations from the *Treatise on Measurement* (1525).

as a fear of fear, is a way of pointing only to the individual agoraphobic, not to the social or spatial contexts of its occurrence. Moreover, reduced only to itself, fear (or anxiety) is also reduced to a single state of being. Whether it is approached as a simplified animal state (the physiological state of autonomic arousal), an abstract phenomenological state (an individual's subjective experience of fear), or a cognitive, bioinformational model (where "anxiety is based on informational structures consisting of stimulus, response, and meaning propositions represented in a network of memory nodes"), fear is conceived as a single state undifferentiated by either circumstances or physiology. It is as if a fearful state induced by separation from a loved one was the same as a fearful state brought on by a life-threatening danger or by an undesired anticipated future event.[18]

In addition to their reductive, self referential function, zero signs point to a hidden organizational dimension. To best grasp its organizing function think of how the zero sign works as the vanishing point in one-point linear perspective drawings. The vanishing point is the invisible point that establishes the grid around which all other signs in its range are organized. The vanishing point reveals how the artist's point of view is inscribed in the frame as the "subjective" point of view from which any other onlooker will also see the world organized. (The optical trick of one-point perspective became naturalized in Western culture since the renaissance: we generally refer to it as an "objective" perspective; see figure 3.) As the viewer imperceptibly takes on the painter's point of view, she learns to objectify herself, to erase a particular subjectivity and take on the subject position of the painter which, in becoming transferable, has itself become an object of sorts. With regard to agoraphobia, the organizing aspect of the fear-of-fear thesis directs all those who would understand the disorder—including the patient herself—to "see" the illness from the perspective of late-twentieth-century biopsychology.

A third characteristic of the zero sign is its capacity to open up a space for dissension. Retrieving the zero sign in painting, for example, allows us to reconstruct the process of the painting. Once the process has been foregrounded, the viewer might note that there are many other positions from which to view the scene in question. The potential for such diversity can then be an invitation for a viewer to consider other points of view. With regard to agoraphobia, the fear-of-fear thesis is a zero sign that, once revealed as such, leads us to consider historical, cultural, feminist, and other critical points of view. These three characteristics of the zero sign—its self-referentiality, the creation of subject/object positions, and the capacity to open up a space for dissention—can all be invoked with regard to agoraphobia. They give us a visceral sense of the powerful spatial rhetoric at stake when agoraphobia is collapsed into the fear-of-fear thesis and public space is "disappeared" from the definition.

*Panic Disorder: The New Description of Agoraphobia Becomes a New Theory of Its Cause*

The second issue raised by Boyd's gloss of Westphal's case histories concerns the new etiology of agoraphobia. In his commentary, Boyd explains how a new description can lead to a new etiology, a new narrative of how the pathology came about. "Description is never simply description," Boyd rightly tells us. "It has embedded in it a certain emphasis,… plac[ing] a priority on some aspects of a phenomenon over other[s]…and thereby a description can suggest a theory of etiology." Westphal, Boyd notes, "made a major contribution in describing a clinical condition. However, his emphasis on the 'fear of open spaces' (such as markets, agora) has not withstood the test of time…. [Westphal] succeeded in describing a complex clinical phenomenon, but failed in terms of selecting which aspect of that phenomenon to emphasize. Can you imagine, for example, where we would be today if Westphal had chosen to emphasize panic attacks, instead of emphasizing wide open spaces, in his original description of agoraphobia? Had that happened then he might have named the diagnosis 'panic-phobia' instead of 'agoraphobia.'[19]

Boyd's discussion explains why biopsychological clinical researchers focusing on the fear of fear in the 1970s were led to study the effects of various drugs not on the avoidance behavior per se, but rather on the physical reaction of panic. *Panic disorder* then came to be the preferred term to describe the general condition under which agoraphobia would be grouped in the new classification of anxiety that came out in 1980 in the third revised edition of the American Psychiatric Association's *Diagnostic and Statistical Manual of Mental Disorders* (*DSM-IIIR*).

The American introduction of "panic disorder" as a category distinct from "generalized anxiety disorder" was confusing to European classifications of anxiety at the time.[20] Thus, Dr. Assen Jablensky of the World Health Organization (WHO) comments on the strangeness of the new American classification of "panic disorder" in 1984, noting that panic states do not form a separate category under anxiety states in the WHO's *International Classification of Diseases.* He points out that "with the exception of English-language psychiatry, the term 'panic' is hardly ever used in Europe. Although the phenomenon of acute attacks or exacerbations of anxiety 'out of the blue' is recognized ... it has received far less attention in non-English speaking psychiatry and certainly has not been regarded as a phenomenon presenting any special problems for classification. For example, the manual to the *Arbeitsgruppe fur Methodik und Dokumentation in der Psychiatrie* (Working Group on Methods and Documentation in Psychiatry) (1982), a widely used methodology for the standardized recording of clinical information, does not contain a reference to panic."[21]

Why was the symptom of panic raised to such prominence at this time in the American context? According to Jablensky, the main reason for the new emphasis on panic is the invention of a new class of drugs; he notes that "until recently the treatment and management of anxiety disorders was rather nonspecific and did not call for fine diagnostic and classificatory distinctions as prerequisites for a rational choice of therapeutic modalities. Only with the advent of the benzodiazepines, the coinage of the new term 'anxiolytic,' and the discovery of a putative benzodiazepine receptor in the brain did anxiety disorders reemerge on the psychiatric *avant-scene. The epidemic of over-prescription and over-use of anxiolytics gave psychiatrists, for the first time, an inkling of the true epidemiological dimensions of the problem of anxiety in the community.*"[22]

Benzodiazepines are certainly the most widely studied drugs for anxiety in the 1960s. But whether their overuse was an indication of the epidemiological dimensions of the problem of anxiety in Cold War Britain and America, as Jablensky suggests, or whether it was their potential market value that led the pharmaceutical industry to play a more significant role in anxiety research in the United States during the 1970s (where studies of anxiolytic drugs on mice and primates continued to refine the work of the British behaviorists), both of these reasons can help account for the refocus of the clinical understanding of agoraphobia in the English-speaking world away from the object of fear in public space and toward the physiology of panic in the fearful subject. Between 1982 and 1986 Upjohn, a U.S. pharmaceutical company, began one of the largest controlled clinical trials in the history of psychiatry to test a new benzodiazepine, alprazolam (Xanax), for U.S. Food and Drug Administration approval. They sought

FDA approval to use their drug for the treatment of the *DSM-IIIR*'s new category: panic disorder. Alprazolam had previously been approved at lower dosages for the treatment of generalized anxiety, but Upjohn's study (the Cross-National Collaborative Panic Study), which involved approximately 1,700 patients and over twenty senior investigators at centers in fourteen countries in North America, South America, and Western Europe, was testing alprazolam at higher dosages for panic. The *DSM-IIIR* redescription of agoraphobia had created a new field for biopsychiatric research. In 1988 Upjohn gained FDA approval, and the expansion of biopsychiatry for agoraphobia and many other psychological problems was on its way.

### *Pharmacological Cognitive Behaviorism: New Treatments to Accompany the New Description*

This brings me to the third point I wish to raise concerning Boyd's commentary on Westphal's case. What new treatments will be developed based on the new etiology of agoraphobia as "panic disorder"? In his article Boyd gives us an example by directing our attention to the work of Donald Klein, a major researcher and theorist in the field of anxiety disorders, whose clinical studies beginning in the early 1960s reinterpret the descriptive phenomenology of "panic attacks." Klein, Boyd notes,

> places a new emphasis on the experiences of breathlessness and air hunger. He points out that we may in the past have placed too much emphasis on the cardiac symptoms. What emerges from this shift in emphasis of the clinical description, is the suggestion of an entirely new theory of the etiology of panic attacks. Klein suggests that the brain abnormalities of panic disorder might be thought of as constituting a derangement of the "suffocation centers" of the brain. The idea is that our brain naturally has a way of sounding an alarm if we are being suffocated, and in some people that regulatory thermostat may have an incorrectly low threshold, such that alarm bells go off internally causing the person to gasp for air and to attempt to flee the place where the suffocation is experienced.[23]

With its alarm bells, broken thermostat metaphors and linear chains of causality, Klein's "suffocation center" theory of panic disorder may appear overly mechanistic in its approach to the complex neurological, emotional, and urban systems that appear to be communicating with each other in the experience of agoraphobia.[24] But this mechanistic quality makes it a good testing ground for a pharmacological psychiatry that will redirect therapeutic concern thereafter toward the regulatory control of physiological "centers." Beginning in the late 1950s and increasingly to this day, agoraphobia in the United States is primarily treated as a physiological problem—despite the high correlation between adult agoraphobia and early separation trauma in childhood and the problems raised by feminists and psychoanalysts on the relation between agoraphobia's high percentage of female sufferers and the culturally gendered nature of public space.[25] Since the development of the "anxiolytics," the dominant mode of therapy for agoraphobia remains a combination of pharmacologic, behaviorist, and cognitive methods: most commonly this takes the form of repeated trips to the shopping mall (the behaviorist desensitization technique of in vivo exposure) with the patient on antidepressants and/or anxiolytics (the most commonly used drugs) as the patient is retrained (through cognitive processes) how to "conquer [note the militaristic metaphor] her fear."[26]

A close study of Dr. Boyd's 1991 translation and commentary of Dr. Westphal's 1872 inaugural study of agoraphobia demonstrates that over the last 120 years the clinical literature can reveal how agoraphobia has lost its connection to social space. More specifically, the clinical literature shows that what has been lost is the connection between agoraphobia and the perception of emptiness in public urban space. Empty space, we see, is both a structure of feeling and an element of the built environment. Without a thorough understanding of the relation between agoraphobia and empty space we can never fully understand the cultural implications of this modern pathology of urban space.

## Affects of Occulted Empty Space across the Spectrum of Treatment Modalities

The brief introductory review of dominant treatment patterns revealed in Dr. Boyd's commentary shows that, lacking a sense of spatial and historical context, the treatments that accept agoraphobia as "panic disorder" end up introjecting the external, public emptiness they ignore into the agoraphobic's sense of self. By reducing the agoraphobic's reaction to modern urban space to a mere fear-of-fear reflex, post–World War II clinical psychiatry posits an abstract interior form of (subjective) empty space which, as it turns out, matches the dehistoricized and abstract form of (objectival) space now ubiquitously appearing in the modernist design of the built environment of postwar European and American cities.

The further abstraction of the agoraphobic's experiential being can be noted in the clinical description of the agoraphobic patient since World War II. From behaviorism to pharmacological/biologic psychiatry, the description of the agoraphobic patient is a mathematical one: statistical in behaviorism and biochemical in biopsychiatry. Thus, the agoraphobic has doubly become an abstract subject in empty, Euclidean space, not only through the dominant treatments but also through the very techniques of looking at and studying her. This is the ultimate irony for the agoraphobic. When the new psychiatric treatments study, desensitize, and reinsert agoraphobics back into fearful domains of public urban space, they reproduce them as (cognitively deluded) subjects of abstract space in order to cure them of their "foolish" fears that urban space is pocked with abstract emptiness.

The following synopses of psychological theories describe the dominant therapies for treating agoraphobia in the United States. While these theories and their specific treatment modalities will be analyzed in greater cultural depth in chapters 6 and 7, an overview of their explanatory models is useful here to demonstrate the extent to which empty space has become an introjected form of mental life and to show where the symptom of panic has become the central focus of treatment.[27]

*Biological Theories*

There are several theories that claim that agoraphobia—in as much as it is a panic disorder—is caused by biological dysfunctions. Various studies based on these theories claim to show connections between agoraphobic panic and abnormal biological processes: defective genetic inheritance, hyperactive or other dysregulative aspects of the central nervous system (such as dysregulation of noradrenergic, benzodiazepeine, or serotonin systems), chronic hyperventilation, abnormally sensitive carbon dioxide chemoreceptors in the brain stem (Klein's suffocation alarm theory), abnormal balance systems, and deficits in perceptual-motor skill. Pharmacological treatments are generally offered when agoraphobia is understood in these ways.[28]

*Cognitive Theories*

Cognitive models stress that agoraphobics misinterpret bodily sensations of panic in a catastrophic way (i.e., the experience of an increased heart rate is thought to be a heart attack). Such cognitive models assume that it is the panickers' conception of these sensations—and not the specificity of the external or even internal triggers—that results in the avoidance behavior of agoraphobia. Consequently, these cognitive models work on changing an individual's thought processes regarding bodily sensations of panic. Other cognitive models focus on changing a person's belief in his own capacity to cope with threatening situations, increasing his sense of personal control, making him more aware of linguistic, memory, or emotional cues associated with his fears, and various other modes of intervention into conscious thought processes that arise in situations where agoraphobic panic sets in.

### *Behaviorist and Psychoanalytic Models*

While cognitive theories focus on conscious thought processes, other psychological models understand agoraphobia in terms of an individual's unconscious processes. Unconscious behavior may be understood in terms of nonsymbolic stimuli around which unwanted habitual responses have formed. From this perspective, agoraphobic avoidance and panic are habituated/conditioned fear responses that behavioral retraining may help to "extinguish." From a psychoanalytic perspective, unconscious conflicts are generally understood as repressed sexual or other unacceptable desires that break into consciousness when the ego's defense mechanisms are not able to shield the person from the danger that these unacceptable desires imply. Anxiety then breaks through to consciousness in a myriad of symptoms. Panic results from feeling totally overwhelmed. Agoraphobia, from a psychoanalytic perspective, is understood as the symbolic substitution of suppressed desires. Studies based on theories of unconscious processes delve into patients' past histories and find that people with panic disorder struggle with repressed feelings of aggression toward parents who were critical and controlling. In women with panic disorder they also find "high rates of sexual and/or physical abuse, the witnessing of family violence, and parental alcohol abuse," experiences that are "likely to lead to the development of personality disorders." Some researchers speculate that "the sense of emotional vulnerability and loss of control can result in neurophysiological changes, which, in turn, render the person vulnerable to panic."[29]

### *Biopsychosocial Approaches*

In the guides to treatments for agoraphobia, one often finds the above theories combined to form a "biopsychosocial" approach. It is worth quoting at some length from one such treatment guide in order to see how the relatively new category of *panic* allows the diverse theories mentioned above to be combined in a seamless way. Summarizing the integrative, "biopsychosocial" approach of behaviorist David H. Barlow, whose work in the 1980s defended the new interpretation of agoraphobia as a panic disorder, Elke Zuercher-White notes, "A biological vulnerability to stress exists, which may involve an overactive autonomic nervous system and/or labile neurotransmitter systems. A psychological vulnerability may involve an enhanced fear of illness or physical injury and a past learned inability to cope with life events that are unpredictable and uncontrollable. Individuals with a biological and/or psychological vulnerability to panic often have their initial attack in the context of a real stressor. Although there is no impending physical threat to the person's life, the fight/flight reaction is as great as if there were one, constituting a 'false alarm.'"[30]

Note that in the preceding integrative model there is no mention of public space. The closest we come is in the notion of "a real stressor," which refers to "stressful life experiences that preceded a first panic attack." "Stressors" are further defined as "triggers" and the most common ones for panic disorder are given as: "marital or interpersonal conflicts, frustration due to entrapment in relationships and unfair treatment by others; illness, death of a loved one, moving, a major change in occupation, and frustration or dissatisfaction with work."[31] The common factor in these "stress triggers" is that the patient is "deprived of all means of control while being subjected to a stressor." Most of the above-mentioned therapeutic techniques, then, aim to give the agoraphobic "control" over "stressors" that, in the case of agoraphobia, have been decontextualized from the larger picture of social space.

Critical observers of therapeutic techniques that train the agoraphobic to gain control over stressors note how strongly the control skills resemble intensified forms of behavior characteristic of bourgeois Euro-American males where self-control is centralized and masterful. The desensitization treatments that help the agoraphobic achieve a sense of mastery over the (decontextualized) self, critics note, look a lot like exaggerations of culturally masculine behavior.[32] Investigating the gendered dimension of these therapeutic techniques will be a major task of the chapters to come. For now, however, we need to consider the relation between culturally masculine techniques of self control and the quality of emptiness so often noted by agoraphobics in the spatial triggers of their disorder. In short, what does culturally masculine behavior have to do with empty space?

## Recovering the Emptiness of Public Space and Its Gendered Existential Dimensions

Having begun the recovery of public space in psychological descriptions of agoraphobia, it is now time to raise some issues concerning the recovery of the public self. When *angst* was translated into *anxiety* and *anxiety* was in turn subsumed by *panic disorder* in the therapies that dominate the treatment of agoraphobia in the United States, the patient's deeply felt perception of spatial emptiness was occasionally noted by clinicians and theorists as a form of existential awareness. But theoretical interest in the existential dimensions of agoraphobia is out of sync with the most common pattern I found in women's expression of the cause of their agoraphobia. In nineteenth- and twentieth-century cases, I found women associating the onset of their spatially expressed anxiety with experiences of marriage, pregnancy and childbirth, nursing, weaning, and the more general care of young children. Psychiatry, on the other hand, when it does examine existential issues of agoraphobia, does so in terms of the experience of death, in particular the experience of soldiers and battlefield neurosis. The therapeutic transference of anxiety treatments for "shell-shocked" soldiers to urban women begs for closer examination, which will come in chapter 5. For now I simply wish to introduce the gender problem in agoraphobia by showing how existential issues associated with the experience of death dominate the interpretation of "emptiness" expressed in the agoraphobic symptom. Thus an entire range of human experience associated with birth and early child care is neglected by the dominant treatment modalities.

While it is true that existential questions are strikingly absent in the cognitive and biological theories of agoraphobia listed above, behaviorists, on the other hand, have given attention to an existential dimension of anxiety disorders by focusing on a general *fear of death*, in particular in the experience of soldiers suffering from war neuroses. Behaviorist clinician Brian J. Cox, for example, has noted the omission by observing that "there has been virtually no investigation into the possibility of a general *fear of death* with regard to the development of panic disorder."[33] Behavioral treatments of agoraphobia that use techniques of exposure to the feared situation are, in fact, based on the treatments developed for World War II soldiers who suffered what had been called, in World War I, "shell shock." This existential experience arose in the battlefield when a soldier encountered either his own near death or the death of a fellow soldier. Abreaction, a treatment that would help a soldier to relive the existential experience, usually under the effect of hypnosis or sodium amytal, was very successful in curing soldiers of neurotic symptoms related to unspeakable encounters with horror and death on the battlefield.[34] The behaviorist development of desensitization techniques that use in vivo exposure for agoraphobia are based on clinical work on abreaction for war neurosis. In other words, the dominant behavioral treatments for agoraphobia have developed out of an intensified realm of culturally masculine behavior associated with the battlefields of World War II.

In view of the fact that agoraphobia has become so emphatically a problem of women in Western modernity, we are led to wonder why treatments that *do* address the existential issues involved in agoraphobia do so by focusing on a *general fear of death*. A review of the clinical literature indicates that for many women the onset of agoraphobia occurs in relation to pregnancy, birthing, nursing, and caring for young children—in other words, with existential relations of life. In the over one hundred years of clinical research that I reviewed, such associations were summarily dismissed by clinicians and never followed up on for research. Gestation, birthing, and childcare, relations associated with physical, emotional, social, and material aspects of the well being of the youngest members of the human family, are obviously not the same as the existential relations associated with death. These are existential experiences of life and the demands of life's beginnings in the world when humans are at their most vulnerable and needy stage. Across cultures women's bodies and women's experiential being in the world differ in various ways from men's. To the extent that cognitive-behavioral-biopsychiatric treatments do not address existential issues, and if so only in terms of a "general fear of death," it is no wonder that treatments for agoraphobia are less than successful and that the incidence of the disorder continues to grow for women in western urban space. Such disregard for the unique conditions under which agoraphobia can arise for women is consonant with larger patterns of neglect of women's bodies in medical science.

In the Western philosophy of phenomenology, existential experience has also been dominated by the experience of death. For phenomenologists, death is foremost an experience of emptiness in space and authentic being meant facing the nothingness which death presented to life (Martin Heidegger, Jean-Paul Sartre). Thus, in various forms of the literary and philosophical writings of the Western twentieth century, anxiety—the state of a subject in relation to nothingness (objectless or free-floating anxiety)—was viewed as a valued mode of being in the world. Heidegger, for example, privileging the experiential world of the mature, independent (male) adult, taught that the authentic person was not born; he was instead "thrown" into being. Even in a phenomenologist like Maurice Merleau-Ponty, who wished to put embodied experience back into the existential equation, the ontology that emerges from his writing is dominated by a problematics of vision (visibility and invisibility) that privileges the sensory experience of vision but, by omission, demotes the experiential world that arrives to a subject through the sense of touch. As the feminist philosopher Luce Irigaray points out (and this is a point I will examine more thoroughly in chapter 4), the words used by Merleau-Ponty to describe the most fundamental experience of our being in the world are dominated by metaphors of fluidity that strongly suggest the subject's first intrauterine experiences. Instead of referring to the human being's first sensory experience of the amniotic womb, however (an experience that is, of course, dominated by the sense of touch and hearing), Merleau-Ponty uses the metaphors of fluidity to describe the relation the subject will form with the world through the visual sense. This gesture of disregard for the intrauterine experience in the fundamental texts of the phenomenology of embodiment seems astounding. Why this neglect of humans' first experience, its sensory domains of tactility and hearing and its relations of dependency with the mother?

In *The Phenomenal Woman: Feminist Metaphysics and the Patterns of Identity*, philosopher Christine Battersby argues that "[p]hilosophers have notably failed to address the ontological significance of the fact that selves are born. Furthermore, there is also a more general inability to imaginatively grasp that the self/other relationship needs to be reworked from the perspective of birth—and thus in ways that never abstract from power inequalities or from issues relating to embodied differences...." The "dominant metaphysics of the West," Battersby continues, "have been developed from the point of view of an identity that cannot give birth, so that birthing is treated as a deviation of the 'normal' models of identity—not integral to thinking identity itself."[35] Formed within Western traditions, psychiatry, which includes all the various models we have touched on above, shares the ontological and epistemological premises of its philosophical inheritance.

A strong picture of this philosophical inheritance appears in the treatments that reinsert a mostly female population of agoraphobics into public urban space. For Battersby, resituating the place of birth, mothering, and parenting in the Western philosophical tradition is a corrective to the tradition:

> Immanuel Kant's "Copernican revolution" sought to rewrite philosophical tradition by placing man—instead of God or the object—at the center of the reality which we inhabit. My own feminist philosophical turn displaces the apparently gender-neutral Kantian self at the center of the knowable world. However, instead of dispensing with the self in ways now fashionable in the postmodern tradition, I am attempting to construct a new subject-position that makes *women* typical. In effect, this means dispensing with the (Kantian) notion that the "I" gives form to reality by imposing a grid of spatio-temporal relationships upon otherwise unformed "matter." Focusing on the female subject involves treating humans as non-autonomous, and instead thinking relationships of dependence (childhood/weaning/rearing) through which one attains selfhood. It also involves thinking the process of birthing as neither monstrous nor abnormal. Mothering, parenting and the fact of being born need to become fully integrated into what is entailed in being a human "person" or "self."[36]

The feminist call for the repositioning of women's experiences in the Western tradition of self and identity formation has great importance for agoraphobia, viewed both as an illness of individual women in Western urban space and also as a larger indicator of a cultural pathology of western modernity. In the present volume we place the connection that agoraphobic women make between their experience of childbirth and child care and the pockets of built emptiness that trigger their panic and fear next to other social and cultural factors in order to paint a broad picture of the spatial demands made by the modern city on all its citizens.

Attention to gender complexity in anxiety disorders certainly goes back to the late nineteenth century, when somatic models predominated medical thinking. Anxiety, for example, which was studied in terms of hysteria and neurasthenia during this period, was often given confused gendered labels. Although the most well-known theorizer of hysteria, Jean-Martin Charcot, generally associated hysteria with middle-class femininity, he also used the term to describe the somatic manifestation of anxiety in working-class males. The American George Miller Beard coined the term *neurasthenia* to describe nervous fatigue among men, but Europeans like Silas Weir Mitchel later used it to discuss nervous diseases among middle-class women. Eventually, anxiety disorders began to be seen as separate from hysteria and neurasthenia, a distinction that culminated with the French publication of Sigmund Freud's *The Justification for Detaching from Neurasthenia a Particular Syndrome: The Anxiety Neurosis* (1895), in which he argued that neurasthenia be broken into neurasthenia proper and anxiety neurosis (*névrose d'angoisse)* characterized by anxiety attacks (*attaques d'angoisse*). Male hysteria on the battlefield was diagnosed in American Civil War soldiers as "soldier's heart" and, during the Russo-Japanese War in 1905, Russian doctors devised specific treatments for nervous breakdown during war. By World War I, the designation of *shell shock*, or combat stress, extended the description of hysteria as well as the legitimacy of psychiatry. At this time Freud's theories of the psyche gained authority, especially his description of a distinct class of anxiety neuroses that placed anxiety as a key to understanding the human psyche.[37]

In the twentieth century, anxiety remains a gender-coded phenomenon in modern psychology, especially with regard to the way the term *panic* has arisen to account for the somatic dimension of anxiety. Previously, we noted that Boyd had cited the work of the American psychiatrist Donald Klein to prove that something he called *panic attacks* were at the bottom of the agoraphobic's disorder. In his clinical studies of patients whose anxiety neuroses were complicated by agoraphobia, Klein had noted in 1962 that a particular drug, Impramine, could suppress acute anxiety attacks but not the long-lasting state of anxiety. This lead him to conclude that what Freud had labeled *attaques d'angoisse* (anxiety attacks) was a physical phenomenon separate from the more general anxiety disorders and should be thus given the separate name "panic attacks." In later chapters I will discuss the sociospatial and gendered repercussions of making agoraphobia a subset of what, since Klein, has been called "panic disorders," but for now we can note that the term *panic* is a relative newcomer to psychology. It comes, nonetheless, with its own historical and gendered connotations. Freud apparently used the term only once—in his *Group Psychology and the Analysis of the Ego* (1921). Others, too have used the term *panic* when analyzing the behavior of the masses, especially in researches conducted by military psychiatry.[38] But sociologists, as well, have made the term *moral panic* a common category of mass reactions to various social phenomena. If Klein aimed in making the term *panic attack* the physiological basis of agoraphobia—and in doing so, separating the agoraphobic's anxiety from normal anxiety reactions—this does not mean that he succeeded in giving the term *panic* (and the designation *panic disorder*) a meaning separate from the broader cultural, and gendered, sphere in which it exists. In other words, somatized anxiety, even when it is called a *panic attack* (a state of pathology) may not be radically different from the state of normal anxiety. That is because panic attacks, from a wider historical and cultural perspective, may not be so easily separated from what we, as a culture, have labeled *panic*. Medical historian Daniel Ussishkin, for example, notes how the medical pretensions of the "homosexual panic defense" in the American legal system rely on both normative and pathological notions of panic. As Eve Kosofsky Sedgwick puts it, "[T]he homosexual panic defense rests on the falsely individualizing and pathologizing assumption that hatred of homosexuals is so private and so atypical a phenomenon in this culture as to be classifiable as an accountability-reducing illness. ... [O]n the contrary ... hatred of homosexuals is even more pubic, more typical, hence harder to find a leverage against than hatred of other disadvantaged groups."[39]

In this volume, I, too, will pay careful attention to the gendered connotations implicit in the terms *panic* and *panic attacks* as they have come to usurp the medical discussion of anxiety with regard to agoraphobia. As we shall see, agoraphobia is a condition that has sometimes appeared in the clinical literature in connection with homosexuality. What is of interest to us here is the gendered way in which public space becomes caught up in both the expression of the agoraphobic's acute anxiety and its treatment.

## Conclusion

Agoraphobia has much to tell us about the way nonpathologized urban dwellers in general are in the process of being molded to inhabit the cities of late modernity. If agoraphobia is a pathology of our urban culture, and not only the pathology of the individual, as we have stated, then pathology must be present in the larger urban culture that organizes our experience of the world. Agoraphobics are the miner's canaries in the public space of our cities. With their heightened sensibility, they may have a more intense visceral experience of what most modern city dwellers face in their everyday use of modern public space. However, I would argue that what they undergo as recipients of the culture's dominant treatments to reinsert them back into public space is merely the intensified version of what modern public space demands of all its inhabitants. Agoraphobics inhabit the zero point of psychology and the zero point of the modern city. They manifest the invisible (because it has been naturalized) relationship between modern urbanites and public space, revealing that the public space of our cities contains pockets of built emptiness that can create certain visceral disturbances and demand certain adaptive skills. What are these pockets of public emptiness revealed by agoraphobic dread? As has been observed by numerous social commentators, public emptiness is a built materiality, a constructed intensification in terms of scale, speed, and homogeneity. We build increasingly gigantic forms of public emptiness in our cities, places whose increasing homogeneity paradoxically creates an increasing spatial instability that requires ever greater speeds in those aspects of our everyday lives that are dependent on them.

Let us return to the dilemma as stated by literary critic Klaus Scherpe (as mentioned in the preface to the present volume): in the literature of Euro-American modernity, empty space appears to be a structuring metaphor for the modern city. Urban narratives built around a central vacuity leave us without an adequate imaginal structure to the city. The imaginal boundlessness of empty urban space is only useful, Scherpe laments, to orient us in the ways of modern architecture and the culture of advertising, practices that build on razed ground or blank surfaces. The current trend in behaviorist treatments of agoraphobia apparently does the same thing. It shares with a trend in modern literature the depiction of urban space as vacuous (a reflection from the built environment) and, like its literary counterpart, it uses this spatial imaginary to insert individuals into the dominant social conditions of urban life. It prepares their reentry into normative urban life by equipping them with a spatial experience of city life as a homogenous surface.

In the following chapters I provide historical evidence for my argument that in the pathology of agoraphobia we have a prism through which to examine how empty space is both a structure of feeling and a key organizing feature of modern Euro-American urban life. Its impacts encompass the larger political economy of urbanization and the deeper social identities of class, race, and gender. Boyd's commentary on Westphal's original German text has allowed us to see how agoraphobia has become a reduced conception of *Platzangst*, a fear without a material object, a "fear of fear." The task of the next two chapters is to return to the earliest cases in late-nineteenth-century Europe and, through cultural analysis, recover and reflect on those spaces which triggered the agoraphobic's reaction. If we can better understand the nature of the earlier fear-provoking sites, we can more effectively compare those sites to the sites that trigger agoraphobia today and better understand the spatial foundation of ourselves as urban citizens and as modern subjects of experience and knowledge.

CHAPTER 2

# The Nineteenth-Century Urban Commons as a Spatial Puzzle

## Introduction

> In Berlin the Dönhoffplatz is the most unpleasant for him; if he tries to cross it, he is struck by the feeling that the distance is very great, miles wide, that he will never get to the other side, and connected to this is the referred-to feeling of anxiety. …
>
> —**Dr. Carl Westphal,** "*Die Agoraphobie*"[1]

In the psychiatric journals of the late nineteenth century, the fearful trigger sites mentioned by agoraphobic patients in Europe are almost without exception like Dönhoffplatz: geometric plazas or squares based on the grand baroque plans of the imperial European capital. When Dr. Carl Westphal's first patient faltered before the gapping expanse of Dönhoffplatz, he was facing a square that by 1871 had become the very reference-point (or zero-point) of the Prussian system of road distance as Berlin emerged as the capital city of the new German state. Dönhoffplatz extended its vastness by opening onto one of Berlin's broad arterial streets, like another nearby open square of this period (see figure 4). These urban commons are characteristic of the neoclassical approach to urban design that placed monumental plazas and squares at the hearts of cities to foster civic pride.[2] The most famous of these designs is Georges-Eugène Haussmann's redevelopment of Paris and Vienna's Ringstrasse. This serialized urban design

**Figure 4** Lustgarten and Old Museum, Berlin, circa. 1890.

movement was transplanted to American cities in the early 1890s, where it can be seen in monumental spaces like the Mall in Washington, D.C., and Grant Park in Chicago. A 1903 imitation of the Place de la Concorde, the immense plaza most cited by French agoraphobics of the last century, still exists in the center of Cleveland, Ohio. The monumental approach to the urban commons went dormant after the turn of the century but was

**Figure 5** Corporate park: offices and parking. Photo from *Suburban Nation* by Andres Duany, Elizabeth Plater-Zyberk, and Jeff Speck (2000). Reprinted with permission.

revived in the 1980s when it became, as one architectural historian has put it, "a motif for corporate headquarters and office parks, combining visual pomposity with ecological sterility" in places that were never built for pedestrian habitation.[3]

The European neoclassical public square is cited repeatedly in the clinical literature on nineteenth-century agoraphobia. I have chosen four such squares from nineteenth-century case histories and offer them in this chapter as exemplary sites at which to begin the task of returning spatial specificity to our understanding of agoraphobia: Place de la Concorde in Paris, Place de la Republique in Lille, Place Bellecour in Lyon, and Dvortsovaya Square in St. Petersburg. From the perspective of agoraphobia these squares are exemplary sites to reveal the cultural logic of empty space in the emergent form of the modern city.

## Place de la Concorde, Paris

Dr. Henri Legrand du Saulle of the Hopital de la Salpêtrière in Paris described the "strangeness" of the following case of agoraphobia in the journal *Le Practicien* (1885):

> I was consulted by a woman of forty-three years (which is quite rare, as the disease is generally only observed in men) who had experienced this fear for the first time in Righi, Switzerland. She immediately returned home to Paris, and was feeling quite well without a further thought of that accident until one day while crossing Place de

**Figure 6** Place de la Concorde, Paris circa 1870.

> la Concorde she found herself crying, reddening and then becoming pale, such that a man came and offered to take her to a nearby pharmacy. In the meantime she quickly recovered but upon arriving back home she felt quite worried, and wondered if she hadn't felt the precursor of apoplexy. Once more the same happened. Finally, she no longer dared cross her own courtyard or climb the stairway without calling the concierge. She began to feel this fear in her living room, in her bedroom such that she had her bed brought into the bathroom. The situation became intolerable. Every doctor she consulted offered different advice. Even myself, at the beginning I was not very affirmative and it wasn't until some time later that I happened to read some observations on this illness and then asked myself if she might not have, by chance, agoraphobia. On my suggestion, she had furniture placed in her living room and now that it looks like an actual bazaar she can safely walk around in it.[4]

The spatial problem faced by the patient was puzzling for several reasons. She had returned from an anxious experience in the mountains of Righi, Switzerland, and now felt her anxiety reawakened in the city by the Place de la Concorde. Also, the psychiatrist recognized that his female patient was having a problem with space that is usually associated with men. The problematic space first appeared in the unbuilt environment—the Alps—but was later recognized in the center of Paris in the Place de la Concorde. This spatial problem became even more extensive as it reached into the patient's living quarters: first the courtyard, then the bedroom, and even the most intimate and private of built spaces, the bathroom. The patient was apparently returning home to a built space of great public and private proportions. After some unsuccessful attempts, Legrand du Saulle finally treated the problem in the very terms of the spatial puzzle established by his patient: he suggested that she dispel the emptiness that threatened her domestic space and make it navigable once again. In rearranging her built space, she filled the living room until it looked like a bazaar where she could once again feel safe as she walked. She appears to have created her own miniature marketplace and thereby taken the first steps to solving—in a safe, private space—a puzzle of public space that had suddenly, for her, lost all proportion. In this way the female agoraphobic mimics the normative public order in a way that makes it feel safe.

The agoraphobic in this case history establishes a special connection between the Place de la Concorde and the Swiss Alps, suggesting a subliminal association between the alpine space of natural precipices and the vast built space of the Parisian neoclassical square. The Place de la Concorde was an expression of the changes in urban space that were occurring in Paris between 1853 and 1870, the time during which our forty-three-year-old patient was learning to negotiate the public space of her city. The population of Paris was growing exponentially, from 1,277,00 in 1851 to 1,970,000 in 1870, an increase of 700,000 inhabitants.[5] Georges-Eugène Haussmann had taken over as prefect of the Seine and, under the direction of Napoleon III, led the reconstruction of Paris. Under Haussmann, historians note, the medieval city with its alley-like streets without issue, its houses without water and slums without light or adequate air was changed into a modern city with regularized streets, a new water supply and sewage system. Medieval Paris was mapped, leveled, and rebuilt according to plans that came to serve as a model of urban development throughout Europe and eventually in the United States. Haussmann's plan for urban redevelopment was marked by the razing of entire neighborhoods for the creation of *la grand croisée*, an urban artery that would link up with monumental rectilinear streets and squares, cutting through the tangled density of urban life. The plan was imitated in many French cities during the Second Empire—Avignon, Lyons, Marseilles, Montpellier, Rouen, and Lille—and enormous *percées* (through ways) were burrowed into provincial cities and given the name Rue Impériale or Rue de l'Impératrice, later to be renamed Rue de la République (or after some well-known opponent of the empire). Historians describe the overall aim of this plan as an attempt to facilitate communications between the central parts of the city and the periphery. The experience of agoraphobics has much to say about the experiential nature of this new transit and nodal space and directs our attention to the role played by empty space as a structure of feeling.

Haussmann's 1890 memoir indicates how much his intentions, on his first day in office in 1853, involved the attempt to deal with empty space: "In order to render accessible and inhabitable the vast empty spaces which have remained unproductive on the furthermost edges of the town, it will be necessary first to pierce it right through, thus ripping open the centre."[6] The percées were intended to connect unbuilt empty space to the urban center, which itself was being emptied of its most dense quarters and transformed into monumental open space. It is as if the unbuilt space of the periphery was in some way folded back onto the urban center where the nodal points or endpoints of these great urban thoroughfares were embellished with monumental empty space. Along with the great railway lines that first entered cities like Paris during this time, the new urban arteries moved citizens through neighborhoods back and forth into built and unbuilt empty space. For many students of modern urban planning, the wide percées of Haussmann's Paris form an ominous precursor to the urban freeway system, the second-most cited trigger of agoraphobic anxiety today.

The Place de la Concorde was fundamental to Haussmann's plan for the redesign of Paris. It was Haussmann who finally completed a project of long standing to build an east-west axis, a *via triumphalis*, from the Louvre through the Place de la Concorde to the Place de l'Etoile (now Place Charles de Gaulle). The Concorde had originally been built as a *place royale*, a "royal square" intended to magnify the power of the monarch. It reflects what some architects refer to as "a change in the purpose of urban space—a shift from economic to political purpose,"[7] a development associated with the regime of Louis XV and his project to build throughout France twenty-two such squares, in the middle of which would stand the equestrian statue of the king. These squares were meant to serve as the symbolic consolidation of Louis XV's regime.[8]

The Concorde represents the very model of the eighteenth-century neoclassical square. Its post-Renaissance rectilinear space marks an architectural shift away from the fifteenth century design of urban commons characteristic of the closed in market town squares of northern Italy. Neoclassical squares are characterized by their open nature. Instead of being removed from everyday traffic, as were their Italian predecessors, neoclassical street systems continue through the square. Architectural historians often refer to the synthesizing role of neoclassical squares: they were built to be "interrelated as closely as possible with the town *as a whole*."[9] In order to integrate the extremely irregular streets of the town with the new monumental square, whole sections of a city might be razed if necessary "and rebuilt around the central space so as to effect its physical integration into the area and its sense of unity with the city as a whole." Thus, they presaged a form of urban continuity that Haussmann would later seek on a much more massive scale. The neoclassical square sought a "continuity of visual or spatial experience beyond the square itself along predetermined sight lines with specified termini. In this way the square with its monumental cross axis appeared to bond itself to the central urban scheme."[10] This continuity is additionally enacted by the identical facades and arcades on the public and private buildings surrounding the square—precursors, perhaps, to the homogeneous facadelike effect of the commercial billboards that today litter the urban freeway system in many modern cities.

The intention of all the place royale projects was to create "open space," in contrast to the closed space of the previous period.[11] The integration of urban elements and landscape—entirely contrary to the practices of the previous century—increased the sense of monumental urban openness. This new ideal of open space in the city was realized by what Paul Zucker and other architectural historians have called "the inclusion of nature."[12] Considering the connection that Legrand du Saulle's agoraphobic patient made between the Place de la Concorde and the gapping expanses of the

Swiss Alps, we are lead to question how "nature" was included in the imperial city's most monumental open spaces as a structure of feeling.

The Concorde is described as standing with three sides "into open space": the Jardin des Tuileries, the River Seine, and the Champs Elysees—an urban park, a river, and an immense boulevard. As Zucker explains, "Its openness on three sides does not actually create a definite space but rather a field of complex spatial relations: *perspectives, not edifices, are its boundaries*."[13] "Nature" in the projects of the places royales is an abstraction, "a field of complex spatial relations" in which abstract, geometric perspectives function as material boundaries. The Enlightenment philosopher Immanuel Kant had noted that abstract representations of complex experiential phenomena are ideas supplied by the imagination. The imagination acts as a mediator between experiential complexity and the grasp of reason, providing reason with a conceptual or abstract representation of something that remains experientially ungraspable. Nature in the Place de la Concorde is such an idea built into the landscape. Kant called these "ideas of reason," as they were products of the imagination meant to bypass the worrisome experiential conundrum that the nonconceptual world presented to the man of reason. Turned into a concept, the messiness of life need not inspire anxiety in the person of reason. With the new place royale design in heavily trafficked nodal points, cities begin to transform nature into abstractly designed open spaces where immense perspectival directives take the task of walking through the city away from the fully sensate person and hand over to the faculty of sight and reason what was once shared with the more tactile modes of knowing. This phenomena reaches its most streamlined instrumental point in today's urban freeways.

All of the squares mentioned by agoraphobic patients in the late nineteenth century were built on the model of the place royale. It is as if the place royale design proliferates in city centers at this time like a kind of urban exercise ground where the pedestrian retrains his sensate being to move according to ever more abstract directives. On the one hand, this lends greater scope to what can be accomplished by relying on reason. The "feeling" of the place is less likely to provide reliable information. For the person whose confidence lies less with skills of abstract reasoning, on the other hand, the diminished authority of the tactile senses could be experienced as a loss of control.

Some clinical studies inadvertently suggest that an architectural abstraction of nature could be a trigger for agoraphobic fear. A 1929 clinical study of the relation between fear of mountains and agoraphobia by Swiss authors A. Bernard and Ch. Jung demonstrated the relation between agoraphobia and the fear of heights, or vertigo (*le vertige des hauteurs*; also called *peur des montaignes*, "fear of mountains"). Their investigation led them to coin a new term for this complaint: *la cremnophobie*—fear of the precipice—from the Greek word for *precipice*.[14] The etymology of the word itself suggests a double meaning: a precipice is "a very steep or overhanging place" as well as "the brink of a disaster," and derives from the Latin *praecipitium*, *praecipit*, *praeceps*, meaning "headlong," and from *prae*, "in front of" and *caput*, "head," implying fear of the headlong fall, fear of the abyss. The case described by Bernard and Jung (cited below) is strikingly similar to that of Legrand du Saulle's patient who had just recovered from her first "anxiety attack" in the mountains only to find the anxiety provoked once again by the Place de la Concorde:

> [A male patient,] 48 years old [tells us,] "Emptiness [*le vide*] gives me an undefinable anxiety [*une angoise indefinissable*]. I feel oppressed, my legs become weak in exactly the same way as when I cross wide open spaces. The phenomena are rather similar but in addition I have a peculiar feeling of being attracted by the emptiness [*le vide*]. By an irresistible force. I feel an emotion that may appear ridiculous but becomes increasingly exaggerated the more I react. I avoid looking down from tall buildings just as I try to avoid deserted streets and squares, etc. …"
>
> The idea of the abyss [*l'abîme*] makes him fearful, but not as much as the idea of the *Place de la Concorde*. …[15]

The comments suggest that the Place de la Concorde, even as an idea, is more terrifying to the patient than the idea of the precipice or abyss. Kant's observations on the relation of nature to ideas of reason are relevant here. When nature functions as an idea of reason rather than a tactile experience, Kant explained in his philosophical exploration of the limits of human reason, we are heading for an encounter with the sublime. The sublime, for Kant, is the representation of that which cannot be represented. The attempt to represent the awesome quality of the unspeakable always carries the possibility of evoking terror. It is the terror of the unknown in the form of what cannot be conceptualized that leads Enlightenment philosophers like Kant to equate the sublime idea of nature with an engulfing experience, with the terror of death. For Kant, ideas of reason, coming as they do from the imagination, are unstable abstractions which threaten to overwhelm reason by challenging its ability to explain the unknown, to "understand" or conceptualize death. In later periods of German philosophy, the romantics and existentialists would come to privilege a person's ability to defy reason by dwelling in the face of the abyss. Facing the anxiety of unreason or absurdity would become the hallmark of the "authentic" person, empowering the lone romantic poet or the existential man. For the agoraphobic, however, the experience of anxiety in a site like the Place de la Concorde is not turned into an intellectual adventure. It is rather an awareness of how unreliable her sensibility to the world has become.

Monumental public space in the modern city of the late nineteenth century is an embodiment of Enlightenment notions of personhood. The successful pedestrian "trains," as it were, in urban commons dominated by abstract, homogeneous space and experiences the successes of being distractedly (or subliminally) directed by perspectival geometries.[16] Such practices hone skills associated with the person's rational faculties and encourage confidence in an unspecified and perhaps limitless power of reason. Agoraphobics, on the other hand, when confronted with the cultural expression of Enlightenment ideals in the built environment, appear to be highly sensitive to the limits of reason. Contrary to the confident pedestrian (what later social critics will call the flaneur), the agoraphobic experiences monumentally abstract urban space as a structure of feeling where the limits of reason are encountered. From a Kantian perspective, when reason fails to grasp an idea that the imagination has presented to it in monumentalizing abstract forms, an encounter with the intense emptiness of the abyss is imminent. The intense emptiness of homogeneous space is, according to Kant, the very ground of reason's capacity for abstraction. An encounter with homogeneous, abstract space can be an overwhelming and paradoxical experience for the agoraphobic's acute sense of the limits of reason. Indeed, the clinical literature shows that generally, reason does continue to speak (reasonably) to the agoraphobic individual engulfed by such situational fears by telling her that what she is experiencing is unreasonable. Unlike the schizophrenic, the agoraphobic maintains a distinction between the reasonable self and her unreasonable fears. As psychologists have long known, the problem for the agoraphobic is that in places of fear, the voice of reason is an entirely ineffective and unbelievable voice. If the person relying on Enlightenment ideals finds herself calmed by the use of reason while crossing the Place de la Concorde, where, as architectural historian Zucker noted, "perspectives, not edifices" are the main demarcations in "boundless" space, the agoraphobic finds the Concorde unnavigable because visual, perspectival cues become unreliable. As we shall see from other case histories in the next chapter, the agoraphobic is most likely to rely on senses other than sight to navigate the square: she turns to touch (the cane) or sound (the passing carriage). The agoraphobic, then, perfectly willing and able to call on reason in sites of monumentally abstract public space, cannot be helped by Enlightenment models of personhood for she finds reason to be an unreliable source of information.

Vast tracts of homogeneous public space were, in the late nineteenth century, the very places where the new idea of the nation and national identity were represented.[17] The Place de la Concorde, for example, became the representative stage on which France celebrates its national events, the site of fireworks and Bastille Day celebrations. It is not a coincidence, then, that the clinical literature shows an overwhelming number of agoraphobic patients who complain of the space of the theater. "He can't stay in a theater because of the space that stretches before him," writes Drs. M. Lannois and C. Tournier in 1898 of one of their patients.[18] The empty space that is required for representation is acutely apparent to the agoraphobic in both its theatrical and its urban architectural forms. Perhaps this is why some agoraphobics use theatrical techniques of mise en scène to work with their fears. Legrand du Saulle's Parisian woman, for example, finds secure space in her apparently vacuous living room only after she makes it look, in the doctor's terms or hers, like a bazaar. Thus she mimics the fearful "outside" by setting up an interior marketplace, participating in the same ironic behavior that feminist critics, as we shall see in the next chapter, have described as a general device of agoraphobic women to gain control over space.

### Place de la Republique, Lille

The Place de la Republique is the representative space of the "Haussmannization" of Lille begun in the 1860s. Formerly the Place Napoleon III, the Place de la Republique was created by boring through the old city in 1870 to connect the new railway station to the former central city square, Grand Place. The name changes of this new thoroughfare—first Rue Imperiale, then Rue Nationale—reflect the political shifts of the times and the attempts to make Lille part of the larger national space with the aid of the new railway system. It is here that a sixty-four-year-old woman, supervisor at a large clothing operation, sees her doctor in the late 1890s because it has become impossible for her to cross wide open squares, especially the Place de la Republique. The following case of agoraphobia is written up in *L'Echo medicale du nord* (1898) by an intern at a hospital in Lille:

> She is a sixty-four-year-old woman, employed for a long time in a major confection house. … She directs the sewing factory and oversees a class of young [female]workers. … At twenty she marries and at twenty-two brings into the world a boy who dies at a young age. She's in good health until around thirty when, thanks in part to menopause, her apoplectic tendencies appear and her long series of miseries begins. In the last three years now … it is absolutely impossible for her to cross the smallest public square. In order to get to work, she daily passes by a not particularly wide square (Jacquart Square in Lille) and finds she must hug the walls, troubled, worried, *angoisse* in

**Figure 7** Place de la Republique, Lille circa 1880.

> her soul and her eyes fixed on the ground. The same for the squares of an even greater surface area, like the Place de la Republique (still in Lille). For many long years now she has experienced this strange problem and she can no longer go across these [squares.] When asked what it is that she feels, ... she declares that she is *no longer the mistress of her movement*; that she can't resist and must blindly obey that internal force. ... She is afraid, she says, "of the openness and *emptiness* [*le vide*] which seems so immense to her. Walls seem to begin marching and houses to do a disorganized dance."[19]

The complaint of this Lilloise agoraphobic has been echoed by French architectural historians, who refer to Lille's Place de la Republique as a symptom of "the crisis of the monument and its symbolization in the space of the city."[20] For the architectural critic the crisis is explained in terms of a growing inability during this period to see the boundaries between the monumental and the nonmonumental in urban space. The situation is aggravated by the fact that in this era of intense French nation building, monumental structures in places royales compete for grandiosity calling on Hellenistic and Roman motifs in a vertiginous game of pomposity and aggrandizement where "everything is exploited to make the space appear noble." "The problem of the monument," note architectural historians commenting on the reconstruction of Lille during this period, "is felt most particularly in the vast spaces cleared out for the new neighborhoods: Place de la Republique, flanked by two huge monuments, the Prefecture and the museum, manages to crush even these monuments with its immensity ... the architect of the Prefecture attempts to rival this dreadful competition of *emptiness* [*vide*] by reducing his building to the role of a monotonous border."[21]

From the perspective of a cultural logic of empty space, what is striking is that architectural critics and agoraphobics alike note that nothing can effectively compete with the emptiness of the square itself, as if emptiness were the pinnacle of monumentality. As giganticism seeks to express itself in a built environment of empty space, we have the same cultural logic we discussed in relation to the Kantian sublime: a doomed attempt to represent the unrepresentable. In the case of the Haussmannization of urban France, the logic of the sublime is associated with attempts to spatially represent the nation as the monumental state, the main city square as the "place" of the republic. As a structure of feeling, then, the homogeneous, monumentally sublime character of public space as empty state space risks collapsing into a space of dizzying and unstable intensity for both the architectural critic and the agoraphobic.

Nature is brought into the intensive gridwork of the Place de la Republique as the "serialization of public parks" that decorates the square. Nature, along with "the arcade ironwork department stores and bargain emporiums [*bazaars*] which border the square" makes this square the commercial center of the city.[22] The juxtaposed proximity of commercial and nature zones in the city center was also noted by Walter Benjamin in his description of the Parisian arcades of this period: the parks lying on the same axis as the commercial center constitute the space of the "flaneur," sometimes landscape, sometimes boutique.[23]

When a contemporary anonymous critic grasps for a metaphor to describe the emptiness of the redesigned nationalist square during this period, he suggests the important, yet little-mentioned, military dimension of these monumental city spaces, noting, "With a certain brashness, urban reformers have set this enormous building (Palais des Beaux arts) facing the Prefecture, leaving in the center a vast denuded square that looks more like an army square than a place for walking. This attempt to give the city a new center capable of rivaling the Grand Place failed."[24]

In monumental squares of redesigned urban emptiness, a sign emerges of a past, and potentially present, function: many cities had standing armies within their perimeters during this period of European state building. For the agoraphobic observer as well, the square's expansive emptiness recalls less a pedestrian pathway than a military parade. We see this in the case of the sixty-four-year-old Lille woman cited above who is afraid of the "openness and emptiness" of Lille's largest squares. As she told her doctor, "Walls seem to begin marching and houses to do a disorganized dance."

From both architectural critics and agoraphobic sensibility certain contours are made palpable in the emptiness of the redesigned national plazas. At the zenith of European state monumentality when empty public space seeks to symbolize the stability of the state, the agoraphobic is the citizen who senses a military presence (the "walls seemed to march") that eventually gives way to a sense of instability (a "disorganized dance"). Thus, the agoraphobic appears unable to set aside the sense of an inherently dangerous potential of vast, homogeneous, monumentalized city space.[25]

## Place Bellecour, Lyon

In 1898, Drs. M. Lannois and C. Tournier in Lyon examined the case of Claude F., a forty-year-old man who was one of several agoraphobic patients:

> He has had a clear case of agoraphobia for the last six to eight months only. He can't cross either Bellecour Square (*Place Bellecour*) or Terreaux Square: if he must cross even a large street, he has the sudden sensation that he is going to fall forward so he straightens himself up and then feels he is going to fall backwards. At the same time he has

**Figure 8** Place Bellecour, Lyon circa 1890.

a feeling of cerebral congestion and then is covered in a cold sweat with intense *angoisse*. He says he can cross bridges by following the parapets: to cross a street he waits for a car to pass slowly by and then crosses obliquely by following as closely as possible. *He can't stay in a theater because of the space that stretches before him* and he sometimes must even leave a sidewalk café due to the movement in the streets. As a particular phenomenon, *he never experiences agoraphobic angoisse in the country where he often goes for his work as a traveling salesman.*[26]

Claude F.'s agoraphobia was treated as an inner-ear problem with two or three sessions of catheter treatments. In twelve days he was crossing streets without thinking about it, but not yet crossing squares. One year later, they report, his dizziness and agoraphobia were gone, although the agoraphobia returned as soon as the dizziness did.

In the case of this Lyonnais patient, two qualities of agoraphobic space are made clear. First, open space in the countryside does not trigger Claude F.'s agoraphobia—only open space in the city does. The urban quality of open space thus appears a key factor in triggering the pathological reaction. Second, for Claude F., Place Bellecour presents the same spatial problem as "the space that stretches before him [in the theater]." In many cases from this period agoraphobics mention the theater as the second most common trigger of their illness (the third most common is the church, arguably an equally theatrical place).

Urban and theatrical, Place Bellecour shares one other feature with the trigger sites found in the clinical literature on agoraphobia during this period: its military overtones. From 1562 to 1688 the vast rectangle (300 by 145 meters) of Place Bellecour was known as the Place d'Armes, a military post. Between 1686 and 1738 it was reworked into a new form of political urbanization after being chosen as the place royale, the ideal backdrop for the equestrian statue of Louis XV. Along with the pivotal presence of the monarchy, the square was furnished with two identical buildings, two similar fountains, and trees planted on the southern side "to mask its irregularity."[27] The construction of homogeneous nature and the designation of place royale launched Place Bellecour's transformation from military to monumental urban space. During the French revolution the square was renamed "Place de la Fédération puis de l'Égalité." The bronze statue of Louis XIV was melted and reformed into the symbols of the new republic and the baroque facades were demolished by the People's Brigade as the square reverted to a military post. Eventually the facades were rebuilt and during the restoration the statue of Louis XIV was remounted.

By the time Lannois and Tournier's patients were faltering at the edge of Place Bellecour, the city itself had been opened up by the railroad system, with, by 1895, magnificent train stations reaching Lyons in seven and a half hours from Paris. Technological innovations opened up tunnels in the hilly city and the first tramway line (1879) connected Bellecour to a larger rail network that was finally electrified in 1884. On its western edge, Place Bellecour, like Place de la Concorde, bordered the city's main river.[28] Place Bellecour was one of a handful of heavily frequented places to be "electrified" in the early 1890s by the city to avoid the risk of gas fires. This was a period of "festivals for the greatest number of people, of gatherings of different social classes."[29] Between 1889 and 1914, the period in which Lannois and Tournier's case was published, Place Bellecour was host to an annual military parade celebrating the Fourteenth of July (Bastille Day), which included "at noon, a revue of the troops in arms and an official banquet" and later "sports and music and fire works in the evening."[30]

The agoraphobic's sense that the empty space of Bellecour resembles the empty space that "stretches before" the audience in a theater suggests that this kind of urban emptiness affects the agoraphobic not only as abstract space (as we saw in Place de la Concorde) but also as space of sheer potentiality, like an empty stage or a blank page that presents a writer with both emptiness and potential. As a contemporary of the agoraphobic Claude F. notes, "Lyon is a city which subordinates moderation (*le mesuré*) to giganticism."[31] Abstract space is homogeneous and measurable. It can be known through rational approaches. Giganticism takes what is measurable in abstract space and submits it to increased size. But increasing

**Figure 9** Dvortsovaya Square, St. Petersburg (engraving circa 1836).

the scale of an abstract spatial schema can do more than increase its size. Giganticism can turn abstract space (*le mesuré*) into a spatial experience that is *démesuré*, unstable, immeasurable with unaccountable effects. That is what the agoraphobic reaction appears to be telling us. It shows us those public spaces where abstract space, through monumentalism and giganticism, is most easily given over to the démesuré.

## Dvortsovaya Square, St. Petersburg

In 1885, Dr. Cherchevsky described the case of a patient for whom "the spacious public squares of St. Petersburg" are exemplary triggers of agoraphobia. The case, reported in the *Revue de medicine*, is worth quoting at length for vivid and yet typical picture it evokes of the late-nineteenth-century agoraphobic man and his relation to the monumental space of the Russian capital.

> N.N. [is] thirty-three years old, robust, muscular, apparently in good health. His parents are healthy and he knows of no neurotic illnesses in his large extended family … of middle income, but not rich, and knowing no superfluousness. Since the age of twenty he has been living an independent life. [He has had] no syphilis or onanism [but is taken to] venereal excesses that rapidly took a considerable place in his life, filling the moral emptiness (*le vide*) left by an incomplete education intended only for his outer life. Thus, he passed five years in which he spent his days at the office and his evenings and nights in orgies where wine held a considerable place.
>
> In December of 1875, after a series of orgies … [he goes] one morning for a walk in the street, and is suddenly struck with strong heart palpitations, … his legs begin to shake and he feels he is going to involuntarily fall. It seems to him that he hears an internal voice that says, "You're going to fall, you can't go any farther!" [He returns home by coach but] dares not cross his rather large room with no furniture in the center. Groping his way along walls and furniture, he makes his way to his bed and finally begins to calm down, still keeping his eyes averted from the center of his room. He stays in bed for several days … and when he finally tries to walk across the center of his room, he is struck by the same palpitations and undefined *angoisse*. He returns to his bed and remains there for nearly one and a half months. [Eventually] he decides to go outside … but despite him having familiarized himself with "the deserted space of his bedroom," *he still feels completely devastated and powerless when going through the wide, straight streets and spacious public squares of St. Petersburg, which, even while full of people, were still "deserted"*

> *enough to trigger those same painful sensations.* ... After six months of refamiliarizing himself with these streets, he begins to go out again ... staying close to the houses, trying to mix in with the crowd going in the same direction as himself and choosing to cross the street in places where there are the greatest number of buses and carriages, even though he risks being crushed there. What really strikes the patient the most at this time is that on the arm of a friend he can walk just as steadily as before, such that even the Field of Mars causes him no apprehension. And that is not all, for with his younger brother, ten years old, he can take long walks with no fear whatsoever. He is surprised to be able to go to Tzarskoe-Selo (a small village twenty kilometers from St. Petersburg) by himself and felt fine walking in the streets of this village. This continued until 1877 when in the spring of that year he passed by a street in St. Petersburg and was immediately seized with the same sensations as before. ... [A trip to the seaside did not help] as "the nearness of a sea without visible limits made him enormously uncomfortable."[32]

The treatment Cherchevsky recommended involved retreat to the country and a regime of regular manual labor, rubbing the body with cold water, and taking arsenic internally in increasing doses. The patient was also advised to stop smoking. After three months of this, he returned to St. Petersburg completely well and remained so in the follow-up period of a few months.

Dvortsovaya Square and the Field of Mars are among the largest squares in St. Petersburg. By the mid-nineteenth century, an Italian architect had completed the tsar's orders to make Dvortsovaya Square "a stage for huge military parades."[33] The Field of Mars, named after the Roman god of war, is perhaps the most literal manifestation of the link between the large public squares of late-nineteenth-century European capitals and the cities' standing armies. War is allegorized in the square's name and it is easy to see how the memory of immense military parades might remain in the minds of St. Petersburg's citizenry.

Among the large public squares of St. Petersburg mentioned by Cherchevsky's patient as sites of agoraphobic anxiety, the Field of Mars is singled out as one of the most challenging. The spatial anxiety he walks us through restates qualities of agoraphobic space we have already encountered as well as some new ones. The Field of Mars is the square he can cross comfortably on the arm of a friend, or even in conversation with his ten-year-old brother. As a relational being he experiences the city's empty expanses "with no fear whatsoever." But as a solitary individual he hears an internal voice that tells him he will fall if he continues. A typical statement echoed in the clinical literature, the agoraphobic's sense that he will fall if he ventures into the cities' most public of spaces by himself, suggests that public urban life has a corollary spatial sense of self. Empty space appears to be a testing ground for this spatial sense of self, since even the emptiness of the Russian patient's rather large furnitureless room can provoke the sense that he is missing some stabilizing element, just as the Field of Mars did. The emptiness of the Field of Mars is also similar, the patient reports, to "a sea without visible limits." Compared to the pedestrian who was helped across the Place de la Concorde by abstract perspectival directives, the agoraphobic appears unable to "read" abstract visual cues; instead, he sees the space's boundlessness. Thus, he takes to crossing urban spaces of immense dread by mixing with the crowd. He goes to busy intersections and risks his life by crossing with moving buses and carriages. It is as if, failing to receive reliable information from his visual senses, the agoraphobic relies on his sense of touch. By default he suggests that the city's most public of spaces demand a sense of self that is not relational but solitary, highly sensitive to space yet restricted to honing the sense of vision for reliable information about that space.

Reading Cherchevsky's patient's written tour of the public spaces of late-nineteenth-century St. Petersburg I cannot help but wonder whether the Russian novelist Fyodor Dostoyevsky's infamous underground man in *Notes From the Underground* (1864), who so reluctantly left his shelter beneath the floorboards to slouch the streets of St. Petersburg, was also—like his contemporary, Edvard Munch—an agoraphobic.

## Conclusion

The monumentalized neoclassical square is the site of the emergence of a modern urban pathology. Agoraphobia emerges as a pathology in relation to the transformations and uses of these monumental spaces. Its occurrence in the late nineteenth century appears inseparable from the urban giganticism that accompanies nationalization at this time, a giganticism where "exterior" social space is powerfully linked with an "inner" social space experienced at the individual level of collective consciousness. The crisis of representation that architectural critics attribute to the excesses of monumental city design had its echo in the appearance of agoraphobia during this period. Most significantly, agoraphobic triggers in public urban space appear to show us where giganticism has taken built environments of abstract space and, through an increase in the scale of empty space, has turned these spaces into intense sites of *démesuré* potentiality, sites to which the heightened sensibility of the agoraphobic will react.

Walter Benjamin has described the secularization of the sacred in the monumental forms of Haussmann's architectural projects. Streets, before their completion, he notes in his essay, "Paris, Capital of the Nineteenth Century," were draped in canvas and unveiled like monuments.[34] Nineteenth-century agoraphobics show us that, for a certain section of the population, these monumental spaces were unreliable guarantors of secular, statist identity. The agoraphobic's experience manifests sublime uneasiness and military overtones. In the next chapter I will analyze further the gendered contours that the nineteenth-century agoraphobic reveals in the built emptiness of modern space and propose theoretical models to better interpret the puzzling relation between urban space and modern subjectivity.

CHAPTER 3

# The Nineteenth-Century Urban Commons as a Gendered Puzzle

> From this epoch stem the arcades and interiors, the exhibitions and the panoramas. They are residues of a dream world.... Each epoch not only dreams the next, but also in dreaming, strives toward the moment of waking.
>
> —**Walter Benjamin,** *Paris, Capital of the Nineteenth Century*

## Introduction

In the last chapter we uncovered common patterns among specific trigger sites of late-nineteenth-century agoraphobia. The dreaded domains of public space that agoraphobics single out are generally neoclassical squares monumentalized to serve as cohesive symbolic spheres for an emergent nationalism. Looking further into their aggrandizement schemes, we saw that expansive empty space, rectilinear adaptations of nature, and abstract, perspectival pedestrian directives were common features. Furthermore, the squares were often palimpsests of military training and parading grounds; chaotic nodal points for urban traffic flow; commercial zones; and stages for national festivals. Introjected onto a public sense of self, these spaces made specific demands that we recognized by default in the agoraphobic: the spaces called for solitary individuals with well-honed visual skills aimed at recognizing abstract, perspectival directives to be followed even as the giganticism swept the abstract nature of the space into a new space of *démesuré* potentiality. In this chapter I will continue to examine the clinical literature of this period for patterns relating the agoraphobic's mental state to public urban space. Specifically, I am interested in gendered patterns, clues to better understand how demands of urban space are also gendered demands on a public self.

Several excellent studies have found gendered patterns in the relation between self and urban space in the nineteenth century.[1] Men's public roles are spelled out with greater clarity than women's at this time and these social roles have been mapped onto public space. With respect to agoraphobia, however, the picture is not so clear, and this important body of social analysis is less helpful. Gendered understanding of public space becomes more difficult in the case of agoraphobia where we are dealing with *emptiness* in public space, the use of vast emptiness as a nineteenth-century architectural medium to achieve both monumental affect and instrumental national unity. Because empty space is closely associated with existential relations of being (as opposed to epistemological relations of knowing) and because agoraphobia shows us that monumental giganticism can transform abstract empty space into an emptiness of intense potentiality, we are no longer dealing uniquely with mapping public space in terms of normative gender relations that could be characterized or stereotyped as stable social roles. Rather, we are dealing with gendered dimensions of specific public spaces that have become increasingly ineffective at giving spatial directives. In our case we are lead to look at how the failed task of giving spatial directives is taken up by social and cultural institutions whose codes are not yet built into these new nodal, monumental forms of public space. What strategies do these other institutional codes use to reinsert agoraphobic men and women back into public spaces whose built emptiness has challenged their sense of public self?

## The Rebus Puzzle as a Heuristic Device to Consider Contradictory Approaches to Gendered Public Space

In the epigraph to this chapter Walter Benjamin presents the architectural historian as an interpreter of a society's collective dreams. Using the metaphor of a dreamscape for urban space, Benjamin invites his reader on an analytical journey in which the urban critic, like an interpreter of dreams, uses explanatory models that are at times contradictory without weakening the overall argument he makes about his complex social object. With a similar aim we can also say that the study of agoraphobia reveals how urban architecture of the last century contains residues of a dream world where we ourselves, inheritors of the European city, were first imagined as subjects in daily relation to the expansive emptiness of public urban space.

The nineteenth-century agoraphobic, in this analogy, is like a sleepwalker whose waking nightmares in the newly opened spaces of urban expansion present us with a sort of rebus or spatial puzzle, the theme of which is the relation of modern urban subjects to the built emptiness of contemporary urban life.

The modern dreamer's attempt to understand his dream was likened by Sigmund Freud in *The Interpretation of Dreams* to the process of reading a rebus.[2] A rebus is a puzzle whose pattern or answer is constructed of the relationships among images, words, and letters. In dreams such relations are opaque. They form patterns that are at once incommunicable and fascinating, enigmatic yet compelling. For Freud this dual pull of the language of dreams reflects the resistance that "the real"—that is to say, the ineluctable and inscrutable experiences such as life and death—exerts against all attempts at representation. Dreams are like rebuses because both are patterned, figural forms of thought that use the tension of spatial juxtaposition to bring words or language into relation with nondiscursive elements; rebuses relate words to images while dreams relate language/understanding to emotions and unspeakable experiences. Key in this analogy is the work of space. All reading of rebuses, all interpretation of dreams involves recognizing patterns created by spatial juxtaposition of incommensurable elements.

Continuing this analogy we can say that nineteenth-century agoraphobics have framed for us sections of European capitals that are, like the old arcades, exhibition halls, and panoramas of which Benjamin spoke, residues of a dream world. As such we may consider them as rebus structures. The analysis that follows in this chapter seeks to locate and interpret patterns in the century-old agoraphobic accounts of dreaded metropolitan space. The patterns make up the agoraphobic's "spatial puzzles," whose theme remains the relation of modern urban subjects to the built emptiness of contemporary urban life. Modern urban life has put metropolitan citizens into everyday contact with invisible forms of built emptiness. Tracking the acute sensibilities of the agoraphobic pedestrian we can recognize these invisible forms of the built environment in particular psychosomatic patterns. Spatial phobics are ancestors who can speak to us about our social subjectivity as inheritors of the empty urban space constructed by modern architecture.

To discern the collective psychic imprint that agoraphobia leaves in urban space we will use tools of psychoanalysis. Agoraphobia from a psychoanalytic perspective is a publicly triggered instance of what modern psychiatry calls "abreaction," the acute reliving of traumatic experiences or events that produce catharsis or cure. Viewed as an instance of abreaction in public space, the agoraphobic's plight brings the body, long neglected in architectural analysis, into a spatial puzzle. Just as psychoanalysis examines the puzzling tension between words and images, we can use some of these basic concepts to analyze the tension between language/understanding and emotions/unspeakable experiences when we look at the agoraphobic's body and its full sensorium reaction to specific kinds of public space. In this regard, the spatial disorder of agoraphobia focuses our attention on the tension between a cultural order dominated by the visual and an experiential body whose tactile skills of knowing are thoroughly neglected in modernity. Psychoanalytic concepts can be usefully deployed to deepen our understanding of this tension.

Where psychoanalytic concepts fail to grasp the complexity of the gendered patterns in the tension between the agoraphobically defined public space and the full sensorium body of the patient, we will use concepts from the antipsychoanalytic theories of Gilles Deleuze and Félix Guattari. Because of the profound concern for the spatial nature of subjectivity in these philosophers, their theories provide useful concepts for discerning what happens when modern urban life puts metropolitan citizens into everyday contact with invisible forms of built emptiness. From both of these analytical perspectives, the acute sensibilities of the agoraphobic pedestrian are recognized in particular psychosomatic patterns. For both theories, spatial phobics are ancestors who can speak to us about our social subjectivity as inheritors of the empty urban space constructed by modern architecture.

In this chapter, then, I approach the nineteenth-century clinical literature with tools of social analysis coming from theories where the formation of a self is understood as a spatial relation. Thus, I borrow from psychoanalysis (object relations theory) as well as from antipsychoanalytic theories (the anti-oedipal, the schizoanalysis of Deleuze and Guattari). Our psychological approach to urban history and gender identities is not unified: diverse theories with contradictory premises are all partially useful in explaining our historical material. In fact, contradictory approaches to the analysis of the emergent urban commons turn out to be necessary tools for a fuller understanding of the gendered nature of these new forms of social space.

## Gendered Patterns of Agoraphobic Collapse in Nineteenth-Century Public Space

While Carl F. O. Westphal's cases of uncertain pedestrians in nineteenth-century Berlin have been cited repeatedly as the inaugural stories of agoraphobia in the modern age, other cases appearing in psychiatric journals in fin-de-siècle Europe have been overlooked.[3] These other cases present an unusual gendered pattern that has ramifications for our understanding of agoraphobia today. Although most doctors of this period regard agoraphobia as first and foremost a male disorder, 20 to 30 percent of the cases reported in the journals I examined concern female agoraphobics. Doctors emphasize that both groups report identical symptoms: immobilizing fear of crossing wide open squares and urban streets, dizziness, a feeling that they are going to fall, and physical signs like heart palpitations, jitters, and profuse sweating, all of which conspire to make patients feel as if they are going to die. These sensations cause both male and female agoraphobics to withdraw from the fearsome public spaces. Reactions to this terror may include the creation of a new map that allows them to continue circulating, or it may mean complete retreat into the safety of the home or even the bed. Common sites of fear mentioned in the early studies of both male and female agoraphobics include the names of dreaded squares and streets as well as theaters and churches. Doctors include these spatial references in the case histories even as they *ignore and advise suppression of these spatial triggers as causes.* While all the above-mentioned conditions are present in both men's and women's case histories, there are certain cases that offer notable, gendered differences.

## The Soldiers' Stories

The following three cases of agoraphobia, one from St. Petersburg, and two from different doctors in Paris, involve agoraphobic anxiety among male military personnel that occurs in the process of moving back and forth between spaces defined as military and those defined as civilian.

Dr. Cherchevsky of St. Petersburg, in the 1885 *Revue de medicine*, published the case history of an agoraphobic who was

> thirty years old, very small in stature, robust, muscular, has all the outward signs of flourishing health … during the summer of 1880 … at this time he began, for the first time, to feel a painful sensation of anxiety [*angoisse*] in the area of his heart, followed by weakness and exhaustion as soon as he found himself in less frequented places. Streets full of people, theaters, dance halls, restaurants all became from this time on inaccessible. Since he lived in St. Petersburg and had to show up daily at his regiment, which was camped just outside the city, the patient, tracked by an ever-growing fear of populated places, began to choose the earliest morning hours to make his trip from his lodgings to the train station. He had his attendant accompany him, even though this entire trip, which, by the way, he took by carriage, lasted only three to five minutes. Despite the presence of his attendant, when he crossed nearly deserted streets he was seized by an indefinable anguish [*angoisse*]

> and a painful anxiety [*anxiete*] as soon as he *chanced* to encounter one or two carriages, or a few pedestrians coming out of a neighboring street. Scarcely master of himself, bathed in a cold sweat, trembling from head to toe, after a few unsuccessful attempts to return home, he finally reached the station; as soon as he entered the station, all the aforementioned phenomena would disappear and a light feeling of weakness would take its place. Analyzing this on the spot and even later when he was calmer … the patient was convinced that, basically, it depended on one single idea: he was afraid of falling, of getting hurt, of being taken for a drunk. … His explanation seemed all the more probable to him since at the limits of St. Petersburg, in "his" railway station in the town where "his" regiment was stationed, he never experienced such sensations, he would walk freely in the streets and parks, lunch and dine in the officers' circle. … *Next to this painful terror of the streets of Petersburg, the patient noted the very remarkable fact that, in these same streets that he could not bear crossing by carriage, he traversed on horseback at the head of the soldiers he commanded without the least disagreeable sensation. He explained this apparent contradiction by the fact that here he was surrounded by "his own" and in fact in the middle of a crowd as numerous as a regiment, he felt imperceptible, all the more since the public is completely absorbed by the general aspect of parading troops.*[4]

The patient was prescribed terebenthine with ether for his liver and was advised to stop drinking and take warm baths daily.

Dr. Henri Legrand du Saulle of the Hopital de la Salpêtrière in Paris described the following similar case in *Le Practicien* (1885):

> One day I was consulted by a twenty-seven-year-old infantry lieutenant who told me that one morning at six o'clock, in front of a square that he crossed everyday at the same time, he could no longer go forward or even go backward. His face began to redden and he started swearing and exhorting himself to walk. After an enormous amount of time, perhaps two minutes, a carriage passed by allowing him to immediately continue on his way. … *If he now comes to this square wearing his saber or on horseback, all is well; but if he is dressed in civilian street clothes* [*en bourgeois*] *terror strikes him.* … [Later] this young officer, whom one could not accuse of being chickenhearted since he had been decorated at the age of twenty for acts of bravery, was stricken in the morning when he tried to cross the courtyard of his barracks. He was made fun of and he immediately took a leave of absence from his post. Since then, he has gone

> back in the service and become captain; today he holds a sedentary post. This man is a homebody type, who, like most people of this sort, is conscious of his condition and is far from having that inflated style of hypochondriacs. … I feel fine, he says, I eat well, but if I have the misfortune of arriving alone at a large square, I am immediately seized with terror.[5]

The doctor commented on the unusual nature of these fears. Like other agoraphobic patients, this patient was apparently in good health and also completely conscious of what was happening to him. Legrand du Saulle notes that if caught early, the disease can be easy to cure: "Most important, take these people seriously and destroy any fear they may have of apoplexy [stroke]. Suppress the cause and give them tonics and potassium bromide. Therapy, in the case of neurosis, must be absolutely authoritarian. You must impose your will on the weak will of the neurotic so that he keeps you in mind. Without this, if you go down the path of conciliations, he will do nothing you tell him to."[6]

Dr. Gros, the ex-chief of medicine at Bologne Hospital, who in all cases he treated traced agoraphobic disorders to heart problems, described the case of an agoraphobic man in *Annales Medico-Psychologiques* (1885):

> I was consulted [in 1875] by D., thirty-two years old, whose heart appeared hypertrophied and who had just left the military, where he had been a drummer. As long as he was playing his drum, he told me, he walked straight and strong with the other drummers at the head of his troop. When he stopped, he became dizzy, staggered in his gait and was often forced to sit down on his drum. If he left his ranks, he would fall down. … [A few years previously,] while fighting with the Versaillais against the Commune … a fall from high up on the barricades had fractured, he was told, the left frontal plate of his skull. … This man died of his heart ailment in the hospital where I worked toward the end of 1882.[7]

All the above cases present agoraphobic men whose military identity gives them relief from the inexplicable collapse of their public self in civilian/nonmilitarized space. There is a significant connection between the military identity of the agoraphobic and the social space he can and cannot venture into. To analyze this further, however, we need a theory of subject formation that positions the development of the self in relation to space. Thus we turn to the psychoanalytic theory of object relations for insight into the specifically spatial nature of agoraphobic cases.

## Object Relations Theory as an Interpretive Framework for the Soldiers' Stories

The work of Melanie Klein, and later, Wilfred Bion and Donald Winnicott, offers a theory of subject formation that is fundamentally spatial.[8] Their work points to an originary safe environment—the mother's body for the fetus and eventually the parent's embrace for the infant—that becomes the basis of an endless series of displacements and substitutions that enable a person/self to feel relatively safe in confronting the world's otherness. This theory reasons that when as children we feel the unspeakable distress of pain or fear of the unknown, the ones who hold us through the experience and call to us beyond our distress are helping us build a foundational psychic space. This inner space and all the forms it eventually takes will allow us to contain our fear and sufficiently modify the need to externalize it, thus allowing us to form relations to the other(s) that are neither paranoid nor excessively controlling. Bion suggests we think of this inner space as a container, a place where anxiety and meaning can be held, as we were once held, and therefore worked on, rather than spilling over into a fear that we visit on the other or even on ourselves since the self may also become that feared or loathsome other.

Such inner space is the place of experience. For Bion it is a precarious place, and subject to pathological turns. Whether it is posited at the individual or at the social level, it functions as a container to hold the fluid-like nature of experience. How it holds our experience varies. As a social medium, it may hold experience in socially bounded ways like routine, ritual, and rule, or it may take the form of physical boundaries, gated communities, and the like.[9] This theory suggests that the process of human and social development hinges upon a reliable container for experience. When we, as individuals or as a social body, have no access to those forms/spaces that can hold together fear and meaning, our experience of ourselves and of social space becomes pathological.

Using object relations theory we can speculate that when the three agoraphobic soldiers noted above identify with the military, they have found a container of sorts to face something that is apparent yet intolerable in the wide open public spaces of the urban experience. The military identification allows these men to enter certain kinds of public space characterized, as we saw in chapter 2, by monumental emptiness, and, acting like stable, bourgeois males, experience encounters with others without being immobilized by fear. The directives to reinsert men of acute spatial sensibility into monumental public squares, then, comes from the military. As members of a military "machine," these men are prepared to enter large-scale public squares as spaces where they may encounter the enemy. What sort of enemy might they run into in the large public squares of the capitals of European nation-states at this historical juncture?

In his essay "Mass Culture as Woman," cultural historian Andreas Huyssen points to the fear with which the European mainstream media of the late nineteenth and early twentieth centuries described the masses. In an age of declining liberalism, fear of the masses "is always also a fear of woman, of sexuality, of the loss of identity and stable ego boundaries in the mass." He continues, "Male fears of an engulfing femininity are here projected onto the metropolitan masses, who did indeed represent a threat to the rational bourgeois order. The haunting specter of a loss of power combines with the fear of losing one's fortified and stable ego boundaries, which represent the *sine qua non* of male psychology in that bourgeois order."[10]

In the case of the bourgeois male agoraphobics described by Westphal and his contemporaries, the fear of the masses may also arise as a fear of the spaces in which the masses are constituted as such—namely, the large, open public squares of the growing metropolitan world. In his 1872 study, Dr. Carl Westphal describes how one of his agoraphobic patients loses ground when approaching a large square in Berlin, noting, "He compares the feeling when crossing an open square with the feeling of a swimmer who suddenly swims out of a moat/*grave [Graben]* into a wide pond and fears to try to make it across the later. The condition improves when he again nears the buildings; if he has crossed the space, it [his traversal] seems to him like a dream."[11] The perceived fluidity of the space and the association of that space with the work of the unconscious in dreams and metonymically with death (through the word *Graben)* reinforces the sense of its having lost its stable boundaries.

Due to an influx of provincials, late-nineteenth-century capital cities of Europe saw their populations increase manifold. In their description of Sweden's capital at the turn of the century, for example, social historians Allan Richard Pred and Michael John Watts remark that Stockholm saw its population increase by 80 percent. In becoming a modern European capital, he explains, national monuments were erected in city squares, and new street names signified a national as opposed to a local identity.[12] This transition from the local to the national that occurred in many overpopulous European capitals at the time was destabilizing in many ways. The use of the new physical structures that were built to contain and channel metropolitan identity toward an allegiance with the emergent state were as impossible to predict as were the crowds. Would the masses become revolutionary or nationalized? Would the cobblestones enable the flow of traffic in the new boulevards or become barricades to keep out the republican army?[13]

Pred and Watts describe walking around in the capital city as a spatial acting out.[14] Agoraphobic soldiers also appear to be acting out their destabilizing encounter with the flux of change materialized in large and open urban spaces. Stabilized by their identification with the military, they draw on a collective hypermasculinized response to ward off the fear of these spaces. Their gendered source of stability suggests that the spectral enemy they encounter in the new form of urban space is not only the unidentifiable, formless masses but also the masses as a feminized other.

The syntax of urban street life in Europe's capital cities at the time also reflects an encounter with the project of nation building. Political style was characteristically secular in tone, its aim to inspire mere crowds to become national masses. In his study of nationalization of the masses in Germany, George Mosse has described the function of national monuments during this period as an attempt to anchor national myths and symbols in the consciousness of the people. The large new public squares, whose construction often entailed the destruction of the narrow streets and small shops of the cities' oldest neighborhoods, were not just built to ease the increasing bulk of city traffic but also as sites for citizens to congregate in numbers hitherto unknown for the cultic rites of public, state-sponsored festivals.

Mosse describes how large areas of open space were often left to stand around national monuments for the purpose of national festivals and mass rallies which would in turn make the monument come alive.[15] Although architects have suggested that such public space functions as "sacred space," modern nation-states, unlike the monotheistic religions of their citizens, have no one authoritative book of stories to stabilize the correspondence between symbol and meaning. States may seek to stabilize their sovereign authority with symbolic national heroes, but such personages or statues, unlike religious icons, cannot function as symbols of a clearly defined politicoreligious hierarchy. Rather, they are allegories of an abstraction. They allegorize the sovereign power of the nation-state. The possibility of referring to ambiguous, unstable, abstract meaning differentiates allegory from symbol and makes it the more suitable form with which to describe the imaginative function of the new spaces for the masses in late-nineteenth-century Europe. These areas of late-nineteenth-century urban space are characterized by their relation to an abstraction, "the masses" or "nationalism," and in this respect they are well serviced by the function of vast, empty space. In his frequently cited study of modern nationalism, Benedict Anderson cites the observation of contemporary social critic Ernst Gellner: "Nationalism is not an awakening of nations to self-consciousness. It *invents* nations *where they do not exist*." Anderson rightly comments that instead of focusing on the creative or invented aspect of nations, Gellner is too quick to juxtapose the "nonexistence" of the nation, being therefore false, with the existence of the face-to-face community, therefore real.[16] Our study of agoraphobia, moreover, shows that "nonexistence" must also be created or invented. A clearing, both material and allegorical, must be created as a basis for the new. Not only are late-nineteenth-century urban spaces marked by the imaginative work of national building, they are also marked by large areas of emptied space in the form of razed neighborhoods and in the formlessness of vast areas of spatial emptiness whose signifying function the agoraphobic reaction makes palpable.

The social function of empty space (*leere Raum*), according to sociologist Georg Simmel in his 1908 work "Raumkonfiguration," was to act as a neutral zone between feuding parties or as a meeting place or common ground for trade or peace negotiations among *enemies*.[17] Likewise, the empty space of wide open urban areas signals the site of an encounter with an enemy. The unrepresentable, allegorical enemy best represented by the emptiness of the capital city's square may be the nationalized masses, inspiring fear with their ambiguously bounded identity. Ambiguous, unbounded identity may be feminized in popular consciousness, so that fear of the masses and their spaces is easily displaced as a fear of women as that unbounded other. The military is for multiple reasons the container in which this fearful encounter can take place, according to the interpretive structure of object relations. The military offers men of acute spatial sensibility relief by allowing their weakened sense of self to identify with a masculine subjectivity that is also a fighting force. Without a strong, collective military identification, the feminized, unbounded space becomes unsupportable for these spatially sensitive types. Dressed in civilian clothing or simply veering from their ranks, they encounter empty space that cannot contain them as individual men and they, their gendered bourgeois self, thus fails/falls. The encounter with the feminized masses is an encounter with a poisonous bad object. It can only mobilize defensive mechanisms such as the identification with the military.

## The Women's Stories

Historical clinical literature also makes reference to the experience of women in the dreaded metropolitan space and of the supports and directives used to treat their agoraphobia. The following excerpts from medical reports of the same period provide details of gendered differences in treatments and onset of the disorder.

In 1898, Drs. M. Lannois and C. Tournier, in the journal *Annales des Maladies De l'Oreille, Du Larynx, du Nez et Du Pharynx*, cite a number of cases of agoraphobia among women. The doctors indicate in passing that for many of the women the onset of the phobic disorder occurs in close connection with the birth or the death of a child. Whereas the experience of death was often cited as an inaugural event for agoraphobic anxiety in the cases of men, I found no reference to the experience of birth of children to be associated with agoraphobia in the case of men. In other respects, however, the symptoms reported by the women are much the same as those of men, including fear of large open squares, streets, crowds, theaters and sometimes churches. As Lannois and Tournier write,

> Mme P. de Darrieu (Ain) forty-two years old. … Nervous and impressionable temperament. … Had three children, all dead, one born dead. Married a second time. Her first husband, with whom she had her children, was alcoholic and epileptic. … The patient lived several years with continuous fighting and fears of being killed. The death of a niece last winter aggravated her problems with her nerves, which consisted of ideas of sadness, crying spells, and *angoisse*. Since seeing her husband's epileptic fit, the patient is terrified of having a fit and this is, it seems to me, how her very clear agoraphobic syndrome developed along with an inability to go out alone. At first, *angoisse*. The agoraphobia persists to this day, but in an attenuated form. She has clearly been given to dizzy spells and sounds in her ears which have been with her for a long time. An examination of her ears revealed a definite diminution of her hearing capacity and sclerosis of the eardrums. …[18]

In spite of the severe conditions of personal crisis that surrounded the onset of agoraphobia in this case, the doctors treated her agoraphobic condition, apparently successfully, as an ear problem. The treatment involved air insufflation by trump (horn), the prescription of potassium bromide (2 grams per day), and sodium bicarbonate, as well as dietary changes.

A London physician, Dr. C. W. Suckling, described in the *American Journal of the Medical Sciences* (1890) a similar case of agoraphobia in a woman, apparently the first he had encountered in nine years in a large clinic specializing in nervous disorders:

> [A] married woman, aged forty, was admitted into the Queen's Hospital [Birmingham, England] on August 29th, complaining of an inability to walk in an open space or strange places, and also of depression of spirits. No history of nervous disease in the patient's family. … The patient has always been a highly nervous temperament, but has never had an attack of the same kind before the present one. She has always had a good home and plenty of food. She has nine children and one miscarriage … *she attributes her illness to having so many children and to over-suckling.*

> Nine years ago, while nursing a relative, and being in a very weak state of health, she was seized one day with a horrible dread and with shivering while going up stairs. A few months later, while walking out of doors she had a fit of terrible fear and palpitation. Ever since she has been subject to these attacks. They begin suddenly and end suddenly and are unattended by any loss of consciousness or confusion of mind. *She cannot walk in an open space*; she can walk out of her house for a few yards, and then is seized with an intense fear that she will never reach home again. She then turns back, and can run better than she can walk, but cannot run in a straight line. If she carries a weight, such as two buckets of water, she can walk straight. *She can also walk well in an entry and walks much better in a room where there are lines along the carpet, far better on a wooden floor than where there is a plain carpet, for the lines assist her greatly. She can go across a ploughed field, but not across a meadow.*
>
> While in the hospital it was found that she could not walk in a straight line even in the ward. She said that this was because it was a large room and strange to her for she could get about her own house very well. … A stick was a great help to her, but it did not enable her to overcome her fear entirely. … *If strangers went into the ward, she said the bed seemed to sway and she felt inclined to scream.* She felt *more comfortable with a screen near the bed. …* The patient complained at times of seeing black spots and flashes of light before the eyes. There was slight deafness of nerve origin, but smell and taste were normal. … The patient had only been in the hospital for ten days when she insisted on going out, saying that she could not make herself comfortable in a strange place. During her stay in the hospital her temperature had been normal.[19]

Iron, salts, arsenic, and bromides were prescribed as treatment, but they in no way improved her condition. Another doctor reported to Suckling that this woman "is indeed better and had been to church since leaving the hospital, this being the first time for five years. … She had continued taking the iron and bromides, the prescription for which I gave her when she left the hospital…"[20] In his case history, Suckling emphasized that "agoraphobia is a symptom only and not a disease in itself … it is the most important of the morbid fears as it completely incapacitates its victims. … The proper treatment is to discover and remove any faulty habit of depressing influence at work, and to prescribe a generous diet, cheerful society and surroundings, change of air, and nervine tonics such as iron, strychnine and arsenic with the bromides."[21] He also remarked that, after reviewing the scanty literature available on the subject, he was "struck with the marked potency of childbearing as a cause of agoraphobia and allied morbid fears." He also mentioned here that the sister of a fellow doctor "was also seized with intense agoraphobia after her first *confinement*. The affliction lasted several months but she recovered after living at Brighton for some time."[22]

In both cases, which are quite typical of the women's cases reported in the medical literature, the onset of agoraphobia is closely associated in the minds of the patients with the death and birth of children. The existential dimension of agoraphobia is rarely addressed by biologically driven therapies, neither in the literature of the late nineteenth century nor in the behaviorist treatments that came to dominate the cure of agoraphobia by the end of the twentieth century. (Today it is common to read that agoraphobic women associate the onset of their condition with pregnancy, death, and miscarriage.) Unlike the soldiers, nineteenth-century bourgeois agoraphobic women do not tend to seek relief from their neurotic symptoms in collective forms of identity associated with their gender, such as motherhood. Unlike in the cases of agoraphobic soldiers, there was no support available to the women in the form of an aggregate identity formation. A retreat to home appears neither safe (Mme P. is subject to her husband's violence) nor restful (the English woman has nine children). Confinement away from home (the rest cure) is the recommended treatment, even though this treatment will ironically direct the patient to do exactly what the disorder is doing: allow her to withdraw to a safe space as the means to cope with her problem of withdrawing to a safe space. In a double twist, the English term *date of confinement* found on maternity medical forms to this day, refers to the date when a woman gives birth, a date subsequent to which the mother will go into a period of confinement and withdraw from public space. According to contemporary literature on agoraphobia, the onset of agoraphobia in women often appears soon after childbirth. How should we interpret this little-recognized part of the pattern of women's experience with agoraphobia?

One way to interpret the agoraphobic strategy of withdrawal from public space after childbirth is to say that it mimics in an exaggerated way the confinement that appears normative in Western bourgeois culture. Contemporary feminist studies of the similarity of agoraphobic and nonagoraphobic women's construction of safe and dreaded spaces, points to this strange mimesis.[23] For some feminists, agoraphobia is not a pathology at all, but instead a symptom of the larger problem of normative societal violence against women. According to their view, agoraphobic women, who today make up close to 90 percent of cases of agoraphobia, are ironic characters: they are playing the role of the "good"—meaning housebound—woman too well, to the point of criticism.[24] Others, such as literary critic Gillian Brown, in her study of agoraphobia in late-nineteenth-century Ameri-

**Figure 10** Artist's interpretation of the experience of childcare in the modern urban highrise. "Spring in the Suburb of Hallonbergen" by Anna Sjodahl (1972). (Courtesy of the Museum of Boras.)

can literature, suggest that agoraphobia is within the range of normative expectations of modernity because it mimics or "epitomizes the structure of individuality in a market economy." Agoraphobia, claims Brown, maps in the individual self the circuits that capitalism must take to make domestic space safe for the extension of the marketplace.[25] Those circuits involve circumventing the space that is resistant to the extension of capital, the home, and then learning how to mimic domestic space in an effort to learn how to cross that bounded territory. Brown shows that domestic space has now, in the late twentieth century, been extended to the shopping mall, a site of intense activity on the part of women and one that provokes the utmost in agoraphobic dread. Brown's argument gains strength in view of the fact that the dominant treatment of agoraphobic women today is a pharmacologically assisted trip to the shopping center.

Regardless of whether one interprets the women's cases as exaggerated forms of normative bourgeois behavior or as an allegory of the relation between modern subjectivity and the capitalist marketplace, the relation of women's experience of agoraphobia to their experiences as caregivers of children in a modern urban context needs to be further addressed. Feminist architects have recently drawn our attention to the psychological affects of modern urban dwellings on women with small children.[26] (See Figure 10.) Again, the cultural expectations and directives built into urban design appear to be at once normative for women and, from the perspective of the women involved, often experienced as pathological. The feminist literature shows that this pattern exists for middle-class women with children whether they are confined in American suburbs or in European high-rises.[27] The relationship between psychological illness and the existential experience of birth and childcare, an association that is generally ignored in the dominant treatment modalities, suggests the importance of considering the cultural directives behind the spatial dimension of human experience at this fundamental point in a woman's life. Because these cultural directives may be within the range of what is normative for women, the theories of spatial maladaptations we saw in object relations are not useful here. We need to more thoroughly reexamine the basis of Western notions of subjectivity and space.

## Anti-oedipal Theory as an Interpretive Framework for the Women's and Men's Stories

The relation between agoraphobic subjectivity and social space can be more thoroughly described with reference to a distinction made by Deleuze and Guattari in their innovative philosophical writings: two kinds of space, they claim, are the basis of two kinds of subject formation. Space that is striated and stable, laying out a gridded network to organize a social world around a central point (much as we saw in our discussion of one-point perspective in chapter 1) gives rise to forms of subjectivity that are centrally fixated, like the oedipal formation described by Freud or, at a larger social scale, the state formations epitomized by the modern nation-state. Space that is smooth and characterized by its mobile aspect, on the other hand (like the ocean, which is characterized by the motion of waves), gives rise to forms of subjectivity that are nomadic, in the process of becoming. These later types of subjectivity are less authoritative in modernity. Indeed, at the larger social level, the modern state has colonized all nomadic tribal communities and contained them legally inside the nation-state. Emergent social identities based on this second kind of smooth space, however, are gaining greater power in the twenty-first century. Deleuze and Guattari persuasively argue that as capitalism becomes multinational and escapes the legal directives of the territorial nation-state it provides new examples of normative becomings in smooth space; likewise, as computer users enjoy the Internet as a fundamental form of community interface, they experience more flexible forms of self-creation that can only arise out of more mobile forms of (virtual) space. Such arguments concerning how global forms of capital and communication are transforming structures of social governance and self-identity are now commonly presented by social theorists. What is interesting for our purposes is how this spatial thinking can be applied to understanding the gendered patterns we are uncovering in nineteenth-century agoraphobia. Certainly we see a general spatial relation between the psychic confort of striated space in both the soldiers' and the women's stories. Consider, for example, how regimented lines assisted the marching soldier to find a public self capable of crossing the vast emptiness of late-nineteenth-century city squares, or how the English woman was similarly enabled to cross open space with the straight lines of wooden floorboards or ploughed fields directing her cautious steps. Certain theoretical concepts about space and subjectivity in Deleuze and Guattari's work may offer insight into puzzling features of agoraphobia as a gendered social pathology. Their main argument—that two different kinds of spaces can be associated with two corresponding kinds of subjectivity—is immediately relevant to the plight of the agoraphobic, which might be spatially summarized as follows: the normal person walks in straight lines; the pathological one falls in smooth space. In Western traditions of being, the "normal" self and the pathological self are also spatial traditions.

To best understand the spatial nature of the Western self in their theory, we need to consider these philosophers' discussion of striated space as a dominant spatial aspect of Western traditions of being in the world. In Deleuze and Guattari's spatial schema, intense forms of homogeneous space such as those singled out by agoraphobics in the monumentalized neoclassical squares present a special case of striated space. For the agoraphobic, we recall, homogeneous space is first encountered as the vast expanse of Euclidean geometric relations it was architecturally intended to be. Then suddenly, the geometric perspectival directives no longer work, the space becomes dizzingly unstable, and visual cues are discarded in favor of more tactile forms of sensory authority to help the pedestrian across. The slippage from a space held in place by Euclidean stability to a space more aptly described by Riemanian mathematics or chaos theory is accounted for in Deleuze and Guattari's model by reference to the mathematician Rene Thom's formula of "retroactive smoothing." Deleuze and Guattari describe this spatial phenomena in their book *A Thousand Plateaus* and, to fully understand its conceptual value for our discussion of gendered patterns in agoraphobia, it is worth quoting at some length:

> The more regular the intersection [of abstract, gridded spatiality], the tighter the striation, the more homogenous the space tends to become; it is for this reason that from the beginning homogeneity did not seem to us to be a characteristic of smooth space, but on the contrary, the extreme result of striation, or the limit-form of a space striated everywhere and in all directions. *If the smooth and the homogeneous seem to communicate, it is only because when the striated achieves its ideal of perfect homogeneity, it is apt to reimpart smooth space by a movement that superposes itself upon that of the homogeneous but remains entirely different from it.*[28]

Analogous to the collapse of abstract, perspectival directives that we have seen the agoraphobic experience when traversing the large open squares of European cities, homogeneous space can intensify its striations such that it "reimparts smooth space." Deleuze and Guattari, in fact, see the perfect example of this spatial phenomenon in the modern metropolis:

> In contrast to the sea, the city is the striated space par excellence; the sea is a smooth space fundamentally open to striation [lines of longitude and latitude], and the city is the force of striation that reimparts smooth space, puts it back into operation everywhere. … The smooth spaces arising from the city are … a counterattack combining the smooth … and turning back against the town: sprawling, temporary, shifting shantytowns of nomads and cave dwellers, scrap metal and fabric, patchwork, to which the striations of money, work, or housing are no longer even relevant. An explosive misery secreted by the city, and corresponding to Thom's mathematical formula: "retroactive smoothing."[29]

Inner-city spaces of bourgeois order and monumental giganticism would not be the only spaces affected by the intensification of striated space in the built environment of the modern metropolis. Outer fringes of explosive city growth across the globe, the philosophers suggest, is subject to the same spatial logic whereby rationally, centrally organized spaces that increase their scale can find that, after a certain point, such increase will no longer produce the same spatial logic on a grander scale. This happens because spatial increase is also an increase in intensity and increased intensity can produce new spatial organizations that do not follow the rational directives of the original abstract, striated spatiality.

The spatial ontology of striated and smooth modes of being and becoming are also associated with a number of other concepts that are usefully applied to the analysis of some of the more puzzling patterns we have noted in the agoraphobic's experience. For example, when agoraphobics in the above cases did find ways to traverse empty homogeneous space, they often did so by finding things, people, noises (passing carriages) to support them in their progress. They did not, could not enter as *solitary*, monadic individuals, but stepped in with the props that would make them aggregates. As Deleuze and Guattari indicate, striated and smooth space favor the formation of two different kinds of aggregates they call "multiplicities": "metric and nonmetric [multiplicities]; extensive and qualitative; centered and acentered; aborescent and rhizomatic; numerical and flat; dimensional and directional; *of masses and of packs*; of magnitude and of distance; of breaks and of frequency; *striated and smooth*."[30] The distinction between multiplicities formed as "masses" and those formed as "packs" is the basis for the authors' anti-Freudian/anti-oedipal social psychology of subjectivity.[31] Following the work of Elias Canetti, Deleuze and Guattari describe masses as crowds characterized by "large quantity, divisibility and equality of the members, concentration, sociability of the aggregate as a whole, a one-way hierarchy, organization of territoriality or territorialization." These adjectives can all be associated with the kind of aggregate subjectivity at home in the striated, homogeneous space we saw in the neoclassical squares that had been overgrown by the giganticism of monumental design. Packs, on the other hand, describe aggregates characterized by "small or restricted numbers, dispersion, nondecomposable variable distances, … impossibility of a fixed totalization or hierarchization, lines of deterritorialization. …"[32] Both masses and packs are phantasmatic modes of orientation characteristic of two kinds of space. If the agoraphobic self enters the overgrown neoclassical squares by forming an "aggregate" with canes, passing coaches, and other individuals, they are, in Deleuze and Guattari's terms entering as "packs" into space that is smooth and characterized by its movement and deterritorializing nature.

The two ways of moving through space, then, enact or respond to two conceptions of space. The first kind of space constructed for the movement of the multiplicity of the masses is associated with state power. This is an Aristotelian concept of space, adopted in the West most forcefully by Renaissance perspectivism. The forms and practices that defy state power are called "nomadic nomos," and these are associated with the second kind of space—smooth or nomadic space. Nomadic nomos describes a form of subjectivity that is without property, enclosure or measure, a subjectivity that distributes itself in a space without precise limits and develops modes of moving through that space. Aristotle described the distribution of being in the same terms as the distribution of visual representation both being distributed hierarchically around one center which forms a sole and elusive perspective. This description, however, did not account for the representation of movement, which is associated with a plurality of centers, with superimposing and mixed perspectives.[33] This plurality of points of view can create a distorting effect in the visual field from the perspective of Aristotelian space. For the subjectivity of nomadic nomos, however, a plurality of centers is not a distortion. It requires a particular way of seeing and sensing, a particular subjectivity. Deleuze and Guattari describe this subjectivity in the figure of the "pack."

Movement in space constitutes that space. And space here is a cultural creation. In the Deleuze and Guattari model the mover, a form of what we've been calling "subjectivity," creates space. But the subjectivity in question here is not that of the individual. Individuals do not create space any more than they create language. Individuals receive space just as they receive language. They become individual poets and city planners in the cultural categories of a larger social order.

Deleuze and Guattari's model of subjectivity is quite different from that offered by object relations theory. Space is not a "container" that holds me as a subject related to a perhaps fearful object. It is not an ideal ego, or an imagined originary environment that will become in time a series of displacements and substitutions. Such formulations, in Deleuzian terms, are based on a *static* relation to *lack*: the lack of the original unity (mother/child) or the lack of the phallic usurper (father). On the other hand, Deleuze and Guattari's anti-oedipal model of subjectivity offers space as a relation of movement, of territorialization and deterritorialization. This relation is not based on the notion of lack, but of multiplicity. Lack and multiplicity are, in Deleuzian terms, two different kinds of "zero." The oedipal zero is an originary lack that generates a series of substitutions. Zero in an anti-oedipal system, on the other hand, is a "threshold of intensity," a moment where a level of intensity is reached that breaks up the aggregate into new forms or new multiplicities. Multiplicities, like subjectivities, are formations of the unconscious. But multiplicities are subjectivities that are inseparable from space. The *pack* is a form of multiplicity characterized by roaming nomadism (wolves or a swarm of bees being an apt example). Packs are related to smooth space. The *masses* are a form of multiplicity characterized by a static relation to striated space, masses being a form of collective identity that exists in relation to the State.

Multiplicities are psychic formations associated with particular areas of the sensorium. The multiplicity of the pack, for example, is associated with the "I feel" rather than with the "I see" or "I think." For Deleuze and Guattari, a self is an instantaneous apprehension of a multiplicity in a given region. A self apprehending itself as a member of the masses is in the domain of representation and knows itself primarily in visual terms. A self that knows itself in terms of a pack is not characterized very well in terms of optics, but rather by the "haptic," the "I feel" rather than the "I think."[34] To apply these concepts to an agoraphobic, we could say that he is a "pack-like" multiplicity who relies more on the "I feel" domain of the senorium as he steps into an urban space that, overgrown with giganticism, is experienced as a slippage from homogeneous striated space to smooth space. Smooth space, according to Deleuze and Guattari, is

> filled by events or haecceties, far more than by formed or perceived things. It is a space of affects, more than one of properties. It is *haptic* rather than optical in perception. Whereas in the striated [space] forms organize matter, in the smooth [space] materials signal forces and serve as symptoms for them. It is an intensive rather than an extensive space, one of distances, not of measures and properties. Intense [space of ] *Spatium* instead of [the Euclidian space of] *Extensio. ... Perceptions in it is are based on symptoms and evaluations rather than measures and properties.* That is why smooth space is occupied by intensities, wind and noise, forces and sonorous and tactile qualities, as in the desert, steppe or ice. The creaking of ice and the song of the sands. [Non visual signs that serve as orienting devices.] Striated space, on the contrary, is canopied by the sky as measure and by the measurable visual qualities deriving from it.[35]

For Deleuze and Guattari, perceptions of space that focus on symptoms rather than measures and properties suggest a space of affect, occupied by intensities, filled by events and haecceties rather than things.[36] This is strikingly similar to the agoraphobic's description of the space of the wide open urban squares. The agoraphobic's square becomes a pond to swim across; buildings dance and move, things do not stay things, but become unmoored from their thingness and begin to swirl in a sea of intensities, nothing stays anchored, and most important, *emptiness is the initial trigger.* Dr. Perroud's account of an agoraphobic patient in the 1873 issue of *Lyon Medical* represents an instance of this phenomenon:

> A (male) patient is subject to dizzy spells or weakness in his lower appendages; he hesitates to venture far from objects on which he might lean in case of an accident; in streets he stays close to the doorways of houses. It's with some apprehension that he crosses a roadway and his apprehension grows even greater if he has to traverse a square; bit by bit, thanks to his neuropathic state, this apprehension becomes morbid and soon turns to terror and *angoisse*, which the

> subject experiences when he feels alone and lonely in the midst of an extended space. It is a sort of *terror of emptiness* [*le vide*] he feels, it is as if he were nailed to the ground, unable to proceed, unable to turn back, convinced that he could not do this without endangering himself. Thus is the agoraphobic made. Should the patient find reassurance in a nearby object on which he might lean, his crazy terror disappears. And thus it is that the mere company of a cane, or the presence of a walking companion is sufficient to restore the patient with the freedom of movement.[37]

Using an anti-oedipal conceptual framework, we would say that the agoraphobic must enter the vast city square as a member of a pack, so to speak. He needs a family member or good friend close by, or perhaps a cane, an umbrella, a passing vehicle, a nearby wall. All these things that do not appear to form any coherent category are in fact part of his identity as a member of a pack. The agoraphobic soldier needs his regiment or a synecdoche thereof, such as his uniform. Agoraphobics become individuals in this space only as a multiplicity, as a member of a pack. For the agoraphobic these places are fluid, boundless, in motion. They are allegories of an unknown fear.

At a broader social level, those for whom the square appears stable, symbolic, and functional are, in Deleuzian-Guattarian terms, those who can become individuals in relation to the abstraction of the undifferentiated masses. Agoraphobic citizens are those who cannot muster a strong sense of public self (individuality) in city squares that function symbolically as civic space for the emergent national masses. The spatial directives of the square itself are not sufficient for the mobilization of their acute sensibility, which instead of identifying with the abstraction of the masses identifies with the quirky aggregate of the pack. What directive, orienting devices from other cultural institutions can agoraphobics rely on to create a public self to navigate the unruly space of the striated square that turns into smooth space before their very eyes? Women, as we have seen, choose the arm of a family member or close friend. So do men, who also apparently choose attendants, passing carriages, and walking sticks. All these options, which are not provided by any strong public institution, are open to both sexes. But men have an additional option, one that is allied with a fiercely regimented, public, social institution—the military. Only agoraphobic men can enter the fear-inspiring space of the masses and be protected by the public social identity of the soldier. Unlike a family member, an umbrella or a cane, the military pack shares with the abstraction of the masses an identity formed in relation to the state. The military embodies the rigidity that is characteristic of the state apparatus. As Deleuze and Guattari describe it, the military is a nomadic form (they call it a "war machine") that has been "captured" by the state. As a "captive" of the state, the military is a pack that serves the ends of the state.

The masses, on the other hand, are an abstraction produced with the help of the stable, striated space that symbolizes the state. From the state's perspective, the masses are a statistical entity known in ways that lend predictability and therefore some stability to their behavior. From an individual perspective the masses are those people who can comfortably identify themselves via the stable and powerful abstraction of nationalism. Individual soldiers can identify with the state through their military affiliation. They need not identify with the masses in order to identify with the state. This makes the military a hybrid pack, trained to navigate both smooth and striated space. We can see that the agoraphobic male's use of the military as his pack is a gendered option of spatial orientation he does not share with women.

The Deleuzian-Guattarian interpretation of agoraphobia adds to what object relations offered us in terms of a theory of the relation between subjectivity and space. Object relations suggested that the source of agoraphobic fear was a disruption in an individual's primary presymbolic relationship to the mother as the model of the container/space. The primary safe place can be extended/displaced to become a collective "container" if we accept that we—as an individual in the case of a particular patient, or as a society in the case of a broader social analysis—have "fallen" from some ideal environment. This line of reasoning becomes a theoretical problem if one's model of the individual or society does not acknowledge the actuality of a utopian past. According to object relations theory, the mother's womb or early caregiving becomes a presymbolic place we have forever lost but continue to seek in the form of substitutes. It becomes a utopian, Archimedean point against which we construct our identity in the world. Deleuze and Guattari's model of subjectivity, on the contrary, has no such utopian, Archimedean point, neither for society nor for the individual. For Deleuze and Guattari, our spatial being is characterized by two kinds of being in the world: the statist and the nomadic. Intrauterine and childhood experiences of presymbolic, nomadic subjectivity do not persist in our lives in the form of a lost utopian moment. They persist and insist as a productive form for the creation of new identities, new collaborations. They are modes of being (modes of *becoming*, Deleuze and Guattari would say) that place greater value on information about the world coming from areas of the human sensorium that are undervalued, even unuseful in homogeneous space.

Nomadic subjectivities like that of the pack aggregate need not be seen as pathological in the Deleuzian-Guattarian model. Just as the military pack is not a pathological subjectivity in this schema, neither is the person who ventures through a public square only on the arm of a friend. This theory of self-formation in relation to space may be useful to the feminist observation that agoraphobic women's behavior is not that different from normative behavior of nineteenth- or twentieth-century Euro-American women in public urban space. Furthermore, the possible connection between female agoraphobics and the existential experience of motherhood and dependent child care—again, a packlike subjectivity in Deleuzian-Guattarian terms—suggests that agoraphobia, on both the individual and larger social levels, can be understood as the plight of a public self whose dependent, aggregate being is given insufficient directives by monumental public space. From the perspective of object relations, such space threatens the agoraphobic because it has moved too far from the type of intrauterine space whose aim was to contain, comfort and hold the self as it met with new experiences in the world. From the perspective of the anti-oedipal psychology, such space threatens because it has no use for the self-orienting skills that come from a self fashioned outside the centralized, individualized rationality of modern public personhood, unless those skills come from the experience of the soldier.

## In Summary: Gender as a Spatial Puzzle

Object relations theory and the anti-oedipal theories of subjectivity elaborated by Deleuze and Guattari deploy antithetical notions of space: space as a static container and space as movement. In terms of empty space, they use what Deleuze and Guattari call two different kinds of zero: the oedipal zero, which is an originary lack that generates a series of substitutions, and the anti-oedipal zero, which is a "threshold of intensity" where aggregates break into new forms of subjectivity or new "multiplicities."

In the analysis of early cases of agoraphobia both notions of space can be methodologically useful even though they are theoretically contradictory. Both space as a container for an encounter with the feminized masses and space as the intensity of an existential encounter with birth and death are useful spatial categories for cultural analysis. Methodological inconsistency may be enabling to social analysis in view of the analogy between agoraphobic space and the rebus. A rebus is a spatial puzzle that brings incommensurable forms into relation with each other. Interpreting a rebus, like reading a dream, requires analytic concepts and procedures which are enormously varied just as the elements being juxtaposed in the spatial puzzle are of great disparity.

The gendered pattern we encountered in these early cases of agoraphobia is not unrelated to the methodological observation made above. In both the soldiers' and the women's cases, we saw that an existential experience of emptiness triggered the agoraphobic reaction, but only in the women's cases was this directly related to an existential experience of birth or child care. Also in the women's cases we saw that both the agoraphobic reaction, the withdrawal to home, and its treatment, confinement, mimicked what was considered normative behavior or practices in the culture. In other words, it may be highly problematic to women to pathologize agoraphobia. From a Deleuzian perspective, agoraphobia may be considered an "intense" form of subjectivity that arises in relation to "intense" existential experience like death, birth, or early child care and may be triggered unexpectedly in one's life when exposed to that very form of space that is the foundation of such subjectivity: intensity that has collapsed into emptiness. This is the kind of space that the agoraphobic was increasingly required to confront on a daily basis in the large public squares and boulevards of late-nineteenth-century European capital cities.

The women's cases suggest that the form of subjectivity that can arise in such instances is, paradoxically, both an aberration and a norm, both pathological and normative. This may be why therapeutic use of paradoxical logic has been found to be an effective treatment of agoraphobia, as we shall see in chapter 4. The form of emptiness we increasingly encounter in public space enjoins us to more paradoxical subject positions. Finding solace in paradoxical thinking may be necessary for the analysis of subjectivity in modernity, because modern subjectivity, whether that of the modern urban pedestrian or of the social analyst of modernity, is formed in a relation to empty space, and empty space in modernity is imagined, conceptualized, built and inhabited as abstract space as well as homogeneous and heterogeneous intensity.

The agoraphobic's description of the large new common spaces in European capitals demonstrated the relation of modern urban subjects to the built emptiness of contemporary urban life. One of the dominant features of almost all of these early cases is the agoraphobic's recognition of a form of "emptiness" at the heart of the large, imposing urban spaces that triggered the agoraphobic reaction. In closing this chapter on the nineteenth-century puzzle of agoraphobic space, the psychoanalytic notion of *the relation to the unknown* lends another meaning to the effects of urban emptiness. In psychoanalysis, the relation to the unknown is a concept associated with the way in which the psyche comes to form a connection or relation, as opposed to a reaction, to that which is unknowable.

In Tom Conley's probing analysis of cartographic writings of the early modern era, this concept is used to demonstrate how the formation of the modern self that emerges in sixteenth-century Europe is connected to the experience of forming a relation to the unknown. Conley finds that the relation to the unknown, considered to be a basic component of the clinical practice of psychoanalysis, "shares much with what might have been one of the principal drives inspiring navigation and the discovery of the world." It

> entails a subject's ever renewed and renewing encounter with the mysteries that foster a desire to seek a sense of identity. Any vital relation to language and space, to life and death, and to both the imagination and the sensation of objective reality of the world (which defies reduction to language and hence is *real*) is spurred by the unknown. … The unknown, graphically inscribed as *terrae incognitae* on the western and southern horizons of early maps, was traditionally included as an important element of the maps' overall depictions. It was to be conquered, or at least to become known insofar as the gain of knowledge was to assure the discoverer's founding illusion of immortality. … Because the unknown was located by being *named*, it became a form of a relation rather than an unfathomable menace or delusion.[38]

If the agoraphobic locates particular urban spaces as sites where the self collapses and is regrouped as an "aggregate" self, she may do so as part of the process of forming a relation to the unknown, experiencing what Conley describes as "the mysteries that foster a desire to seek a sense of identity." Modern architecture, in constructing urban commons as vast abstract spaces for the gathering of the masses and the experience of the individual as a citizen of a modern nation-state, has built into our daily life a form of empty space that allows not only for the emergence of statist subjectivity, but also for the self to encounter the unknown either in the form of the stranger—as the sociologist Georg Simmel told us in the late nineteenth century—or in the form of a directionless, disorientating empty space. Either encounter might require or enable a new form of identity, a new mode of subjectivity.

The descriptions psychoanalysis offers of the relation to the unknown bear close affinity to the agoraphobic's plight. Conley, following psychoanalyst Guy Rosolato, notes that the relation to the unknown induces an obsessional perspective with "the trauma and mystery of birth, with the spectral presence of death, and finally, with the vital drives of sexuality, which also include madness (a spatial experience) and the brute resistance that the real exerts against language, knowledge, or representation in general. … The unknown declares itself to be that which escapes recognition."[39]

Conley finds this psychoanalytic concept useful in his interpretation of the growth of cartographic representation in the sixteenth century, with its transformation of the three-dimensional world of the cosmographer into that of the abstract, two-dimensional world of the mapmaker. It is equally applicable to our interpretation of the late-nineteenth-century neoclassical squares singled out by agoraphobics as sites of monumental emptiness. In our case, however, the agoraphobic woman has perhaps more in common with the native inhabitants of the New World than with the sixteenth-century navigator. The indigenous peoples found their humanity unrecognized by the European adventurers, their lands valued only as *terra nullius,* land that belonged to nobody, and *terra vacantis*, land empty of recognizable labor. The only puzzle that remains today—and it remains a gendered one—is what happens in public space to the skills of a self not formed in relation to striated space, without the option of military recuperation.

CHAPTER 4

# The Twentieth-Century Urban Commons

## *The Urban Freeway*

Imagine for a moment you are driving down the freeway. Suddenly, for no apparent reason, your heart begins to race. Your breathing becomes labored. You find it difficult to swallow. Feeling light-headed, you grip the steering wheel and notice that your hands are perspiring. A feeling of panic washes over you. … You try to distract yourself by listening to the car radio or focusing your attention on the traffic around you. Another wave of panic! … Terrified … you head for the nearest exit. …

This episode could have taken place in a shopping mall … or any number of other places. *You have experienced a panic attack.* …

Chances are, you associate the panic episode with the freeway and you begin to generalize: *If it happens on the freeway, it could happen elsewhere.* … Helplessly caught up in a panic–avoidence cycle, you are now dealing with the phenomenon known as agoraphobia.

—**Judith Bemis and Amr Barrada,** *Embracing the Fear: Learning to Manage Anxiety and Panic Attacks*

### Introduction

The shopping mall and the urban freeway are the most cited instigators of contemporary agoraphobia in the United States. Already by the mid-twentieth century, journals began to report a new and different picture of agoraphobic patients and the sites of their urban fear. In one Belgian study of nineteen agoraphobic patients published in the *Journal belge de la neurologie et de la psychiatrie* in 1941, Dr. Th. Henusse reported that one place his patients will not go is the theater, followed by the cinema, then cafés, and finally the street. What about the great squares of his city, Brussels? He comments, "As for those vast, open air squares which gave their name to our syndrome, it seems they have lost much of their terrifying power since the classical [cases]. Place de la Concorde, [where] [Dr.] Legrand du Saulle's patient had experienced the very acme of his *angoisse*; he dared not set his foot upon its cobblestones. [By contrast,] only two of our patients needed to hug the walls as they crossed Place Rogier; all the others, without hesitating, opted for a diagonal across. 'It's faster,' they said."[1]

In addition to the fact that these open squares had lost their power to terrify, another major change in the clinical perception of agoraphobia at this time, according to Henusse, was the fact that it was more common in women: "Agoraphobia," he writes, "is observed much more frequently among women than men."[2]

These two observations—that agoraphobia is predominantly a woman's disease and that its urban triggers are no longer the neoclassical square—are not coincidental. Vast urban empty space is agoraphobia's general object of fear, but its specific object will change along with changes in the modern urban landscape. Empty space in modernity is continuously reinvented. As the "commons" form of public space is opened up by new building technologies, the spatial imaginary that facilitates our entry and orientation in that space also changes. In nineteenth-century Europe, empty space was recognized by the agoraphobic as the evolving *place royales* and the wide new boulevards that made monumental squares heavily trafficked urban nodes. In twentieth-century America that emptiness takes shape in the shopping mall and the urban freeway.

The fact that women came to dominate the patient population of agoraphobia sufferers in the later twentieth century reflects the increasing number of women entering the industrial city and its workforce and being socialized into urban and suburban life. By the early 1970s the incidence of agoraphobia had increased exponentially, accounting for more than 50 percent of all phobic or psychoneurotic disorders seen by British psychologists.[3] It is "the most common and most distressing phobic disorder seen in adult patients," writes Dr. Isaac Marks, the British doctor whose clinical work on agoraphobia has helped establish the most commonly prescribed treatments today.[4] As women now make up the majority of patients treated for the disorder, those treatments can provide clues as to how gender functions in socialization processes that orient all modern urbanites, both agoraphobic and not, who enter these changing forms of emptiness in public space.

Nineteenth-century medical cases of agoraphobia were treated by doctors without reference to public trigger sites, their architectural design, or allegorical function. Contemporary doctors continue to neglect spatial triggers, as they propose a wide array of new treatments that range from the psychoanalytic and behaviorist to the cognitive, biomedical, and pharmacological. In this chapter the clinical literature of the twentieth century is examined for its assumptions about space, gender, and the public self. We take a cultural look at cognitive and psychoanalytic approaches to agoraphobia and consider them next to proponents and critics of modernist city design and the urban freeway. Therapies that provide new directives to a self fearful of dwelling in these forms of public space are therapies that hold cultural assumptions about normative demands made by public space. I begin this chapter with a look at how, in the 1980s, drug trials to medicate one of agoraphobia's key symptoms—now called "panic attacks"—suggest that an international, cross-cultural extension of agoraphobia may follow in the tracks of global pharmaceutical marketing initiatives as well as modernist city design. Contemporary treatments for agoraphobia reveal how the modern Euro-American city imagines us as subject/citizens in daily relation to this latest manifestation of emptiness in our shared public space. By juxtaposing the clinical material with writings of architects, city planners, and urban geographers, we can note the social patterns and schemas that arise as key indicators of the "feel" of the urban commons in late modernity.

## The Global (and Cross-Cultural) Extension of Agoraphobia

In the twentieth century, agoraphobia became increasingly "globalized," in the sense that it can now be located and described universally with little regard to cultural difference. To the extent that psychiatry follows Western biomedicine it deemphasizes cultural diversity and stresses a common biological heritage of humanity. Cross-cultural psychopathologists treat psychological illnesses such as agoraphobia on the same model as physical diseases with universal symptoms, such as smallpox. However, they apparently overlook the ironic fact that biology is itself a source of diversity at least as much as of uniformity.[5] Such research often begins with diagnostic measures developed in Europe or America that are then translated for use in non-Western cultures.[6]

The following are cross-cultural and cross-national psychopathology studies that involve agoraphobia. Both demonstrate the worldview/epistemological assumptions and the political economy of the Western research project itself and provide insight into the roles played by space, subjectivity, and emptiness as cultural features of the Western spatial imaginary.

*Upjohn's Cross-National Collaborative Panic Study*

The Cross-National Collaborative Panic Study commissioned by the pharmaceutical company Upjohn in 1982 and completed in 1986 was one of the largest controlled clinical trials in the history of psychiatry.[7] The study involved approximately seventeen hundred patients who were studied for eight weeks by over twenty senior investigators at centers in fourteen countries in North America, South America, and Western Europe. Upjohn commissioned this wide-reaching study to test an anxiety drug, alprazolam (Xanax), for approval by the U.S. Food and Drug Administration (FDA). Alprazolam, a benzodiazepine, had hitherto been used at low dosages for generalized anxiety but new work in the field of biologic psychiatry, especially coming out of the United States, had been trying to demonstrate the existence of a physiological cause for certain symptoms of anxiety often seen among agoraphobics that American researchers were calling "panic attacks." According to one of the doctors participating in the studies, the psychopharmacology research unit at Upjohn ran many studies during this period both to get approval for their FDA new drug application and to provide a general scientific foundation for the drug treatment of panic disorder.[8] Up until this time, it was apparent that the notion of agoraphobia as a subcategory of "panic disorder" was of American origin. (European languages have the term *panic*, as was noted in chapter 1, but non-English-speaking European psychiatrists were not using it or its conceptual framework as a key descriptive feature of agoraphobia at this time.) Nor did the International Classification of Diseases have a special category for panic states as a disorder that should be specifically differentiated from anxiety states generally.[9] The American Psychiatric Association had brought into being the new category of "panic anxiety" in their 1980 revised third edition of the widely used diagnostic manual, Diagnostic and Statistical Manual of Mental Disorders (*DSM-IIIR*). In other words, Upjohn could have a wider international market for alprazolam if it could be proven effective at higher dosages in treating the emerging field and subfields of panic disorders.

Among other new theories of a biological cause for agoraphobia, the work of Donald Klein, in particular, promoted the view that agoraphobia is not so much a fear triggered by particular kinds of public space but rather one that is triggered by defective "suffocation centers" in the brain that make agoraphobics more susceptible to overwhelming fear of the experience of fear itself. This suggestion opened up three new territories of panic in the *DSM-IIIR* for occupation by Upjohn and other pharmaceutical companies in the early 1980s: (1) panic disorder uncomplicated; (2) panic disorder with limited phobic avoidance; and (3) panic disorder with extensive phobic avoidance (also called "agoraphobia with panic disorder"). The new classification also created an additional group subject to "agoraphobia without panic disorder," but it was a group with few members. Subsequent to the new classification schema, agoraphobics could now be described as subject to panic disorder.

In 1988, based on the results of the Cross-National Collaborative Panic Study, Upjohn won approval from the FDA for its new drug application for alprazolam. This marked the beginning of a more intensive era of pharmacological psychiatry, most forcefully active in the United States today. The Upjohn study represented a tremendous expansion of the pharmacologically treatable territory of agoraphobia. It is no accident that it coincided exactly with the moment when public space was removed from the diagnostic understanding of the illness. Paradoxically, the marginalizing of space as an incidental and insignificant aspect of agoraphobia actually functioned to increase the space in which the illness could now be found. This is due to the fact that the Upjohn study is called a *cross-national* study, not a cross-cultural one, the emphasis being on national space, a territorial mode of population organization that arises from the historical experience of Europe and follows its colonial expansion, in this case into South America. National space differs substantially from the diverse forms of spatial organization practiced in the world that would include, for example, village communities or the routes of nomadic peoples. All the centers that participated in the Upjohn study were located in modern cities that had followed the urban development patterns of Western Europe and the United States. All these nation-states were potential markets for Upjohn's product, alprazolam (Xanax). The spatial extension of international capitalism, in which markets are unified by the value structure of the dollar, follows the trajectory of Euro-American forms of urban modernization and the trajectory of biologic psychiatry. These overlapping trajectories helped to create the impression of isomorphic, universal space and they constituted the best explanation for why, with respect to agoraphobia, homogeneous space underwent a dramatic expansion at this time.

In the medical community, significant protest accompanied the disappearance of public space as a significant factor in the etiology of agoraphobia. Resistance to the new approach, particularly among British behavioral psychiatrists, has lasted to the present day. Most textbooks in psychiatry will explain the current divide in the following way: "American research tends to define agoraphobia as an especially disabling variant of panic disorder. European research follows Marks in England who defines agoraphobia as 'fearful avoidance of a characteristic cluster of public places'."[10] The *DSM-IIIR* focuses medical attention on panic itself as the etiology of the disorder—the "fear of fear" thesis in which panic is defined with or without avoidance—but the original trigger has been completely removed from the diagnostic picture. Objects of anxious avoidance like spiders and snakes, for instance, now have the same value as urban freeways and shopping malls. The British psychiatrist Isaac M. Marks, who had pioneered behavioral treatments for agoraphobia in the 1960s and '70s, was a particularly outspoken critic of the Upjohn study. When the Upjohn results were published in the prestigious journal of the American Medical Association, *Archives of General Psychiatry,* Marks and his colleagues responded extensively in the prestigious *British Journal of Psychiatry,* their opening comment, "In our view, this study's elephantine labour has resulted in the delivery of a mouse."[11] Alprazolam, they argued, was hardly unique, as the study had claimed in order to gain FDA approval. In fact, it was in no way more effective than other drugs in its class of benzodiazipines that function to depress anxiety while the patient is on the drug but create withdrawal problems and rebound of panic afterward. As Marks and his colleagues argued,

> Despite its randomized design, with many patients and measures, its analysis is scanty and biased towards alprazolam ... the superiority of alprazolam was almost non-existent. ... The size of the drug effect was small even at week 4 and by week 8 it was almost invisible. ... the percentages of panic-free cases [at 8 weeks] were: alprazolam 78%, imipramine [Valium, another benzodiazapine] 81% and placebo 75% ... despite FDA approval of alprazolam for "panic" disorder, ... *the greatest part of the improvement is attributable to the placebo effect, which improved panics greatly. ...*
>
> The report claims "well tolerated" side-effects. However ... more alprazolam than placebo cases reported sedation, memory problems, and ataxia/*impaired coordination. Did this affect driving and similar activities?*[12]

In addition to the medical contradiction, Marks noted a cultural contradiction in the new pharmacologic direction of psychiatry for agoraphobia. The extreme desensitization of alprazolam has reported side effects of ataxia/impaired coordination—meaning, presumably, that agoraphobics and the numerous other individuals now included in the expanded diagnosis of panic disorder should stay off the roads while medicated. This contradicts one of the express purposes for taking the drug in the first place—namely, that it should put the agoraphobic back into public space. The urban freeway systems that have come to make up part of everyday space for so many Americans during this period are, for agoraphobics, the second most avoided sites, according to the clinical literature. Could this mean that the medicated agoraphobic will be physically impaired on the urban arteries so essential to negotiating public space? If so, would not this make those freeways even less safe and legitimately more fear-inspiring for the general public?

In addition to these potential drawbacks, the criticism of Marks and his colleagues also pointed out that "the [Cross National Panic] study is a classic demonstration of the hazards of research funded by industry." Taking alprazolam offered no improvement over the use of a placebo, they argued, writing, "The Upjohn company funded a series of panic studies … in the hope of obtaining FDA approval of an alprazolam indication for treating panic disorder. The company succeeded. … Yet none of those studies … found a greater antipanic effect on completer analyses than was obtained with imipramine [Valium] or placebo. Pharmaceutical marketing and science are different disciplines."[13]

The issue of the placebo effect is almost never addressed by the dominant treatment modalities for agoraphobia. Yet the studies showed 75 percent of the placebo control group in the Upjohn study were panic free at the end of the study, while 78 percent of the alprazolam group were panic free. In a later randomized double-blind international study conducted by Marks and his colleagues, alprazolam is tested again against a placebo and this time against the behavioral exposure therapy Marks pioneered in the 1970s. "In panic disorder with agoraphobia," they found, "panic improved so much with placebo that neither alprazolam nor exposure added benefit."[14] The results again show the effectiveness of placebo for agoraphobia. The placebo effect challenges some fundamental premises of biomedical psychiatry, since it suggests the inseparable nature of the mental and physical body, a terrain that is relatively unexplored in biological psychiatry. We will return to this subject in our final chapter.

By 1991 Xanax, with its aggressive marketing campaign , had overtaken Valium as the most widely used benzodiazepine, accounting for almost one-fifth of Upjohn's worldwide sales. Also by the early 1990s researchers began discovering and warning patients about its addictive nature. Xanax was eventually only recommended for short term use, a problem for agoraphobics whose anxiety troubles are often chronic. Today the drug might be recommended for immediate, short-term anxiety relief. As Dr. Peter Tyler, a professor of psychiatry at St. Mary's Hospital Medical School in London and a longtime benzodiazepine researcher, noted already in 1993, Xanax might be used "[f]or example, if someone has been in a car accident and is nervous afterward when he goes out into the street, he could take *Xanax* for a short time after that."[15]

The paradoxical achievement of the Upjohn Cross-National Study is the international expansion of anxiety drugs into areas where agoraphobia could then be treated as a fear of fear (in other words, as a fear unrelated to expansive forms of public space). The "fear of fear" thesis that gained sway in the *DSM-IIIR* in the 1980s functions like a zero sign: it sets up a new, expansive grid of subject/object relations that are organized around intensely homogeneous, cross-nationalist, capitalist, universal space.

### *The Exception to the International Classification of Anxiety: The Aboriginal Peoples of the Western Australian Desert*

While the Upjohn study demonstrated the expansion of homogeneous space across nations, several steps had also been taken since World War II to standardize the assessment of anxiety states across cultures.[16] Between 1968 and 1973 the World Health Organization initiated an international program for the standardization of psychiatric diagnosis, classification, and statistics that resulted in a quasi-manual, the *International Classification of Diseases*. Research psychiatrists, prior to the reclassification of agoraphobia as a panic disorder, were contributing to this effort by studying the incidence of anxiety disorder in places as diverse as rural and urban Iran, Ethiopia, India, Norway, and Aboriginal Australia. One study by Harvard Medical School professors, titled "Culture and Anxiety: Cross-Cultural Evidence for the Patterning of Anxiety Disorders," found that Australian aborigines were the one cultural group that did not fit the predominant pattern for the incidence of anxiety disorders. It noted that "with the exception of the aborigines … anxiety disorders were diagnosed at a rate of 12 to 27 cases per one thousand population. … *The studies of the aborigines provide the single sharp contrast to this pattern. Here, in population surveys of 2,360 persons, only one case of 'overt anxiety' was found, and this in the most Westernized individual in the group.*"[17]

The Harvard professors suggested that the exceptional status of aborigines indicated a different relationship between subjectivity and space in this culture. They referred to a study titled "Psychiatric Disorders among Aborigines of the Australian Western Desert," published in 1973. In it the subjects surveyed were described as follows: "This group contains some of the most primitive to be found in Australia now. That is, it contains many of those *least affected by western influences* and may thereby give some indication of psychiatric disorders pertaining among these people at the time when they were nomadic—now there are virtually no fully nomadic aborigines left. … Virtually all Australian Aborigines have now *abandoned* their nomadic existence and live in semi-permanent camps around missions."[18]

Despite the enormous epistemological problems with all cross-cultural studies done by anthropologists during this period, when the Aborigine study finds that only nomadic peoples, those who inhabit space in motion, are exceptional—that is, they apparently never experience anxiety neurosis or conventional phobias—it conversely suggests that the stationary experience of space known to sedentary peoples may have some special relation to anxiety.[19] At bottom the study suggests that anxiety is linked with culturally appropriate causes. As its authors note, "The term 'overt anxiety' has been used to describe the syndrome of persistent apprehension with restlessness, tremor and excessive sweating. Such a syndrome is seen when Aborigines are afraid, as they often are: of spirits, the dark, witchcraft, strangers and so on. This fear is short lived and goes when the cause is removed. No intractable symptoms of 'overt anxiety' without a culturally appropriate cause were found."[20]

Here nomadic space is described as a domain where irrational causes—such as spirits, witchcraft, the dark—are treated as rational causes, such as strangers. All triggers, though they may appear paradoxical from a rationalist perspective, are, from the Aboriginal viewpoint, appropriate or normative triggers of anxiety in nomadic space. The study finds that nomadic space is one in which a full spectrum of fear-causing objects are sensible: a full human sensorium, not just vision, may be reliably engaged and a full human intelligence, not just rationality, may be counted on to deal with feelings of fear triggered by spatial sites. In nomadic space, an anxiety-stricken Western urbanite, a "modern" subject, may see nothing, but an anxious Aborigine of Australia's Western Desert may sense something. The "modern" subject, encountering this pocket of nothing/emptiness, may then only form a pathological relation to his objectless fears while the nomadic subject might rely on various rituals or any number of culturally appropriate actions to regain a nonanxious relation to the space. The Aborigine's fear is "short-lived and go[ne] when the cause is removed." If we follow the logic of this cultural comparison, we might come to the conclusion that in "modern" space dominated by rational approaches, such encounters with objectless anxiety create pockets of emptiness that do not exist in the realm of movement and imagination that is nomadic space. Both notions—a diminished sensorium and spatial emptiness—characterize the relation between the self and space in what Gilles Deleuze and Félix Guattari describe as striated space (see chapter 3). Smooth space, on the other hand—a domain of intensity that facilitates paradoxical connections—resembles what cross-cultural psychopathologists claim to have found in Aboriginal nomadic culture.

The study of Aboriginal peoples "least affected by Western influences" betrays a corresponding set of assumptions about the modern Western subject and his relation to space. It assumes a modern, secular subject whose experience of objectless anxiety is an experience of nothingness in space. However, as German philosopher of modernity Martin Heidegger has noted, modernity also asks the modern subject to know himself only as a being and not as a being in relation to space, or what Heidegger calls *Dasein*. Because of this neglect of his spatial "being there," Heidegger decries the modern subject, who undervalues his spatial experience of nothingness by calling it a pathology, a nothingness that is not really "there," a nothingness that merely exists in his (presumably) pathological mind. Heidegger despairs that the modern subject is compelled to try to rid himself of the nothingness, to be cured of its anxiety-inducing effects. Heidegger, on the contrary, champions this nothingness. In the existentialist tradition, he privileges the spatial experience of nothingness and recommended that its encounter count as humankind's authentic relation to being.[21] The cross-cultural study of Aboriginal anxiety and the Heideggerian theory of the role of anxiety in modern consciousness share similar assumptions about modern space. These two aspects of the modern epistemology of space—the psychiatric one that pathologizes nothingness in space, and the philosophical one which privileges nothingness in space—can be contrasted with an agoraphobic notion of space that places the self by necessity in touch with empty space as a form of tactile intensity (recall that without resorting to tactile modes of proceeding, the agoraphobic would fall). With respect to the Aboriginal, nomadic sense of anxiety and space, these other two epistemologies have much in common. Unlike the Aboriginal view, both the psychiatric and the existentialist epistemologies locate an emptiness at the heart of modern space. Whether it is pathologized or made heroic, it is a spatial sense that shares a corresponding form of subjectivity, a corresponding notion of self.

While the cross-cultural studies of anxiety from the 1960s and '70s are now considered by most anthropologists as a chapter in the history of a Western colonial imagination projected on non-Western peoples, Upjohn's cross-national study of alprazolam (Xanax) suggests that they may rather have been simply another step in a continuing project to advance a global jurisdiction for judgments about a normative self in relation to modern space.

## Cognitive Treatments and (Their Mirror Image) Paradoxical Intention

In the United States especially, anxiety medications are generally prescribed alongside other treatment modalities for agoraphobia today. One treatment regularly offered is cognitive therapy, an attempt to convince the patient that there is no rational basis for her agoraphobic fears. Little persuasion is generally needed, however, for one thing that distinquishes agoraphobia from other phobic disorders is that the agoraphobic is already convinced that her fear is irrational. The cognitive therapist offers skills to train the self to deal rationally with irrational fears. For many critics, however, this is precisely why cognitive therapies are less effective: rational knowledge by itself is insufficient to quiet the demands of the irrational voices the agoraphobic hears.[22] Thus, cognitive approaches are generally combined with behavioral ones to achieve a better effect.

One treatment generally categorized as cognitive in fact warrants separate status, in my view. That is the treatment known as paradoxical intention, or logotherapy, associated with the work of Viktor Frankl.[23] Paradoxical intention differs from most cognitive approaches in that it does not attempt to correct false interpretations of anxious reactions nor does it seek to give patients control over their symptoms by helping them to rely on rational thought processes. Dr. Amr Barrada, a psychotherapist specializing in anxiety disorders at a large inner-city clinic in Minneapolis, Minnesota, has successfully used techniques of paradoxical intention to treat agoraphobia. The description of the modality below is based on interviews I had with Dr. Barrada about his treatment techniques, as well as from his writings.[24]

Barrada explains that the highly rational "voice" that agoraphobics use to tell themselves that their fears are completely irrational is a "dominant and self-destructive feature" of the disorder. We have already seen this same rational self-observation in many of the early case histories, where psychiatrists note that their patients seem to be totally aware that their fears of large public squares and crowded places are "silly." The highly rational voice makes the agoraphobic fear that he is going insane. In psychology, such split consciousness is characteristic of a group of phobias referred to as *psychoasthenia,* an incapacity to resolve doubts or uncertainties or to resist phobias, obsessions or compulsions which one knows are irrational. For cognitivists, it is precisely because agoraphobics are able to speak of the "irrationality" of their fears that their disorder may be labeled a "fear of fear" or, more specifically, a rational fear of irrational fear. The object of the fear—say, empty public space—is replaced by a subjective experience (panic) because the spatial referent of this complex, baroque mode of intrasubjective signification, this "self-talk," as Barrada calls it, is so hard to ascertain.

In his practice with agoraphobics, Barrada seeks to undo the binary operations of reason and unreason in what he describes as one mode of the agoraphobic's self-talk, what he calls "A-Talk." He explains that "one outstanding feature of A-Talk is that it is extremely logical. It is replete with logical equations. Unfortunately, when it comes to dealing with human emotions logic does not work well; in fact, more often than not, it becomes an instrument of self-abuse." He continues, "A-Talk cannot be gotten rid of [just as the symptoms it generates cannot be gotten rid of], and attempts to do so only reinforce it. ... trying to get rid of the A-Talk is itself an A sort of strategy and cannot therefore work. ... The strategies of A-Talk are probably extremely internalized. … They are automatic [have a life of their own independent of our will]; and they are covert, so that much of the time we really have no clear access to them."[25]

For Barrada, A-Talk is contrasted with B-Talk, which involves a different set of cognitive strategies of a paradoxical nature. "One way to bring about a reduction of A-Talk is by directly generating B-Talk, and setting it up to be in competition with [rather than replacive of] the strategies of A-Talk," he notes. "Another way is to manage one's A-Talk by applying to it the strategies of B-Talk. Since the strategies of B-Talk are necessarily paradoxical there will often be a rather comical effect. For example, instead of trying to get rid of A-Talk (which is itself an A sort of strategy and cannot therefore work) one can try to leave it alone and be permissive of it."[26]

Given his belief that agoraphobics often have legitimate fears of the modern world that should not be reasoned away, Barrada's treatment of the disorder contrasts sharply with certain cognitive-behaviorist treatments. Cognitive behaviorism, Barrada explains, understands the development of child to adult in terms of control. A child is a creature on the way to learning to control or master itself and its environment. Cognitive behaviorists thus explain that women make up the majority of agoraphobic cases because in our society women have long been infantilized. For Barrada, however, mastery may not be what children need to learn to become adults. Furthermore, he questions whether mastery is the appropriate relation for humans to have to their environment. Thus, his therapeutic approach encourages patients to forget about controlling or mastering their panic either by means of drugs or with behaviorist techniques. In a world where control and mastery are the dominant approaches to the real, Barrada seems to feel that the best chance of finding a living space in-between reason and panic is to take comfort in paradox.[27]

We will return to the spatial implications of a self trained in paradoxical and cognitive approaches later in this chapter when we examine the built environment of the urban freeway, the skills it demands of the public self and the way in which urban growth patterns in U.S. cities have lead from "highway rationality" to "highway irrationality."

## Psychoanalytic Treatments of Agoraphobia: Freud and Lacan

In the early twentieth century, agoraphobia was often treated as a consequence of syphilis, or as a symptom of optical illnesses or diseases of the inner ear. However, agoraphobics were also frequently treated by psychoanalysts as if the disease were a symbolic disorder. The literature on agoraphobia from the psychoanalytic perspective is abundant. It has evolved from Sigmund Freud's early work on anxiety as nonsymbolic blockage of energy quantities, and his later work on the symbolic dimensions of neurosis, to the cultural analyzes of urban space that rely on the psychoanalytic theories of Jacques Lacan.

*Freud and Empty Space*

Freud treated several cases of agoraphobia, his most famous being the case of little Hans, a five-year-old boy who developed a fear of going out into the streets and squares of Vienna. For Freud the spatial issue in agoraphobia was not empty space but urban or social space. Anxiety neuroses like agoraphobia were understood to involve repressed desires or fears masquerading as spatial ones, thus attaching themselves to various elements of the built environment.[28] Buildings and squares—which Freud noted had no intrinsic symbolic value, no inherent architectural meaning—became convenient symbolic substitutes for repressed feelings. "Desire, thwarted by prohibition, transfers itself by metonymy to a nearby object."[29] As Esther Da Costa Meyer notes, Freud explained, "'In the case of phobias one can see clearly how this internal danger is transformed into an external one … The agoraphobic is always afraid of his impulses in connection with temptations aroused in him by meeting people in the street. In his phobia he makes a displacement and is now afraid of an external situation. What he gains thereby is obvious; it is that he feels he can protect himself better in that way. One can rescue oneself from an external danger by flight, whereas an attempt to fly from an internal danger is a difficult undertaking.'"[30]

Despite the preponderance of male cases of agoraphobia written about at the turn of the century, Freud had theorized in his early writings that agoraphobia was a female disorder. In his 1897 essay "The Architecture of Hysteria" he wrote "Agoraphobia seems to depend on a romance of prostitution."[31] Women secretly desire or fear sexual promiscuity, which they associate with the street. In a typical phobic displacement, Freud theorized, the street becomes the neurotic object of women's repressed desires or fears. The cure for this disorder is to bring the patient toward consciously recognizing the relation between the street and his unconscious desire or fear. Once brought to consciousness, the patient can manage or even dispel the somatic symptoms.

Many later case studies built on Freud's interpretative framework and analyzed agoraphobia as a displaced desire or fear stemming from an unresolved oedipal complex. This produced case analyses such as the following reported by a doctor in Rome to the *International Journal of Psychoanalysis* in 1935[32]:

> One patient, whose principle anxiety related to large open squares (she could not endure great "empty spaces"), once dreamt that the

> analyst had to have intercourse with her, but to her deep disappointment it turned out that he had no penis: there was simply *"an empty space"* where the penis should have been. (This was the patient's own expression: *un vuoto.*) He then changed into her mother, for whom it was normal to have an "empty space" instead of the desired organ. This dream shows that open places, from the dread of which the term agoraphobia is derived, signify the castrated mother. *Probably some inner urge prompts us to put a statue, an obelisk and especially, a fountain in the middle of squares.*[33]
>
> ... A certain agoraphobic patient in Rome has an anxiety attack in the busy Via Nationale. He succeeded in reaching the building where the Fascist Exhibition was being held, and this set him daydreaming. He phantasized that he had done great things for the Fascist cause and imagined the Duce [Benito Mussolini] clapping him on the shoulder in a commendatory way. As these thoughts passed through his mind, he suddenly realized that his anxiety had vanished, and he went on his way in good spirits and with head erect.[34]

From a psychoanalytic perspective, men and women deploy different strategies with respect to empty urban space. In the above cases, the man can identify with Mussolini and form a phantasmatic relation that will enable his threatened ego to cross the large Roman boulevard (the Via Nationale). The doctor also reported a case of an agoraphobic male patient who had a large collection of photographs of the king "taken in every possible position," while another had a similar collection of photos of Mussolini.[35] For men the ambiguity of national identity at the level of the individual ego—an ambiguity we have already seen surface in the anxiety triggered by nineteenth-century monumental urban space—can be concretized by giving a "face" to the abstract nation. For the woman, issues of the emptiness of urban space are not resolved by the mediation of the "father's" face; they are more likely mediated by another part of the father's anatomy to which she cannot form an identification, at least theoretically, expect by associating her lack. From this perspective, the woman's fear of empty space can only be mediated by her own symbolic emptiness. The happy resolution of the female agoraphobic, from this rather crude version of the psychoanalytic perspective, would have the woman internally mimic the emptiness she experiences in the street. In such a symbolic world women themselves would be associated with empty space and become anxiety-provoking objects themselves as they trigger castration anxiety in men. One finds cases in the psychoanalytic literature where the symbolic interpretation of empty urban space is introjected in this way, leading to descriptions of female agoraphobics who, when able to go out in the street, are "liv[ing] out the fantasy of walking erect, of being the penis." Note the following cases, published in the *International Journal of Psycho-Analysis* in 1961:

> These two … cases, both married, and *both with children*, had, in addition to the agoraphobia, severe claustrophobia; one of them, in her deepest regression, developed an anorexia nervosa, reducing herself to emaciation and almost threatening her life. The second, too, when regressing, developed a partial anorexia. …
>
> For both the street symbolized independence, and forbidden heterosexuality; in addition, however, it had a rather cannibalistic oral symbolic function. Both patients, in attempts to compensate for the narcissistic injury of castration, had strong desires to be dancers, with the body symbolizing the phallus. In both of these, the street symbolized the dangerous vagina dentata and there were fears of the walls closing in. At the moment of agoraphobic crisis the patient, while walking, would live out the phallic fantasy, i.e. identity at one instance with the father or the father's phallus; at the same time there was also a partial identification with the mother or the greedy, all-incorporating vagina of the prostitute. If one or the other parental figures were there as a companion, the patients' anxiety was reduced, *but they still unconsciously lived out the fantasy of walking erect, of being the penis*; the helpless anxiety was also an accusation that the mother had deprived them of a penis.[36]

Crude as these psychoanalytic analyses may seem, they do highlight an interpretive worldview in which all monumental public space is a projection of patriarchal values and all ego-threatening experiences of boundlessness in space are feminized. The emptiness we are led to by agoraphobics, from this perspective, would always be gendered, feminized, and dangerous to the ego. Many feminists, as we shall see, criticize this interpretive structure which, they argue, cannot offer to reinsert agoraphobic women with any confidence into public space.

### *A Lacanian Model of the Subject's Relation to Empty Space*

A more complex version of this interpretive structure is found in the work of one of Freud's most well-known intellectual descendents, Jacques Lacan. Because Freud had for the most part focused on individual pathology, his work on agoraphobia did not make any larger correlations between this pathology and society. Lacan's work, on the other hand, is often used as an interpretive framework in academic cultural analyses to understand the connection between psychological illness and the larger cultural system. While I am unaware of any Lacanian analyses of agoraphobia per se, there are authors who rely on Lacan's well-known essay of 1949, "The Mirror Stage as Formative of the Function of the I," to analyze the relation between ego development and urban space.[37] Generally speaking, these works show how modern public space acts as a kind of mirror in which the dominant, patriarchal society recognizes its normative self.

Lacan described a mirror stage in the development of the modern ego as a stage in which the infant, between six to eighteen months, still a bundle of sensations relationally bound up with the experiences of the womb and of the mother's care—the touch of the breast, the taste of the milk, the sounds of the mother's voice—first comes to recognize its body in the reflection of a mirror. The mirror image gives the infant a sense of being in the world that is different from that of the sensory being it knew before. The mirror, Lacan reasoned, lends the child a sense of being as a separate entity with distinct boundaries of its own. It is the visual aspect of the sensorium that experiences the self as a well-delineated being. Smell, sound, touch, and taste become less meaningful in this cultural schema, in which the experiential body is developing a sense of self. The new visual regime in which the body is hereafter caught has a new set of relations that will now "hold" the emerging self together.

Lacan theorized that this new set of relations involves the child's realization, on the one hand, that the mirror image is "empty," and, on the other, that it can laughingly play with the gestures and movements it sees rebounding from its reflection. To the extent that the child comes to identify its own body with the imagistic body in empty, virtual space, it will soon acquire through play the false sense that mastery over the mirror body gives it a form of mastery over the real, physical body. This play and mastery takes place within the unreal or empty surround space of the mirror, so that the whole experience of this form of the self's "wholeness" or "boundedness" is caught in the relationships established between a real sensory body and its virtual image. The self is formed as a relation between the virtual and real worlds, the latter of which, of course, still includes other people and the child's environment.

According to this theory, the relations with the mother (what Freud had called the "oceanic" experience of the womb) as well as the cascade of other sensory experiences—all of which Lacan calls the "real"—will now exist in a sort of parallel universe to the new imagistic, visual regime that Lacan calls the "imaginary."[38] This formative stage in the development of the self will be supplemented at a later stage when the child, as it acquires language, begins to be formed in relation to the dominant, patriarchal cultural values contained in the language it will adopt. This later stage, which Lacan called the "symbolic," is similar to what Freud called the oedipal stage, wherein the child develops by forming a relation to the father. In Lacan's model, all three levels—the real, the imaginary, and the symbolic—coexist in the modern person's sense of self, the earlier ones persisting through the later ones.

Psychoanalytic therapies, like cognitive-behaviorist ones, insert the agoraphobic woman into public urban space by explaining her—or training her in the case of cognitive behaviorism—in culturally masculine behavior. This makes sense according to the Lacanian model of ego development, because the mirror stage holds the "imaginary" sense of a whole self together in a very particular way. It does so by relating a sensory body to a space that is empty of all sensory experience except sight. This splitting of the experiential world into two realms—a material full bodied, or real one and an image dependent, imaginary or virtual one—engenders a complex set of dialectical relations for the child that will be with it for life. First, there is the relation between embodied self and virtual self, the former associated with the full sensorium and dependency, the relations with the mother, and the latter associated with a diminished sensorium. This relation fosters a false sense of mastery over the self that can only be seen or "realized" in a "derealized," virtual space. Second, there is the relation between this split self and the everyday world. The experiential world itself takes on this dual aspect. This is experienced not only in the form of hallucinations, dreams, and fantasy, but even, Lacan proposes, at the level of all appearances that will be reinterpreted in terms of the mirror experience. Consequently, all appearances, everything the self sees, will take on the dual aspect of being both there and not there, both situated and abstract, both real and unreal. Finally, the child knows that there is always a blind spot in the two-dimensional mirrored world, a blind spot that hides that part of the three-dimensional body the child cannot see in the mirror even as it knows that others in the environment can see it. This knowledge that others can see a part of the imagistic, mastery-engaged self that the self cannot see forms the ground for a paranoid relation to the world.[39]

## An Anthropological Interpretation of the Psychoanalytic Model of Subjects in Empty Space: The Person of Surplus Sensibility

Before the social through language even makes its mark, the child is engulfed, from a psychoanalytic perspective, in relations of derealization and alienation. The mirror stage describes how a dichotomy emerges between a child and its reality, an inner world and its external world. The experience of an external world, in this model, is predicated on the child's anxiety in response to its visual experience of a body that is incomplete, part hidden and part visible. All external things, Lacan surmised, pass through this structure of a child's mental development, which peers anxiously at a world that is dualistic, unstable, incomplete. If the child does not develop tactics to protect itself against this schism in its world, such as strong ego defenses to override the ego's experience that its wholeness and autonomy is a misrecognition, it will succumb to psychic disorders such as schizophrenia (the mind in pieces) or hysteria (the body in pieces). Based on this schema, agoraphobia is a disorder wherein the whole sensorium self is not successfully socialized into the two largest cultural pieces of the Western self, the mind/body dualism. This dualism is maintained, according to Lacan, by socializing the child to invest in the visual sense, mirror stage, to obtain true knowledge of self and the world. The agoraphobic, from a Lacanian perspective, must be the urban person who for some reason has slipped through the looking glass and experienced a full sensorium self that will not become reorganized around the sense of sight, which would have honed perspectival techniques to makes its way through space. And when the senses of hearing, smell, and so on are not sufficiently subservient to the authority of the visual, this person of what I will call "surplus sensibilities" will experience herself as "oversensitive" in an urban world designed and built in the reign of the visual era. This person of surplus sensibilities, then, may find that she is more apt to be disoriented in a world built for those highly trained in visual technologies of the self, as Michel Foucault would express it. And since that world is becoming more and more characterized by abstract, Euclidian, gridded space, the agoraphobic will not *re*-cognize herself there, will not feel strong and readily able to act there. From a Lacanian perspective, losing or never having sufficiently developed skills for entering such space may make the agoraphobic avoid public space, become dependent on a domestic space that will accommodate her surplus sensibility. Unfortunately, that forces her into an extremely restricted life.

From this psychoanalytically inspired, Lacanian-inflected perspective—I will call it the "agoraphobic perspective"—we can understand many so-called tactical ego defense treatments for agoraphobia as treatments that retrain the unruly and incapacitated full-sensorium person, a person who in the modern era has become the person of surplus sensibility. The behavioral desensitization techniques, from this modern "agoraphobic perspective," are what Foucault labeled "technologies of the self," techniques which aim to get rid of the surplus. Cognitive behaviorism, for example, teaches the agoraphobic how to rationally interpret bodily sensations and emotions. It also trains the patient with in vivo exposure—that is, deliberate, repeated exposure to the fearsome object, a technique that cognitive behaviorism claims can "exhaust" or "extinguish" sensory reaction. When accompanied by medications that physiologically block biochemical processes, cognitive behaviorism achieves somatic desensitization to what has become phobic space. From a psychoanalytic perspective, on the other hand, these are tactics that "protect" or desensitize the ego from the experience of extreme anxiety that arises when encountering those abstract and empty qualities of public space that symbolically remind the agoraphobic of the fragility of the split self.

The psychoanalytic perspective has deepened our understanding of how agoraphobia might be related to the vast architectural expanses that have been built into modern cities. Since the Second World War, with the popularity of Le Corbusier's now ubiquitous International Style, the transformation of public urban space into a sphere of abstract and empty qualities appears to demand new skills to keep the visual/perspectivally oriented self on top of the game of modern city life. When a person's visual relation to his environment is so crucial to his sense of self, and that environment's visual aspect is increasingly dominated by monumental, abstract, empty space, the conditions are set for an eruption of anxiety over the vision-dominated self's loss of control. In the clinical literature of the twentieth century, the loss of bodily control in public is the agoraphobic's single most common complaint.

From an anthropological perspective, however, the more complex issue remains that knowledge and self-knowledge are so dominated by the visual in Western culture that the model of ego development that depends upon mirrors needs to be examined with a broader cultural lens. In the context of an anthropology of modernity, Lacan's mirror stage is less a theory of ego development than an illustration of how all reflection on the modern Western self is influenced by the realm of the visual. As cultural critics in many domains have pointed out, modernity, perhaps beginning with the Italian Renaissance but certainly intensified in the architectural designs and constructions of Enlightenment city planners, is synonymous with an increasing one-point perspective visualization and organization of the world. In his essay "The Age of the World Picture," Heidegger referred to the problems of understanding ourselves so completely through visual schemas. Similarly, the art historian Ervin Panofsky, Heidegger's contemporary, has described modernity as an "anthropocracy" warning that "[p]erspective, in transforming the *ousia* (reality) into the *pheinomenon* (appearance), seems to reduce the divine to a mere subject matter for human consciousness."[40] This reduction does not do away with the divine, Panofsky explains. Rather, it incorporates it into a terrestrial perspective that lends new powers to human beings who can now act without explicit otherworldly reference.[41] Psychoanalytic theory describes a world in which a culturally masculine gaze holds those formerly divine powers from a zero point that organizes the visually dominant, image-laden culture of late modernity.

## A Feminist Interpretation of the Psychoanalytic Model of Subjects in Empty Space: Revaluing Tactile Modes of Knowing

The gender component of agoraphobia can be restated as follows. If the highly skilled visual domain of Western culture is dominated by a patriarchal worldview and that worldview demands constant tactics of ego reinforcement to protect itself from the increasing triggers of built emptiness in public space, the culturally feminine tactics of urban women may be increasingly less effective in protecting the fragile dualistic relations of the modern ego. Two options are open to a woman. Either she chooses an intense, even parodic, adoption of culturally masculine forms of socialization, which is exactly what cognitive-behaviorist approaches appear to advocate, or she orients herself to an even more intense, even parodic, adoption of culturally feminized forms of socialization, which is what the agoraphobic syndrome appears to do. The former, suggested by Arnold Schwarzenegger as the bodybuilder turned movie star turned governor of California, allows the ego to keep inserting itself—despite the emptiness—into public space, while the latter allows it to withdraw.

Agoraphobia has often been described as a parodic form of femininity because the anxious, housebound person exaggerates the stereotyped behavior of affluent, urban women. Domesticity becomes immobility, helplessness, and infantilization.[42] This intensified feminine behavior seems to offer a safe, nonthreatening way to withdraw from an increasingly fractured public space, marked by pockets of emptiness and actual threats of violence. Feminists on both sides of the Atlantic have described gender-specific types of neurosis as outlets of resistance to patriarchy.[43] Whether or not they are successful in such opposition, it is certainly true that disorders—such as hysteria in the nineteenth century, and anorexia nervosa and agoraphobia today—display exaggerated forms of the cultural norms of femininity.

Agoraphobia provides further insight as well into human beings as they develop under conditions in which the world and self are known so exclusively through the dimension of the visual. For the normative modern subject, vision is privileged, to the extent of acquiring divine-like status, while the knowledge produced by the other, neglected senses is devalued. For the agoraphobic, on the other hand, the visual becomes an unreliable sense. When the disorder strikes, she becomes dizzy, sees double, needs to lean on walls or various other supports to make her way. It is the tactile sense that serves her by way of support when she is faced with the crisis of agoraphobia. But she lives in a culture for which the tactile dimension of knowing is a mere surplus sensibility. Modern technologies of the self focus on honing our visual relations to the world. Other senses and ways of knowing are undervalued and neglected by our culture. Skills that could tap into our bodies' resources to know the world—its magnetic pull, its polluted effects—meet enormous resistance on the road to becoming legitimate knowledge. This leads us to an important question about gender and embodied knowing: If patriarchal gods could be enshrined in humanistic knowledge that privileges the visual, what culturally gendered powers of knowing are dispelled when the sense of touch is culturally neglected?

This is a question Luce Irigaray answers in her critique of the French philosopher Maurice Merleau-Ponty's important work *The Visible and The Invisible*. Many feminists have found Merleau-Ponty's brand of phenomenology, one that focuses not on the split between mind and body but on their interrelatedness, to support their own consideration of embodied knowing, even if they remain critical of generalizations about subjectivity that tend, according to philosopher Elizabeth Grosz, to take men's experiences for human ones.[44] Irigaray's observations examine the gendered metaphors Merleau-Ponty uses to develop specific ontological notions about embodiment and embodied knowledge. This offers useful evidence of what happens to emptiness and lack once an appreciation of tactile knowing is given its due. As Grosz succinctly summarizes Irigaray's critique of Merleau-Ponty in her book *Ethics of Sexual Difference*, "[Irigaray's] objections to Merleau-Ponty's reworking of being in terms of the flesh revolve around three major claims: first, that the privileged, indeed dominant, position of vision in his writings, in overpowering and acting as a model for all other perceptual relations, submits them to a phallic economy in which the feminine figures as a lack or a blind spot; second, that the concept of the flesh is implicitly coded in terms of the attributes of femininity; and third, a related point, that Merleau-Ponty disavows the debt that the flesh owes to maternity."[45]

Irigaray claims that when Merleau-Ponty privileges vision in his writing, he does so with metaphors that more appropriately refer to the sense of touch and the experience that all humans begin with in the womb. When he describes the intimacy of the relation between the seer and the visible, Merleau-Ponty speaks of the indeterminacy of the relation between "the sea and the shore."[46] The metaphor of fluids, Irigaray claims, refers more appropriately to the domain of touch. It implies not only the "formlessness" of feminine *jouissance* (a Lacanian psychoanalytic term referring to both orgasm and to the embodied sense of the real) but more specifically it implies "the amniotic element that houses the child in the mother's body and continues to be a 'watermark' etched on the child's body" throughout her life.[47] The experience of the womb and the earliest relations between mother and child—relations that precede and enable the relations that will emerge with the sense of vision—precondition the operations of vision. This function of intrauterine darkness is something that Merleau-Ponty's work, notes Irigaray, does not and cannot address. Nor should this darkness or invisibility of the maternal be understood as an absence of vision or a lack of light. For Irigaray it is a positivity—namely, the realm of tactility. When Merleau-Ponty refers to the sense of touch, he does so to explain how the visible and the tactile have a relation of reciprocity and mutual dependence. Irigaray, on the other hand, demonstrates that the characteristics of the tactile are not generalizable to all the senses. Vision operates differently.

Irigaray's understanding of the relation between the two senses has been effectively summarized by Grosz, who writes,

> The map provided by the tactile is not congruous with that provided by the visual. In [Irigaray's] understanding, the visual and the tactile function according to different logics and rhythms, although it is clear that there is some interchange between them. There is, she claims, a surreptitious reclamation and reordering of the tactile by the visual, which subordinates all the other senses to its exigencies and forms. Irigaray denies that the visible can be situated within the tangible or that the tangible is situated through the visual: theirs is not a relation of reciprocity, for the tangible provides the preconditions and the grounds of the visible. In brief, her claim is that the visible requires the tangible but the tangible is perfectly capable of an existence autonomous from the visible (a case that is perhaps best illustrated in the existence of blindness—one cannot conceive of a case of a tangible equivalent to blindness, where touch no longer functions while the other senses remain operative; if the tangible does not function, the subject is in a state of unconsciousness.) In her understanding, the tangible is the unacknowledged base or foundation, the source of the visible that renders any comparison between them false: they are not comparable for they occupy different logical positions—one is the foundation and the origin of the other. The tangible is the invisible, unseeable milieu of the visible, the source of visibility; it precedes the distinction between active and passive and subject and object: "I see only though the touching of the light" (Irigaray, p. 155).[48]

For Irigaray, Merleau-Ponty and Western philosophy have undervalued the role of the human experience of life in the womb, the sense of tactility and the other relations that intrauterine life provide. Unlike the schema of the world that is built around the sense of vision, the experience in/of the womb does not organize relations of subject and object, a seer and a seen, with one being subordinated to the other. Instead, Irigaray notes, there are relations of osmotic exchanges within the maternal world, "an alchemy of substitution of a placentary nourishment."[49] This means that our first experience of life in the womb stays with us. The nourishing relationship we had with the placenta persists in life, acting as a template of tactility that will be adjusted throughout life as we learn from experiences that involve the sense of touch. But learning also involves social instruction and cultural judgments. If the dominant culture of a society is generally dismissive about the legitimacy of the sensibility that is grounded in intrauterine life, there will be little chance of recognition for those who become skilled in these ways of knowing, and little chance for understanding those who maintain heightened capabilities from within this most foundational sense of self.

This new conceptualization of the foundational quality of the sense of touch forces us to reconsider the agoraphobic syndrome. Irigaray's commentary provides a sort of corrective to the psychoanalytic model that, in its focus on pathology, tends to neglect the ways in which humans' previsual and maternal relations to the world are modes of organization that give rise to forms of nonpathologized knowledge. This neglect of the role of tactile knowing is not unique to psychoanalysis; we see it in almost all of the treatment modalities that serve the agoraphobic today. This is most likely the reason why agoraphobia has, since Carl Westphal's days, been so often treated as a uniquely visual disorder, sometimes to comic effect. For example, consider the treatment of agoraphobia as an optical problem with the "attention antenna," a contraption invented in the 1970s by Dr. Monte J. Meldman at the Chicago Medical School out of a pipe cleaner that attaches to the patient's eyeglasses and extends horizontally for about three inches into the field of vision. Though it probably contributed little to helping the agoraphobic appear "normal" in public space, the device was meant to give a constant reference point to the patient's perambulations in wide-open urban space. It apparently helped reduce the dizziness caused by the agoraphobic's purported inability "'to synthesize visual stimuli into a coherent figure-ground pattern.'"[50] It is surely not a coincidence that this Rube Goldberg contraption also reinstitutes the one-point perspective that dominates Western perception.

Within the field of psychoanalysis there are those who recognize that agoraphobia gives us clues about a wider social problem stemming from our patriarchal culture's devaluation of maternal experience. Looking closely at the metaphors of their critique, we see that, like Luce Irigaray, they, too, are speaking of the problem with a symbolic order that associates emptiness with the womb. For example, in their 1983 study of agoraphobia, authors Robert Seidenberg and Karen DeCrow—one a psychiatrist and practicing psychoanalyst, the other a lawyer involved in city government—call for psychoanalysis to develop new listening techniques capable of locating the dreaded (empty) space in external rather than internal sites. "Conflicts about gender may be the core problem in agoraphobia," they state, and for psychoanalysis this means that descriptions of women's ego development must be reevaluated in terms of symbolic notions of inside and outside.[51] Even the enlightened Erick Erickson, they note, had to describe women as lacking an outward display of their difference (i.e., a penis). For Erickson, women "must turn inward for ego sustenance." As Seidenberg and DeCrow elaborate,

> Whatever value [a woman] has must be on the inside, if anywhere. Erikson might have said "inside her skull," but that was not to be. Anatomy refers only to genitals in this developmental scheme. ... Erikson writes that the body image of the girl "includes a valuable inside, an inside on the development of which depends her fulfillment as an organism and as a role bearer. *This fear of being left empty*, and, more simply, of being left, seems to be the most basic feminine fear, extending over the whole of a woman's existence. It is normally intensified with each menstruation and takes its final toll during the menopause."[52]

Although they do not focus on this point, Seidenberg and DeCrow rightly demonstrate that the association that psychoanalysis and patriarchal culture has long made between emptiness and women is not only based on the women as lacking a penis, but also on the cultural notion that the womb, a biological characteristic of women, is a site of emptiness. Not only is it empty when it is not filled with new human life, but, as Irigaray points out, even when it is housing new life, the womb is not appreciated as a form of positivity. It is darkness understood as a lack of light and it instructs us through the devalued senses of touch and hearing: "More primordial than vision, the tangible is also the necessary accompaniment of the earliest sensations, those in the blackness of the womb, those to do with hearing."[53]

With Irigaray's insight, we can read Seidenberg and DeCrow's corrective for psychoanalysis in a new light. "Often," they write, "the psychoanalyst is still listening with a third ear [the transferential dimension] when the times call for a fourth ear,"[54] a technique of listening that would take psychoanalysis out of its genital stage and move it into the analysis of the social. From a spatial perspective, we can add that the fourth ear would be also listening for the *maternal voice*, a term we will give to the voice that comes from a space that is no longer dominated by the visual, a space where we receive legitimate information from the tactile dimension of our existence—from our being in space, our *Dasein*, as Heidegger might have said—except that this time the relation is not between being and nothingness. It is a relation among being and feelings, sounds, smells and tastes, all of which may give clues to the agoraphobic's sense of where something is wrong with modern public space. With this ontological insight we can add to the psychoanalytic paradigm. At an epistemological level we can agree with Seidenberg and DeCrow when they say that agoraphobia is a "metaphorical disease." "[The agoraphobic] is a living caricature of what she is living through," they tell us. "She has it within her power to relinquish the symptom whenever *she feels* it is the proper time and place."[55] To this we can add that the techniques that may help her relinquish the symptom may come from her tangible sensibility, a form of embodied knowing whose skills have, for a number of reasons, not yet been transferred to and developed for modern public space.

Helene Deutsch, not only the first woman psychoanalyst to study agoraphobia, but also the first psychoanalyst to analyze the architectural imagery of the house, found that for many agoraphobics, the act of leaving the protective walls of the home and finding oneself "outside" was strongly associated with the act of giving birth.[56] We have already noted cases where agoraphobic women in the nineteenth century trace the onset of their disorder to the birth of their children. The same neglected reference to pregnancy, childbirth, and child care appears as well in many twentieth-century clinical studies of agoraphobia, including those with a feminist agenda.[57] The researcher avoids consideration of the possibility that the spatial experience of maternity might provoke a heightened sense of the undervalued tactile sense Irigaray has described so well. It is worth emphasizing the obvious fact that the experience of intrauterine life is shared by both men and women. Both sexes may experience an agoraphobic crisis of the visual/perceptual self that falls back on an undervalued and thus socially underdeveloped sense of tactility. But women in pregnancy and childbirth will experience intrauterine life differently. As adults, the experience offers a conscious sense of embodiment that echoes many of the agoraphobic's most heightened sensibilities—such as leaving the house, as Deutsch discovered, but also the experience of boundlessness, of being paradoxically both one and another. The experience of the self's expanded boundaries is heightened in pregnancy and childbirth, and persists in the relationality of child care, which, of course, is shared by both men and women, although it remains to this day largely a maternal domain. The self may also not have developed the social skills that would allow a person to accept the positivity of this experience—as Irigaray reminds us, the intrauterine experience is not one of emptiness, or of lack. Under common conditions such as these the potential for a crisis of the self seems greatly intensified.[58] The visually dominant aspect of modernity heightens this situation as well. In the most redundant images of intrauterine experience in the Western world today, the ones enabled by the technological developments in photography during the 1960s and widely circulated in U.S. popular culture (images such as the one that famously appeared on the cover of *Life* magazine in 1965 entitled "A Child is Born") show a fetus in a background of empty space. Because the visual representation of this most fundamental tactile experience is so often *re*-presented to us in empty space, it enters the image repertoire of our collective cultural unconscious and lends a virtual divine reality to the psychoanalytic description of woman as lacking.

## Le Corbusier: Architect of Modern Emptiness in Gendered Space

Empty space is not only one of the West's great "psychological" exports. It has also become a global material phenomena in the architectural movement known as International Style. In the past fifty years this style of building and urban planning has stenciled European architectural modernism on cities around the world. It may seem obvious that the ubiquitous, gigantic glass-and-steel structures and vast concomitant networks of urban freeways so typical of International Style are linked with an increasing incidence of agoraphobia. Perhaps less obvious is the relation between International Style and gendered assumptions about space.

The work of Le Corbusier, the twentieth century's most renowned architect, epitomizes the structure of emptiness in the contemporary built environment. Le Corbusier, whose towering steel-and-glass boxes have become the global signature of metropolitan modernism, is the father of what is called International Style. But this style includes much more than the signature skyscrapers we see on most metropolitan horizons. Its larger vision includes blueprints to raze pre–World War Two urban neighborhoods and rebuild entire cities from the emptiness of "ground zero." The ratio of empty space to buildings was reversed in the modern city as planners opened dense older neighborhoods for urban freeway systems and monumental architectural projects and designed a suburban life completely dependent on the automobile. One of Le Corbusier's most well-known designs—for Brasilia, the modern capital city of Brazil—shows how the tactile sterility of empty space took over the look of the modern city (see figure 11).

Le Corbusier's seminal text *The Radiant City* proposes a rationalist city that dehistorizes the particular and offers itself as a universal model for city planning. The plans for *The Radiant City* were presented at the Congres Internationaux d'Architecture Moderne (CIAM) in 1933 and became influential in postwar American architecture and urban planning thanks to their rationalized vision of a totally functional modern city.[59] The CIAM philosophy concentrated on four functions of the city: *housing, work, recreation*, and *traffic*; later, an *administrative* function was added to the list. One of the most developed embodiments of Le Corbusier's vision is found

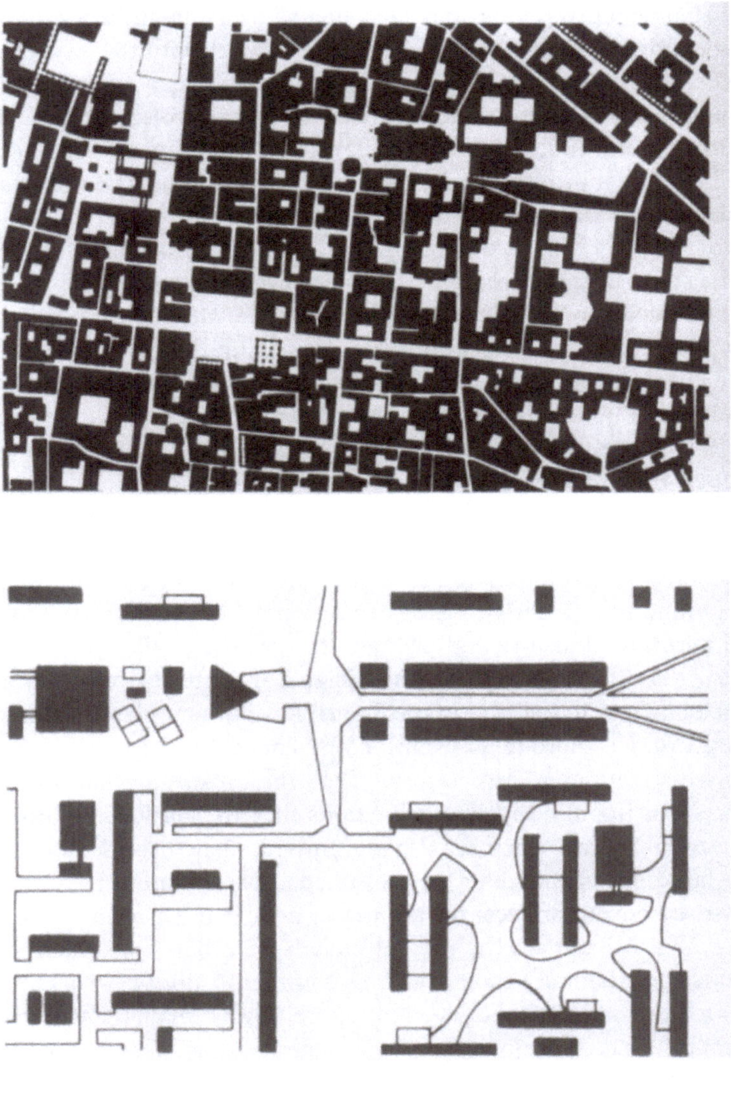

**Figure 11** Empty space to building ratio changing in the modern city: figure-ground plan of Parma (1830) and Brasilia (1960) from James Holston's *The Modernist City.* Courtesy of the author.

in the new, post-war capital city of Brasil, Brasilia. Anthropologist James Holston's account of the construction of Brasilia points out how the modernist city manages to unite mutually antagonistic social and political programs under a single architectural program. He writes, "Brasilia was planned by a left-center liberal, designed by a communist, constructed by a developmentalist regime and consolidated by a bureaucratic authoritarian dictatorship each claiming an elective affinity with the city. Precisely because the CIAM model manages to unite such dissident interest, its brand of modernism has come to dominate development projects worldwide."[60]

Holston shows how modernist land-use planning in Brasilia separated capitalist process from planning theory and practice. Taking the modernist vision out of the political economy of modernization and out of the everyday needs of the city's inhabitants, the plan created sterile structures that remained in place even as the practices of everyday life began to undermine the plan's modernist logics. But how did it happen that capitalists and communists simultaneously recognized their vision in the same set of architectural symbols to begin with? As urban geographer Michael Dear explains "The peculiar genius of the modernist city plan lies in its "empty vessel" quality; anyone can pour identity or signification into that vessel."[61]

For sociologists of modernity like Zygmunt Bauman, Le Corbusier's vision is the outcome of an architectural imagination that arose in the wake of the French Revolution and the state's attempt to begin from year zero and ground zero in designing the perfect capital city, a city that implied "a total rejection of history and razing to the ground of all its tangible remnants."[62] From the surveyor-geometrician F.-L Aubry's project for a "city named Liberty" in year five of the French Revolution to Jeremy Bentham's panopticon (so thoroughly examined by Foucault), the modern impulse is to see society at a "degree zero." The urban planning that historically reflects this impulse involves habitations that are sterile and elitist, even though in most cases their avant-garde aims may have been democratic and their buildings intended for the presumed tastes and uses of the masses—high-rise housing projects for the urban poor being a primary example. According to Bauman, the present globalized urban space that runs on circuits, global finance capital, and telecommunications networks extends this architectural metaphor of empty space. For Bauman, the visualization of empty urban space offers us a "near perfect metaphor for the crucial facets of modernization of power and control."[63] Le Corbusier's vision was an essential component in the realization of this urban schema.

Among the many architectural historians and critics who have analyzed Le Corbusier's contribution to modern urban life, Anthony Vidler's analysis is especially pertinent. In the chapter on Le Corbusier titled "Men in Space," in his *Warped Space: Art, Architecture and Anxiety in Modern Culture*, Vidler analyzes the projections of masculinity in architectural space and the relation between these projections and the perceived emptiness of the urban commons and reveals the larger cultural logic at stake in the agoraphobic's pathologized perception of urban emptiness.

Vidler introduces Le Corbusier with a quote from Sigfried Giedion, an architectural historian and contemporary of Le Corbusier who championed his work: "'Our period demands a type of man who can restore the lost equilibrium between inner and outer reality. This equilibrium, never static but, like reality itself, involved in continuous change, is like that of a tightrope dancer who, by small adjustments, keeps a continuous balance between his being and empty space.'"[64]

Vidler goes on to describe the key terms associated with Le Corbusier's modernist vision, writing,

> The pathologies of agoraphobia and claustrophobia, joined if not caused by their common site in metropolis, provided ready arguments for modernist architects who were eager to reconstruct the very foundations of urban space. Arguing that urban phobias were precisely the product of urban environments, and that their cure was dependent on the erasure of the old city in its entirety, modernist architects from the early 1920s projected images of a city restored to a natural state, within which the dispersed institutions of the new society would be scattered like pavilions in a landscape garden. Reviving the late eighteenth-century myth of "transparency," both social and spatial, modernists evoked the picture of a glass city, its buildings invisible and society open. The resulting "space" would be open, infinitely extended, and thereby cleansed of all mental disturbance: the site of healthy and presumably aerobically perfect bodies. As Sigfried Giedion figured it, this would be the space of a "tightrope dancer," balanced between individual "being" and "empty space."[65]

We have already met the failed version of this tightrope walker in the nineteenth-century agoraphobic who lacked the brinkmanship to make it across the Place de la Concorde. Vidler shows how the acrobatic demand on the urban citizen was connected to a modernist sublime in the writings of Le Corbusier, referring to Le Corbusier's daydream concerning a space he calls *l'espace indicible*—ineffable, undefinable, inexpressible, indescribable space. Like his modernist contemporary, Ludwig Mies van der Rohe, who envisioned an endlessly gridded universal system of three-dimensional graph paper, and Bruno Taut who attempted to fabricate crystalline cities out of the Alps, Le Corbusier—in his concept of l'espace indicible—also celebrated the vocabulary of the romantic sublime. Vidler recounts how Le Corbusier, in his famous address to an international meeting of architects in 1933, revealed his debt "in almost Nietzschean terms" to the Athenian Acropolis, how Le Corbusier "[remembered] his first experience of the hill and its ruins as overwhelming, how he left 'crushed by the superhuman aspect of things on the Acropolis,' by the sight of the Parthenon, 'a cry hurled into a landscape made of grace and terror.'"[66]

Le Corbusier's address was first republished in 1948 in an English review of Le Corbusier's life and work called *The New World of Space*, the first chapter of which is a translation of the essay "L'espace indicible." As Vidler notes, "with the concept of "l'espace indicible" Le Corbusier completes his acropolitan trajectory, finally assimilating the unassimilable to his architecture."[67] Reading from his work, one is struck by the similarities between an agoraphobic's description of the fearful emptiness of public space and Le Corbusier's celebration of l'espace indicible:

> The essential thing that will be said here is that the release of aesthetic emotion is a special function of space.
>
> ACTION OF THE WORK on its surroundings: vibrations, cries or shouts (such as the Parthenon on the Acropolis in Athens), arrows darting away like rays, as if springing from an explosion; the near or distant site is shaken by them, touched, wounded dominated or caressed. REACTION OF THE SETTING: the walls of the room, its dimensions, the public square ..., the expanses or the slopes of the landscape even to the bare horizons of the plain or the sharp outlines of the mountains—the whole environment brings its weight to bear on the place where there is a work of art. ... Then a boundless depth opens up, effaces the walls, drives away contingent presences, accomplishes the miracle of the ineffable.[68]

Le Corbusier compared his architectural vision of modernist space to a sounding board that resonated and reverberated. Modernist urban space "generated force fields, took possession of space ... made it cry out with harmony or pain." This space, claimed Le Corbusier in 1946, was discovered by modernity; it was the fourth dimension: "The fourth dimension is the moment of limitless escape evoked by exceptionally just consonance of the plastic means employed." Vidler notes Le Corbusier's qualified contempt for those who do not recognize this dimension: "[the fourth dimension] is a veritable world which reveals itself to those it may concern, which means: to those who deserve it."[69] The combination of a feeling of the transcendent boundlessness of space—what Freud had a few years earlier called an "oceanic" feeling—and a feeling of contempt for the undeserving inhabitants of this fourth dimension is further expressed in Le Corbusier's work and might evoke some righteous anger among agoraphobics around the "new world of [urban] space."

Le Corbusier's infinite space, writes Vidler, would be the instrument of suppression for everything modernists hated about the city, "if not the agent of repression of their own highly developed phobias: claustrophobia in the face of the old city, of course, but also, and linked to this, that fear identified by Simmel—the fear of touching."[70] When Le Corbusier states his contempt for the old city space that should be cleared away by modern design in an 1929 essay titled "The Street," his words are reminiscent of the agoraphobic pedestrian:

> The street is full of people: one must take care where one goes. For several years now it has been full of rapidly moving vehicles as well; death threatens us at every step between the twin curb-stones. But we have been trained to face the peril of being crushed between them. On Sundays, when they are empty, the streets reveal their full horror.... Every aspect of human life pullulates throughout their length ... a sea of lusts and faces. It is better than the theater, better than what we read in novels. ... The street wears us out. And when all is said and done we have to admit it disgusts us.
>
> Heaven preserve us from the Balzacian mentality of [those] who would be content to leave our streets as they are because these murky canyons offer them the fascinating spectacle of human physiognomy![71]

These remarks not only contain all the descriptive metaphors used by nineteenth-century agoraphobics, but also the dream of the solution to come that would be equally nightmarish for twentieth-century agoraphobics: urban highways balancing on concrete stilts high above city streets. Today's metropolis, which combines urban highways and steel-and-glass skyscrapers, realizes Le Corbusier's dream: it aims to get those who can afford to up and off the streets, making those very streets unnoticeable from above. As Le Corbusier wrote,

> Reason, and reason alone, would justify the most brilliant solutions and endorse their urgency. But suppose reason were reinforced by a well-timed lyricism. ... [Imagine] you are under the shade of trees, vast lawns spread all round you. The air is clean and pure, there is hardly any noise. What? You cannot see where the buildings are? Look through the charmingly diapered arabesques of branches out into the sky towards those widely spaced crystal towers which soar higher than any pinnacle on earth. ... translucent prisms ... [they] are huge blocks of offices ... those gigantic and majestic prisms of purest transparency rear their heads one upon the other in a dazzling spectacle of grandeur, serenity and gladness....[72]

"Here," Vidler adds, "Le Corbusier touches on the principle that will dominate all others throughout the history of modernism, whether expressionist, functionalist, metaphysical, or idealist: transparency ... [a]

transparency that extend[s] the universal panopticism of Benthamite ideology. ..."[73] It is this combined rational and lyrical transparency that is offered to "cure" the streets of the neurasthenic disorders that so many early-twentieth-century metropolitan doctors had noted.

The medical literature of this era, on the other hand, is not entirely convinced of the connection between the city streets, on the one hand, and phobias and neuroses, such as agoraphobia, referred to as neurasthenia, on the other. In a 1928 journal in which Le Corbusier described his vision of a new Paris, the old doctor Maurice de Fleury, whose work on neurasthenia had long supported Jean-Martin Charcot's hereditary thesis of mental illness, contributed an article on "urban neuroses" in which he denied any relation between pathological disorders and urban life, claiming that all the so-called neurasthenic diseases were in fact hereditary. In his description of the beneficial role of the city's external stimuli, Fleury sounds like the nineteenth-century male agoraphobic whose faltering footsteps were cured by donning his military uniform or by simply marching into a monumental square along with his troops. Fleury writes, "'These external stimuli [of the city] which from all sides assail us, are like a bath of vital energy. They play for us, at our behest, the beneficent role of military music which relieves the step of the tired soldier, or of the orchestra whose rhythmic accents unleash the muscular strength of the dancers. Let us not fear urban life too much.'"[74]

For the first half of the twentieth century, the masculinized descriptions of city space and their solutions to the illnesses provoked in those spaces are well-documented in Vidler's careful analysis. It is a culturally masculinized vision that informed the key architectural themes of the twentieth century—transparency, rationality, mastery over nature, contempt for the feminized masses, an aesthetic of the sublime. Le Corbusier bequeathed us the experience of the urbanite as a tightrope walker who balances himself between being and empty space. This legacy is epitomized in an early 1960s photo I once saw of Le Corbusier in New York City, shaking hands with Robert Moses, the city engineer whose monumental postwar redevelopment projects brought about the ruin of many multiethnic neighborhoods and the abandonment of the inner city as those who could afford it followed the new urban freeway into the suburbanizing metropolitan fringe. In the urban space emptied by Moses's vision, New York City lost many architectural treasures like the original Pennsylvania Station and many of its ethnic neighborhoods, which were replaced with large scale urban housing projects like that of Red Hook, Brooklyn; massive skyscrapers like the World Trade Center towers, and urban freeway systems like the Cross Bronx Expressway. Le Corbusier's vision of speed and functional efficiency is also built into the freeways that now tunnel through every large American city.

## The Urban Freeway

Dr. Amr Barrada's insights on the therapeutic value of paradoxical intention for agoraphobia discussed earlier in this chapter make even more sense when we consider that the agoraphobic's dilemma with public space involves an urban freeway system whose rational beginnings have devolved into an irrational system in many American cities by encouraging urban sprawl, longer commutes, and less time for family and leisure. Unlike many of his colleagues, however, Barrada has also suffered from agoraphobia. When I interviewed him for this study, he described to me his first experience of agoraphobia. "I was in Massachusetts at the time," he told me, "and had just taken a job as a professor of English and linguistics in a small college in upstate New York. I had decided to take a drive down to New York City and was just pulling onto the freeway. I recall looking to the right and seeing the openness of the horizon stretching before me. Suddenly I froze. I felt completely alone. I had to return home immediately and never made that trip down to the city."[75]

For Barrada, this was the beginning of a lengthy struggle with the disorder. It would eventually lead him to change careers and retrain for a doctorate in psychotherapy. When reflecting on those first overwhelming experiences of fear in the public space of the urban freeway, he had a practical explanation. On the one hand, he found a somewhat personal story of the fear an individual might feel when encountering (a spatialized metaphor of) that first step into what our culture sees as adulthood—independence, aloneness. On the other hand, the fear is deeply connected to a larger social story of how new immigrants might respond moving into ethnically homogeneous, predominantly white towns in America. Barrada is an Egyptian Arab who had come to the United States to study and was about to make a new life in a small northern—and predominantly white—college town where he was probably justified in fearing a xenophobic reception.[76]

Lisa Capps and Elinor Ochs begin their 1995 ethnographic book *Constructing Panic: The Discourse of Agoraphobia* with the case of a woman they will interview who is similarly terrified of the freeway and has been unable to give them directions to her house: "'I'm afraid I can't really tell you how to get here from where you are. It's been so long since I've been on the freeway.'"[77] The most intense and momentous panic attack of her life, she tells them, was when she got stuck in traffic on the freeway.

Henri Lefebvre, the great philosopher of urban space, offers us some insight into why the vast, homogeneous expanse of the urban freeway should provoke such fear for the modern self. In *The Production of Space*, Lefebvre gives the example of a nonanxious, presumably "normal" driver on the freeway who finds that all the road signs are perfectly intelligible. The freeway's signs direct and connect him to the country or the city as a whole, enabling him to understand urban space and its arterial pathways as one immense totality, like a two-dimensional map. The problem arises when this driver does not realize that the transparency, rationality, and easy directives she enjoys on the freeway are only good for moving through the rationalized space of the freeway. Spatial and mental skills learned for highway use are not necessarily transferable to the space of cities. If the urban freeway driver through force of habit comes to expect that the signs in the city are a text that directs our movements with similar clarity and predictability, allowing us to have a sense of the city "as a coherent whole, a unity," he will be living in an illusion that is only maintained thanks to the dominant everyday experience of freeway driving, which reduces space to a surface (the freeway) and teaches us to accept ourselves as subjects of that abstract space.

Of this subjectivized state Lefebvre asks, "So what escape can there be from a space thus shattered into images, into signs, into connected-yet-disconnected data directed at a 'subject' itself doomed to abstraction? For space offers itself like a mirror to the thinking 'subject,' but after the manner of Lewis Carroll, the 'subject' passes through the looking glass and becomes a lived abstraction."[78]

Taken in the aftermath of our discussion of the Lacanian mirror stage and the experience of urban emptiness, Lefebvre's analysis allows us to wonder, along the same lines, whether the agoraphobic may well be the one who, when "passing through the looking glass," does not become "a lived abstraction" to identify with and thus traverse the homogeneous surfaces of modern urban space.

The U.S. highway system that was built after the Second World War completely changed the layout of America's urban life. Both the Highway Act of 1954 and the Housing Acts of 1949 and 1954—the results of intensive lobbying by the real estate, building, and automotive industries—brought a massive suburbanization to American cities that followed vehicular patterns.[79] In the inner cities the freeways created gigantic urban pathways by razing older neighborhoods, often creating even deeper spatial boundaries along lines of entrenched segregation. Connecting the city's neighborhoods in this way allowed a driver to experience the expanding metropolis as a functional whole, "as a totality," even if this experience was *en passant* rather than *in vivo*. Critics of this era's urban planning are emphatic on the negative role played by empty space. The "functional" city, architectural critic Bernard Huet writes, was conceived as a "space of Euclidean abstraction regulated by quantity and industrial repetition, a space whose three fundamental characteristics are homogeneity, isotropy, and fragmentation, and which presents itself as the absolute antithesis of the space of the 'historic' city. The model of the 'functional' city is the most accomplished expression of a 'scientific' urbanism which progressively detached itself from the practices of urban art at the beginning of the twentieth century and whose exclusive object is the rational administration of housing the masses in industrial society."[80]

Interstate networks, with their commercial pathways, provided a similar spatial experience of the country as an increasingly homogeneous whole. The motel and fast-food chains that cropped up along these routes have only expanded in recent times. While reconstructed postwar American cities adopted a functional approach to urban life—separating daily life into discrete functions with assigned places—the urban landscapes they created were increasingly considered dysfunctional by more than just agoraphobics.

The transformation of the American road film by German (and sometimes Hollywood) filmmaker Wim Wenders's *Paris, Texas* speaks to the human consequences of the normalization of the urban freeway in everyday American life. The main character, a man who has become asocial as a result of a traumatic fire, is seen in the opening shots of the film wandering in a disoriented crisscross, off-road, through the emptiness of the west Texan desert. His cure is slow, and Wenders shows his character's gradual reentry into mental health by allowing the character to tentatively begin walking and then driving along rural highways. Eventually he is observed regaining "normalcy" in lengthy scenes depicting his arrival by automobile in Los Angeles to reunite with what is left of his family. As if to highlight the metaphorical space of the freeway as the ontological condition of normal urban subjects, Wenders has the character hold an important conversation with his young son under a node of overpasses along the Los Angeles highway system, its vast concrete expanses stretching out and forming the horizon of what Wenders appears to say is the very backdrop of the modern face-to-face relation (see figure 12). The urban freeway is the zone of roaring white noise within which the "normal" citizen must learn to be comfortable.[81] Becoming normal in this road film is to become increasingly desensitized to the feeling and effects of both personal trauma and public space. The urban freeway is the perfect spatial expression of this normative demand.

This filmic observation of the (negative) effects of modern roadways on the communal psychic disposition of Americans has also been echoed by urban planners since the early 1960s.[82] Here is one recent version of the complaint:

**Figure 12** A still from Wim Wenders's *Paris, Texas* (1984).

> The highways and parking lots built since the 1950s have so separated, segregated, and isolated the American people that we have become pockets of hostile aliens. The garage door has replaced the front door, the parking lot the public steps to City Hall, and the underground garage the office building lobby. The suburban majority lives in isolating communities, increasingly walled, gated, guarded and protected by limited-access roadways. …
>
> We do not communicate or forge connections as a people and we have few public places left to do that, even when we choose to do so. We have all but eliminated "public places" from the physical and mental geography of the country. Without the variety of common grounds on which a diverse people mix and mingle in an unplanned manner, the health of the commonweal is undermined. Genuine "public places"—whether a town square or downtown sidewalk—are where planned, chance, formal, and informal meetings occur, the opportunity for people to come together, to hear about new ideas, share concerns, understand the dilemmas of others, listen to differing opinions, debate proposals for change, and, perhaps, even resolve differences. Without a variety of true arenas for public meeting and discourse, people feel isolated, frustrated and powerless.[83]

The authors go on to describe the physical urban landscape shaped by cars and highway engineers as a "homogenized America." "The nation's built landscape," they say, "no longer differentiates between places." Where this "look of anywhere" prevails, these urban planners lament the ontological outcome: "If people don't know and feel where they are, they don't know who they are."[84] A space of everywhere being described as a space of nowhere creates an urban commons of general cognitive confusion.

The urban freeway has become a quintessential form of public space in America. In 1973 Ray Banham described the freeway system in language that is reminiscent of a city commons. In *Los Angeles: Architecture of the Four Ecologies* he divided the Los Angeles landscape into four ecological niches: "surfurbia" (the beach cities); "the foothills" (the privileged sectors of Beverly Hills, Bel Air, and the like) and two others that help us picture the agoraphobic's dilemma today:

> The plains of Id: "An endless plain endlessly gridded with endless streets, peppered endlessly with ticky-tacky houses clustered in indistinguishable neighborhoods, slashed across by endless freeways that have destroyed any community spirit that may have once existed, and so on … endlessly"; and
>
> Autopia: "As the car in front turned down the off-ramp of the San Diego freeway, the girl beside the driver pulled down the sun-visor and used the mirror on the back of it to tidy her hair. Only when I had seen a couple more incidents of this kind did I catch their import: that coming off the freeway is coming in from outdoors. A domestic or sociable journey in Los Angeles does not end so much at the door of one's destination as at the off-ramp of the freeway, the mile or two of ground-level streets counts as no more than the front drive of the house. … [The] freeway system in its totality is now a single comprehensible place, *a coherent state of mind*, a complete way of life."[85]

Banham's astute ethnographic observation demonstrates that city space is compressed by the urban freeway, which now provides us, as Lefebvre has also noted, with the single most coherent sense of the city. From an agoraphobic perspective, we can interpret this further. Note that the girl checking her reflection in the car mirror is, for Banham, the sign of a division between indoors and outdoors, a parodic replay of the division between nature and culture where the body of the woman is the paradoxical sign of both sides of the split. (In the car she is in a private space, checking herself in the mirror, but she is also at the same time in public space, observed by all around her). For Banham she is the marker of a collapsing distinction between public and private space. The experience of collapsing spatial boundaries is one of the agoraphobic's main visceral complaints about modern public space. If this seemingly private but utterly public space of the car is fast becoming the very form that provides the normative urban citizen with her most coherent sense of urban life—it is, after all, as Banham notes, "a single comprehensible place, a coherent state of mind, a complete way of life"—to the agoraphobic it never achieves this coherence. Rationally, she may know that the urban freeway should be a rational, coherent urban experience, but for her it is not. Banham's urban vignette is a rich source of cultural norms. When we add the agoraphobic perspective, we see that the urban freeway system is more like the surface of the mirror: it is the flat, homogeneous background that gives us the sense or imaginary feel that the city we are looking at is a coherent, bounded whole, "a comprehensible place."

Since the early 1970s the Los Angeles freeway system has grown and a new kind of descriptor—*postmodern*, some might say—appears more appropriate than what Banham and Lefebvre were able to use in 1973 and 1974 when they commented on the freeway's ability to give a sense of (false) coherence and rationality to urban space. In 2000, Michael Dear, an urban geographer who teaches in and writes about Los Angeles, described the cognitive dissonance engendered by the California urban freeway system. For nearly two centuries, Dear notes, Los Angeles had a history of land-use planning that was built on various rationalities that included the Roman city planning principles used by Felipe de Neve, onetime governor of Spanish California; the transit rationality of the streetcar network (by 1925, Los Angeles had the largest electric interurban railway system in the world), and finally the urban freeway system, which handed the political process of city planning over to the new "science" of traffic engineering in the 1950s. But as transit rationality was replaced by freeway rationality, and "the signature landscape of modernist Los Angeles [became] a flat totalization, uniting a fragmented mosaic of polarized neighborhoods segregated by race, ethnicity and class," the freeway system that had promised speed and leisure led to massive traffic jams in which suburban commuters remained trapped in traffic for hours before finding the off-ramp to their late dinners and neglected children.[86] Highway rationality, Dear explains, has become highway irrationality. After a century-long trend in which the planning profession had slowly been absorbed by the State, land-use planning in the city became privatized and urban sprawl intensified.[87] The social contract is gone, laments Dear, and "all urban place-making bets are off; we are engaged, knowingly or otherwise, in the search for new ways of creating cities."[88] While Los Angeles is by no means the model of all American cities, it does appear that in the twenty-first century, its freeways no longer give the city its—even false—sense of coherence and rationality. *Highway irrationality* is perhaps a better way to describe the contemporary metropolitan driver's everyday encounter with these vast concrete networks of homogeneous space. With approximately 40,000 automobile fatalities a year in the United States, the agoraphobic perspective comes to resemble that of the normal urban driver, who simply dreads driving on the urban freeway.

## Conclusion

Paradoxical intention appears to be a therapy whose notion of healthy (paradoxical) subjectivity is well matched in the vast tracts of empty yet baroquely intensified, homogeneous yet increasingly irrational, forms of public space that we have examined so far in our look at the urban freeway. The urban freeway and its visionary corollary, International Style, have transformed the structure of modern cities and made demands on their citizens. In this chapter we have seen how the twentieth-century agoraphobic patient was reimagined as he was statistically recategorized in far-reaching pharmaceutical trials and in population studies. Psychoanalytic frameworks also refocused the agoraphobic patient by proposing a mirror (image)-based model of subjectivity that, as we have seen, emphasized the sense of sight in the formation of the modern Western self, and neglected the foundational role of touch as mere surplus sensibility.

CHAPTER 5

# The Twentieth-Century Urban Commons

## *The Shopping Center, Laboratory of Behaviorism*

Imagine you are going out the front door of this house. ... You turn left and walk in the direction of the shopping center where you have to go and buy something. ... You are walking there alone. ... You begin to feel rather bad now. You become dizzy. ... Now you have to cross the street. There is a string of cars and you run between them. ... You are sweating terribly, you take another couple of steps and then you fall. You fall there in the middle of the street.

—(Imaginal scene used in a clinical study to induce fear in agoraphobic patients. **Walter Everaerd, Hanneke Rijken and Paul Emmelkamp**, "A Comparison of 'Flooding' and 'Successive Approximation' in the Treatment of Agoraphobia")

### Introduction

After World War II, biological and hereditary models of mental illness gained sway in the diagnosis and treatment of agoraphobia. Psychiatrists began to experiment with medical, biochemical, and behaviorist techniques, eventually combining them to form the pharmacological and cognitive-behavioral approach that dominates the field today. In this chapter I take a close look at behavioral approaches to agoraphobia—in particular, the technique of "flooding," which uses public space to induce a powerful and little understood force called "abreaction" in the cure of the agoraphobic symptom. Behaviorism played a pivotal role in the 1960s and '70s in training citizens to inhabit the intense transformation of public space brought on by the new scale of consumerism in everyday life. At its most fundamental level, behavioral psychiatry studies the human being's relation to the world with a scientistic vocabulary that describes behavior in terms of reactions to stimuli. Behavioral treatments function to insert agoraphobics back into changing forms of public space by training them with new behaviors practicing on the modern urban individual a kind of cultural training to inhabit modern empty space.

Many have argued that the techniques of behaviorism helped to produce a new sense of self that was emerging in postwar Britain and the United States at this time.[1] Behaviorism intervened in previous techniques of self-making established for centuries through religion, rituals, and codes of manners, many of which also offered their own cathartic forms of experience, not unlike those we will encounter in the abreactive technique of flooding. With the authoritative voice of science behind it, behaviorism became a powerful operator in postwar culture and should be viewed as a historical event in the creation of the modern self. During the 1950s and '60s in particular, behaviorism brought the sterile environment of the laboratory, the rigor of experimental methods and statistical measurements, and the objectivity of the white-coated psychologist into everyday behaviors of urban citizens. The current predominance of behavioral methods in the United States and Britain went hand in hand with the postwar move away from the explanatory and interpretive procedures of psychoanalysis. Following Michel Foucault, sociologist Nikolas Rose argues that behaviorism produced "technologies of the self," specific mediations by which people can engage in self knowledge, self transformation, self maintenance and self governance. At this time in Britain in particular, certain behaviors, specifically those of alcoholics, anorexics, bulimic, phobics, obsessives and the anxious, were given over to the new field of behavioral psychology, and the treatment methods used could include rewards and punishments in the form of tokens or even money.[2]

This new form of psychology initiated a shift away from a "disease" model of human problems to an "educational" model: the behaviorist's model of health was based on the project of learning to be a self through the employment of various skills. The phobic patient, for example, was a person who simply needed to acquire a new set of social skills. Behaviorism introduced the idea that information about an individual's personal or social history was no longer required to solve many mental problems. Doctors and patients were encouraged to stay on the surface, as it were, judging the success or failure of treatments only by gauging the discrepancy between the behavior produced and the behavior desired. The

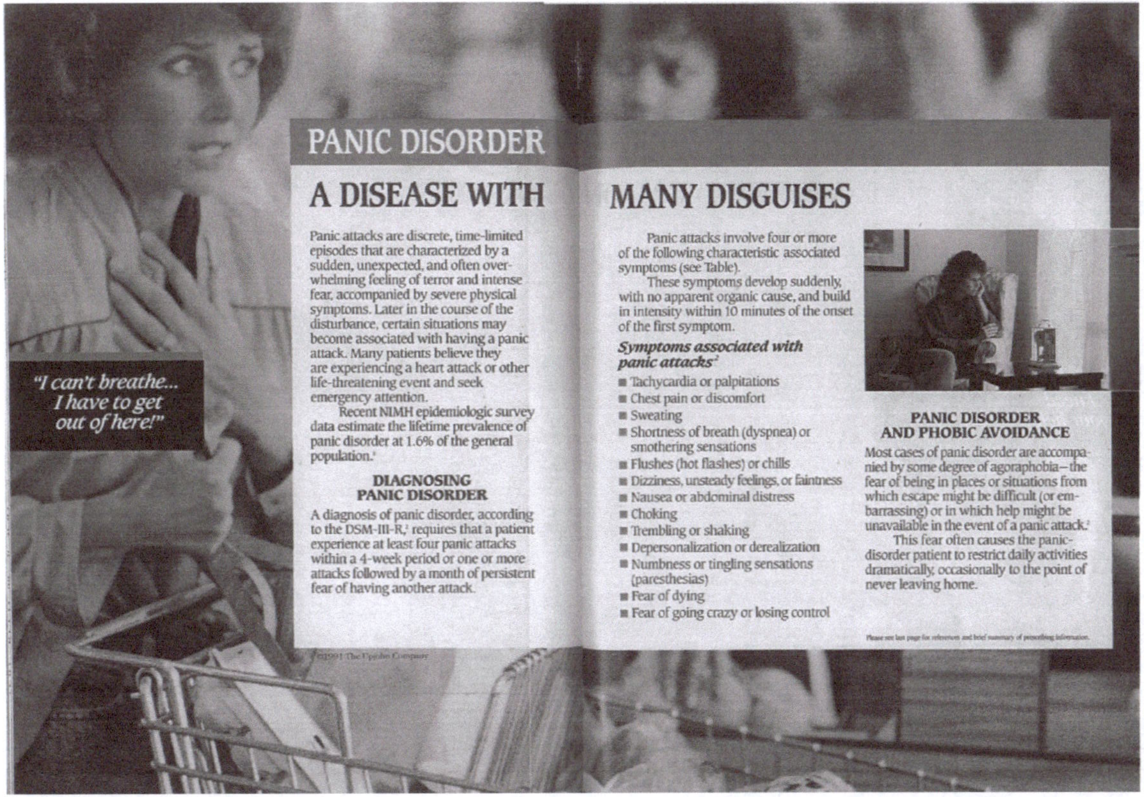


**Figure 13** A woman with a shopping cart in a Xanax advertisement. This image captures the agoraphobic at her most common trigger site. Published in the *Journal of the American Medical Association* (1991).

patient's illness itself became less of an issue as the behaviorist focused on the patient's misshapen psyche and sought to reshape it through processes that are considered "normal."[3] In the case of agoraphobia, patients whose anxiety problems manifested at the shopping center were retrained to go shopping (see figure 13).[4] From a broader social perspective, however, we know that the big box, warehouse shopping center—what eventually became the Wal-Mart of our day—was just appearing at this time in the United States, Britain, and France. Its appearance changed long-standing traditions of small shop, neighborly, face-to-face interaction in the daily routines of procuring food and other material needs. Marketing reports and consumer surveys of the time show that agoraphobics were not the only citizens having trouble adapting to this new form of social space, but they were the only citizens taken there by behaviorist therapists to publicly display their anxiety in ritualized acts of abreaction.

In Britain, the incubator of behaviorism, a handful of doctors have performed significant experimental work on agoraphobia.[5] The most important and prolific figure associated with this group is Dr. Isaac M. Marks who, along with his colleagues at the Maudsley Hospital/Institute of Psychiatry in London, did clinical studies using the techniques of desensitization on agoraphobic patients, most of whom were women.[6] Marks's research studies in the 1960s and '70s led to the development of a behavioral technique called *flooding*, in which agoraphobics were deliberately exposed to urban sites of dread, the most frequently cited of which is the shopping center. There is probably no treatment of agoraphobia today that does not rely to some extent on exposure techniques whose validity was established by the research work of Marks. Clinical studies reported, in 2004, the success of flooding for phobias in children, and it appears that the technique is finding new terrains of deployment in the population as a whole.[7]

Marks began his clinical work on agoraphobia with techniques of gradual exposure called *desensitization*. Lack of success with these techniques led him to try the more intense form of flooding, which produced striking success insofar as it removed for significant amounts of time the main symptom of withdrawal from public space. Behaviorists speak of exposure to phobic sites in terms of a spectrum that goes from gradual (desensitization) to immediate (flooding). As Marks explains, "We can wade into cold water bit by bit or just dive in. … Similarly, exposure to fear cues can be gradual, starting with slightly frightening cues and slowly moving to terrifying ones (that is, desensitization). Or it can begin at the top of the hierarchy, with the most alarming first (that is, flooding)."[8] Marks's techniques for flooding were influenced by the work of Joseph Wolpe, who had studied abreaction and desensitization as treatments for combat veterans suffering from shell shock, also known as battle fatigue or war neuroses, during World War II. Wolpe was a British Army medical officer in South Africa during the war. He had become dissatisfied with the psychoanalytic paradigm dominant at that time, and had turned to the experimental work on laboratory dogs done by the Russian researcher Ivan Petrovich Pavlov in order to develop a technique to provoke an abreaction and systematically desensitize the afflicted soldier from the remembered site of his wartime fear. After years of research, Marks came to regard flooding in vivo—that is to say, intense periods of exposure leading to abreaction in real-life trigger sites, without medication if possible, as the most effective treatment for agoraphobia. His studies proved the effectiveness of this method and theorized that its success might be explained by three different but overlapping theories of human and animal behavior: extinction, adaptation, and habituation. In this chapter I will take a broad social and cultural perspective on the technique of flooding in Marks's clinical work and in the various theories and studies offered to explain its success. Flooding is a "technology of the self" that can tell us about normative and gendered assumptions for urban citizens in public space. In the behavioral technique of flooding we look closely at a treatment originally developed to cure psychologically wounded combat soldiers suffering traumatic brushes with death, and eventually used to reinsert agoraphobic women into shopping malls.

Marks's original work on agoraphobia is of fundamental importance to our study of this illness as a pathology of modern space. While Marks's work on intense exposure in vivo continues to inform the dominant treatment modalities for agoraphobia today, later clinicians use Marks's key contribution, flooding, in contexts that focus on a measurable chemistry or physiology of panic or on the mental habits of cognitive processes. These pharmacological, cognitive-behavioral appropriations of flooding techniques practice a stark mind/body dualism. Marks's work, on the other hand, while it participates in the dualist conception of the human being, also leaves room to challenge this dualism. It does so by virtue of four things. First, Marks's behavioral understanding of agoraphobia maintains that public space is an essential element of the psychopathology, unlike other cognitive and biomedical therapists who claim that public space is incidental to the true structure of the disease which is either faulty thinking habits or faulty brain chemistry. Second, Marks's work on flooding for agoraphobia proposes that abreaction, a little-understood, nonrational process, may be an essential aspect of why flooding enjoys a higher success rate than either cognitive or pharmacological approaches. Third, Marks's work is important because it allows us to challenge the theory of abreaction as it originated in the work of Sigmund Freud and his cathartic psychoanalytic method and to examine its nonsymbolic functions in view of psychopathology and public space. Fourth, Marks insists that flooding, with its mysterious abreactive, cathartic potential, affords the best cure for agoraphobia when the patient is unmedicated. The dominant treatments today, even those that use flooding techniques, use drugs to alter the agoraphobic's anxious state of being. We have already looked at the way pharmacological solutions have driven the market in clinical research on agoraphobia. Marks, as we saw in chapter 4, was an outspoken critic of the Upjohn study on alprazolam (Xanax) associated with the relabeling of agoraphobia as a subcategory of panic disorder and the subsequent increase in pharmacological approaches to the treatment of agoraphobia in the United States since the 1980s. In his criticism, Marks noted that alprazolam's success was not significantly different from the remarkable success of the mysterious placebo in controlled studies. Medication was sometimes called for in treating agoraphobia, Marks thought, but not in the way it is used today. In this chapter we use Marks's clinical work as a window into the era before pharmaceutical treatments gained wide-spread popularity for agoraphobia. From this window we can observe indissociable links between the metropolis and mental life, between the public self and urban space.

A brief portrait of the agoraphobic person in postwar England will help set the scene for our close look into the pioneering behavioral studies of this period. Medical literature of the period reveals that the pathoscape of agoraphobia was growing. "The agoraphobic syndrome is the commonest and the most distressing phobic-anxiety disorder encountered in adult patients," notes a British medical journal article published in 1975. Estimates put the number of "phobic anxiety state suffers" in the British Isles at this time at four million, 300,000 of whom are agoraphobics (although "this might be an underestimation as agoraphobia is a condition that many sufferers tend to conceal"). There were several popular lay organizations that dealt with phobias in this period in England. A correspondence circle for agoraphobic sufferers called the Open Door, for example, started in 1965 with 1,600 members and in one decade grew to over 72,000. Nearly all studies at this time show that 75 percent of patients with the agoraphobic syndrome were women whose average age at onset was between 18 and 35 years. The condition could arise suddenly, the literature shows, yet "in a substantial number of cases the condition clearly starts after traumatic events such as a serious illness in the patient or a relative, leaving home, bereavement, marriage, pregnancy, divorce, miscarriage, childbirth or an unpleasant scene in a shop, street or bus."[9] The link between miscarriage and childbirth and the onset of agoraphobia was often noted in the literature but was typically ignored.

One agoraphobic patient seen at a British clinic in the early 1970s gave the following account of her personal experience, and I cite it for the detail it offers about symptoms and place:

> I was inside a very busy shopping precinct, and all of a sudden it happened: in a matter of seconds I was like a mad woman. It was like a nightmare, only I was awake; everything went black and sweat poured out of me—my body, my hands and even my hair got wet through. All the blood seemed to drain out of me; I went as white as a ghost. I felt as if I were going to collapse; it was as if I had no control over my limbs; my back and legs were very weak and I felt as though it were impossible to move. It was as if I had been taken over by some stronger force.
>
> I saw all the people looking at me—just faces, no bodies, all merged into one. My heart started pounding in my head and in my ears; I thought my heart was going to stop. I could see black and yellow lights. I could hear the voices of the people but from a long way off. I could not think of anything except the way I was feeling and that now I had to get out and run quickly or I would die.[10]

In the early 1970s, prior to the reclassification of agoraphobia as a panic disorder, the anxiety attacks that accompanied agoraphobia could be described in the clinical literature as an intensification of "free-floating anxiety." Intense bouts of anxiety could be eased by having a companion along or some tactile support in the form of "inanimate objects such as walking sticks, umbrellas, prams and shopping baskets. …" The above narrative indicates that the agoraphobic's sense of sight could become untrustworthy, causing her to depend more on the sense of touch in the form of props she could carry. Agoraphobics are "hypersensitive to their environments," the literature generally notes. In the conclusion of one medical article, the fate of the agoraphobic in late-twentieth-century public space is succinctly summed up: "The patient may rapidly seek aid, and drugs will be given. …"[11]

## Lobotomy: Disconnecting with the Mind

### *The Early Clinical Climate for Behaviorists: Of Lobotomy, Women's Labor, and Emergent Forms of Commercial Public Space*

A review of the clinical literature in the 1950s and '60s reveals that lobotomies were an acceptable treatment for agoraphobia. Many psychiatrists, including Isaac Marks, studied the "effectiveness" of lobotomy for the overwhelmingly female population of agoraphobics who were treated by this surgical procedure. A brief look at some of Marks's early work on the use of lobotomy for agoraphobia presents a good picture of the clinical climate for psychiatrists and agoraphobics in England during the period when behaviorism gained popular support.

While prefrontal lobotomies—or *leucotomies*, the early medical term for lobotomy—were increasingly carried out in the 1940s and '50s (up to fifteen thousand were performed in Great Britain alone during this period), they were generally reserved for severe, regressed, and supposedly untreatable cases of schizophrenia.[12] It is startling to discover, however, that lobotomies were also used for agoraphobia, which has always been considered a neurotic, rather than psychotic, disorder. As late as 1974, one finds statements of support for the use of psychosurgery to treat agoraphobia. For example, in a lead article titled "Agoraphobia" in the prestigious *British Medical Journal* in 1974, the editors reviewed the current treatments and commended the use of psychosurgery, writing that

> severe agoraphobia, which is one of the most disabling of the neuroses … has a definite onset usually in the 20s or 30s, and the patient, usually a woman, develops symptoms of severe anxiety in public places. …
>
> The management of agoraphobia is difficult, but there have been advances in recent years. First of all, a patient with an acute attack of agoraphobia which does not respond rapidly to adequate doses of a benzodiazepine should be referred to a psychiatrist because of the great danger of chronicity. Many patients who appear in the psychiatric clinic have been housebound for 10 or 20 years, and by this time, intractable habits of avoidance may have been superimposed on the original illness. …
>
> Benzodiazepines and other anxiolytics are of only limited benefit for the longstanding case because of the development of tolerance. … Tricyclic compounds are ineffective, although no controlled trial has yet been reported. A recent trial suggests that the monoamine oxidase inhibitor phenelzine may be helpful. *There is also evidence that psychosurgery may be beneficial. A retrospectively controlled trial showed benefit from lower medial quadrant leucotomy [lobotomy]. …*[13]

Dr. Isaac Marks is the lead author of the "retrospectively controlled trial" referred to above. That study, published in 1966 in the *British Journal of Psychiatry* and titled "Modified Leucotomy in Severe Agoraphobia: A Controlled Serial Inquiry" is a report of the outcomes of prefrontal lobotomies performed on twenty-two agoraphobic patients—four of them male, and eighteen female. The study finds that, over a period of five postoperative years, lobotomy patients did significantly better than control patients in several areas, most markedly in the area of "work adjustment."[14] The study claims that lobotomy appears to interfere with the agoraphobic patient's ability to arrive at a state of severe anxiety. Unable to produce anxiety, the agoraphobic cannot attach this extreme emotion to a particular, feared public setting. Because the authors believe that, in the case of agoraphobia, "general anxiety … is attached [only] *secondarily to its setting*"[15]—that is, that the public setting does not in itself provoke anxiety—they also believe that the solution lies in literally severing the connection which the agoraphobic body has made between the setting and her fear. The connection must be eliminated from consideration since it is precisely this connection that will interfere with the success of the emergent behavioral therapy called desensitization. The study remarks that

> this fairly homogeneous group of severe agoraphobics … generally respond poorly to other forms of treatment, including behavior therapy (Marks and Gelder 1965; Gelder and Marks 1966). A common history in these cases is that the patient begins to improve and then has a sudden unexpected attack of panic, in, say, *a crowded shop*, after which the patient will not venture out again into the shop for fear that the panic attack will recur there. *Once severe general anxiety has occurred it is attached secondarily to its setting* and a phobia has developed. In patients with much general anxiety, desensitization becomes a Sisyphean task because of the repeated regeneration of phobias. In the present series, *as soon as leucotomy had reduced anxiety this obstacle was removed, and desensitization could then be applied usefully. …*
>
> These findings indicate that the leucotomy operation should be part of a wider treatment programme. Once anxiety falls after operation, patients should be retrained to go out. …[16]

Once the agoraphobic has been lobotomized, the behavior treatment of desensitization works. How was success measured? In the above study a psychiatric social worker or doctor evaluated the psychiatric hospital notes of lobotomized agoraphobic patients. In some cases the evaluation included interviews with relatives of the patients, as well as general practitioners. The data was then compiled and the patients' progress was evaluated in the following six categories: phobias, anxiety, depression, obsessions, work, and social activities. The conclusion was, "Leucotomy patients did significantly better than controls with respect to phobias and anxiety; depression remained mild; *work adjustment improved markedly*. Personality changes after operation were mild and not related to outcome."[17] The fact that work adjustment improved markedly is significant, in view of the relation between public urban space, gender, and the treatments proposed to normalize/ insert citizens into public space. A great majority of agoraphobics are women, and women were lobotomized in much greater numbers than men, just as today more women than men are medicated for depression, not only in this study but in Western society in general. If work is the place where lobotomies most help to normalize agoraphobic women, it is important to know where these women are working and what this kind of work reveals about the relation of women to public space.

Outside of the information given about the sex of the patients in the study—"4 male, 18 female"—the authors do not calculate any of their results in terms of gender differences. Only when offering a specific example are the authors compelled to indicate the patient's sex, thanks to the gendered pronouns in the English language. They write, for instance,

> Thus after six months' follow-up, more patients in the leucotomy series showed increased outspokenness or irritability, apathy or emotional blunting, and poorer memory or concentration. These were pronounced in only one patient, who complained that *his knowledge of foreign languages* had become impaired. One woman who said *her* memory and concentration were poorer nevertheless managed to pass *nursing* examinations two years after the operation. …
>
> Eight patients showed increased outspokenness and irritability; this produced difficulties occasionally, e.g. one *school teacher* found that in the first year *she* had an impulse to swear which could be difficult to restrain. …
>
> It must be noted, however, that *no patient in either series did highly skilled work*; leucotomy might have impaired this more. For *relatively undemanding occupations*, however, the amount of personality change produced by leucotomy with these operations was not usually excessive, and did not prevent the patient from leading *a reasonably normal life* again when the symptoms subsided.[18]

If lobotomy helps agoraphobic women adjust to their jobs, jobs typically done by women, and if these are "relatively undemanding occupations," the medical literature says as much about cultural notions of women's labor as it does about agoraphobia. Strikingly, in this study no information is provided about how many of these women also worked in the home taking care of children and other domestic chores, although it does indicate that "[m]ost of the patients contracted stable marriages and were living with their families when treated."[19] Apparently, according to the study, the patients generally experienced anxiety attacks when going to "a crowded shop." It is highly likely that these women were not only shopping but also raising children, a culturally gendered job that is constantly demanding and, according to British research carried out not long after this leucotomy study, a major factor in depression among women at this time.[20] In other words, the study appears to demonstrate that lobotomy reinserted women to a "reasonably normal life" especially with respect to their (domestic) jobs of caring for children and their (public sphere) jobs of grocery shopping, teaching, and nursing.

The greatest success of lobotomy then is shown in work performance. But the study also mentions that of the six factors doctors evaluated in their lobotomized patients, "work performance was the most difficult to assess."[21] "Work adjustment" was also the very category that proved lobotomy successful at getting agoraphobics into the public sphere. The researchers apparently have difficulty attaching value to women's work. The fact that women's work comprises the work of child care, a profoundly invisible form of women's labor in industrial, patriarchal society, accounts for some of this difficulty. Whereas child care is domestic labor, in an urban context it also includes grocery shopping, which regularly brings women into the public sphere. This study provides clear evidence of the way in which women's labor is undervalued by researchers. In stating that lobotomy does not affect the performance of women, even when these women are performing wage or salaried labor in the public sphere as teachers and nurses, the researchers dismiss the intellectual demands of these generally female professions, because they are "not highly skilled." The lobotomy study, then, gives empirical evidence to one of the most common claims of feminist scholars: women's labor is, for the most part, invisible in capitalist economies. The public space that develops in line with the economic needs of capitalism also does not recognize women's labor.

Feminist architectural historians emphasize this problem of modern urban space. As Esther da Costa Meyer comments,

> [t]he synchronicity of the appearance of agoraphobia with the rise of the metropolis also anchors it firmly within capitalism. The Industrial Revolution required, among other things, the sexual division of labor and the separation of dwelling from workplace. As a result, the social identities of men and women came to be constituted differently. Yet the doctrine of separate spheres—a male public sphere and a female private sphere—cannot be accepted today except as *ideology*. Numerous historians have underscored the continued presence of women in the public realm throughout the centuries; *it was only to men that they had been invisible.*[22]

And as Lauretta Vinciarelli professor of architecture, notes,

> With the rise of the middle class and the capitalist economy, segregation of women became more successful. The notions of public and private spaces as we know them today, did, in fact, spring from

> capitalism. Limiting my observation to central Italy, I can safely say that, as long as agrarian values have resisted the pressures of emerging middle-class values, the majority of public space has been understood and used as an extension of private space, and has been almost entirely controlled by women. Even today, I have seen this phenomenon in Gradioli, a little town north of Rome, in Latium, where 90 percent of the public space is still controlled by women. They inhabit it, they work in it, and they enjoy leisure in it. ...[23]

The public realm, as the term *agoraphobia* reminds us, has always included the *agora*, the marketplace, the place of assembly. It is a space that historically, before the separation of dwelling from workplace in modern European urban life, belonged to both men and women who lived above their street-level shops. When the agora became the shopping center during the postwar suburbanization of metropolitan life, it did so as an *extension* of that separate sphere of middle-class life known as the suburb. As an extension of the female private sphere, the shopping center might become an invisible site of women's labor. But the shopping center is at the same time *not* an extension of women's domestic sphere, since after all it is privatized and more truly an extension of the industrial relations of mass production under capitalism into the built environment. It is an extension of the relations of consumption. As such, it is a space that is initially *for* middle-class women but not *of* women. It is certainly not controlled by women. In this respect it differs radically from the extension of private space into public space characteristic of the neighborhoods described by Vinciarelli, in which agrarian values have resisted the pressures of middle-class values. It appears the skills that women have traditionally developed to do their jobs well, the skills of women's culture that are useful and empowering to women in the kind of small scale public space described by Vinciarelli, are unrecognized in public spaces where the values of middle-class urban life have become dominant. When a person trained in that kind of women's culture steps outside her door into the new shopping spaces of middle class life, it is as if she were stepping into a universe of nonrecognition.[24]

During the period when lobotomy was recommended for agoraphobia, doctors found that skills of desensitization were useful for women whose "hypersensitivity" led them to withdraw from public space. Lobotomy increased the effectiveness of behaviorist methods of desensitization, but for the most part only when success was measured in terms of work improvement, and only assuming that the work involved was "not highly skilled" women's work, including extended domestic labor. Desensitization, which for behaviorists is a form of habituation, worked when it was used to condition (or accommodate, habituate, or break in) women to their spheres of labor—spheres that were mostly invisible to men even when they included work sites outside the home. The most daunting of these work sites, it turned out, was the shopping center. Lobotomy made it easier for severe agoraphobics to accustom themselves to the transformation of everyday British shopping habits in the 1960s as the small-scale face-to-face shops disappeared in favor of warehouse-sized, depersonalized shopping centers. Lobotomies helped acclimatize certain very sensitive women, and some men as well, to the challenges presented in these new forms of built environment.

By 1987, some twenty years after Marks's lobotomy study, the seemingly casual and undisputed consideration of lobotomy for the treatment of agoraphobia and other psychological disorders was no more than a dark and repressed spot in the medical literature. However, Marks did refer to it in a passing comment on the role of psychosurgery in his exhaustive retrospective work *Fears, Phobias and Ritual,* a book that attempts to synthesize modern experimental work in behaviorist psychiatry, pharmacology, ethology and sociobiology. Here, in one small paragraph at the end of some five hundred pages, Marks mentions his own 1966 study and another one from 1971 that also commended lobotomy. "These studies," he writes, "were done before effective behavioral treatment had become available for phobic and OC [obsessive-compulsive] disorders. Today, psychosurgery would never be recommended for these conditions except for a tiny minority of chronic cases in whom adequate *systematic exposure and drug treatment* had been repeatedly tried and failed."[25]

Today surgical lobotomy is no longer an acceptable treatment for agoraphobia. Drug treatments appear to be doing what the lobotomy once did: they make gradual desensitization treatments more effective and improve "work adjustment." With lobotomy, women were seen to habituate better to the extended sites of "women's work."[26] In the postwar period, when middle-class values related to commercial and suburban life extended into the built environment on a massive scale, women in Britain experienced an apparent increase in agoraphobia. Skills that were appropriate to women's traditional forms of labor were devalued as women entered new forms of public space and new modes of medical observation.

### *The Chemical Lobotomy of Spatial Sensibility*

The fact that today desensitization is rarely applied without medicating the patient suggests that the dominant behaviorist treatments exist in some important synergy with the physiological work done by both lobotomies and by the drugs prescribed for anxiety. Significant links among lobotomies, antianxiety drugs, and the various desensitization treatments for agoraphobia lie in their ability to disable patients' sentient responsiveness, to disable their sensibility to public space.

Marks's 1966 research demonstrated that only after lobotomy did desensitization of severe agoraphobia really work: "as soon as leucotomy had reduced anxiety, this obstacle [of attaching anxiety to a particular setting] was removed, and desensitization could then be applied usefully." The operation not only disabled the patients' frontal lobes, but also their faculty for responding to fearful public space. Lobotomy's success for agoraphobia may be more revealing than the British and American biomedical communities in the early 1970s recognized. Lobotomy obviously shows that cutting off parts of the brain can be a form of desensitization therapy. But it may also suggest that an entire dimension of the human sensorium functions primarily as a mode of knowing oneself in relation to space. The psychosurgical experiments on agoraphobics demonstrate that this sensibility may be closest to what we consider from the Western perspective of five senses to be the sense of touch/tactility. The lobotomy study may indicate that we have a faculty of spatial relations, an environmental sensibility, that cannot be conceived in terms of a separation of mind and body. Once disconnected, this spatial sense becomes the basis for a successful round of behaviorist desensitization retraining. As Marks learned in his lobotomy study, "leucotomy" could be "part of a wider treatment programme [because once] anxiety falls after operation, patients [could] be retrained to go out. …"[27] By the mid-1960s, then, both behaviorist and biological medicine appear to agree that the effectiveness of psychosurgery derives from the fact that it severs the connection between anxiety and space. Once this has been accomplished, the behaviorist techniques of desensitization can be gainfully applied. Some medical researchers critical of the overuse of prescription drugs have claimed that this disconnect is replicated in pharmacotherapy.

Today agoraphobics do not undergo lobotomy to sever the connection between anxiety and space. Clinical studies show that they accomplish this disconnect with the environment through medication. Almost all of the clinical literature I examined on current behaviorist treatments of agoraphobia makes it clear that the patients are medicated. In their 1992 guide to the psychological treatment of agoraphobia, where they use the new vocabulary of "panic attacks," authors Jeffrey Hecker and Geoffrey Thorpe are typical in noting that "*pharmacological intervention may be the most common form of treatment panic disorder clients receive*. Clients who present themselves at our clinic for treatment of anxiety and who are not on any form of anxiolytic medication have become the exception."[28]

The pharmacopia of antianxiety drugs is diverse. According to the 1997 manual *Treating Panic Disorder and Agoraphobia: A Step-by-Step Clinical Guide* the preferred drugs in order of frequency of use are: since the mid-1990s, the selective serotonin reuptake inhibitors fluoxetine (Prozac), paroxetine (Paxil) and sertraline (Zoloft). When these are not sufficient, the older tricyclic antidepressants that we have seen in the 1960s cases are sometimes added: imipramine and chlordiazepoxide (Librium) or diazepam (Valium). A stronger class of antidepressants, of which researchers in the mid-1960s anticipated great things, was the monoamine oxidase inhibitors. These can result in a fatal hypertension crisis if combined with foods that contain tyramine, such as aged cheeses, red wines, yeast, liver, bananas, chocolate, and yogurt, and for this reason are only occasionally used even though some researchers believe "they are the most powerful medications for treating panic."[29] Benzodiazepines such as alprazolam (Xanax)—referred to in the previous discussion of the Upjohn Cross-National Panic Study—and clonazepam (Klonopin), the most widely studied drugs for anxiety in the 1960s, are the medications used today for immediate results in relieving panic attacks. They are generally used in combination with antidepressants, which take several weeks to begin working, often with the hope that patients will be weaned off them as soon as possible. In fact, despite the proof that benzodiazepines can cause depression and memory loss, the medical literature shows that many patients are unable to discontinue use of the product. Studies have confirmed patients' complaints that after withdrawing from these drugs their anxiety attacks have worsened, which leads some doctors to suppose that the drugs in fact increase anxiety sensitivity, a situation that paradoxically leads to further dependence on the drugs.

Several researchers have found that the effects on the brain of antianxiety and antidepression drugs are similar to those produced by lobotomies. In his 1997 book *Brain-Disabling Treatments in Psychiatry: Drugs, Electroshock, and the Role of the FDA*, especially in chapter 2 "Deactivation Syndrome (Chemical Lobotomy)," medical researcher and practitioner Dr. Peter Breggin cites several reports from the mid-1980s demonstrating the presence of brain atrophy ("benzodiazepine-induced persistent cognitive deficits or brain damage") with long-term use of benzodiazepines.[30] Despite their popularity—antianxiety agents (anxiolytics) are among the most commonly used drugs in both medicine and psychiatry, Breggin states, citing studies that estimate that "15% of American adults use these or similar sedative/hypnotic agents during any given year, usually through a physician's prescription" while "almost 2% of the population may use benzodiazepines more or less chronically"[31]—their effectiveness in suppressing anxiety is generally maintained as long as the drug is taken. The longer the drug is taken, the greater its toxic effect on the brain. The class of drugs most popular today for anxiety disorders—Prozac, Paxil, and Zoloft—were not available in 1966. According to Breggin, their effects are also similar to those of lobotomy since they work by maintaining a level of toxicity that shuts down operations of particular regions of the brain. Like the anxiolytics, they, too, need to be taken regularly to maintain their effectiveness. For the treatment of agoraphobia both the serotonin reuptake inhibitors and the benzodiazapines must be taken uninterruptedly. That is most likely why some agoraphobia studies advise that agoraphobia should be treated like asthma, epilepsy, or cardiovascular conditions in which patients are advised to simply tolerate the side effects of medication because the disease is presumed to be chronic and to require lifelong medication.[32] As noted in his chapter title, "Chemical Lobotomy" is what Breggin calls the drugs that form the basis of the dominant treatment of agoraphobia today.

### *Analyzing the Contradictions of Pharmacological Treatments for Agoraphobia*

Today drug treatments appear to go hand in hand with behaviorist treatments in a trend that apparently goes back to the 1950s and '60s. However, this has not always been the sole method of treatment. During the 1970s behaviorists like Marks began experimenting with a new form of exposure therapy, called flooding, and discovered that it is particularly effective without medication. In his 1987 book *Fears, Phobias and Rituals*, Marks concludes that of all the exposure techniques for treating agoraphobia—including gradual desensitization—the technique known as flooding works best. Not only is it the most effective treatment, but it is notably most effective when not accompanied by the use of drugs. To emphasize this point, Marks cites an example of popular health advice from the newsletter of a British agoraphobics' correspondence club:

> *Use no pills or alcohol.* Give yourself time to work on your goals one by one, be persistent, and practice, practice, practice. *It may be easier to practice returning home by yourself than to leave home alone.* Let your feelings come, don't run away from them, expect and accept the panic—don't fight it or run away but instead just stay your ground. Do anything that helps you remain in the phobic situation and concentrate on it until your fear is easier. Only use distraction if it is essential to remain where you are—for instance, *feel the coolness of coins in your hands, look at your reflection,* study a design on your dress or a leaf on the ground, *pretend a stranger on the bus is traveling with you.* Expect many setbacks and use them as cues for further exposure.[33]

Important differences exist between the way in which agoraphobics advise each other in the practice of flooding and in the way clinical doctors in their studies train patients to advise themselves; the doctor advises the patient, generally for the needs of a scientific method that seeks to control all variables, to go out unaccompanied, to accept his aloneness in public space, and to let go of any props or distractions that might lessen the experience of fear. For the benefit of the agoraphobics' correspondence club, on the other hand, members are encouraged to do quite the contrary. It is as if, outside the clinic, agoraphobics have reappropriated the treatment that had been streamlined and isolated for purposes of scientific verification in a laboratory and made it a ritual of their own. Club members insist that the agoraphobic "use no pills." Given the abundance of clinical literature disputing the effectiveness, and even the safety, of the antianxiety drugs, it is worth asking why behaviorist desensitization techniques today are almost always accompanied by medication.

Several possible reasons can be suggested, of which the first is economic rationality. The pharmaceutical industry boasts profits at 14 percent, nearly double that of other industries. By the year 2000, the pharmaceutical industry, with marketing budgets that far outstrip money spent on research and development, was the new engine of growth in the United States after the collapse of the "dot-com" economy of the 1990s. In 2002, Georgetown University published a study, including data from both Europe and the United States, showing that 20 percent of prescription drugs are marketed with instructions for use that must later be corrected by the manufacturer—almost always to lower the dose. "Drugs," they found, "are being studied at excessively high doses to emphasize their effects, and then marketed at the same high doses to maximize profits."[34] When doctors lower dosages based on their patients' reported side effects, the studied effectiveness of the drugs may no longer apply. In view of the fact that most medical research in the United States on the effects of pharmaceutical drugs is done by the drug companies themselves, and that, because these companies are the legal owners of the research they produce, they are not required by law to publish the results, it is clear that the side effects of popular antianxiety drugs may not be easily available for scrutiny by the medical community.[35] In other words, the increase in drug prescriptions may in no way be an adequate indicator of a drug's effectiveness in the general population.[36]

A second reason that behavioral treatments for agoraphobia are so often practiced on medicated clients appears to be ideological. Many studies have pointed to the social problems arising from the steadily increasing reliance on psychiatric drugs. The problem is certainly compounded by the core ideology of biological psychiatry, the view that mental states, from unhappiness to schizophrenia, have a primarily biological, or even genetic, origin. The view is increasingly accepted, although not scientifically substantiated, and detractors of biological psychiatry caution that medical approval for the treatment of a physical disease, such as pneumonia or diabetes, is very different from approving the use of specific drugs for expressions of human suffering that are psychological and social in origin.[37] Biological psychiatry is the dominant form of psychiatry in the Western world, and its influence spreads far beyond actual treatment. It has quickly become the leading approach conceptualizing most forms of human distress and eccentricity, and its aura of certainty makes it very hard to challenge, even in the treatment of agoraphobia, where its effects mimic lobotomy and its track record is less hopeful than advertisers would have us think. With commercial profits higher than in any other industry, the pharmaceutical industry controls scientific research on drugs. The cultural implications are even more complex if we consider that many of the drugs prescribed to improve performance in social situations, in school, and even in sports are changing the normative expectations of what it means to be a successful person in societies of advanced, flexible capitalism.[38] Biological psychiatry affects women much more than men.[39] Some have reasoned that this is perhaps due to women's greater willingness to discuss personal problems, or to the fact that their behavior, when interpreted within a patriarchal bias of modern medicine, does not measure up to a longstanding standard set by white, middle-class men. In any case, there is a growing concern that this medicalized psychology has, on balance, produced more harm than good.[40] It puts women at greater risk for mistreatment, and this has certainly been the case with agoraphobia.

Finally, the third reason that behaviorist techniques of desensitization are so often employed with medication is a more properly cultural one. We are culturally unprepared for the demands that the new expansive and shifting forms of modern time and space make on our sense of self. Lacking skills from the wider culture, medications may be called on to help create a sense of self for persons whose behavior is increasingly called on to meet the demands of the current economic world, where capitalism has been made flexible by new electronically mediated technologies of speed. The anthropologist Emily Martin, for example, has noted that certain mental conditions such as manic-depression and attention deficit hyperactivity disorder have been recently reconceptualized, even popularized by media commentators who point out that such hypersensitive disorders display personality traits shared by some of the United States' most wealthy and successful businessmen, chief executive officers who are at once hands on, nonstop, control freaks and subject to constant mood swings. While such mental conditions may appear to mimic the exigencies of labor in late capitalism, the overuse of drugs to control such behavior in the general population suggests that we are as yet culturally unskilled to deal with ourselves when acting in these ways. The popularity of medications such as Ritalin, then, for disorders that appear to mimic the demands of flexible capital, may have a close parallel with the increase in medications dispensed for the predominantly female population of agoraphobics whose disorder, with its free-floating panics and fears of depthless space, also mimics changes in a now almost ubiquitous style of increasingly homogenous forms of public urban space.

Lobotomy, whether surgical or chemical, is more than just a metaphor for the way that desensitization treatments for agoraphobia have developed in behaviorist psychology. Such treatments disable the patient, preventing him from developing the very social skills needed to receive tangible information about the urban environment. The evolving biopsychological-behaviorist treatment appears to support the larger culture's devaluation of the sense of tactility as a legitimate means of knowing. Much of what has generally been in the domain of women's culture, on the other hand—in particular those skills associated with nonindustrial labor such as child care, food preparation, and the like—engages tactile sensibility in highly skilled ways. When given expression in public space, as in the small towns of Italy where women extend and indeed control their labor as it moves into the public squares, these skills remain associated with useful knowledge. When women's labor enters the public spaces of urban industrial societies, however, these skills appear to fall into disuse. Behavioral techniques appear historically in the gap created when the modern public self lacks a tradition of skills to negotiate changing forms and demands of public space. The contradictions of pharmacological methods are many, but one of the most important is surely the unresolved problem of widening the gap that modern urbanites feel between self and environment. If agoraphobics withdraw from these new forms of public space for want of social skills, many of the medications we have looked at in this section succeed in reinserting agoraphobics into common society by means not dissimilar to those of the lobotomy: paradoxically, they reinsert by furthering the disconnect; they bridge the gap by severing connections between feeling and public space.

## Flooding: Disconnecting with Space

Public space is recognized as a powerful structure of feeling in the behavioral technique of flooding, engaging the body in a mysterious act of self-cure that is most successful when the patient is not medicated. For flooding to work, public space and the full sensorium person must be brought together. Unlike biological psychiatry as it develops in the United States, where the environment is eventually erased from treatment altogether, early behaviorist studies like those of Marks maintain a certain curiosity about the spatial object of agoraphobic fear. For Marks and British researchers generally, agoraphobia never becomes an entirely objectless phobia and this is a key to the relative success of the technique of flooding. As Marks comments in his 1987 book, "To diagnose agoraphobia, some fear of and tendency to avoid public places is a *sine qua non*: *the fear of fear or of harmful consequences to oneself are frequent concomitants but not essential features. A woman who avoids public places because they frighten her is agoraphobic even if she is not afraid of fear itself or of going mad.* Similarly, someone who fears panic but goes out freely into public places is not agoraphobic but rather has an anxiety state (panic disorder without agoraphobia)."[41]

Public space remained an important feature of Marks's experimental work on agoraphobia. Two behavioral techniques he studied, desensitization and flooding, actually use space to help the agoraphobic disconnect from her fear-driven self.

Flooding is a form of exposure to phobic sites that, in the case of agoraphobia, uses public space as an immersion experience to trigger a full-blown anxiety attack. Flooding differs from desensitization, which is a gradual technique of exposure that does not force the patient into a phobic reaction. Early in his experiments Marks saw that flooding was a far more effective technique for agoraphobia, but he was unsure why it worked better or what caused it to work. He questioned what distinguished flooding from desensitization and whether the mechanism of its success was habituation, adaptation, or extinction.

Adaptation, habituation, and extinction are behaviorist terms to explain change in human behavior. Adaptation and habituation are rational explanations for why techniques like flooding work. Adaptation explains a technique's success in terms of a biological need of the human species to adapt to its environment. If flooding worked through adaptation, the agoraphobic would be cured when she finally adapted to what is, after all, her environment. Habituation, on the other hand, explains the success of a behavioral technique by claiming that enough repetition will inevitably change behavior. If flooding works through habituation, the agoraphobic has changed her behavior with regard to urban space because the repeated exposures have become habit forming, they have changed her habits. The last theory Marks considered to explain the strong effects of flooding is known as extinction, which in behavioral parlance refers to the fact that prolonged exposure to stimuli can eventually, for some unknown reason, extinguish the very reaction it once provoked. Psychologists and psychoanalysts have studied this phenomenon variously as catharsis or abreaction (Sigmund Freud) and as paradoxical intention (Amr Barrada, Erick Erickson, and Viktor Frankl).

For behaviorists, abreactions and paradoxical reactions are viewed as sudden releases of blocked energy that accompany the acute reliving of a traumatic experience. They have been known to be accompanied by mysterious somatic phenomena, as when the body spontaneously reproduces marks such as redness on the skin where a long buried physical trauma had originally occurred. From a materialist perspective, behaviorists might describe extinction as changes in brain-wave patterns, but as they readily acknowledge, the psychosomatic phenomenon remains more complex and mysterious. If flooding works on the principle of extinction/abreaction, then it also engages this complex, nonrational, and little-understood phenomenon of modern experience that behaviorists recognize in other cultures and historical contexts as the domain of powerful religious experience or trance-induced "acting out."

Marks eventually came to think that extinction was the ground for the success of the technique of flooding. He further hypothesized that flooding was not merely a more intense form of desensitization. The gradual exposure of desensitization techniques had a high rate of relapse for the agoraphobic. Marks judged this to be because desensitization worked by the weaker mechanism of habituation, creating new habits that allowed the patient to adapt to the once fearful environment. Similarly, when flooding was practiced in conjunction with antianxiety drugs, it produced the same low rate of success as desensitization. Marks thus considered that medication stopped the production of a powerful extinction effect. Adding medication to flooding, then, changed behavior in a weak and unstable way by training a patient to form new habits. But flooding by itself made use of the body's mysterious power for self-cure through extinction.

In the following sections, we will consider how public space is engaged for the agoraphobic through the successes of flooding. Close readings of several of Marks's clinical studies in the late 1960s and 1970s take us through his discovery of the usefulness of this technique and point out how specific public places become therapeutic devices in gender-specific ways. Shopping centers are the laboratories where behaviorists see their most powerful method succeed. As we reflect further on what behaviorists consider to be the mechanism of flooding's success, we see that this treatment exists in a long history of cathartic therapies leading back to the behaviorist treatments of soldiers suffering war neurosis and to Freud's early work on *abreaction*—a term he coined with his colleague Dr. Josef Breuer. In our genealogy of the behaviorist technique of flooding, we see that military overtones are therapeutically carried into new forms of urban architecture that adapt industrial-scale mass production and capitalist marketing strategies to the domain of food and other goods—in short, they are carried over to the shopping center. This suggests a larger cultural picture about the agoraphobic's complaint and the recovery of the public self.

*Recovering Public Space in Exposure Treatments: Flooding versus Desensitization*

Public space plays an important role in how the self is recovered with behavioral techniques. A close examination of some of Marks's key clinical studies reveals how flooding came to be distinguished from desensitization and how both methods emerged from unexamined assumptions about the dark successes of lobotomy. Beginning with the study published by M. G. Gelder and Marks in 1966—the same year as the lobotomy study—we can deploy a careful reading to discover how cultural assumptions about the public self and its relation to space are built into the emergent behavioral techniques of desensitization.

The 1966 study is titled "Severe Agoraphobia: A Controlled Prospective Trial of Behaviour Therapy." As in the lobotomy study, the patients in this study are referred to as having "severe agoraphobia ... severe enough to require treatment in hospital."[42] As in the lobotomy study, it is the same diagnosis, the same publication year, the same doctors running the study, and the same psychiatric hospital, but there is no mention of lobotomy as a current treatment for agoraphobia. The report begins, "Severe agoraphobia is difficult to treat. Encouraging immediate results have been reported with diverse treatments, including intensive psychotherapy (Friedman, 1959), acetyl choline injections (Sim, 1964), anti-depressant drugs (King, 1962), and more recently with behaviour therapy (Wolpe, 1958). It is this later claim which this paper examines."[43]

There is no mention of lobotomy among the list of treatments with "[e]ncouraging, immediate results." In this study twenty patients participated in a controlled test of desensitivization techniques—five men and fifteen women. The behavior therapy group received "graded retraining ... with systematic desensitization in imagination." These patients receive "desensitization" sessions with a therapist in which they are induced to imagine for long periods of time, and in exquisite detail, the places they are most afraid of. They must also take assisted field trips to various sites in the city that they would otherwise avoid. The control group received "supervised, psychotherapeutic interviews directed mainly to current interpersonal problems, relating these to past experiences." The authors note that they are using a "brief, re-educative [version of] psychotherapy" only to "serve as a control." In other words, in order to compare the effectiveness of behavioral treatments to the effectiveness of psychotherapy, the patients receiving behavioral treatments must not be engaged in any talking therapies. Here we see how the behavioral treatment technique initially develops more out of concern for the exigencies of the scientific method than out of concern for the needs of the patient. The over-anxious agoraphobic patient receiving behaviorist treatments is placed in fearful environments without the solace of a trusted person she can talk to. Drugs, on the other hand, are not controlled for in the study. In both the behavior group and the control group, all the patients are receiving either antianxiety or antidepressant drugs, as if the mechanism of physical disconnect achieved in lobotomy was, from the experimenter's point of view, an assumed, perhaps even necessary part of any therapy (see table below).

| | **Men** | **Women** |
|---|---|---|
| Behavior Therapy | 2 | 7 / 8 |
| 6 received antianxiety drugs | | |
| 3 received antidepressant drugs | | |
| Psychotherapy (Control Group) | 3 | 7 / 8 |
| 7 received antianxiety drugs | | |
| 3 received antidepressant drugs | | |
| Total | 5 | 15 |

Three quarters of the patients in this study are women, but, as in the lobotomy study, we are not explicitly told much about the gender differences among the patients. When we are introduced to more information about the patients there is no reference to their sex:

> These patients with agoraphobia complained of intense fears of going out alone into open spaces, into streets, shops, crowds, cars, trains, etc, or of remaining alone. All were severely handicapped by their symptoms which had been present for many years. *Three quarters* were unable to leave the house unaccompanied, and their symptoms made it very difficult for them to work, shop, take their children to school, or enjoy their leisure. … *Sexual difficulties, mainly frigidity, were present in three quarters.* … All but four were married, and all the married patients had children. *Clinical features closely resembled those of Robert's (1964) "housebound housewives"* and of the agoraphobics studied retrospectively by Marks and Gelder (1965). Interpersonal problems were common. … The mean age of the patients who received behaviour therapy was 34.5; mean duration of illness 7 years.[44]

The study reveals more about the patients' gender and social circumstances than did the aforementioned lobotomy study. For example, we are told that the married patients all had children (so a demand for the generally "invisible" labor of child care was present in all these households). All references to "three quarters" of the patients seem likely to be references to women since we know that three quarters of the patients in the study are women. Similarly, we might assume that women make up the "three quarters" who could not leave the house, the same group that the study calls "frigid" and "housebound housewives." The researchers never explain why all the patients in this study—whether in the group receiving the desensitization behavior treatment or in the control group receiving only psychotherapy—were medicated with either antianxiety tranquillizers (sodium amytal and Librium) or antidepressant drugs.

The results on desensitization therapy "disappoint" the researchers: the study lasted six months with a one year follow-up. There appeared to be a slight improvement in the behavior group, once again with respect to "work adjustment"; we discover that "five patients receiving behaviour therapy (against just two receiving the control treatment) made useful, although limited, gains in ability to make one particular journey, usually to work."[45] We aren't told whether the success stories are men or women, but the authors do say that, once again, scoring something like improved "work adjustment" was "difficult" because "it attempts to take into account both the work difficulties of a housewife and those of a wage earner." Still, the authors conclude, "by the time of the six months follow-up … both [groups] were left with considerable difficulties in carrying out their work."[46] After one year, the study reports, both groups were pretty much back where they started from, making desensitization less effective than lobotomy at this time. We read, "Behaviour therapy is not useful for all agoraphobic patients: on the other hand *a few patients did very well* with this treatment. … Our experience is that patients with mildly perfectionist personalities co-operate well with the treatment, which is precisely formulated. … [and] patients mainly seeking a *direct attack* on symptoms will co-operate more readily than those seeking help with wider problems."[47]

Despite these dismal initial results, with most of the patients relapsing within one year, the intensified version of this treatment—the employment of flooding while on anxiety medication—went on to become one of the most popular behaviorist techniques for agoraphobia today. In the 1966 study no discussion is made of the lobotomy study, even though Marks and his coauthors have noted elsewhere that lobotomy remained the most successful treatment to combine with desensitization in changing severe agoraphobic behavior with respect to work performance. The repressed connection to lobotomy and the unexamined role of medication in this early desensitization study cannot be overlooked when considering how this treatment has developed into a sort of model for agoraphobic treatments today. Also, there is no indication of whether the few patients who "did very well" with medicated desensitization techniques were men or women. These details would be addressed in the study that appeared seven years later.

In 1973 Dr. Marks published another study, "Brief and Prolonged Flooding: A Comparison in Agoraphobic Patients," this time in the *Archives of General Psychiatry*, with other colleagues in association with the same psychiatric institute and the same hospital as in the lobotomy study. The exposure technique was now called flooding, and appeared to be a refinement of what was used in 1966, only now the patient was taken to sites that trigger extreme fear and kept there longer in a state of prolonged exposure. As the study explains, "Flooding denotes confrontation of a patient with the stimuli that distress him until he gets used to them and may also include the evocation of intense emotion during treatment. This confrontation can take place in a patient's imagination (implosion) or in real life. There are many variants of flooding. …"[48]

In this study there were seven male and nine female patients whose mean age is thirty-six and whose average experience with agoraphobic symptoms is eleven years. The treatments involved flooding in both fantasy and in practice. In the fantasy sessions patients were subjected to eighty-minute tapes of "flooding scenes," such as, "Imagine you are standing on a bus and the bus lurches forward throwing you off your feet. You are sweating, your heart is pounding, you are pouring with sweat, and your legs feel like jelly. …"[49] The flooding tapes were then followed by "neutral tapes" that consisted of, for instance, "a published investigation into the merits of different automatic washing machines." Already we might have a potentially gendered choice for the material in the fantasy flooding: public mobility or stationary domesticity. (Upon reflection the investigators would consider that the medium itself—the tape recorder—was probably the reason why the fantasy flooding technique proved less effective: electronically reproduced narratives engaging only the sense of sound with the patient's imagination did not provoke the desired full sensorium state of anxiety. As we will see in chapter 6, however, once the visual element is added, with television, the electronic simulations of fear provoking scenarios in everyday settings like the agoraphobic's living room suggest a gendered response in fantasy reactions.)

The in vivo flooding sessions—those done in practice, in real life—reveal that the patient is being taken to the shopping center:

> A typical long-flooding practice session was a 20-minute bus journey to *a shopping center*, accompanied if necessary by the therapist, and 80 minutes shopping, during which the therapist left the patient for as long as the patient allowed. … Patients were told before the session that they must expect to experience palpitations, sweating,

> and other unpleasant anxiety symptoms, but that no physical harm would befall them. The importance of remaining in the situation was stressed. … The therapist both reassured the patient and encouraged him to remain alone in the phobic situation. … other methods were improvised to prevent the patient avoiding the phobic situation.
>
> In short flooding in practice … the patient was taken to *a large shopping center* in the therapist's car, which was parked outside. *Agoraphobic patients usually feel safe inside a car, and advantage was taken of this to use the car as a base from which timed expeditions to the shops were made.* … patients were instructed to return after 30 minutes.[50]

In all the behavioral literature I read where exposure was being used to treat agoraphobia, if any exposure site was mentioned it was a shopping center. Shopping centers were indeed becoming notable sites of fear for the agoraphobic at this time and, as we will see in chapter 6, the general public also registered discomfort with the palpable giganticism and alienation introduced into British shopping habits by this new architectural form.

In the 1973 study, the activity of shopping is only mentioned as a triumphant achievement of exposure therapy when the patient is a woman. In the section on results, the authors mention five specific patients who were helped by the therapy, and thanks to gender-marked pronouns in English we can tell that two of them are women, the other three men. I have put headings on these excerpts to emphasize the different spaces that the patients give as an example of conquering their agoraphobic fear:

**Female: Supermarket**

> The rationale of flooding was explained to all patients. … They had previously avoided phobic situations, e.g., as soon as one woman entered a supermarket and experienced anxiety, she hurriedly left, which made reentry very difficult; to improve she needed to return to the shop and stay there till the unpleasant feelings subsided. Before flooding in practice she would be asked to imagine herself venturing into shops.[51]

**Male: Public Transportation**

> One patient actually remarked: "I respond better to the longer treatments; you see, the first 20 minutes is sheer agony but after awhile you get acclimatized and the panic attacks bounce off you. …" He volunteered to go home by public transport alone after his first treatment session, although he had not done so for the previous ten months. Later, he reported that he continued to have panic attacks

but no longer had to leave the situations in which they occurred. He had learned to tolerate the unpleasantness of panics without avoidance.[52]

**Female: Shopping Center**

Most patients were initially reluctant to enter the phobic situation but were pleased after doing so, and often quite elated after a session.

"Thank you for pushing me into it," said one patient after returning from a shopping expedition which was part of her flooding in practice in the third session. After the first two sessions the patient had not wanted to continue with treatment. Seven other patients were reluctant to carry on after two sessions, but all were persuaded to continue. Often the patient telephoned the therapist to say that she could not go through with the treatment. Several others said they were "too tired," while others frankly admitted being too frightened to continue.[53]

**Male: Waterloo Bridge**

Two patients stressed that the fears they had to face in treatment were much greater than in their normal lives and this may have been important. During treatment, one patient had to stand in the middle of Waterloo Bridge in London. On completing treatment, he stated that he would still avoid Waterloo Bridge, but small bridges, streets, open spaces, and bus stops no longer presented any difficulty.[54]

**Male: Classroom; Public Transportation**

In real life, improvement after practice implied that patients could resume everyday activities they had hitherto avoided, eg, an agoraphobic lecturer was able to resume teaching his class and travels alone by public transport.[55]

The male patients are enabled in the use of public transportation, and in teaching classes. The women are enabled in shopping. The gender/social space dimension of behavioral treatments using flooding at this time appear the same throughout the clinical literature. For example, in another behavioral study done in Utrecht, Netherlands, and published in *Behaviour Research and Therapy: An International Multi-Disciplinary Journal* (also in 1973), Dutch clinicians testing the efficacy of flooding report on the imaginal flooding scene they gave to fourteen agoraphobic patients (twelve women, two men) whose average duration of complaint ranged from two to twenty-three years. After having the patients make a list of the phobic situations and "the cues that were relevant for the client [patient]," the patients were given five forty-five-minute sessions of flooding in the imagination, followed immediately by forty-five minutes of flooding in vivo where "the client was instructed to enter the anxiety-arousing situation. The therapist and the client agreed upon a route through the city … which the client had to follow alone." Here is the study's reported imaginal scene, which preceded the agreed-upon walk through the most dreadful sites of the city, ending at the shopping center:

> Imagine you are going out of the front door of this house. You walk through the front garden and then you are in the street. You turn left and *walk in the direction of the shopping center where you have to go and buy something.* Imagine it as well as you can: the houses you walk past, the cars that rush past you. You are walking there alone and you are going in the direction of the railway crossing. … you walk on and *arrive in the shopping center.* It is fuller there, there are more and more people. You begin to feel rather bad now. You become dizzy. You feel it in your legs. But you nevertheless walk on, because there is nowhere you can go there on the street, you cannot flee inside anywhere. Now you have to cross the street. There is a string of cars and you run between them. On the other side of the street there are still more people. Now you are feeling completely dizzy. Your legs are heavy. But there you are walking in the middle of the pavement and there is nowhere you can go. You begin to panic and you think, I want to go away, I want to go home, but you cannot go home. You hold onto a gate for awhile, but you can't manage anymore. You are sweating terribly, you take another couple of steps and then you fall. You fall there in the middle of the street. People come and stand around you and are wondering what has happened. And there you lie, in the middle of the street.[56]

It is important to note that *walking* to the shopping center, both imaginally and in reality, is not something that city planners would have made much provision for. The shopping center is generally located at the intersection of a major roadway with high traffic volume; thus, its large parking lot and warehouse size is designed for large quantities of purchases that would be taken home by car. As a pedestrian destination it would be a challenge for any urban citizen. The use of the fantasy scenario as a first step into city space is an important feature of the technique. It shows that behaviorist researchers understand what literary critics have long noted about the important function of literature and film in public life, that a culture's narrative descriptions of urban life provide the imaginal means with which a citizen can insert himself into the city. If, as we saw in the introduction to this volume, a dominant literary trope for the city's coherence in modern Euro-American fiction is indeed a "central vacuity," as Scherpe noted, then we citizens are being prepped in many powerful ways to enter and abide in vast zones of homogenous urban space, such as the shopping centered described in the Dutch behaviorist urban fantasy delineated above.

The Dutch study, like the British study, proves that flooding is an effective treatment. As in the case of Marks's 1973 study, the patients are now apparently unmedicated (no mention of drugs appears in either study). The literature begins to show at this time that it makes more sense not to medicate patients for flooding because the goal of the technique is to have the patients experience the full physical and emotional impact of their situated fear and recover from the self-induced cure of it alone, without the aid of spouses, pets, or props. In a similar study two years later, one of the same Dutch clinicians emphasized the importance of the patient being alone in flooding: "The client had to walk alone [on the agreed upon route through the city] without any aid which might reduce anxiety (e.g. umbrella, bicycle, hand-bag, sunglasses, dog, etc.)"[57] Furthermore, researchers avoided providing any feedback during their sessions, so that the efficacy of the technique of flooding could be determined, without confusing it with elements of psychotherapy. As a result, during the period of work with flooding, the therapist would avoid discussion with these mostly female patients of the relations between agoraphobic fears and personal problems: "When a client brought up an interpersonal problem during a therapy session, the therapist in principle tried to postpone the discussion of this problem until the completion of the investigation. When this proved impossible, the therapist went into the matter briefly."[58] The behavioral techniques that were thus developing around flooding include attempts to socialize patients who are mostly women, into culturally feminized spaces (shopping centers) by training them in culturally masculine behavior such as being comfortable as a solitary individual in vast, crowded urban spaces; venturing into public space without props, not even a handbag; discouraging anything but the briefest discussion of interpersonal issues; and accepting aloneness as a normative, albeit heroic, existential experience of one's being in the world. With these techniques for inducing culturally masculine behavior through flooding exercises, behavioral clinicians demonstrate that flooding works.

In the years since in vivo flooding was introduced, it has been streamlined into self-help programs that could be cost effective for the general population so that it no longer makes high demands on the therapist's time. Marks, working within England's socialized medical system, was instrumental in this regard.[59] In 1978 he wrote a self-help manual, *Living with Fear: Understanding and Coping with Anxiety*, that could be handed out in emergency rooms or distributed to housebound agoraphobics. Following a general trend in behavioral treatment programs toward reducing the involvement of the therapist, the program used just one session of therapist-assisted flooding in vivo training, as well as structured diaries, peer group sessions, and telephone conversations with therapists. This follows a general trend in behavioral treatment programs toward reducing the involvement of the therapist and moving the patient toward techniques of self-fashioning.

Since that time, clinicians treating agoraphobia have tested several other therapeutic approaches against the baseline practice of flooding/exposure in vivo—treatments such as "rational-emotive therapy, paradoxical intention, and progressive relaxation, [but these have] not consistently enhanced the effectiveness of exposure *in vivo*."[60] In this way, the techniques of exposure in vivo with and without medication became standards in the treatment of agoraphobia.

*Why Does Flooding Work? Habituation versus Abreaction/Extinction*

Two dominant theories have been proposed to explain the relative successes of flooding techniques: habituation and abreaction/extinction. Behaviorists who argue that flooding works by habituation give reasons like those of the Dutch researchers, such as, "It is not clear by what mechanism flooding … operate[s] … [however] one (important) factor [is that]… the client is exposed to the phobic situation *in vivo*. In flooding, the client's exposure to the situation is prolonged and may *not* be avoided. … It had been suggested elsewhere … that this exposure in vivo is the essential element of the treatment, which may eventually bring about *habituation*."[61]

Whatever one's explanatory model for why it is that flooding works, all researchers acknowledge the primary function of public space in this treatment: flooding shows that exposure *in* vivo—that is, in reality and not simulated exposure—is the key ingredient. The full effects of reality, then, have a significant if unclear role to play in the cure. Behaviorists who support the thesis that flooding eventually cures agoraphobia by habituation argue that the agoraphobic has become comfortable with the previously phobic space by sheer force of repetition. Habituation means that fear has been overcome through repetition.[62]

In their 1973 study, Marks and his colleagues entertained both the habituation and the abreaction/extinction theses. Habituation was a possible explanation if the repetitions of flooding had some cognitive value in helping the patient rehearse, in advance, her approach to the fearsome public sites. But abreaction, a little understood process that acknowledges an "unknown factor" in the experience of flooding, could not be ruled out as a major reason for its effectiveness:

> Why were prolonged sessions more potent than shorter ones? The duration of exposure as such may be less important than that of intervals between exposure. Incubation effects are known to be important for the acquisition of fear in animals. They might be equally important for its extinction in humans, but answer of this point requires a different design from ours. *Cognitive rehearsal* between periods of exposure might affect incubation processes.
>
> Another possibility is that prolonging sessions increases the chances of some critical *but unknown* processes occurring which facilitates improvement. *A similar idea might lie behind past emphases on reaching the point of emotional exhaustion during abreaction of war neuroses.*"[63]

The idea that the stronger effect of flooding may have been brought on by "cognitive rehearsal" means that, like animals in fear studies, when humans *know* through anticipation that another session of intense anxiety is due to occur, they *habituate* or adapt themselves to the situation. Following this line of thinking, the doctors reasoned that perhaps the interval between exposures—that is, the periods in between trips to the shopping center when patients knew what was coming up—allowed patients time to cognitively *rehearse* their fears and coping strategies; in other words, they had time to think about what they would do. Habituation remains to this day a common explanation among behaviorists as to the question of why flooding works as well as it does.

Marks's later work rejects the thesis of habituation based on the general failures of cognitive therapies in the treatment of phobic disorders. He notes, "A major research effort in many centers has produced disappointing results from cognitive therapies for phobic-OC [obsessive-compulsive] problems, both in patients and in volunteers. *Cognitive approaches added almost nothing to the value of exposure for agora- and specific phobics, and had limited effects alone*...."[64]

As Marks rejected the theory of habituation, especially as it is elaborated in terms of "cognitive rehearsal," he came to embrace the idea that the process of flooding worked by means of "some critical but unknown processes" known generally since Freud's day by the term *abreaction*.

### *Flooding as Abreaction, and Its Significance for the Relation of the Public Self to Modern Urban Space*

Abreaction, with its core of mystery and energetic materiality, is, as Marks has noted, an "unknown process" that involves the full sensorium in an acute reliving of key experiences and events. It provides a sharp contrast to the rationalist, mechanical theory of habituation and suggests an entirely different, nonrational and potentially curative relation of the public self to modern urban space. On the other hand, abreaction also proposes a comparative link between the battlefields of the twentieth-century European wars and the dominant places to which agoraphobics are being "exposed" in the clinical literature: the shopping center. It is true that prior to the rise of behaviorism in the 1960s all clinical work on abreaction in Britain and the United States was done in relation to the traumatic experience of the soldier on the European battlefield. In the United States after the end of the Vietnam War, work on abreaction returned to focus on the soldier's experience in what became known as post-traumatic stress disorder. In the meantime, throughout the 1960s and '70s, abreaction was studied mainly in the behavioral technique of flooding. "Abreaction (catharsis)," notes Marks, "originally denoted the intense emotion that may accompany a revival of traumatic memories under hypnosis. More recently it has come to mean any intense emotional experience during treatment. The emotion can be of many kinds, not only fear, and may involve problems unrelated to the trauma that precipitated the distress (Wilde 1942). Much was published about abreaction for traumatic phobias (post-traumatic stress disorder during and after the two world wars. *Since then relevant reports have mainly appeared in the literature on flooding.*"[65] As abreaction became a topic of scientific inquiry for those researching in vivo flooding, it was being perfected as a technique to take the agoraphobic into the new public spaces of the shopping center.

For behaviorists, abreaction is associated with what they call "organic memory." As opposed to conscious or even unconscious memory in the psychoanalytic models, organic memory is a somatized form of remembering whose symbolic content need not be engaged in order for its curative power to operate. Behaviorists focus on descriptions of abreaction. Marks, for example, writes,

> Intense abreaction may be accompanied by "organic memories" or "somatizations." [Examples of somatizations recorded in the medical literature include:] A hand blanched at the time a memory of past injury to it recurred (Edkins 1949) [or the case of] a man [who while] reliv[ing] the experience of being tied up 12 years previously, [experienced] rope marks appear[ing] on his forearm (Moody 1946); a few minutes later weals appeared on both forearms and gradually became indented, and finally fresh petechiae were seen along their course. These marks lasted for several hours after the abreaction had ended. In a woman, skin lesions appeared during her abreaction of trauma from many years before (Moody 1948); hyperemia began minutes after the abreaction started, followed by edema, petechiae, and then

> slight flaking of the epidermis. The changes lasted up to a day after abreaction. Trained observers witnessed them several times during repeated abreactions of different traumata, and each time the area affected was the bodily part involved in the abreacted memory.[66]

In other eras and cultural traditions the phenomena of a spontaneous, somatic sign produced in an altered or otherwise detached state of consciousness has been variously recognized by terms such as *religious stigmata* and *spirit possession*. In nonwestern medical traditions like acupuncture, for example, red spots appearing on a patient's skin during treatment are somatized signs that Qi energy (the Chinese term for the body's vital force) has become unblocked and the body is moving back to a state of health. As interest in abreaction enters the vocabulary of psychoanalysis, somatizations are studied in terms of hysteria. Later, somatic conversions are discussed with regard to the experience of soldiers traumatized on the battlefield. Behaviorists enter this discussion after the Second World War through scientific observation. In his general audience book, *Fears, Phobias and Rituals: Panic, Anxiety and Their Disorders*, Marks explains abreaction by quoting from R. L. Moody's physiological explanations of somatic phenomena:

> "Neural pathways undoubtedly exist by which psychic contents may be projected on to the body *in a highly specific manner*; and it is reasonable to suppose that, in such cases, the psychic content or image, with its emotional charge, acts as the afferent side of a reflex arc the efferent counterpart of which is [autonomic]. … Such traumatic experiences are not restricted to adult life or to the battlefield. They may occur also in the formative years of early childhood and may involve regions of the body other than the skin and subcutaneous tissue."[67]

Behaviorists take a new direction in the psychological description of abreaction, however, when they use the objective rhetoric of science to take medical interest far from the symbolic content of abreactive phenomena. Attaching meaning to such somatic signs, a long-standing practice in many cultures, becomes less important for behaviorists who do not seek to understand the force (and curative potential) behind the body's encrypted language. With regard to flooding, for example, behaviorists note that forgotten memories in chronic phobic patients have been documented after flooding/exposure treatment and "relief of phobias has also occurred after chance encounters prompted the return of long-forgotten worries related to the onset of the fear."[68] For behaviorists, however, examples of "organic" (embodied) memory are there as a reminder to the prospective behavioral therapist that he "*need not* spend much time probing for meaning, which in any case may emerge as exposure goes on."[69]

The lack of attention to meaning is not out of keeping with the general thrust of behaviorists' methods of cure, since the cure will be noted in the patient's changed behavior, not in her changed interpretations of symbolic material.[70] With regard to the use of flooding techniques to cure agoraphobic patients of their pathologized withdrawal from certain forms of public space—space that is becoming widely recognized in the broader culture as asocial and even conducive to pathological reaction—we are no longer talking about only a medical problem. If the behavioral adaptation of abreaction as a somatic release of some energetic materiality is used to relieve both the therapist and the patient from the burden of finding the words to name the relation between such overgrown forms of public space and repeated bouts of anxiety, we have an ethical dilemma. If finding *les mots pour le dire*, the words to tell us about the relations of body, mind, and social space is no longer a necessary part of the agoraphobic cure, this is an indication of a wider social problem. In this case the body itself becomes a "speaker" on the pathological effects of this most intense, commercial form of modern common space, but a "speaker" who can only use a language that needs no interpretation. It needs no interpretation, however, not because its meaning is self-evident, but because no one understands it: it is "mysterious," an energetic "charge" that can bring about cure without the mediation of understanding, similar to the so-called placebo cure we saw in the Xanax study in chapter 4. The symptom of agoraphobia functions, then, as both a representation of the unrepresentable and as a *differend*, as the philosopher Jean-Francois Lyotard called it in a juridical context—a complaint that can be spoken but not heard. To suspend meaning in flooding treatments and let the body take care of the cure is, on the one hand, to collapse mind into body. But it also provides an excuse to ignore the relation of this body to a particular, increasingly ubiquitous and suspect form of homogeneous social space.

### *Borrowing Abreaction from Freud: From the Private Experience of Cathartic Method in the Therapist's Office to the Public Spectacle of Flooding in the Shopping Center*

To fully explore the cultural dimensions of abreaction in the behavioral treatment of agoraphobia, the notions of mystery and energy it assumes and ignores, the embodied spatial metaphors it sets up between military and commercial zones of late-twentieth-century urban life, we need to better understand how behaviorists came to appropriate and define abreaction. *Abreaction* describes an empirical phenomenon long recognized in Western and other cultures linking physical pathology and its cure to strong emotional display. However, when behavioral theorists borrowed the term from the early work of Freud and combined it with the work of Pavlov they ended up with a new, original understanding of the phenomena steeped in cultural assumptions of mid-twentieth-century medicine.

The term was first coined by Freud and Breuer in *Studies on Hysteria* (1895). Like other neurologists of his day, Freud had originally conceived of emotions in physical terms as quantities of energy channeled through our neural networks like electrical currents. Initially, Freud had argued that any sudden emotion not immediately evacuated through the system could lead to pathology, what he early on termed "neurosis." From *coitus interruptus* to a trauma that stuns or an illicit desire put in check, Freud theorized that such experiences constituted a surge of energy that when blocked or repressed would be expressed in neurotic symptoms. The aim of psychological therapy was to finally bring about a discharge of blocked energy. During this early period of his work, Freud used two terms to describe his therapeutic technique: *abreaction* and its predecessor *cathartic method*. This new concept of abreaction enabled Freud and Breuer to show deference to the mechanistic physiology of neurology in their day while also legitimating a new direction. By adding the Latin-Germanic prefix *ab* to the word *reactio*, which already had a prefix (*re*), they intensified the more common, mechanistic sense of the word *reaction*. In his *Autobiographical Study*, Freud attributes the linguistic innovation to Breuer. "Breuer," he writes, "spoke of our method as *cathartic*: its therapeutic aim was explained as being to provide that the quota of affect used for maintaining the symptom, which had got on to the wrong lines and had, as it were, become strangulated there, should be redirected on to the normal path along which it could obtain discharge (or *abreaction*)."[71]

The term *catharsis* had long been part of the medical lexicon up to the nineteenth century. The works of Hippocrates and Galen, as well as most pharmacopeias, contained references to *cathartic* drugs, also known as "purgatives" or "evacuants," but Freud is apparently the first to use the word *catharsis* in psychology.[72] Friedrich Nietzsche had briefly mentioned the word *catharsis* in *The Birth of Tragedy* (1871) but Nietzsche did so to point out that when Aristotle used the word in his poetics—referring to the way a successful tragedy could purge the audience's passions by bringing them to experience terror and compassion in the safe, bounded setting of the theater—his use of the term was ambiguous and philologists were not sure whether the discharge referenced medical or moral phenomena.[73] When later in his work Freud adopted a psychological meaning for the term *catharsis*, he dropped the reference to abreaction and substituted the term *psychoanalysis* for *cathartic method*.[74] Psychoanalysis then focused on the symbolic dimension of the blockage. Instead of energy it was meaning itself that was stymied and deferred by the quasi-poetic mechanisms of the unconscious—displacement, conversion (metaphor), and condensation (metonymy). It was meaning that needed to be discharged.[75]

With a focus on the symbolic dimension it became less the immediate and explosive experience of cathartic release that produced the psychoanalytic cure but rather the long and painstaking experience of constructing a story that could allow the patient to form a relation to the perhaps unknowable traumatic dimension that had produced the psychosomatic problems in his or her life. Freud eventually abandoned the terms abreaction and catharsis in order to emphasize the symbolic process of what psychoanalysis calls the "talking cure," what Freud called *durcharbeiten* or "working through." Abandoning the terms *catharsis* and *abreaction* Freud also dropped the literary connotation that connects abreaction/catharsis to the collective emotional experience of a spectator, in a safe, bounded space (the theater), witnessing the public dramatization of traumatic events in the lives of culturally mythic individuals—that is, characters widely recognized within a shared cultural framework. From a historical perspective, psychoanalysis effected the transformation of fundamental features of the abreaction/catharsis experience by turning it into the individualized experience of a solitary patient revisiting personal trauma in the safe, bounded space of the analyst's office. Behaviorist theory transformed the idea even further when catharsis/abreaction were integrated into the technique of flooding.

Flooding takes catharsis back into a collective public space, although that space is neither theatrical nor medical, but instead, I would argue, the space of an atomized and alienated ritual. This is the increasingly unbounded sphere of the modern shopping center, with the agoraphobic herself as both the actor/spectacle of anguish and a member of the audience/spectator of her publicly displayed reaction—behavior she will therapeutically reflect on in increasingly private ways with her therapist and, following the self-help manuals, in her diaries—until the technique of in vivo flooding comes to look like a normal shopping expedition.[76]

### *Abreaction in Behaviorism: War Neurosis*

Half a century after Freud and Breuer, behaviorists picked up the term *abreaction*, disassociating it from catharsis and hysteria studies and emphasizing its connection to Pavlovian theory and war neurosis. The use of the term in connection with women's bodies faded as the notion was increasingly associated with what was called "shell shock" in World War I, "battle fatigue" in World War II, and "post traumatic stress disorder" after the Vietnam War. With the behaviorist appropriation of the term, it was no longer used in connection with women's bodies and the dramatic, curative powers that could accompany somatization. When Isaac Marks and Richard Stern suggested in their 1973 study that the success of flooding in the treatment of their mostly female patients with agoraphobia could be explained by the process of abreaction, they did not footnote Freud and Breuer's 1895 hysteria studies, but William Sargant's 1957 book on his experience treating soldiers suffering from the trauma of World War II, *Battle for the Mind: Introduction to Physical Methods of Treatment in Psychiatry.*

Sargant's book explains his success in using "drug abreaction" to treat patients suffering war neuroses after World War II. Referring to both Freud and Pavlov, Sargant elaborates a new behavioral paradigm explaining not only the psychological structure of battlefield trauma but also the psychology behind a wide array of phenomena, such as the symbolic ritual of North Carolina's religious snake handlers, the popularity of Chinese communist leaders and the appeal of rock and roll music to British teenagers. Sargant's writing was used by Marks to explain the effectiveness of this most important technique of the behavioral arsenal with respect to agoraphobia. "Abreaction," Sargant writes, "dat[es] from the time of Breuer and Freud's early studies in the treatment of hysteria, when they observed that some patients were helped by 'just talking it out.' Freud had found that 'affectless memories without any release of emotion' were almost useless; meaning that unless a doctor could get his patients to relive the emotions originally associated with a repressed experience that had caused a neurosis, the mere fact of his remembering the experience would not constitute a cure."[77] He adds that, in 1920, "William Brown had suggested that emotional abreaction was often a far more efficient means of curing a war neurotic than simple suggestion under hypnosis. 'Suggestion removes the symptoms, but abreaction removes the cause of the symptoms by producing fully adequated re-association.'"[78]

In World War I the same abreactive treatment had been successfully used on soldiers, usually together with hypnotism rather than drugs, Sargant notes. During the Second World War, Sargant, together with several other British military doctors, reported that barbiturates were successful in evoking abreaction, to cure traumatized survivors of Dunkirk and the London Blitz. In 1944 they began using ether to attain "a far greater degree of explosive excitement" in their wartime hospital.[79] Notes Sargant,

> It then occurred to my colleague Dr. H. J. Shorvon and to myself that this collapse phenomenon, which we were now repeatedly observing, might correspond to Pavlov's 'transmarginal inhibition,' which occurs when the cortex has become momentarily incapable of further activity. We remembered how, in some of Pavlov's dogs, the Leningrad flood [when water seeping into the laboratory brought an unplanned trauma to the canine experiments] had accidentally

abolished the conditioned behavior patterns implanted by him, and how this allowed other patterns to take their place. Was the same thing happening in some of the patients who had collapsed. If so, we might also expect others to become more suggestible or show reversal of previous patterns of behavior and thought, because a *"paradoxical"* phase of brain activity was being produced. ...[80]

The proximity of abreaction to the concept of catharsis brought a dramatic dynamic to the phenomena known as abreaction, but the same did not occur with Pavlov's "transmarginal inhibition." Describing trauma as a shock that—while bringing the self beyond the limit of its prior experience—may induce a kind of zero state that could wipe clean, as it were, the previously recorded patterns of everyday life, all the metaphorics are there to further translate trauma, using the technology of the day, into measurable units like brain waves. Pavlovian experiments and treatments for war neurosis took the theory of abreaction farther from the cathartic method and closer to its current home in electric shock treatment and biochemistry. According to behaviorist theory, the self is a mechanically organized, rational structure that can break down when confronted with paradoxical stimuli. The "paradoxical phase" is produced, Sargant explains, when the patient has a reverse reaction, such as collapse or diminution of agitation, brought on by the very stimuli that triggered the agitation in the first place.

While the practice of transmarginal inhibition may seem similar to a treatment like paradoxical intention, in one important way it is not. Therapists like Amr Barrada who use techniques of paradoxical intention with phobic patients need not postulate a zero state of brain activity, a "cortex" that "has become momentarily incapable of further activity" in order to explain how paradox may trigger a productive change. Paradoxical intention differs from transmarginal inhibition in the same way that a Zen master's use of the paradoxical structure of a koan differs from an electroshock treatment. The former is part of a long cultural tradition of skills that can bring about personal change and lead to enlightened thinking; the latter destroys brain matter and forces upon the patient a violent form of forgetfulness. Transmarginal inhibition is a treatment method with little regard for linguistic or symbolic meaning. Its evolution into electric shock treatment is also the most violent cultural adaptation of the idea of abreaction. It is no wonder that it is developed in a military context.

Sargant's descriptions of wartime abreactions tell powerful stories of soldiers, psychologically broken from unspeakable battlefield experiences, who relive scenes of horror and emerge from the drug-induced abreaction ready to articulate their experience and ultimately let go of it. There are stories of civilians petrified months later from the experience of having been buried alive under buildings collapsed during the London blitz, finally able to resume normal daily life after recalling the terror in a drug-induced state. Timing mattered in this treatment which worked best, Sargant found, when it was done as soon as possible after the initial trauma. Its effectiveness diminished as the period between treatment and initial onset increased. Sargant also found that, curiously, the patient did not always need to recall an initial traumatic episode. In some cases it was enough for the doctor simply to use powerful suggestion when the patient was in an altered state in order to produce a state of fear that would lead to the kind of emotional collapse that could bring about a cure. So, while timing mattered, space in some sense did not. It did not in the sense that the relation between the trauma and its situatedness, were not thought to be a necessary component in the clinical production of abreaction. The traumatic memory could be held in the body without maintaining a strong connection to a remembered story of the original traumatic events.

The practice and theory of abreaction evolved from its initial psychiatric use on female hysterics in the late nineteenth century to its later application involving soldiers in the twentieth-century European battlefield. Eventually it was integrated into the technique for treatment of agoraphobia known as flooding. Freud, who had initially believed that his hysterical patients were recounting real incidents of sexual abuse in their childhood, eventually came to regard those stories as fantasy. The patient's situated knowledge of her story was replaced by a mental location in fantasy. Some feminists have argued that this theory served to mask the child abuse that was really taking place in the Victorian household, and that the truth of the trauma of abuse should be uncovered, or that at least its possibility be investigated.[81] However, in both cases—the early psychoanalytic work with hysterics and the later work on abreaction in war neurosis—researchers found that neurotic behaviors could be "successfully" treated with fantasy replacements for the "real" environmental story of initial trauma. The only logistical consideration with abreaction is the temporal one: the sooner one treats the neurotic symptom, the better the chances that abreaction will work. With electric shock treatments, original triggers are completely out of the picture since the theory has evolved to say that any story, any physical act that provokes a state of agitation equal to that of the initial trauma might work to produce a cure. Thus, when Marks points to the "organic memories" or "somatizations" that can sometimes accompany abreaction, he does so more as a reminder to behavioral therapists that they "need not spend much time probing for meaning, which in any case may emerge as exposure goes on."[82] Even the spatialization of memory as a bodily mark is ignored as a meaningful moment in the abreactions of agoraphobics undergoing flooding.

In the behaviorist approach to abreaction, the qualitative aspect of a trauma, its nonlinear situatedness in time—that is, its historical emplacement—is discarded. Instead, behaviorist theories and techniques place value on the quantitative aspects, the linear time frame that tells how long it has been since the actual traumatic event took place. Rather than maintaining the connection between environmental and mental states, behavioral theorists that built on the premises of abreaction, like their earlier psychoanalytic colleagues, pursued a theory that separated subjectivity and social space. Both groups relocated sources of neurotic behavior—one in a mechanistic notion of patterned brain activity, the other in the symbolic dimension of experience. Both the symbolic and the mechanistic could be studied and treated independent of their relation to social space. Behaviorists like Sargant theorized that physical modalities such as electric shock therapy and even lobotomy were all ways in which brain patterns could be altered and neurotic symptoms dispelled. This disposable connection between self and space is what Marks had in mind in 1966 when he wrote, following psychoanalytic thinking, that "general anxiety ... is attached [only] *secondarily to its setting*,"[83] meaning that the public setting does not in itself provoke anxiety.

*Behaviorism and Space: Habits without Habitats*

Behaviorism, like psychoanalysis, finds that the agoraphobic's anxiety is only secondarily attached to place: it is a somatized memory of a trauma that can be viscerally recalled by public space, but its relation to public space is utterly unrelated to the original trauma. Public space is unrelated in the sense that public places are not the original scenes of the trauma. In Freudian terms the place tells us that the psyche has "displaced" the memory, away from the original source and onto another seemingly unrelated site in order to throw the conscious mind off track and (paradoxically) leave a trace of how to find the way back by choosing a site that the psyche can nevertheless recognize because it has some motivated relation to the original trauma. Finding the motivated relation is something that the talking cure will help the patient do. In behavioral terms, the displacement is also a means of throwing the psyche off track, but the connection with psychoanalysis stops there. For the behaviorist the patient's motivation in "choosing" a particular trigger site for phobic reactions need not be of any interest with respect to the cure. The only value of the trigger site to the cure is that it can be used to provoke a physical reaction that can then be treated as a mechanistic behavior that can be altered with specific mechanistic skills. My argument in this book is that both of these approaches are wrong with respect to the role of public space. Both approaches say that the patient unconsciously "chooses" the trigger site. I am saying that the trigger site—monumental space—chooses the patient. And then the patient chooses to avoid the trigger site.

This is an important distinction. Psychoanalysis creates a therapeutic technique that uses the trigger site as a symbolic value detached from its actual place. Behaviorism creates a technique that uses the trigger site as an actual place dissociated from its symbolic value. The greater success of behaviorism could well be the fact that it understands something about the material value and active power of place in the disorder. The fact that it also dissociates symbolic values from place—it makes no value judgment about whether monumental public space with its gapping emptiness is something that urban citizens have valid reasons to withdraw from—turns behaviorist methods into skill-training techniques in order to habituate patients to the status quo.

The failures of both the behaviorist and the psychoanalytic methods point to the need for a method that can both value the power of public space and teach the patient to make judgments about the self in relation to these powerful spaces, judgments that are not merely reactive but full of awareness of the power of space and its affects on the self. In other words, the agoraphobic appears to need skills to recognize the social and physical power of place and the demands that such space will place on the self. A treatment that is embedded in the built environment as a spatially powerful site recognizes not only the symbolic features of public space but also the intensely interactive physical features of this space. Because the intensity of public space makes demands on the self as a collective and historically given entity, the individualist notions of self so important to psychoanalysis and behaviorist treatments cannot address the larger self that is so forcefully called on by monumental and modernist-inspired forms of public space.

Behavioral treatments of agoraphobia point to the contradiction between the power of public space and the psychological theories of the modern self. Thus, we are brought to a historical moment when spatially disembedded theories of abreaction inform the understanding and treatment of agoraphobia, one of the most persistent and spatially embedded of all neurotic disorders. As it is now, the agoraphobic can only stand trembling in public sites that refuse to recognize him.

While Marks was by far the most vocal advocate for the connection between agoraphobia and public space, he did not see the public sites his patients complained of as holding any special power over the citizenry as such. In his work there is no sense that shopping centers and urban freeways are difficult places for the modern self to inhabit. And with regard to abreaction as the force behind the skills he passed on to his patients through flooding, here, too, Marks's position is not strong. He is unsure in the end whether it is abreaction or merely habituation that explains the limited successes of this intense-exposure in vivo method. He writes, "Short sallies into agoraphobic situations from brief efforts of willpower lead to only temporary gains unless *pressed to the point of habituation* as is done in a concerted program of exposure treatment [i.e., flooding]."[84]

Behavioral experiments using flooding point to both habituation and abreaction as theoretical explanations for the curative powers of this technique. In my mind, habituation is a better explanation for what agoraphobics who are lobotomized or medicated experience when intensely exposed to public space: their affect is dulled and their behavior can resemble an almost mechanical form of repetition. Intense exposure in vivo without surgical or chemical lobotomy, on the other hand, does appear to provoke the curative release of abreaction. And yet, abreaction repeated time and again in commercial spaces that overwhelm with their scale and intensity may lose its curative power and become, after all, mere habituation.

All in all, treatments of intense in vivo exposure—whether they achieve habituation or abreaction—are still based on the assumption that space and subjectivity are inseparable phenomena. Regardless of how the theoretical explanations neglect or misjudge the role of public space in the use of flooding to recover the public self, the term *in vivo* means precisely that the cure cannot be effected without public space. Both kinds of treatments are inseparable from space. To return to another explanatory model (previously discussed in chapter 3), we might say that, while habituation describes subject/space phenomena in terms that resemble the Deleuzian-Guattarian notion of subjects in repeatable striated space, abreaction comes close to what Gilles Deleuze and Félix Guattari describe as the nomadic subject in smooth space because it describes mysterious phenomena that confounds the rational mind/body frameworks that have long stood as the foundation of modern medicine and of so much of Western thinking. For this reason the limited successes of flooding stands out, as does the sickness of agoraphobia, as signs that the self is inseparable from space and that certain forms of space are, as the medical literature puts it, pathogenetic to certain kinds of selves.

### *Flooding as Systematized Abreaction: A Ritualized Commercial Interruption that Recovers the Person of Surplus Sensibility as a Consumer Self*

The role of abreaction in behaviorism is rarely noted apart from the possibility that repeated abreactions lead to habituation. Marks puts it this way:

> Abreaction and exposure are overlapping phenomena. They share theoretical conundrums though fear reduction from abreaction appears to be more erratic. The effects of abreaction seem similar whether the emotion is induced by drugs or psychological means or occurs spontaneously. Symptom relief may result from several mechanisms. …
>
> … . *The exposure principle has been recognized for centuries but was only systematized recently in behavioral treatment.* …[85]

Abreaction, Marks explains, is more erratic than the exposure in vivo method of flooding. It is, he seems to be saying, a force in and of itself, recognized for centuries. Flooding is the modern, systematized version of abreaction, a mode of harnessing the erratic force of abreaction through repetitions. An agoraphobic patient undergoing flooding will experience that shopping center repeatedly. If the first experience is an abreactive one, the tenth one may not be. Thus, flooding is an abreaction that may become habituation, enacted less frequently for dramatic, cathartic effect and more frequently as a skill to be acquired. When abreaction is systematized and made to resemble habituation, the mysterious relationship that our emotional life has to our bodies, the relationship that seems to be at the core of the abreaction's power to effect a self-cure, is systematized as well. When this happens, the power of the abreactive experience may be simply functioning as a modern form of cultural ritual that turns a self of surplus sensibility into a consumer self.

In the 1970s, when behaviorism introduced the technique of flooding and repeatedly brought the agoraphobic woman to the shopping center, the combined affect of abreaction and habituation made the cure for agoraphobia strategically related to the perfection of the consumer self. As a cultural ritual, abreactive flooding appears to function like a commercial interruption in an otherwise normative program of shopping. Flooding harnesses the somatic intensity of an abreacted emotion and fits it into the shopping experience much as a commercial break that arouses conscious or unconscious desire fits into a televised melodrama or comedy: its disruptive incidence need not be related in anyway to the story being told. Culturally we learn to segregate these moments from the temporality of storytelling, just as with flooding the agoraphobic learns to separate the experience of abreacted emotions from the everyday demands of shopping.

We know that agoraphobia often manifested itself in the 1970s as an inability to shop. An interview with an agoraphobic patient in the United States that was printed in the *Syracuse Post-Standard* in 1978 provides a typical tale. "'Suddenly,'" the patient tells us, "'I found myself unable to go places I used to go to. I couldn't grocery shop. I didn't want to go to the store. And if I did, I was just very, very scared about leaving the house. ... I could go to work but as far as shopping was concerned, I'd get so sick before I'd have to go that my heart would pound, I'd get watery knees. I just sensed danger all around me. I felt that I was going to be mugged or beaten, that something terrible was going to happen to me. ...'"[86]

Similarly, it is common to see the demonstration of a successful cure for agoraphobia at this time framed as the relearning of shopping skills. Here is an excerpt from a booklet published in the 1970s titled *Agoraphobia: Symptoms, Causes, Treatment* and written by Arthur Hardy, an American doctor who specializes in the treatment of phobic disorders. Reporting on the dramatic cure of an agoraphobic patient, he writes, "Once freed of her fears, Anna did many other things she hadn't dreamed possible, including blowing $1,200 in a department store in her elation over being able to shop without anxiety."[87]

In both of the above cases, the patients were reportedly cured of the unreasonableness of their fears by the behaviorist techniques of flooding. It is easy to see how this intense form of exposure in vivo is as much an educational skill being learned as a medical cure undergone. "[B]lowing $1,200 in a department store" is not simply a sign of being cured of agoraphobia, but more accurately a form of reward for having successfully learned to play the new role assigned to the middle-class consumer in the 1970s: shopping on credit.

Considering this larger social picture of how behaviorism operated, we should not be surprised when we come to find that behaviorist techniques and vocabularies of self-management were now entering the new social form of the shopping centers by way of agoraphobics engaged in flooding practice. In the techniques of flooding, behaviorism takes abreaction far from the psychoanalytic field where intense somatic reactions were channeled in cathartic method. Abreactive flooding is a modern ritual, one of whose aims is to purge what is considered the "surplus sensibility" that arises in homogeneous space. In this case, it purges the sensibility that interferes with a well-functioning consumer self.

## Conclusion

In this chapter I have argued that behavioral techniques to treat agoraphobia appear at a particular historical moment when the modern public self lacks skills to negotiate changing forms and demands of public space. The behavioral treatments for agoraphobia show us how those who, with great anxiety, inexplicably withdraw from the our era's most common sites of assembly—our shopping centers, our agoras—can most effectively be reinserted there. Lobotomy, I pointed out, is not just a sad chapter in the history of agoraphobic treatments. It is more likely related to the most common treatments for agoraphobia today: drugs that sever the connection between our most refined tactile capabilities, our feelings, and social space. Abreactive flooding is a technique that, unlike pharmacological remedies, maintains the connection between the agoraphobic and public space. But it maintains this connection paradoxically by training the agoraphobic to not make symbolic connections between her anxiety and her surroundings. Importantly, the techniques of flooding, we have seen, transfer skills effective in recovery from the trauma of war zones to commercial zones where surplus sensibility has interfered with normal shopping. The shopping center that enters the everyday life of so many urban dwellers during the 1960s and 1970s has "chosen" the agoraphobic, it appears, and in the next chapter we will explore why.

CHAPTER 6

# The Twentieth-Century Urban Commons

## *Neoliberal Universes of Nonrecognition*

> … freeways, airports, supermarkets, but also the airways and seemingly less material and indeed more abstract space, such as message- and image-bearing screens, cable networks, radio waves, satellites. Such spaces are the opposite of places, in whose organization cultural anthropologists were wont to read or decipher—or think they could read or decipher—people's identities, their reciprocal relations, and the symbols of their common history. In these "non-places," one may decipher neither identity, relation, nor history.
>
> —**Marc Augé,** *Non-Places: Introduction to the Anthropology of Supermodernity*

Paradoxically, many U.S. metropolitan areas are both recovering from their transformation into sprawling edge cities (the new light-rail plans to promote densification in cities and curtail automobile use in large cities of the Midwest and Southwest attest to this) and also dysfunctionally growing without regard to the broader ecological niche they inhabit. In terms of architectural style, we can track the two trends through the transformation of the modern shopping center. By the mid-1990s the postwar, state-financed modernist city, with its "degree zero" planning, had given way to new alliances between public resources and private profiteering, leading to both the gigantic version of the shopping center, the megamall—that intense, island of entertainment in an asphalt ocean—and the new urbanist version, the privatized simulation of a prewar town commons. Overall in the United States, public space has been increasingly privatized in the neoliberal economic order of the last few decades.[1] American urban critics warn that even in Europe, the source of modern city design, where neither the scale of commercialization nor the scope of modernist urban renewal ever reached what it did in the United States, a "McWorld" of urban transformation is not long in coming.

A common pattern connects the new forms of "dysfunctional" growth and the new behavioral treatments for agoraphobia with their retraining programs to desensitize and most often medicate the patient for reentry into public space. Where urban critics use terms like "free-floating" and "depthlessness" when referring to the transformation of public space in recent decades in land-grabbing cities like Houston, Los Angeles, and Phoenix, the American Psychiatric Association's Diagnostic and Statistical Manual (editions III and IV) reduces the symptoms of agoraphobia to "free-floating" panic unrelated to public space. Increasingly, the treatments for agoraphobia reflect the same neoliberal public/private alliances we see in today's city planning, but here it is an alliance between medical science and pharmaceutical companies. Neoliberal capitalism provides a shared spatial imaginary to both urban and medical phenomena: in descriptions of both the so-called postmodern city (Los Angeles) and the dominant treatments for agoraphobia, the urban experience is depicted as increasingly "depthless," a virtual public space that both overwhelms and gives authority to one member of the human sensorium—the sense of sight—while it "desensitizes" or numbs the other senses through a paradoxical combination of dull, vast, homogeneous structures and intense, sensory-overloaded surfaces and interiors. The result is a proliferation of public sites where citizens become adept at techniques of self-desensitization or become persons of surplus sensibility. The tactile sense is perhaps the most devalued and deskilled of the senses in this new form of urban space, as pedestrians venture through cities of sprawling spatial homogeneity less on foot and increasingly behind the wheel of a car or, as an armchair traveler, in front of a TV screen.

In this chapter we continue our study of the transformation of public space as a structure of feeling by following a genealogy of the shopping center from its post-war exportation to Great Britain and France to its present evolutionary points in the megamall and the new urbanist town center. We then consider this history of the built form and the demands it makes on its shopping subjects in the light of agoraphobia treatments that use techniques of abreaction/flooding. Paying close attention to issues of gender, we consider the clinical literature detailing treatments for agoraphobic soldiers and women in the second half of the twentieth century. The ethnographic fieldsite offered by the clinical literature suggests that urban inhabitants of modernity's most technologically mediated forms of homogenous public space create gendered public selves suitable to what the anthropologist Marc Augé has called "a universe of nonrecognition."

### Reconnecting the Feel to the Form of Dreaded Public Space: Early Behaviorist Treatments and the European Import of the U.S. Shopping Center

The behaviorist treatments of agoraphobia point to the shopping center as the best site at which to study changes in public space as changes in a structure of feeling. Shopping centers were just beginning to appear in the everyday space of Londoners at the time that Dr. Isaac Marks and his colleagues were escorting their female patients on therapeutic shopping expeditions. As in the North American case of the postwar urban freeway system, agoraphobics were not the only ones to voice fear of the new form of commercial space cropping up in the everyday experience of public life in Britain. Nonpathologized voices of dissent were coming from urban residents. In shopping market surveys of this period we see that women spent much more of their out-of-house time—their "public sphere" time—in shopping centers than men, and the complaints they registered about the new form of space were similar to those of agoraphobic women.

The modern supermarket was exported to Europe and other places across the globe after the Second World War, in large part by the overseas division of the U.S. National Cash Register Company.[2] In France and Britain, the new architecture of the modern supermarket introduced dramatic changes in the everyday experience of grocery shopping. The small-scale, two-person exchange of the vendor and buyer in the stalls and small shops that characterized most European food markets at this time was transformed by the new behavior—known as "self-service"—through which customers could wander freely through the aisles of the gigantic warehouse structures picking up and examining potential purchases at their leisure. The American entrepreneur M. M. Zimmerman was one of the main vehicles of this expansive new approach to food selling. Indeed, his buzzwords continue to resound, to this day, the American gospel of self-service. Zimmerman described his National Cash Register Company's sales of tills to foreign countries in terms of a generous American foreign policy: "acting with enlightened-self interest," he claimed, the U.S. company "served its retailing clients in far flung places by helping them into their initiation into American Super Market know-how, thus demonstrating the democratic co-operation possible in American private enterprise."[3] "Shoppers are the same the world over," wrote Zimmerman in 1955 by way of a caption for a photo of customers using a till from the National Cash

Register Company at the checkout of a new store in Nigeria, as if a shopper were a ubiquitous and universal cultural category. The new American model of food retail required both a new architectural structure and a new sales psychology. The new shopping markets thus provide us with a mirror in which to examine the relation between the new type of consumer and the new forms of built environment.

The salesmanship textbooks of the period reveal that the new psychology appeared on the scene just as the salesperson dropped out of the experience of food shopping and the interaction changed from a two-person exchange between buyer and seller to one between buyer and goods. Cultural historian Rachel Bowlby describes how "the salesman [becomes] an obstacle rather than a facilitator. But what he is obstructing is a process that in the 1950s came to be seen as potentially *automatic:* it occurs when certain 'responses' to universally effective aesthetic stimuli can be set in motion. If only buyer and goods can be given the chance to 'meet' in private, without the need for words or the presence of a third, then the requisite purchase-desires will be aroused in the buyer *as though by nature*, by the sheer *force of sensory attraction* exerted by the product or its display."[4]

A more intense role in making judgments was thus given over to the visual senses as the postwar "science" of salesmanship psychology, using behavioral "measurements" of stimuli and response, was applied to fill the gap where the salesperson once stood in the two-person, face-to-face shopping exchange. Salesmanship practices became marketing "techniques" based on a pseudoscience of "identifiable" and "repeatable" conditions that promised to make knowledge of customer behavior predictable in advance. Customers were no longer viewed individually, as individual personalities passing the window or crossing the threshold of the store to be strategically sized-up and handled by a savvy salesperson. In the new shopping center, customers "have multiplied into a '*mass*,' and the mass is conceived of as undifferentiated, divisible into identical units and much the same psychologically wherever you tap it. In applications of *behaviourist psychology* in the 1950s, all customers are thought of as reacting in the same way to the same stimuli: some things they will automatically want, and others they will find they want once their resistances—often described as the 'inhibitions formed by their culture'—have been removed."[5]

While the customer was rationalized to become a predictable subject habituated to universal stimuli, using concepts from behaviorist psychology, a new figure emerged on the scene: the researcher who will observe the customer at a distance trying to puzzle out her choices in the form of statistical and other calculations. Thus a new form of two-person engagement emerged on the scene: "the ubiquitous clipboard survey of post-war market research" which will "either chart customers' movements without them knowing it, or present a set of questions and possible answers that are already settled and planned."[6]

Techniques of behavioral psychology thus began to operate extensively outside the clinic and in the public domain at this time. The behaviorist techniques of self-making were entering the shopping center through many paths, not only through the clinical experiments of our reluctant agoraphobic, who was brought there for the repeated abreactions of the "flooding" technique. The new material structures of the shopping center brought new demands on the self, demands that came in the form of treating the customer as a part of the market-targeted masses. The new architectural form introduced by mass-marketing of food involves a concrete, warehouselike structure in which huge quantities of goods could be displayed without window dressing or any conventions that would interfere with the consumer's view that she was getting goods for a bargain. Industry documents of the era show that the warehouse grocery was the outcome of marketing debates in which it was determined that the real interest of consumers always came down to cheapness. Ironically, for some supermarkets this resulted in dissimulation: the store must appear to spend nothing on it appearance. The store had to do this, even as it spent money to present itself as a kind of circus.

According to the era's American-based mass-marketing guru, Bernard Trujillo, supermarkets had to put on a permanent show, like a fair or circus.[7] A description of the eleventh store in a Carrefour chain of *hypermarchés* (super-supermarkets) built in France in the early 1960s that even outdid the American model in sheer square footage, parking lot size, and diversity of goods offered alongside food items, tells us that "the eleventh Carrefour opened at Creteil new town, to the south-east of Paris, in late 1968—this one had thirty-six checkouts, fifteen hundred parking spaces and a selling area of 7,000 square metres. Its chief architect spoke in Trujillo's language of the 'show where the customers are the actors,' of how 'we give them *a stage which conditions them, we put them in a can whose colours, smells and sounds set all their senses going.' The customer is 'conditioned' for buying as the product is 'conditioned' or packaged for selling.*"[8]

The introduction of the supermarket brought along a new spatial form in the built environment, the warehouse as grocery store. In many ways, the supermarket chain store was a predictable, homogeneous space filled with an ever greater heterogeneity of goods. The shopper had a new role in this space of paradoxes: from the top down she was rationalized as a mass consumer. And yet her full range of senses, her sensorium, was treated like a pincushion, with more and more intense demands on her sensory system. She was engaged as a new kind of sensory-heightened social actor who appeared to require a new kind of sensory-social self. For both the nonpathologized shopper and the more vulnerable agoraphobic at this particular historical moment, the shopping center was a place where sensibilities were being experimented with: how much "heightened sensibility" could a customer handle without becoming overwhelmed? What happened to the shopper under the influence of heightened sensory experiences? From the agoraphobic's perspective, the shopping experience engaged her as a person of "surplus sensibility," and this was an unfortunate side effect of the new sensory-social self.

Yet agoraphobics were not the only customers who abhorred the new shopping spaces. Contemporary critics of these shopping innovations include Vance Packard, whose famous 1957 book on the new marketing psychology, *The Hidden Persuaders,* described "the new jungle called the supermarket," and French novelist Jean-Marie Gustave Le Clezio whose characters in *Les Géants* (The Giants, 1973) wander in a hypermarket world that is pure system, a universal network of the electrical grid. Metaphors of the supermarket that appeared in the critical literature of this period include those of a jungle, a trap, a giant computer, a prison, and a labyrinth.[9]

While the shopping center was quickly becoming a common feature of the urban landscape in America and France at this time, the British supermarket made a slower appearance, apparently having a harder time creating the new sensory-social self. A 1963 sociological report called "Shopping in Suburbia" commissioned by a British supermarket chain and several high street stores to produce a "report on housewives' reactions to supermarket shopping" offers statistics related to opinions and feelings about supermarkets gleaned from interviews with consumers. The report calls the new shopping experience a "post-war revolution in retailing" and a "minor revolution in social habits."[10] The report's findings help us better imagine the sites to which Marks's behaviorally treated patients were most probably taken on their desensitization and flooding expeditions. The study focuses on the difficulty of following in the footsteps of American practice, where both cars and supermarkets are fundamental to the newly built postwar suburbs. The chief problem for British supermarket development, it appears, was that Britain's older suburbia had local shops for customers on foot. In Britain people did not yet shop by car, and this created problems for carrying all those items that the gigantic warehouse supermarket made available at lower cost. Marks's patients were all taken to the shopping center by public transportation or were driven in the car of the practitioner. In the 1963 report, each shopper is described as a "'housewife,' a title that starts at the age of sixteen and applies universally to the female sex. There is not a non-housewife, male or female, to be seen among the survey's respondents."[11] Those interviewed describe supermarkets as "maze-like," and it is clear that the new environment is not always a happy one for the British housewife. One in six of those interviewed describe it "as a place where you are being watched in case you take anything without paying." In addition to the feeling of anonymity, the feeling that "nobody knows you in supermarkets," customers were faced with feeling of being "lost, lonely or under suspicion."[12] The report paints a picture of the 1960s British shopping center as a space where even nonpathologized, "normal" British women feel uncomfortable and vaguely threatened.

Another problem uncovered by the 1963 survey is that customers feel that the supermarket is a place where "impulse shopping is at its height." Clients express the sense that entering the shopping center is like entering a den of iniquity, and they might be unable to resist the lure. "It is striking," Bowlby writes, "that when supermarkets have not yet established themselves definitively in Britain, 'impulse buying' has already entered everyday language, in the form of *an infection to be avoided—or even a latent instinct to be resisted*."[13] In the survey shoppers complain not only of loneliness, but also of the aggressive behavior of other shoppers: pushing and shoving is regarded as a problem by almost one-third of those interviewed. One respondent mentions that "some of the women push and push with wire baskets and once I was pushed into some butter and then I swore I wouldn't go there again—but I was there the next week."[14] Despite the industry's efforts to create a carnivalesque atmosphere—more than fifty Tesco store openings in the single year 1966 were characterized by promotions, gimmicks, and glitz, sometimes featuring a knight named "Sir Save-A-Lot"—the early 1960s survey, Bowlby argues, shows that "supermarket shopping in Britain was still regarded as *a skill* to be acquired."[15] Considered in this light, the new exposure treatments for agoraphobia at this time were functioning as a training mechanism used to teach perhaps the most sensitive women the skills to inhabit and shop in this new and rather threatening space. The agoraphobia material shows that flooding/exposure in vivo could be understood on a continuum of training techniques offered to produce the new sensory-social self that will inhabit these new forms of homogeneous space.

The appearance of the shopping center at this time marked the beginning of an era when all aspects of food production—from its agricultural beginnings to its retail ends—would be industrialized and commodified. Mass production and distribution of food represented a new engine of economic growth, a new arena for capitalization. In all these areas, for better and for worse, we see men and women swept up in the rationalization of social habits and the homogenization of social spaces associated with a new heterogeneity of food. The British example tells us that the recorded increase in the incidence of agoraphobia for women at this time may be related to the experience of women's abrupt insertion into what we have theoretically been calling, following Gilles Deleuze and Félix Guattari, homogeneous space—space that is increasingly "striated" to the point of such extreme intensification and instability that it becomes, for certain inhabitants, "smooth" space, space that is unbounded movement, with pockets of intense emptiness that, for the agoraphobic, are certainly unsupportive and unsafe. Again we need to emphasize that shopping centers do not cause agoraphobia. Like the nineteenth-century *places royales*, they are not causes, but triggers, of agoraphobia. Both sites demand a particular kind of sensory-social self, and as such they raise important ontological issues about how the sensory-social body must change to inhabit these new conditions of social life. Both sites offer historical perspectives on how public life and the public self is being transformed in relation to new forms of social space.

### The Consumer Saturation of Gigantic Space: The Megamall

Agoraphobics of the last century referred to the emptiness of public squares in much the same way that contemporary architectural critics of the time referred to the emptiness of the monumental form in the age of giganticism. In the case of the nineteenth-century public square, this involved the problem of creating a space and a corresponding subjectivity for the nationalized masses. In the last decades of the twentieth century the problems of the public self created in relation to the giganticism of the shopping center are problems of creating a mass identity for the consumer. In the U.S. context we can see a subtle shift of the signs of national space onto private palaces of consumption where they become marketing themes using an allegiance to national space in an economic order that is in fact eroding national borders in the process of creating a globalized neoliberal economic order. Increased size is the most dramatic change in the design of the North American shopping center since the 1960s, when Marks's patients were being "flooded" in its interiors: shopping malls are simply bigger versions of shopping centers. At the same time, the bigger malls are "holding themselves together," as it were, with fantasy themes that often use national and patriotic symbols.[16] These symbols function like the fantasy scenarios of the behaviorist therapist who used imaginal scenes as preliminary techniques to acclimate the agoraphobic to the walk she would eventually take in the real shopping center. As literary historian and critic Klaus Scherpe argued about contemporary novels and the narrative function of their descriptions of city space (see Introduction), "themed" shopping centers and flooding in imagination all point to the power of imaginal means as devices that mediate the way we insert and assert ourselves in urban space.

**Figure 14** Red, white and blue logo over the entrance to the Mall of America (2002). (Photo courtesy of Mall of America.)

A good way to investigate the social relations embedded in this new, themed form of public space is to analyze the space of one of the biggest malls ever built to date. The "Mall of America," which opened in 1992 just outside of Minneapolis, boasts of being the biggest shopping mall in the world. The public relations press kit for the new structure situated the megamall within the pantheon of European civilizations: "It is five times larger than Red Square and twenty times larger than St. Peter's Basilica: it incorporates 2.3 miles of hallways and almost twice as much steel as the Eiffel Tower."[17] This megamall is also a hypernationalist space: its name, "Mall of America," uses the patriotic signifier par excellence and the local newspapers boasts of its function as a "national tourist attraction" that serves not only its regional and national constituency but also foreign shoppers—especially Japanese and European tourists. The ritual opening of the mall included a rendition of the patriotic anthem "America the Beautiful" sung by the famous blues musician Ray Charles (who had sung for both the Ronald Reagan and George H. W. Bush presidential inaugurations) followed by a laser light show, fireworks, and an appearance by Miss America. The mall's logo—a red, white, and blue star bisected by a red, white, and blue ribbon—can be found everywhere: it adorns coffee mugs as well as the sides of city buses (see figure 14). Recalling A. Bernard and Ch. Jung's agoraphobic patient who found Paris Place de la Concorde to be even more horrific than the Swiss Alps (see chapter 2), the Mall of America's director of tourism described the mall as an institution on the scale of Disneyland and the Grand Canyon, revered symbols of the United States.[18]

The Mall of America is an example of giganticism that engages vast tracts of homogeneous space. The parking lot itself, like the lots of most U.S. malls, needs a mnemonic zoo of direction signs to make its empty landscape navigable. Motor vehicle drivers tend to compensate for the disorientation with personalized radio antennae. But disorientation in space is not the only feature the Mall of America shares with other large shopping spaces. Many social critics have argued that "mall-land" is designed to remove its visitors from mundane space and time: you will be hard pressed to find a clock on any wall; there are no windows to tell you how the sun is proceeding across the sky or whether the weather is changing. Shoppers are often shocked to look at their watches and find how quickly the hours have passed in the act of shopping. Television viewers complain of a similar experience when they glance away from their screens only to find they have just spent four hours in a virtual reality. As one critic pointedly observed in his description of the opening of the (mega) Mall of America, the arrows on the well-lit store maps signaling "YOU ARE HERE" are more inclined to raise existential questions and existential angst than to offer directional comfort.[19] Not surprisingly, many women treated for agoraphobia in Minneapolis cite the Mall of America as particularly terrifying.[20]

The inscription of social values in the structure of the largest malls has undergone significant changes in the last two decades—changes that reflect shifts in the economy to a global and flexible capitalist order where traditional demarcations of class, in particular, begin to fade. The prototype for the Minneapolis megamall was the West Edmonton Mall in Edmonton, Alberta. Built in 1981 by the same developers, the Canadian mall has a clear social hierarchy reflected in its spatial arrangement; discount stores like Walgreen's are found on the bottom floor, along with fast food eateries like McDonald's and Burger King; on the second floor, middle-class department stores appear next to yuppie-style restaurants; finally, on the top floor, elite stores like Saks Fifth Avenue are side-by-side with opportunities for elegant dining.[21] The Mall of America makes no such obvious economic distinctions in its shopping space. Underground, however, out of the sight of shoppers and in an area that is strictly for employees only, can be found a recycling station staffed by disabled workers, according to one reporter who was able to make the descent. (Because they are disabled, the contracted waste management company can pay them less than the standard minimum wage.) Above ground, however, the megamall boasts environmental correctness. Browning-Ferris Industries, the company hired to manage the mall's seven hundred tons of monthly garbage, has a small boutique on the second floor that displays a blueprint of the mall's system of garbage shoots, encouraging patrons to sort and throw their varieties of brown, green and clear glass to the recycling station below. A haunting snapshot on the boutique wall shows a scene reminiscent of Fritz Lang's modernist film *Metropolis*: a basement conveyor belt, along which stand workers in protective masks and yellow plastic gloves sorting through the garbage produced in the palace of consumption above.

The Mall of America is characteristic of public spaces that are privately owned and managed for the shopping culture in the United States. Malls have their own security systems separate from that of the municipal police force; they have their own codes of behavior for what is tolerated as licit and illicit public action. Given their status as centers of social congregation—teens, for example, meet for movies and general hanging out; mall walkers and retired people use them to escape the vagaries of the outdoor climate—the mall in the United States have often been described as the modern town hall. However, there is no social contract to ensure that the public's interests are served in these sites. Unlike the city's streets, groups and individuals do not get permission to speak or to stage demonstrations in mall atriums unless their message is inoffensive to mall management and to shopping culture in general.[22] In his book on Los Angeles, Mike

Davis describes how the mall security systems in Los Angeles have turned the city's public spaces into high-tech surveillance centers not only to protect the merchandise but also to sell the idea that mall space is safe.[23] Most megamalls are equipped with a special security that can simultaneously lock all outside entrances and exits in the complex in cases where a missing child is feared to have been abducted (cases of children abducted from the mall being a well-circulated urban legend).

Before even bringing the agoraphobic into this discussion, we can see that the modern agora, still a place of assembly, is hardly a neutral social space. It is explicitly nationalized, as in the case of the Mall of America, but also implicitly nationalized in its self-presentation as a normative space of contemporary civic commerce; it is offered as a site at which to enjoy democracy, as if one of the American citizen's most precious rights was the right to shop. Mobilizing rights discourse for consumer freedom is a commonly heard argument in U.S. culture, as in the following snippet from a radio broadcast in New York City in 1987:

*ANNOUNCER:* Celebrating the bicentennial of the United States Constitution, this is "A More Perfect Union: Prominent Americans Reflect on Our Constitution."

*MOREHEAD KENNEDY:* My name is Morehead Kennedy. In 1979, I was the acting head of the economic section at our embassy in Tehran, and I was held hostage for 444 days. You don't appreciate what freedom is until you've been deprived of it.

When I came home my first instinctive reaction was to go shopping. I sort of sashayed around: maybe I was going to buy this and maybe I was going to buy that, but what I was exercising was purchasing power. The Constitution, we often forget, was designed to ensure that consumers could get a wide variety of things by breaking tariff barriers between the states. These are critical things we often take for granted. Until you've been deprived of them, you don't know what they are.

*ANNOUNCER:* "A More Perfect Union," from WOR Radio 710.[24]

The megamall reveals the contemporary agoraphobic's empty space to be nationalized but mostly as an extension of America as the land of freedom to shop. Homogeneous space is achieved at the megamall less as an affect of visual perspectives, as in the places royales, than as an affect of temporal nondirectives, the well-planned lack of indicators that time is passing: constant lighting; lack of windows to a world where the sun might still indicate passing time; and the absence of clocks, which are elsewhere ubiquitous in Western culture. No wonder mall space is an agoraphobic's nightmare. It is a form of homogeneous space that is constantly becoming smooth space.[25] If it were not for the abstraction of money that regulates almost all exchanges here, the homogeneous quality of mall space would have precariously few visual supports. If not for its vast parking lot, few people would be able to note the mall's particular form of emptiness given that its space is saturated with consumer goods and, usually, shoppers.

### The New Urbanist Antidote to the Shopping Center: Mashpee Commons

While the megamall exemplifies the continuing trend of giganticism in consumer space, new urbanism—a design-oriented approach to planned urban development proposed primarily by architects and journalists[26]— is a more recent but simultaneously occurring architectural trend away from those signature, monumental warehouse buildings set in expansive plains of asphalt. Academics and planning practitioners carry forth the projects of new urbanism—which is primarily known in the United States and, to a lesser extent, in Great Britain[27]—and these projects have the support of a popular movement aimed at stopping the alienation and ecological devastation of suburban sprawl. New urbanists aim to create a close-knit social community through spatial design. The ideal plan allows diverse elements to interact, and includes a variety of building types with mixed uses, intermingling of housing for different income groups, and a strong privileging of the "public realm." The basic unit of planning is the neighborhood, which is limited in physical size, has a well-defined edge, and a focused center. "The daily needs of life are accessible within the five minute-walk," notes James Howard Kunstler.[28] This is the ideal. The actual developments must rely on private developers, and they generally run short of new urbanist aims. Diversity is more easily reached in the spatial arena of mixed building types but rarely achieved with regard to the integration of class, race, and ethnicity.[29]

Whatever its actual flaws in achieving social integration in suburban developments, when the principles of new urbanist design are applied to the traditional big box shopping center, they could have been drawn up by the British agoraphobia club Closed Door. Architects of the new urbanism sound much like the agoraphobic when criticizing the urban conditions that make new urbanism a desired solution: "Asphalt is a social problem. … the more there is, the greater the distances between destinations and the grimmer the landscape. Gradually, people stop walking. Neighbors even stop talking," notes one architect, whose firm, Fields Point Development Company, has been retrofitting shopping centers in American suburbs by

**Figure 15a** Mashpee Commons before: the old shopping center, 1970s. (Courtesy of Mashpee Commons Limited Partnership.)

**Figure 15b** Mashpee Commons after: following the tenets of new urbanist design (1991). Photo from *Suburban Nation* by Andres Duany, Elizabeth Plater-Zyberk and Jeff Speck (2000). Reprinted with permission of the authors.

turning the sites into town centers whose new look fashions itself after the pre–World War II town square. By the mid-1990s Fields Point had thirteen such projects underway throughout the United States. Mashpee Commons, in Mashpee, Massachusetts is one of their projects. Formerly the New Seabury Shopping Center, it was a typical American mall set in an asphalt vastness that shoppers had to traverse to get inside and then renavigate when they left. Fields Point razed the warehouse structure and rebuilt the site with streets, storefronts, sidewalks, benches, a small library, a church, twenty-four apartments that have been earmarked for a balanced mixture of families (with children), senior citizens, single professionals, and so on. In short, Mashpee Commons is a complete simulacra of a small town (see figure 15 on the previous pages).[30]

Only an ethnographic study would show whether or not a shopping complex like Mashpee Commons could more easily integrate the agoraphobic into the shopping experience than the traditional shopping center or the megamall. For instance, would a therapist be able to use Mashpee Commons as the site of a flooding exercise? From a purely spatial perspective, however, many of the agoraphobic's problems seem to be resolved in the new design. It seems reasonable to imagine that, just as a nonpathologized person might choose the small-scale Mashpee Commons over the megamall, so might the agoraphobic. Other issues, however, may remain unresolved about this new kind of space. How, for example, are civic order decisions made within a privatized framework whose primary aim is profitable consumption? How is it decided as to who can live in Mashpee Commons, which religious denomination will inhabit the church building, and which books will be in the library? Since it is privately owned, what does this mean for the range of public activities that are permitted on its grounds? Yet all purely spatial indicators suggest that the new urbanist shopping experience would not disorient the person of surplus sensibility to the same degree that a megamall would.

One criticism made about the new urbanist claim to create community purely by creating appropriate space is that it is a utopian one. Diversity of space does not necessarily create diversity in terms of race, class, and ethnicity. Would the two-dollar cookie be a problem for the agoraphobic of limited means? Would lack of money to shop translate for the sensitive agoraphobic into lack of rights to walk in the pedestrian zones and to sit calmly beside the buildings of such appropriate human scale? While recognizing the important correctives that new urbanism offers to the megascale of modernist city design, retrofitted shopping centers like Mashpee Commons are still subject to the "giganticism" of corporate structures that, under neoliberal regimes, increasingly control domains of public space.[31] The Mall of America and Mashpee Commons, the megamall and the simulacra of the small town, are examples of two simultaneous design trends for the urban commons at the end of the twentieth century in the United States. The agoraphobic sensibility registers the former as a threat. For the latter, the agoraphobic may no longer be able to spatially register threats to public space coming from a privatized simulacra of the public.

The age of modernism has come to an end, but the professional and public critique of its spatial legacies continues apace in the United States and Europe, where pedestrian zones are reemerging in central urban areas that were once subordinate to the car.[32] Whether pedestrians will show up in the clinical literature on agoraphobia waits to be seen.

## A Gendered Reframing of Flooding and Abreaction: Soldiers' Stories and Women's Stories

Modernism no longer reigns in the world of urban design, and as many architects and planners discuss the successes and failures of new urbanism and other proposals to recover from the wreckage of modernist ideals in the built environment, one group in particular is consistently underrepresented in the public debates: feminist architects and planners. The lack of attention to the histories, complaints, and proposed solutions coming from analyses that uncover the particular problems women face in public space is strikingly mirrored in the clinical literature on agoraphobia. Here too, as we have seen in both the nineteenth and twentieth centuries, women's particular problems arising from fears of public space are largely ignored in the dominant treatment modalities. Practice is lagging behind scholarship in both planning and medical domains.

Feminist scholars who complain about this situation in the professions of architecture and planning note how "Gendered histories (Hayden; Greed) and histories that include gender (Birch Wirka; Leavitt) in urban planning have not been able to create a paradigm shift similar to that of Rachel Carson's *Silent Spring* (1962) in environmentalism or to make inroads into policy as occurred when Michael Harrington's *The Other America* (1962) foreshadowed the 'War on Poverty.' Nor did any books, such as Dolores Hayden's *Redesigning the American Dream* (1984), widely heralded as it was, have the power to launch a movement outside of planning or architecture."[33] Despite the production and availability of excellent scholarship documenting issues faced by women in the built environment, the lack of serious attention to these works in mainstream venues is often linked to the lack of women in the profession of architecture and planning. As Sherry Ahrentzen notes,

> quantity of publication does not translate into clout or transformation within the discipline of architecture. In the professional office, feminism (and even the idea of gender) is often highly suspect, even disdained. Many women seeking acceptance in this still male-dominated field—in the United States, 17.5 percent of architects (U.S. Bureau of Labor Statistics 1999) and 15.8 percent of full-time architecture faculty are women (Anthony 2001)—disassociate themselves from talk of gender or even sex difference. Yet certainly something serious is happening when all annual Pritzker Architecture Prize winners are men, as are all winners of the American Institute of Architects (AIA) Gold Medal, an award given annually since 1907.[34]

In the professional realms where the built environment is designed and planned, interest in issues of gender and public space is devalued. Given this wider environment, it should come as no surprise that the pathology of agoraphobia increases for women and the dominant treatments offered to agoraphobic women have a poor record of listening to her complaints and finding an effective remedy.

What urban design scheme should come after modernism? Given their prescient role in mapping emptiness in the modern city as a pathological structure of feeling, agoraphobics should have something important to say in the matter. The treatments offered to them have consistently been ones honed in the experiential domain of the soldier, as if the implicit metaphor for urban life is the battlefield. Perhaps that was the case for the heroic existentialist philosopher of postwar Europe who lived through the bombing and rebuilding of cities. In the United States, where the dominant treatment modalities for the agoraphobic's anxiety are pharmacological, the treatment of soldiers' post-Vietnam and post-Iraq experiences are redefining the meaning of *battlefield neurosis* in a technology-driven era of guerilla and urban warfare. The soldier in the First World War experienced a death rate of approximately ninety soldiers to ten civilians; by the Second World War, the civilian and solider death ratio was around fifty/fifty. In Vietnam, the rate of civilian deaths to soldiers' deaths went up dramatically, and in the current Iraq War, we see ninety civilian deaths for every ten soldiers' deaths.[35] This has changed the soldier's experience of war. As was noted in the introduction to this volume, clinical trials for anxiety medication related to traumatic memory initially developed for Vietnam veterans are now being run in the urban emergency room, where patients suffering from car accidents and rape—urban traumas that occur on a daily basis in our cities—are offered a drug that will block the traumatic memory from lodging itself in a visceral way. The idea is to prevent the trauma from becoming a phobic reaction. Given the direction of clinical research we need to ask, What is the relation between the soldier's experience and the experience of agoraphobia?

In late-twentieth-century behavioral treatment of agoraphobia we see a pattern that was encountered in the nineteenth-century cases. In both centuries, in urban space designated as threatening to the person of surplus sensibility, skills of self-fashioning related to soldiers have some symbolic or experiential advantage. Wearing their military uniforms, the young Frenchmen and the officer from St. Petersburg discussed in chapter 3 could cross through wide open squares that their agoraphobia had prevented them from traversing *en civile.* Similarly, the flooding treatments given to agoraphobics since the 1960s and the rise of behaviorism show that what works (in however limited a way) to recover the soldier's sense of self is what also works to insert a mostly female population of agoraphobics into the new space of the urban shopping center.[36] We have also noted that flooding as a technique of self-management has been criticized by feminists for offering culturally masculine methods of coping with extreme anxiety.[37] We saw how the early, clinically based training programs for flooding in vivo aimed to produce isolated individual selves who could shop alone without purses, friends, or discussion of their inner lives—like military scouts, purged of all relational being except their identification with the consumer masses, armed only with a solitary, confident self. What more can we find that helps us to better understand the relation between the experience of war and the experience of agoraphobia?

### *Soldiers' Stories*

Abreaction, agoraphobia, and the experience of the battlefields of the Second World War in postwar Europe are literally connected in the clinical literature in several cases from the 1950s and '60s where it is discovered that, after years of agoraphobic fear and avoidance of particular public spaces, a patient is cured of agoraphobia by an abreaction that reveals a previous war experience. Let us look at a few such cases.

The first case involves urban space as a trigger of agoraphobia. In 1960, Dr. Jacques Galibert publishes his case study of a French patient whose severe agoraphobia can be traced back to the experience of bombings, as well as Nazi detention in occupied Paris during World War II. The patient, Jean, is a thirty-seven-year-old man who had already been suffering from severe agoraphobia for ten years when he sought treatment in 1959. Jean cannot leave his apartment, and has not done so for several years. Seeking out the "wider problems" of his patient's condition, Dr. Jacques Galibert reports that Jean's first anxiety attack (*crise d'angoisse*) occurred in 1949, when he was in the metro (subway). He had gotten off at the first possible station and had not made use of that means of transportation since. Although the patient "has no idea of the reason" behind the abrupt "*etat d'angoisse*" he experienced at this time, it did leave him with "*un etat de malaise*" that would resurface every time he found himself alone in the street. (Note that this case occurred before the American subsumption of agoraphobia into panic disorders. The word *panic* [*panique*] exists in French but was not used in this article to describe Jean's experience).[38] Within just a few weeks after that initial attack he was unable to leave his apartment by himself. During his first session of therapy, eleven years later, under the influence of a therapeutic dosage of barbiturates and amphetamines, a barrage of stories emerges unsolicited. As Galibert tells us, "He remembers … in 1944 undergoing a police check in a metro station where he was treated as a culprit. One year before, in 1943, during an aerial bombardment, he had spent two days in an underground metro station that had been transformed into a shelter. 'There were dead and wounded in every corner,' he remarked."[39]

After this first session, Jean was so noticeably relieved that he was able to take up his therapist's suggestion and return home "crossing half of Paris" on foot by himself. After several sessions, Galibert notes, Jean was "cured," and remained so during four years of follow-up. Galibert diagnosed his agoraphobia as a classical case of "conditioned reflex," an early behaviorist concept from the research of Ivan Petrovich Pavlov. An initial fear situation occurred while the subject was held immobile, Galibert explains, without the possibility of either escape or self-defense. Two repetitions of a similar fear stimulus in the identical situation of immobility produced a conditioned stimulus. Thereafter, all places in the city that could produce this situation of immobility—buses, the metro, crowded streets—became conditioned stimuli, or agoraphobic triggers. For Jean, the cure for inexplicable bouts of anxiety in certain public spaces was an abreaction that produced memories and a pattern that was recognizable to his therapist. With the emergence of his personal narrative and ten sessions of therapy, his neurotic symptoms disappeared.

Abreaction in Jean's case led to the release of wartime stories that, according to his therapist, provided the means to "decondition" or desensitize him. The example from postwar France suggests that in Britain some of Dr. Isaac Marks's patients may also have been operating in a state of somatically remembered fear for years after the German bombardment of England during World War II. Several cases of agoraphobia published in Britain in 1960, fifteen years after the end of the war, show male patients connecting their wartime experiences with their current phobic fears of space. One doctor noted the cases of four patients he had treated in Sheffield for agoraphobia related to outer space. While many psychologists would not include outer space phobias in the category of agoraphobia, I would argue that, since the launch of Sputnik in 1957 and the Cold War nuclear-arms race, public space has extended itself into a newly technologized outer space. This is broadly reflected at the level of the collective culture in the science fiction films of the period where cities are routinely attacked by alien invaders. In the clinical literature too we see agoraphobics showing up with fears of public space that extend infinitely upward. These may well be unusual variants of agoraphobia, as Dr. Marks notes in his 1976 article "Space Phobia: Syndrome or Agoraphobic Variant."

For the male patients in the 1960 British study published in the *Journal of Mental Science* the link is indeed to the war. The attending doctor, R. J. Kerry, notes that for "a business man of 40 … the fears first became troublesome in 1940 immediately after the 'blitz' on Sheffield, where he was stationed on army service. … His first complaints were of feeling frightened when he was out, when he would break out into a sweat, having to run wherever he was going. He then developed a fear of the world spinning round which was accentuated in open spaces. The fear was worse on route marches. He went sick with these fears at the beginning of 1943 and he was seen once by a psychiatrist…."[40]

When asked to speak about his current fears of outer space some fifteen years after the war had ended, the patient said, "there is so much talk (about outer space) these days—it makes you boggle to think about it. I boggle at the idea of satellites being put up—they are stationary space stations and yet they are going round and round—I can't sort it out."[41]

Similarly, a thirty-three-year-old male patient who had been at one time an elementary school geography teacher felt unsafe because, as he described it in the 1960 study,

> "the earth is a ball spinning round and I am on it." … He became completely incapacitated and had to be admitted to hospital with the fear of "going to disappear into outer space." He felt that his feet were on the ground and that the sky was above and he had to keep reminding himself that the force of gravity was keeping him down—"otherwise I would float into space." … Phrases which commonly occurred included: "It's space that's getting me—the curvature of the globe makes everything insecure." "We are surrounded by *a hostile envelopment*—if I think about it, I want to run for cover. I feel more vulnerable standing still than walking. The globe is a globe and I think of the underneath as well." *At this time he went through a particularly distressing time due to daily reports about the Transantarctic Expedition.* … He would ask, "Can you imagine you are walking on

something unstable" and he would talk of "taking cover from all the space around."[42]

This patient, too, was a soldier, "a navigator in the R.A.F.," during the war, "but [he] does not relate this to his illness," the doctor reports. "He remembers that when [his illness] started he was a geography master using a globe and looking at it as though from outer space."

These men were possibly experiencing what behaviorists describe as *conditioned reflexes*, responses traceable to wartime experiences. In both cases, however, there is also a new awareness of global, empty space in evidence, a new spatial sense owing to satellite technology and Cold War posturing. Both patients report that the radio broadcasts of the Transantarctic Expedition provoked nervous anxiety. A new kind of empty public space—beginning with the radio-transmitted sound images of the Antarctic and ending with outer space—is now notably registering in the popular psyche. These expeditions marked the first extension of international sovereignty into the Antarctic region, officially "colonizing" it as a space that belonged to no one and could therefore be opened to territorial claims by the British and others. (The Antarctic was declared *res nullius* [space belonging to nobody] in 1959 and Britain announced its plan to jointly govern the region with eleven other nations.) News of this new, truly unpopulated *terra nullius* ("no-man's-land," or empty land) came at the same time that Britain was losing its vast overseas colonies, which had been acquired in its imperial era by similar terra nullius–like strategies that declared lands open for occupation because they were *res nullius,* "belonging to nobody." Radio descriptions of the explorers' experience traversing the vast, barren space of the Antarctic must have entered the collective consciousness of all citizens who heard the British Broadcasting Corporation's radio broadcasts, suggesting images of a new form of terra incognita. Meanwhile, Britain was becoming a nuclear power and entered the Cold War, whose battlefields could only be distantly recognized in the often nuclear-powered satellite reconnaissance orbits that altered the night sky over England, as well as in 1950s science fiction movies, with their extraterrestrial invaders. Under Cold War conditions, Antarctica quickly became a terrestrial version of outer space. The agoraphobic reaction to news of the Transantarctic Expedition suggests that, in the popular imagination, Britons were trying to get a handle on the unimaginable vastness of the emptiness that their tax dollars were protecting and their politicians were seeking to govern. It is no surprise that this emptiness should register so strongly in the psyches of spatially sensitive phobic people.

This was a period in which international law was used to bring various areas of vast open space into governable form by labeling it *res nullius.* As

Western legal thought forged its relation to this vast, empty space there was a correlative attempt to produce an epistemic image of this space, one that would register at a collective cultural level larger than the legal sphere. This production of an epistemic image cannot be considered the result of the labor of individual lawmakers; it is instead the product of a much larger cultural sphere. In exploring the modern pathology of agoraphobia in relation to the spheres of res nullius it is possible to recognize how Western culture produces an epistemic imaginary of modern space that is held in "common," both at the discursive level of its various professional languages—legal, geological, psychological—and at the material levels of its technological extensions into space and its physiological extensions into the human mind/body. The epistemic imaginary forms the basis of how modern culture begins to "think" of public space, *res publica*—a space that must be, by its very nature in a secular world, shared with others. The agoraphobic sensibility, in this context, functions not only as "surplus sensibility" but also as a modern registry in which larger cultural processes having to do with public space—space that is just becoming perceptible (due to technological innovations, in this case)—make their mark.

Either as a "conditioned reflex" in a traumatized individual or as a modern registry of new forms of material and cultural space, the imprint of spatial phobias on men in postwar France and Britain reverberates with the soldiers' experience of World War II. War and death, then, are dominant associations with new forms of public space made by the agoraphobic patients in our examples, associations that arise with existential experiences over which humans generally feel they have little control. The experience of agoraphobia allows us to document the relationship between severe nervous anxiety and the changing experiences of space. A drastically changed relationship of the human individual to various forms of public space occurs not only as the result of war experience—a change that for the soldier is not always acknowledged, recognized, or accepted by civilian society—but also as a result of transformations in the popular awareness of space and of material changes in the built environment. Not only places royales, shopping centers, urban freeways, but also outer space and Antarctica: these are all new forms of public space that are characterized by their monumental vastness and by their capacity as cultural forms to hold, as it were, emptiness.

As a cultural form, emptiness may be held or "constructed" in a culture's built environment, in its legal imaginary, or in popular narratives and media descriptions. Culturally given emptiness can circulate in novels and films set in alienating modernist city design, or in radio reports of a trek across Antarctica. From our study of agoraphobia we see that if an individual does not have the proper skills in self-fashioning, the encounter with cultural schemata of emptiness is an encounter that can easily call forth existential anxiety. What are the proper skills to encounter a culture's framing of the very thing it cannot yet name? Agoraphobia suggests that cultures supply their own forms of self, their own sets of skills to encounter such representations of the unrepresentable. The soldier, with his rigorous training, his weapons and uniforms, his cohorts and commanders, appears to be one such form fit for the encounter with built emptiness. It is a form that has wide recognition in the general social order and in public space, especially where troops parade on a regular basis through the city, or in living rooms on the TV. For our nineteenth-century agoraphobic, it was enough to simply put the uniform on or to walk in rank to be able to face the built forms of emptiness that monumental architecture was throwing in his everyday experience at an increasing rate as the modern city grew in size and population.

Modern psychology, from the work of Sigmund Freud to the behaviorists and the biomedical specialists, has taken a special interest in what happens when the soldier's self breaks down, as it often does in the battlefield. These professional fields of self-technology have focused on creating ever new sets of skills to recover the soldier's self. What has been striking in our study of agoraphobia is how these medical skills, from catharsis to flooding, from Xanax to cognitive reasoning—skills sometimes evident in other cultural traditions for other uses, but honed in our own to repair the battle weary soldier—have been handed to nonmilitary selves who are broken under other, very different, circumstances like early marriage, pregnancy, childbirth, and early child care. The circumstances women cite as sources of their sudden experience of unsteadiness in public space are not at all like those of the battlefield. And the skills they might need to recover a public self, given their changed circumstances, may well be completely different than what they are medically offered—unless, of course, what they are offered is what the dominant culture recognizes as the skills necessary for any self recovering from an encounter with the most ubiquitous forms of built emptiness in modern urban space.

### *Women's Stories*

Agoraphobia has allowed us to document anxiety-provoking cultural forms of built emptiness in modern urban space. In addition to the shopping center and the urban freeway, the clinical literature shows that women make other spatial associations with their urban anxiety. One associative element that stands out for the one female patient in the 1960 article on space phobias is an element we have seen in several other cases of female agoraphobia from the nineteenth century. A married woman, twenty-nine years of age, with two children, Kerry reports, associated her agoraphobia with the experience of birthing and caring for children:

> Two children close together (ages 1 and 2 years) were suggested [by the patient] as a reason for worsening of the symptoms. She said she was afraid of "the universe," getting tense when she thought of being upside down and spinning around. She had to listen to space programs on television, "but it's a nuisance when you are interested in things and they frighten you." "The world is unstable and may collide and blow up." She felt that there were peculiar things happening in the universe, e.g. there was *too much radiation*, and there might suddenly be insufficient air. She became worried "about all the collisions there might be up in outer space because of all of this indiscriminate sending up of satellites."[43]

This woman, along with the two former soldiers mentioned earlier, was treated by Kerry in the 1950s as an outpatient at a Sheffield clinic. We are not told whether they received medication, only that they received group therapy. They were tested for physical illness, such as dizziness, inner-ear problems, and the like, and were all found to be physically healthy. As far as this patient is concerned, the worsening of her spatial disorder is clearly linked not with the existential experience of death but rather with the existential demands of new life. In my review of the twentieth-century clinical literature on agoraphobia I found many cases where the onset of the disorder in a female patient occurred at the moment when new child care responsibilities began.[44] Researchers generally ignore this significant piece of information. Numerous studies address or investigate the relationships between agoraphobic women and their spouses or the possibility of a genetic link between children with school phobias and mothers with agoraphobia. With the exception of a comment by the psychoanalyst Helene Deutsch, however, I have found no mention by therapists of the relationship between agoraphobia and the experience of childbirth and child care. This is a significant omission for a disorder whose high incidence in women is strongly linked with the period after marriage and during childbearing years.

Surveys in the United States report that the group most likely to say they are fearful in public urban space is women with young children, a finding that should be understood in a broader cultural context. In the United States and Britain, social critics point to the ways modern urban life has increasingly viewed children as a profitable commodity market while failing to include them in other significant domains of public life. Feminist philosophers (as noted in the Introduction) have demonstrated how the existential import of the experience of birth and child care has been neglected in modern Western philosophy. And feminist architects, city planners, and geographers have also complained of the way in which the built environments of modern cities show little regard for the everyday lives of children and their caregivers. *The Economist* magazine recently went so far as to carry a leader in which it argued that children in public places were a nuisance to everyone except their parents and constituted a "negative externality."

> Governments typically respond to … market failures in two ways. One is higher taxes, to make polluters pay the full cost of their anti-social behaviour. The other is regulation, such as emission standards or bans on smoking in public places. Both approaches might work for children. For children, just like cigarettes or mobile phones, clearly impose a negative externality on people who are near. [45]

Massive civil-engineering projects that cut a wide swath through multiple communities in postwar Euro-American cities allow some people to speed through public space in their cars or others to market their products on billboards while those on the ground find they have lost safe walking space and playing grounds for children.

The public self for which modernist architects and city planners have designed and constructed much of public space is caught in an ideology of instrumentally rational individualism in which the notion of *person* is legally regulated, biomedically treated, and has clear boundaries of inside and outside—my body, your body. The experiences of pregnancy, miscarriage, childbirth, and nursing present women with the inadequacies of that sense of self. Agoraphobia was set off in increasing numbers in postwar Britain, and the literature suggests that many of these women may have associated the disorder with existential experiences related to their roles as mothers and child-care givers. This indicates that the kinds of ubiquitous public space we have been examining through the agoraphobic's maps of the modern city are out of sync with the experience of many women, even as these public spaces become more unavoidable in their everyday lives. Techniques of self-fashioning that enable insertion into the changing forms of public space documented in this book—that is, forms of intense, homogeneous space such as the urban freeway and the supermarket or shopping mall—appear inadequate to the task of inserting those whose sensibility registers the emptiness of these cultural forms. There is a dialectical relationship between public space and the individual's sense of self, between space and subjectivity. When a woman undergoes experiences that so defy the dominant spatial thinking that supports the instrumental rationality of so much of the everyday built environment, she finds it hard to recognize herself in these new forms of public space.

Referring to the study of small-scale societies, the anthropologist Marcel Mauss long ago described the bounded cultural domain of the ethnographer's study as a "universe of recognition" for the inhabitants. This volume's study of agoraphobia suggests that important areas of public space no longer provide a universe of recognition. Such forms of public space could easily become terra incognita, triggering anxiety that bears on other fundamental aspects of modern personhood. A person venturing into such a universe of nonrecognition might experience problems with orientation. She may have trouble simply walking there, standing upright in its abstract and/or intensely saturated dimensions. The more sensitive among us might succumb to psychosomatic reactions. We would then have to eventually form a relation to that everyday space that more properly mirrors the relation one forms with the unknown, the unrecognizable. The modern agoraphobic shows us that constant contact with spaces of nonrecognition affect the way a person experiences her everyday being. We have seen that the agoraphobic women whose common existential experiences include pregnancy, miscarriage, childbirth, nursing, and child care can often find that the most common forms of public urban space are not built to recognize her. The treatments we have reviewed thus far show that often, when agoraphobic women are offered skills to enter public space, these skills are ones that undervalue and indeed dull tactile sensibilities. Flooding and other desensitization treatments appear best suited to the needs of the shopping center and the urban freeway, public places that are among modern society's most technologically complex forms of everydayness. It thus becomes clear that the skills to create self identity in universes of nonrecognition are not the skills traditionally learned by those engaged in face-to-face affective labor. It also becomes clear that technologically complex public spaces demand selves that can live comfortably in a universe of nonrecognition.

The successful behavioral treatments we have studied with regard to agoraphobia, I would argue, are also successfully deployed for a more general public learning to become comfortable in a universe of nonrecognition. The 1960 case of the Sheffield woman, for example, documents how new forms of technologically opened public space (such as outer space) can call on behavioral techniques to create new social skills to quell the anxious perceptions of a population living in a universe of nonrecognition. The Sheffield mother, we recall, feared "too much radiation" and "insufficient air" in the atmosphere which is, of course, legally regulated as a global commons, one of our most vast forms of public space. Radiation is, from a purely spatial point of view, an impossible phenomenon for the sensory self in modern public space. It is invisible, has no scent or sound, and is not palpable. How can citizens recognize it when it enters their public space?

The agoraphobic woman who fears too much radiation lived in a world that preexisted the emergence of a historical consciousness that would eventually become the basis for Earth Day and a popular environmental movement that could disseminate political language and other skills by which common citizens could recognize and speak about invisible contaminants in their environments. Even a half-century later, when the low-level radiation emitted from the nuclear power plants that lie downwind and downstream of many industrialized cities has been associated with rising cancer rates in these areas, the nonpathologized public self finds few legitimized skills or tools with which to deal with the threat. Epidemiological studies cannot "prove" causality, and public laws do not yet sufficiently protect citizens from the growing potential for harm to their health. Everyday citizens lack the means to cope with this empirically difficult substance in their urban midst. By 1964 the Sheffield woman's fears of a falling satellite were indeed realized when an American nuclear-powered satellite broke up and released quantities of plutonium in the atmosphere.[46] Even closer to the time of her first complaint, during the 1950s, England's Sellafield Nuclear Power Plant, located one hundred miles downwind of Sheffield, was the site of one of the largest leaks of radiation in history. While the public knew very little about this at the time, as if the whole deathly incident took place in empty, ungoverned space, in terra nullius, reports today claim the toxicity of the surrounding countryside as equal to that of the area around Chernobyl after the nuclear leak there.[47] What kind of relation has the public formed today to Sellafield's nuclear power plant? The plant has become a tourist site. After major marketing campaigns to sell the idea of safety, the plant transformed its gift shop into a simulated reactor core where tourists can enter in fake protective gear, wear plastic gloves, and pick up pretend radioactive material. This is flooding in vivo gone awry, a desensitization gimmick that borrows from behaviorist therapy.

After the 1950s, when nuclear reactors become more familiar sights on the horizons of metropolitan centers in eastern and western Europe and the United States, the issue of invisible radioactive fallout and effluents in the environment that can be secretly measured by government-controlled scientific instruments begins to be indirectly registered in the clinical literature on anxiety. As an article in *Connecticut Medicine*, a journal of psychiatric medicine, written by an American doctor during the height of the Cold War, in 1959, delineates, "The initial phobic reaction is a devastating experience. Wholly unexpected, it follows a period of unrecognized emotional strain. Often the patient has not previously recognized his neuroticisms. To such a weakly integrated personality, an acute phobic reaction is *an atomic bomb*. Confusion, inability to think, indecision, weakness, a sense of unreality and strangeness suddenly *attack* such a personality and he *seeks a permanent bomb shelter*—a chronic neurosis. After several such experiences the individual develops other neurotic reactions and is surrounded by *neuro-active 'fallouts'* as far as he is concerned."[48]

There is in both the agoraphobic complaint and the therapist's description an unconscious metaphor of the failure of U.S. and British civilian defense policy during the 1950s. Years later, citizens would come to realize that nuclear states have routinely and secretively made use of *res nullius* public space as test sites to release radioactive elements under and above the earth and high seas.[49] The techniques of behavioral psychology that have gained widespread popularity since the 1950s must take their place next to the more direct dissimulating attempts to desensitize citizens to the dangers that surface in public space that has become a universe of nonrecognition. The clinical literature on agoraphobia reveals one particularly disabling way that real but often imperceptible dangers register in the surplus sensibility of citizens whose everyday lives are lived in close contact with these recent forms of public space. Behaviorism, and the psychopharmacology that often accompanies it today, can participate unwittingly in the normalization of newly created forms of violence. High rates of agoraphobia, in this respect, are a sign that a certain urban sensibility has been both developing and suppressed.

To the extent that agoraphobia in our age registers as predominantly a woman's problem, we are led to agree with the position of cultural critic Camilla Griggers, who describes the overmedicated population of American women as victims of a kind of social machine of "surge suppression."[50] Griggers follows anthropologist Michael Taussig in referring to the concept of a "nervous system" in the social body that somatically, in terms of an energetic charge, registers reactions and then checks effects through a surge-control mechanism. In terms of the treatments of the agoraphobic's surplus sensibility described here, the theory of surge suppression provides a useful framework in which to think of how experiences that are becoming more common with the expansion of the kind of emptiness that characterizes homogeneous spaces are experiences that register in primarily "energetic" ways because in a universe of nonrecognition there is no symbolic content to attach to these experiences. Even the new popularity of yoga and Eastern forms of "energy medicine" such as acupuncture, tai chi, and chi gong in the United States and Europe take on new meaning in this light.[51] Abreaction, then, is perhaps on a spectrum with these other techniques of energy medicine, all of which are apparently the right therapies for this particular historical moment. They are right because they are effective treatments for a whole range of somatic disorders associated with trauma and with that catchall cause "stress," conditions that the modern psychologized self does not have cognitive skills to reflect on as a rational individual. Energy medicine, like abreaction, allows the individual to become part of a larger collective entity, the embodied self as an energy system inseparable from its environment. As the mind becomes embodied in these energy therapies, a whole new range of phenomena can be recognized and treated because the semantic field of "energy" allows them to be approached as nonsymbolic forms of intensity. Acupuncture, for example, is a form of energy medicine that comes from a particular symbolic world of Asian cosmologies. In the Western context, however, patients can be completely unaware of the symbolic framework and still feel beneficial results. (Even biomedical doctors, for that matter, can and do practice the technique without using the symbolic system of yin/yang balance that is, after all, acupuncture's cultural home). This is not to say that the introduction and sudden popularity of Asian medical systems in Western culture and in biomedicine is not an important phenomenon that may even lead to the expansion of fundamental understandings of organic life and thus push the boundaries of basic science in Western thinking. Energy medicine clearly has this to offer. What I am pointing to, however, is the social moment at which energy medicine becomes a popular and successful form of treatment in the West, often for many conditions whose etiology is either unknown or related to the black bag of the "unconscious" or "stress."

The clinical literature on agoraphobia shows that the experience of agoraphobic women not only serves to register a dominant anxiety in the population at large (sometimes related to phenomena that is imperceptible only to citizens whose government keeps its dangers secret), but also reflects a socially suppressed response to the experience of violence. In a 1976 case study of agoraphobia in Rome, for example, the report of two Italian doctors in a journal of behavioral psychiatry reveals a much wider gendered assumption about violence, fear, and public space. The doctors analyzed the marital relations of fifteen male agoraphobic patients and found that, aside from their agoraphobic syndrome, all the men in the study had successful personalities: they were "socially extroverted, ambitious, self-assertive and aggressive with high levels of aspiration and good levels of occupational achievement." The element that is most interesting comes with the doctors' description of the men's wives. While the wives showed no signs of agoraphobic behavior, they were nevertheless described by the doctors as "socially introverted," and even defective in one important respect: As the doctors report, "[Their wives were] calm about physical illnesses and able to face situations in which other family members were ill with calmness and efficiency. … However, they shared a fear of any expression of aggressive behavior. For the majority this fear amounted to *a phobia of violence. They were unable, for instance, to watch violent scenes on television or films.*"[52]

This observation is completely overlooked by the authors but fundamental to our concern with a seemingly gendered cultural sensibility that registers the normalization of violence as a relation to empty space. The husbands are described as aggressive, and this is categorized as a component of successful behavior. The wives, on the other hand, "[none of whom] suffered from psychiatric illness," were found for the most part to have "a phobia of violence." This pronouncement appears to base itself on the piece of evidence that they "were unable to watch violent scenes on television or films." Assuming that psychologists in a medical journal are not using the term *phobia* in a figurative manner, the doctors are implying that the normal citizen, both male and female, *should be* capable of watching violence. A sensibility not configured to watching violence, therefore, is considered pathological and, the doctors seem to imply, is somehow related to the women's choice of husbands, who attach enormous fear to actual public space. Watching violence on electronically mediated surfaces, a daily, if not hourly, experience for the average citizen today, reflected a new relation to public, urban, space in the 1970s—new because this public space was produced by a relatively new technology that created a virtual commons that citizens were entering with sensibilities still honed in the spatial dimension of an actual commons. And it must be said that the new virtual commons, like the actual commons built in the postwar period of modernist city design, has emptiness as a main feature. The television screen is fundamentally an empty space, if one considers that the on-and-off nature of the electrical current behind virtual reality is nothing if not the experience that the animated screen depends on a blank surface for its showing: empty space of the modernist period transforming to empty space of the virtual age.

Increasingly in our visually mediated culture we witness the demand for normative skills for watching violence as a representation. The 1978 agoraphobia study tells us that where insufficiently normalized women avert their gaze, well-functioning men (both agoraphobic and not) should be able to watch. Culturally constructed masculinity here acts like the soldier's uniform did for the nineteenth-century male agoraphobic: the soldier wore it like the magical cloak of fairytales, finding powers in its cloth that allowed him to venture into places otherwise inaccessible to the person of surplus sensibility. The 1976 study is both a cultural document of the technologically mediated modern gendered self and a description of the modern city as a place where the successful inhabitant, in order to be successful, must acquire skills to watch violence in relation to the backdrop of public, empty space. The demand for these skills will only grow over the following decades as the pedestrian experience of the modern city dweller, as was noted in the introduction to this book, often owes more to the cinematic traveling shot than to the experience of his feet on the asphalt. Like many modern citizens, I travel comfortably in this technology through virtually visited city streets the world over. In the European and American cities where I have actually lived, but much more so in large American cities of the Southwest with meager public transportation systems like Houston, Los Angeles, and Phoenix, people are coming to know their streets and the streets of a globalized world less through walking and more through the windshield of their car and through the television screens in their living rooms.

Film and television are technologies for the normative alignment of the self. Research into agoraphobia in the mid-1970s, a time by which most households in Europe and North America would own a television set, raises questions about how the big and little screens, by providing us with a visually mediated way to insert ourselves into a "story" of the violent modern metropolis, are also providing us with the visual techniques to insert ourselves into offscreen metropolitan space. As the behavioral clinical literature on agoraphobia has also shown us, the ways in which we imagine our relation to our cities are also means to insert ourselves into city space.

### Conclusion to the Behavioral Literature on Agoraphobia

The above stories of soldiers and women can help us summarize our findings about the behavioral treatment of flooding for agoraphobia and its relation to the social functions of empty space at the end of the twentieth century. In the broadest of terms the stories suggest that in postwar Europe men were treated with flooding for agoraphobia often in relation to extreme wartime experiences on a battlefield while women were treated for agoraphobia that they often associated with "normal" experiences, such as mothering or marriage, whose difficulties are evoked somatically at the shopping center or urban freeway. The behavioral treatment for both the ex-soldier and the housewife is derived from research and therapy on abreaction in soldiers; in its theoretical and clinical beginnings, extreme techniques of exposure in vivo arose from a reinterpretation of the psychoanalytic concept of abreaction/catharsis as applied to soldiers suffering war neurosis from the battlefields of World War II. Later, in the clinical literature of the 1960s and '70s, we see that both male and female agoraphobics are treated the same with flooding therapies in all but one respect: the public spaces they are reinserted into are different and gendered. Men are to be returned to main streets and public transport, classroom podiums and business offices while women relearn to function within shopping centers and on freeways—spaces that are undergoing enormous cultural and social transformation. These places are possibly modernity's greatest urban crucible for the experiment of transforming diversity into homogeneity. To avoid an otherwise threatening experience, entry into the shopping center, the freeway, and televised violence demanded new social skills for women, much as entering the battlefield required a newly trained self for men. Outside of these specific skills of the self, all else becomes surplus sensibility. Behavioral techniques of flooding and exposure in vivo are systematically used during this period to re-adapt the sufferer with "surplus sensitivity" to the newly normative spaces of the urban life.

The evolution of behaviorist treatments for agoraphobia—in particular, those habituating methods that use flooding/exposure in vivo with various medications, can be seen in studies of behaviorist techniques for post-traumatic stress disorder. In their 1992 book *Agoraphobia and Panic: A Guide to Psychological Treatment*, authors Jeffrey Hecker and Geoffrey Thorpe explain that post-traumatic stress disorder (PTSD) differs from agoraphobia and other anxiety disorders "in that it has its origins in a genuinely distressing event, beyond the bounds of typical human experience." They note,

> In the case of combat veterans of the Vietnam War whose PTSD is related to memories of the battlefield, it can be acceptable to follow an imaginal flooding procedure in which the stimuli presented are frightening scenes from combat. Because the client is unlikely to encounter wartime conditions again, and because the anxiety disorder is so obviously linked to images and memories of combat, it has been acceptable to clients, therapists, and the wider community to make aversive reactions to war experiences the target of psychotherapy. … Similar points can be made about the victims of civilian disasters or automobile accidents who develop PTSD in the aftermath of their traumatic experiences. … When a client develops PTSD after victimization by sexual assault or other abuse of this kind, the selection of treatment targets is a more controversial matter. But a client whose PTSD was precipitated by chronic sexual abuse in childhood, *is it appropriate to desensitize her to sex offense perpetrators, or to scenes of rape? Such a treatment plan would be inappropriate because it would seek to treat reasonable fears and concerns as if they were unreasonable ones.*[53]

The phrase "to treat reasonable fears and concerns as if they were unreasonable ones" bears repeating, because architectural critics and urban planners have for the past decades been demonstrating why it is perfectly reasonable to think that ubiquitous forms of public space—the urban freeway and the shopping mall—have negatively transformed the urban community. From this point of view, the behavioral treatment of agoraphobia raises an ethical dilemma. It would appear to be uncontestable at this point that these pathologically indicated sites of modern space threaten not only the urbanite of acute sensibility but also the average metropolitan commuter who turns on the radio to hear the daily death toll on the morning and evening traffic report. At the shopping mall, moving among the surveillance and high-tech security systems so flouted by American mall operators to convince consumers that mall space is safe space, the metropolitan citizen will be reminded that fear is a reasonable undertone. These new spaces of modernity arouse a complex set of emotions, fear being one of those that is apparently most in need of treatment by modern psychology.

The study of agoraphobia and its treatments reveals one dimension of what it feels like to live in a city whose built environment is functionally structured around a central vacuity as Ernst Bloch would say of postwar Berlin.[54] The clinical techniques behaviorists developed to insert Britain's overwhelmingly female population of agoraphobics into the new postwar material form for the industrialized, mass-marketing of food, and those techniques (with their latent ties to the practice of lobotomy) that today combine habit-forming drugs with desensitization practices like flooding, raise serious ethical issues in as much as these methods also lead many health practitioners to "treat [women's] reasonable fears and concerns as if they were unreasonable ones." Similar ethical issues would follow the international marketing of these medical practices for urbanites of acute sensibility who increasingly need to venture into the ubiquitous domains of intense, homogeneous space in modern cities.

The types of urban space we have been led to by the agoraphobic's faltering footsteps are similar to what French anthropologist Marc Augé refers to as "non-places." In *Non-Places: Introduction to an Anthropology of Supermmodernity* he writes, that non-places are "our most technologically developed daily environments," spaces that cultural anthropologists are only just beginning to analyze, such as "freeways, airports, supermarkets, but also the airways and seemingly less material and indeed more abstract spaces, such as message- and image-bearing screens, cable networks, radio waves, satellites. Such spaces are the opposite of places, in whose organization culturalist anthropologists were wont to read or decipher—or to think they could read or decipher—people's identities, their reciprocal relations, and the symbols of their common history. In these 'non-places,' one may decipher neither identity, relation, nor history. They seem characteristic of a period, ours, that I have proposed to call supermodernity [*supermodernité*]."[55]

Supermodernity, Augé notes, is an era dominated by excesses of time (ever more information from a worldwide time frame that makes it impossible to get a historical handle on our immediate past); excesses of space (through faster modes of travel and communication that paradoxically shrink and expand the globe); and excesses of self (an increasing tendency to individuate experience and hand over to singular egos the task of interpreting the complexity of their world, a task that in small-scale societies is reserved for a larger cultural collectivity). In studying the behavioral treatments for agoraphobia we see evidence of these three kinds of excess; we see how they feed into the creation of a person of surplus sensibility, and how they are treated when they manifest as acute anxiety in specific public places of contemporary urban life. In our study of behaviorism we have taken up Augé's challenge to the social anthropologist: to decipher, as it were, identity, relation, and history in those very "non-places" that present themselves as being universally efficient modes of space-making, meaningless in themselves without cultural specificity, and therefore exportable to all modern cities.

Our study shows that the behaviorist treatment of those urban citizens most sensitive to the environments of what we have been calling "built emptiness" reveal new modes of sociality. To the extent that behavioral techniques are linked to pharmacological ones, we find ourselves approaching a version of what Paul Rabinow has called "biosociality": the reorganization of human life based on scientific categories of human biology.[56] Behavioral techniques that produce abreaction without drugs, on the other hand, can be viewed as modern social rituals aimed at purging surplus sensibility that interferes with smooth functioning in a universe of nonrecognition, that universe being comprised of homogeneous space, the "non-places" like shopping centers and the urban freeways that require their own particular kinds of urban subjectivity.

Flooding as treatment keeps public space in the pathology of agoraphobia. Unlike many of the other remedies we have seen in the clinical literature, flooding keeps specific public spaces on the agoraphobic's map of the dysfunctional city. For this reason the genealogy of flooding has helped us as cultural analysts to recover a history of changes in the pockets of emptiness in the built environment, and by extension, a history of the changes in the recovered public self. These spaces of urban emptiness—the urban freeway and the shopping center—are fundamental training grounds for the late modern self. Psychoanalysis and cognitive approaches, when they worked, recovered a public self who could make symbolic and rational sense of their relation to the massive expanses of public space. Flooding and pharmacological approaches, on the other hand, recovered a self that could dispense with symbolic and cognitive systems in relation to these forms of urban space. For the normative public self these approaches are also significant. The successes of flooding and its relation to the phenomenon of abreaction suggest that these massive spaces are terra incognita, spaces where citizens do not need to recognize themselves so much as to form a relation (as opposed to a reaction) to the unknown. Those who form relations to these spaces uniquely through cognitive processes—that is, who rationalize their necessity and find their effects innocuous—generally find themselves ignoring their actual threats. As Henri Lefebvre predicted, the rationalist risks wrongly assuming that the signs allowing us to navigate the abstract space of the urban freeways are the same as the signs that will enable us to live in the city as such. If Georg Simmel's uneasy metropolitan type found further rationalization to be the most successful mode of dealing with the anxiety of everyday urban life a century ago, today's anxious agoraphobic is not greatly helped by the rationalizations of cognitive treatments. Abandoning symbolic approaches to anxiety arising from today's most common forms of public space is a significant change in the treatments.

The change in recovery modes for the anxious public self occurs alongside changes in the economic system enabling the transformations of public space. The urban freeway system and the massive urban engineering projects of the nineteenth century were managed and paid for by the economy of the centralized state. The continued giganticism of today's shopping malls and the smaller-scale new urbanist town (shopping) centers, on the other hand, are the product of a privatized, neoliberal global capitalist economy. Flooding techniques produce a public self that accommodates both economic orders, trimming surplus sensibility that challenges the status quo of either. Here we can suggest that the public self recovered from the nonsymbolic abreactive techniques of flooding is one who is better suited to the open systems of flexible capitalism, and better suited to "non-places" in a universe of nonrecognition.[57]

The therapeutic successes of flooding suggest that, at the larger cultural register of modern urban life, problems related to the increasing expectation that citizens live in everyday relation to empty, intensely homogeneous space cannot be treated effectively by rational, cognitive means. Such an epistemological approach deals with the problems of empty space in urban modernity as problems within our systems of knowledge. The successes of flooding, however, suggest that empty urban space is not only something we know about, but also something we feel. It is a structure of feeling, and as such raises ontological questions: How is our sensorium engaged in this particular kind of space? From what other experiential domains do we find transferable skills that will enable us to inhabit built spaces that, due to their massive scale and scope, have become universes of nonrecognition with respect to traditional cognitive skills? From an ontological perspective, if we habituate or adapt ourselves to the pockets of emptiness, do we form a relation to them through habits that demand a desensitized sensorium, one that is especially compromised with regard to the tactile function and its associated knowledge skills? Habits without habitats; the successes of flooding in recovering the agoraphobic's public self suggest that the public self molded in relation to these forms of public space adopts a mode of forgetfulness and thus loses a sense of how changes in urban space are in fact transforming us as urban citizens. The feelings of fear and dread that arise for a significant mostly female part of the Western population in urban spaces marked as spaces of emptiness by agoraphobics for the last century call for significant changes in city design and in the kinds of social and sensate skills needed to venture or navigate there. It is important to note that the spaces that set off the agoraphobic's fear have always been the very spaces that have served as the "urban commons" in modernity.

CHAPTER 7

# Alternative Treatments for the Twenty-First-Century Urban Commons

## *Horror Vacui, Solvitur Ambulando?*

### Introduction

What can alternative therapies for agoraphobia tell us about the relation between urban anxiety and the ongoing transformation of empty space in our cities' most public sites? The clinical literature shows that agoraphobics, like the general patient population in the United States and Europe, are using alternative therapies at a precipitously increased rate since the 1990s.[1] Alternative treatments for agoraphobia often involve attempts to bridge the mind/body split characteristic of Western biomedicine.[2] Achieving this, neurophysiologists and body therapists reinsert the anxious urbanite into public space via therapeutic skills that call forth a psychosomatic self whose sense of consciousness is radically different than that inherited from either the Freudian/psychoanalytic tradition (with its split conscious/unconscious self) or the Western biomedical one (with its mechanistic split between a conscious mind and a nonconscious body). In this chapter I examine several treatments that come under the heading of *bioenergetic therapies*.[3] These therapies view the agoraphobic's acute anxiety as a problem of kinesthetic knowing, where an embodied self uses nonstoried, nonsymbolic psychomotorial cues to communicate with itself and its environment. Therapists use biofeedback techniques to train patients how to use a subtle, felt sense of bodily awareness to intervene in or disjunctively communicate with the body's autonomic processes, to change heart and breathing rhythms, to modulate hormones, to discharge or reroute energy bound in disruptive patterns. In the clinical literature, bioenergetic awareness is sometimes associated with Asian practices of nonconceptual, mindfulness training. Neurophysiologists who study the relation between emotions and the moving body, on the other hand, speak of a person's proprioceptive capacity to change affective states.[4] In this chapter I am interested in how the increasing popularity of such practices for the agoraphobic are indicative of a changing Western notion of public self. Bioenergetic treatments with success in treating agoraphobia, then, with their new (and also ancient, nonmodern) skills of spatial awareness, should also reveal how the embodied self is being successfully adapted to life in vast, homogenous forms of once dreaded urban space. After examining these treatments for what they can tell us about new approaches to spatial consciousness, we consider other kinesthetic-based treatments involving public space, as well as new features of European city design, all of which raise important issues for our broader interest in public space and the public self, its cultural, gendered, and biological relations.

## Successful Biofeedback Treatments for Agoraphobia and the Questions They Raise for the Modern Self

Several alternative therapies give the agoraphobic skills to work consciously with the body's biofeedback mechanisms to effect a cure. In the field of neurophysiology, for example, biofeedback techniques are used to train agoraphobic patients how to use electroencephalogram (EEG) and magnetic resonance imaging (MRI) brain scans to virtually monitor their brain wave patterns when aroused by memories of phobic spaces.[5] Patients learn specific skills, such as how to regulate their breathing rhythms, and they use these skills to intervene in (or, we could say, to communicate in nonsymbolic, nonlinguistic ways with) the externalized, visual simulation of their heightened emotional states. Emotional states are technologically virtualized as rhythmically active, networked brain states, and patients learn to enter the network and "stabilize" uncomfortable rhythmic patterns. In one study of the effectiveness of EEG feedback techniques for agoraphobia, researchers note that

> [s]tabilizing the brain against excursions such as panic attacks is quite readily achievable with EEG biofeedback training. … As in the case of migraines, such stability is difficult to achieve with pharmacological means. One striking and illustrative case must be mentioned. A woman who had been in treatment for panic anxiety and agorapho-

> bia for ten years, with repeated hospitalizations, long-term psychotherapy, and extensive pharmacological intervention, was eventually given EEG training by the same psychologist who had worked with her for ten years. After only eight sessions, she was able to vacation with her husband in Las Vegas, mixing easily in crowds, and declaring later that she felt anxious only once. On the basis of cases such as these, panic attacks are seen as fundamentally issues of brain instability rather than of psychological state.[6]

The technique invites patients to use a relatively recent technology (EEG or MRI) and a new vocabulary, that of brain instability, to approach their emotional lives. In the above example, the authors continue to conceptualize brain instability (body) as distinct from psychological state (mind). Nevertheless, the techniques train patients to consciously communicate in nonlinguistic ways with "brain states," thereby going in practice beyond the mind/body dualism still found in the medical terminology. The skill-based practice challenges other long-held assumptions concerning the brain's electrical constitution and mental health. As we saw in chapter 5 on behaviorist treatments for agoraphobia, the instability of the brain's electrical networks has more often been approached with the crude instruments of electric shock therapy, which sends a jolt of electrical current through a patient's body to wipe out brain activity associated with pathologized behavior. Like the drug propranolol, which works at the molecular level on the brain's chemical interlocutors, shock therapy aims to re-create the brain as a blank surface. Both treatments seek to dull and erase memory. Brain-wave biofeedback, on the other hand, trains the patient to enter the brain's subtle energy networks and communicate with them suggesting a *tabula rasa* is not a precondition for a cure of chronic phobic conditions like agoraphobia.

Unfortunately, researchers in neurophysiology note that the newly recognized phenomenon of the brain's flexible rhythmicity has attracted little attention in the medical community: it "appears as 'noise' in the search for the genetic basis of behavior," notes Siegfried Othmer, Susan F. Othmer, and David A. Kaiser in their study of EEG biofeedback therapy.[7] Networked brain patterns are likewise (mis)recognized as mere "noise" in research that traces behavior to molecular, membrane, or cellular levels of the body.[8] Thus, biofeedback techniques, despite the empirical information showing their clinical success in the treatment of agoraphobia, have not yet been integrated into the scientific models supporting dominant pharmacological treatments like propranolol or Xanax. A growing number of scholars, however, are working to bring these newfound connections between the body's physical and mental states into dialogue with dominant biomedical and psychoanalytic models of human emotion and behavior. These scholars point to the discoveries of the early work of Sigmund Freud who, before he turned to a psychic explanation of somatic phenomena, had studied the cellular structure of the nervous system in lower vertebrates and speculated that what differentiated primitive from advanced nervous systems was not the cellular elements per se, but the way in which they were organized. Similarly, revisiting the work of the philosopher Henri Bergson, scholars have found conceptual tools to discuss human and nonhuman behavior and embodied knowing within a broader spectrum that challenges concepts of the self in both Western psychology and philosophy. Psychoanalysis and other psychotherapies, they suggest, have more to learn about the human autonomic system from nonhuman life and its modes of communicating with a wider environment.[9]

For many social critics, the turn to biology to explain sociopsychosomatic behavior signals a reductive materiality, a manner of looking at human behavior stripped of its cultural and social forces. But scholars, including feminists, who study neurophysiological clinical work done with biofeedback therapies are wondering anew what novel modes of embodiment might become legible if biological reductionism is tolerated and explored, and if cultural, social, linguistic, literary, and historical analysis are better integrated with biological analysis. Some of the most remarkable questions about hysteria—notably, the phenomena of somatic conversion—they remark, have remained unanswered.[10] We do not know, for example, how the body "remembers" a traumatic episode by converting the event into a paralyzed limb, a disturbed inner ear, a pounding heart, a brief retinal irregularity. How is it that the body "communicates" in these precognitive ways with the world and with the various parts of itself?

Neurophysiologists conducting therapeutic work on agoraphobia have asked these questions about psychomotorial phenomena such as eye movement. Previously recognized as mere reactionary body gestures, the rapid to-and-fro eye movements that sometimes arise in the context of psychotherapy are now being used as a biofeedback tool. Research shows that involuntary eye movement may be more than a passive indication that a deeply charged emotion has been recalled. It may also be actively engaged as a strategic mode of intervention into seemingly unrelated somatic and emotional problems. The therapy, known as "eye movement desensitization and reprocessing" (EMDR) is recognized as one of the fastest growing methods in the history of psychotherapy, and one of the most controversial.[11] In EMDR sessions, therapists help patients become aware of involuntary small motor movements, sometimes called "body starters," that, for agoraphobics, would be associated with the triggers of an anxiety attack. (Shifting eyes were the original mechanism, but later other bilateral gestures were noted.) Patients are taught to consciously repeat these gestures at strategic points in a therapeutic session to intervene disjunctively in the way the central nervous system holds deeply charged memories and distributes their charge through the body's autonomic system as it does during an anxiety attack.[12] According to the theory, "body starters" operate on a different plane from the cognitive, symbolic understanding of a patient's emotional life. Getting the patient to attend to the disjunctive occurrence of both the body starter and the symbolic dimensions is like "the challenge of the childhood game of tapping your head while rubbing your stomach."[13] While the mechanism behind its reported success is still not clear, some researchers conjecture that these minute gestures function like rapid eye movement during deep sleep, which is to say they synthesize at a subconscious level otherwise disparate phenomena of daily life. In EMDR therapies, however, the body's synthesizing mechanism is no longer treated as "subconscious." It becomes a conscious tool to communicate with a psychosomatic self. Patients and therapists report that after as little as one session, long-held somatic responses can sometimes completely disappear. The speed of recovery, they find, often leaves a patient bewildered about the grip and duration of a somatic symptom on her life, challenging long held cultural notions of what constitutes their conscious self.[14]

Francine Shapiro, who discovered and developed the technique, relates the following case of a successful EMDR treatment reported in 1996 by Dutch therapists working with a woman who appears to have developed panic disorder with agoraphobia along with a dental phobia. She writes of a woman who

> avoided dentists for over 30 years. … The fear was established when she was 8 years old and a dentist had tied her arms with towels to the dental chair to restrain her during drilling. She also developed panic disorder later in life. A year of behavior therapy provided no relief from her symptoms. After one session of EMDR, the patient felt competent enough to go shopping for the first time after a long period. After a second session of EMDR, she was able to start dental treatment. At 2-year follow-up she was still free of panic attacks and had completed her dental work.[15]

The fact that a researcher offers a shopping trip as evidence of the treatment's early success should remind us of several cases examined in chapter 5, where Dutch clinicians some thirty years earlier took their agoraphobic patients to the shopping center to test the effectiveness of flooding therapies. In the early clinical studies of flooding, the shopping center was the environment par excellence, where the agoraphobic patient's full-blown anxiety attacks were both triggered and cured.

Shapiro originally believed that the EMDR method of curing phobias through conscious work with an exposed body starter involved the same mechanism at work in the success of flooding—systematic desensitization through intense exposure, the explanation given by the early behaviorist Joseph Wolpe, who first developed and theorized on the mechanisms behind flooding based on his work with combat soldiers in World War II (see chapter 5). But because practitioners now report quicker results with EMDR than with more traditional flooding methods, new questions have surfaced about the relation between the spectacular displays of flooding/catharsis and the more subtle displays of many EMDR cures. In a study titled "The Rhythmic Integration Project in Panic," panic-disorder patients successfully learned to identify and use the minute rhythmicity of their body starter in one ninety-minute session, and to find ways to circumvent the body starter's access to the full-blown physical dysfunctions of anxiety attacks even when specific charged memories were discussed.[16] Does EMDR work on the same principle as flooding? Compared to EMDR therapies, behavioral in vivo exposure methods of flooding begin to look like crude tools to engage what appears to be a more various and subtle rhythmic language involving the body's autonomic system. EMDR appears to give the agoraphobic more complex tools to speak psychosomatically with her environment rather than, as with flooding, to allow the environment to speak through her embodied self.

There are also those who remain more cautious about EMDR for agoraphobia. In one placebo-controlled clinical trial on agoraphobic patients in the United States, EMDR was shown to only have worked better than nothing—that is, better than what was given to those in a group waiting for treatment but receiving nothing. The study also showed that EMDR worked just as well as a placebo. This would at least place EMDR on a par with Xanax, whose clinical performance in the early Upjohn study we examined in chapter 4 was not significantly different from a placebo. Even those who criticize EMDR's effectiveness as a repeatable, scientifically valid technique appear to highlight, once again, the mysterious, psychosomatic power of the placebo effect as a therapeutic mode of intervention.[17] At the very least, these emergent treatments raise many questions about how self-consciousness is involved in physical processes. In agoraphobia, the question concerning self-knowledge and the rhythmicity of embodied communication can be placed in a broader social context of public space: What can the effectiveness of treatments engaging brain scans and psychomotorial interventions reveal about the relations among anxiety, the urban commons, and the public self?

## Initial Explanations from the Neurobiology of Locomotion

We can begin to answer these questions by considering EEG, MRI, or EMDR biofeedback strategies as skill-based modes of nonsymbolic communication that selves use to negotiate environments they move through in daily activities. With these treatments agoraphobics learn skills to communicate with deeply agitating and perplexing environments they have not been able to integrate into their daily lives. Why would agoraphobics need nonsymbolic, nonverbal skills to communicate with these environments? Are such precognitive skills needed/used by all embodied selves, normative and pathologized, to integrate and move with ease through their surroundings? Furthermore, if biofeedback treatments that work with embodied consciousness are so effective, what can their biologically grounded explanations add to the kind of social and cultural explanations we have offered thus far to explain the higher incidence of agoraphobia in women and the insufficiency of the dominant treatment modalities? We have already discussed how dominant treatments like flooding and beta-blocking drugs take the trauma-recovered soldier as the norm for all persons recovering from traumatic experience and how they infuse expectations for culturally masculine behavior into their expectations for normative, nonpathologized behavior during their cures. Do the biofeedback strategies do the same? How does a neurophysiological approach address gender differences in agoraphobia and, if so, what can this add to our discussion of the public self and urban space?

At the Laboratory for the Physiology of Perception and Action at the famed Collège de France, researchers Alain Berthoz and Isabelle Viaud-Delmon have studied agoraphobia and anxiety disorders in order to better understand the role of emotion in spatial orientation.[18] In the past, brain mechanisms underlying spatial orientation have been studied mainly in static conditions. At the laboratory researchers study how brain system mechanisms work when subjects are actually navigating space. When motion is included in brain system function, researchers find that emotions play a more important role than previously thought. Moving through space a person uses anticipatory strategies to gauge what is ahead. Even in simple movements through space, the research shows that anticipatory strategies engage memory, as well as emotion. The complex psychomotorial nexus of emotion and memory in anticipatory strategies engages what neurophysiologists call *proprioception*, the kinesthetic mode by which a person senses itself in space. Proprioception is a multisensory system that engages both cognitive processes and, as the French researchers are showing, the affective, autonomic responses of the limbic system with its gendered hormonal modes of regulation.

Like taste, smell, touch, vision, and hearing, the sense of proprioception has a keen relation to memory. It is well known that the French novelist Marcel Proust, a person of noted agoraphobic tendencies, probed the link between taste and involuntary memory with the famous example of his autobiographical character, Marcel, who receives a rush of intricately connected childhood memories and their emotional resonances upon tasting a particular pastry, the Madeleine. But Proust also tracked how his character could just as suddenly access the cascading images and sensations of involuntary memory by a disturbance to his sense of proprioception—that is, by losing his balance after tripping on a cobblestone or by accidentally stepping off the curb while walking in the streets of Paris.[19] Neurophysiologists at the French laboratory have likewise focused on how disturbances of the sense of proprioception are related to intricate networks involving memory and emotion. Their research takes us beyond traditional physiological understanding that would have dysfunctional spatial orientation be caused by either physical defects of the inner ear (vestibular system) or visual irregularities. The new research suggests that in a simple act like walking, proprioception can be thought of as a multisensory activity that integrates other somasensory systems like the limbic system, which communicates between the environment and the body through hormonal fluctuations.

Once hormones have entered a communicative arena integrating space, memory, and emotion, we are dealing with a notion of the self that has not yet been adequately dealt with by those who examine gender differences from a strictly social constructivist position. Neurophysiologists studying spatial orientation as an integrated, multisensory operation are beginning to look at gender and its socioenvironmental role in new ways. Given our need to better account for the gender discrepancies in agoraphobia, it is worth citing at some length from the neurobiological research to see how gender is observed as a neurophysiological factor with regard to spatial orientation. Citing some of their own research, Berthoz and Viaud-Delmon note,

> There are several sources of individual differences in space orientation, the most recognised of which is gender. Differences in space orientation between males and females have often been approached in terms of differing spatial abilities, but some studies indicate that gender differences in sensory integration could also exist. Evidence for gender differences in circular vection (i.e. the illusion of self-motion when viewing moving visual surrounds) exists … , and could be related to the greater susceptibility of females to motion sickness. … The "mal de débarquement" syndrome (the sensation of rocking and swaying that persists after sea travel) also appears

> to be more common among females. The etiology of this syndrome is unknown, but it has been thought to result from an inability of the brain to integrate and adjust to new spatial surroundings. … In an experiment on sensory adaptation, female subjects were found to recalibrate their vestibular perception to a lesser extent after exposure to conflicting visual–vestibular stimuli. … All these findings consistently suggest gender differences in the central processes dealing with visual–vestibular interaction and internal strategies of spatial orientation and spatial memory.[20]

The authors do not rule out the possibility that the observed neurobiological gender differences might be produced by socially given roles, that differences between men and women in terms of their "ability to maintain a sense of self-position in relation to the global shape of the environment" are a matter of social forces. Nevertheless, clear empirically observed differences in sensory integration exist between men and women. The authors note, "Several studies have demonstrated that females use distal cues for spatial orientation in a different way to males" and that gender differences in the structure of the hippocampus (an area of the limbic system) caused by the effects of sex hormones "could represent a neural correlate of the [gender] difference in spatial ability, even though the neural substrates of the difference in sensory integration are unknown."[21] Neurophysiologists, the authors tell us, will need to plan further research using magnetic and metabolic brain imagery methods to understand the underlying differences between human males and females in the processing of spatial information.

Neurobiology takes us beyond the traditional dichotomy placing spatial disorders like agoraphobia either in a person's (pathologized) mind or in her (defective) anatomy. As a cultural anthropologist studying agoraphobia treatments for what they reveal about a historically situated public self and contemporary urban space, I do not see the idea of integrated somasensory systems (including emotion, memory, and the fluctuating rhythmicities of hormones and brain waves) working together to orient us in space as a move to biological reductionism. Bringing psychomotorial therapies and neurophysiologic research into our discussion of the public self is rather an opening to reconsider what is meant by self and consciousness as spatially embedded notions at this historical moment in the West.[22]

## The Psychomotorial Self: A Challenge to Western Notions of Self and Consciousness

Psychomotorial research on agoraphobia shifts our attention from the psychotherapeutic, symbolic dimensions of the malady as well as from the molecular level of the patient's reactive brain chemistry. Unlike the cognitive, psychoanalytic, and pharmacological therapies we have looked at thus far, biofeedback interventions that work with psychomotorial strategies build the skills of a person's conscious—but not necessarily cognitive (i.e., symbolic or conceptual)—self. Psychomotorial skills allow agoraphobic persons to consciously communicate with their autonomic systems, their limbic systems, their embodied memory systems and their urban environments, disrupting severely limiting patterns of behavior that have taken over their lives. Using biofeedback strategies, a self need not necessarily probe what we in the West call "the unconscious," but neither does the self have to abandon communication with this subconscious system. What, then, do we mean when we say that all these disparate systems "communicate" with each other using psychomotorial skills? What kind of consciousness are we talking about?

Those who use imaging technologies to peer into the workings of the human brain refer to nonconceptual communication of this sort in terms of where it shows up in images of the brain's two hemispheres. In the broadest of terms, activity that registers on the left side of the brain is linked to conceptual processes like analytical thinking or the creation of narrative causality. On the right side of the brain researchers note connections to modes of processing associated with kinesthetic knowing and psychomotorial skills:

> Recent findings from observing caretaker/infant pairs have confirmed what body therapists have known for a long time—that early attachment experiences are encoded in the right brain where they remain unsymbolized and available through communication with the body … this work focus[es] on the right brain to right brain communication that occurs between the infant and her caretaker. These empirical findings indicate that memories during these preverbal years are stored in the nonverbal right brain. They are remembered in terms of body states, without a story. Out of a desire to understand and apply coherency to these feelings the person may later construct a narrative for these feelings.[23]

For body therapists, the persistent and visceral power of embodied memories of early childhood trauma is explained by the communicative strength of "kinesthetic knowing"—its flexible capacity to communicate with other systems—autonomic, limbic, emotional, and cognitive. Psychomotorial treatments for agoraphobia point to the environment as another system with which kinesthetic knowledge communicates. In these models, the disjunctive intervention of bioenergetic, biofeedback therapies for agoraphobia appear as right-side-to-right-side brain communication between "body states without a story" and certain kinds of public, urban spaces. And to push our thinking on this even further we could say that the wide open spaces of empty urban environments constitute systems that communicate most powerfully with the embodied consciousness of citizens in nonstoried ways.

Neurophysiologic research on kinesthetic knowing provides new material for a cultural anthropologist to synthesize when asking questions about the gender issues associated with agoraphobia. Why, for example, do women so often associate the onset of their agoraphobia with the experiences of childbirth and early child care? Is this a time in their lives when they are simply more susceptible to the communicative power of kinesthetic knowing? In what ways might this susceptibility be related to hormonal and other biological differences of women? In what ways might this susceptibility be connected to cultural and social modes of communication that are gender coded? These are interdisciplinary questions that will demand more research. For now, however, we can open another set of questions concerning gender and agoraphobia lead by these discoveries in psychomotorial, kinesthetic knowing.

What kind of consciousness is involved with the communicative abilities of the psychomotorial? The French philosopher Luce Irigaray has recently approached this question for Western philosophy by reflecting on her own experience as a practitioner of yoga. Yoga trains a person to focus conscious awareness simultaneously on respiration, breath control, and body position, key elements of what we have discussed as the proprioceptive mode of self-knowledge. For Irigaray, this ancient Eastern tradition is a mode of knowledge transmission that imparted "another rationality" different from the Western tradition of cultivating the mind through words and texts.[24] Notably, it brought her to an utterly different understanding of consciousness than what she had learned from her training as a philosopher and as a psychoanalyst:

> This [other mode of knowing] has nothing in common with the discovery of some unconscious. To tell the truth, my first encounter with a yoga teacher, which was rather conflictual, took place around the possibility of everything becoming conscious, as he declared to his students. As a psychoanalyst, I made him understand his naïveté. I could not see my own! And no more the fact that we were speaking starting from two different horizons. The practice of respiration, the practice of diverse kinds of breathing certainly reduces the darkness or the shadows of Western consciousness. But above all it constitutes the mental in a different way. It grants more attention to the education of the body, of the senses. It reverses in a way the essential and the

> superfluous. We Westerners believe that the essential part of culture resides in words, in texts, or perhaps in works of art, and that physical exercise should help us to dedicate ourselves to this essential. For the masters of the East, the body itself can become spirit through the cultivation of breathing. Without doubt, at the origin of our tradition—for Aristotle, for example, and still more for Empedocles—the soul still seems related to the breath, to air, But the link between the two was then forgotten, particularly in philosophy. The soul, or what takes its place, has become the effect of conceptualizations and of representations and not the result of a practice of breathing.[25]

The kind of consciousness involved in learning psychomotorial skills such as focused breathing in the yogic traditions is of a different nature than the understanding of consciousness and unconsciousness that comes from Western philosophical traditions and their intellectual legacies in modern psychology. For Irigaray, this difference must be traced to the way in which Western philosophical traditions "forgot" the importance of breath.

Breath, Irigaray argues, entered into Western philosophy as a concept through the work of the nineteenth century German philosopher Arthur Schopenhauer. In his classic work *The World as Will and Representation*, Schopenhauer referred to the fundamental role of breath in Vedanta Hinduism and Buddhism to support an innovative concept of life force he was introducing to Western philosophy. Schopenhauer reinterpreted the Eastern idea of breath as life force and gave it the label of *will*, a term he defined as a nonconceptual, driving force of human nature to reproduce the species and thus overcome death. Schopenhauer's notion of will foreshadowed and laid the groundwork for Charles Darwin's theory of evolution, Friedrich Nietzsche's will to power, and Sigmund Freud's concepts of the libido and the unconscious mind. But, as Irigaray points out, Schopenhauer's "biological materialism," his idea that "the life of man is dominated by a blind passion [he called will], that of reproducing himself,"[26] is far from what the Eastern traditions meant when they pointed to breath as the fundamental force of life. One of the most important elements of Schopenhauer's misunderstanding was certainly his cultural tendency to assume that the texts he read on Hindu or Buddhist teachings about breath could be understood separately from the meditative breathing practices that trained the breath to be an experiential teacher throughout a lifetime. In the nonconceptual practice of cultivating breath, the Eastern tradition taught that life's forces, including consciousness, could be cultivated to hone a person's relations to body, world, and spirit in a lifelong project of becoming individuated (to the point of eventually going beyond one's own personal reincarnation).

Schopenhauer's access to Eastern thought took place without any practical knowledge of breath. Thus his textual, restricted, conceptual understanding of breath as will was developed without the additional knowledge acquired by the nonconceptual Eastern practice of mindful breathing. And this separation of theory and practice, Irigaray argues, brought an utterly different dynamic into Western metaphysics: Schopenhauer's metaphysics "resides in the dynamism of reproductive chromosomes that tear man away from his individual being. I am—Schopenhauer asserts—projected outside of myself by my will to reproduce the species."[27] Consciousness and the world of ideas became for Schopenhauer, as it did for his intellectual heirs in the West, mere servants to a larger aim. That larger goal was driven not by a person's becoming individuated (as in the Eastern traditions) but by their becoming the larger grouping of species. The psychomotorial, experiential knowing and becoming associated with breath in the Eastern tradition was thus "forgotten" as it became Schopenhauer's dynamic, species-propagating will in the Western tradition.

The Western tradition's comfortable separation of theory from practice, of word from gesture, helped turn the psychomotorial experience of breath into the concept of an underlying, unconscious drive of humankind to perpetuate the species. To fully understand the consequences of such thinking for the psychological treatments of agoraphobia, in particular for the overlap of military into civilian remedies in the dominant treatments for anxiety in public urban space, we must follow Irigaray's further observation that the translation of breath into will that we see posited in Schopenhauer and developed in Nietszche, Darwin, and Freud is part of a larger tendency in Western philosophy to place death at the center of our thinking about life. For Irigaray,

> Schopenhauer reveals to us, among other truths: philosophy is a matter of death. A philosopher living and thinking life is a priori suspect in our philosophical culture. Thus begins [Schopenhauer's] chapter "On Death and Its Relation to the Indestructibility of Our Inner Nature" (2:463) in *The World as Will and Representation*: "Death is the real inspiring genius of Musagetes of philosophy, and for this reason Socrates defined philosophy as *thanatou mélétè* (preparation for death; Plato, *Phaedo* 8Ia). Indeed, without death there would hardly have been any philosophizing. It will therefore be quite in order for a special consideration of this subject to have its place here at the beginning of the last, most serious and most important of our books." (23)

Schopenhauer not only places death as the guiding light of Western philosophy, but also makes Western metaphysics into a project of transcendence of death through a species' will to reproduce. Furthermore, Schopenhauer is clear, Irigaray tells us, that the will he is speaking of here is "a masculine will to reproduce."[28] For Schopenhauer, "what we designate generally as a duty to reproduce, to give birth, is linked to the most obscure and elementary passion of man. Of man, in effect. Because the will is, according to him, masculine."[29] Schopenhauer's "blind pathos of the reproduction of the species" is, however, also a metaphysical task. Man is the guardian of the reproduction of the species. He transcends himself in and by reproduction. Irigaray notes that for Schopenhauer, "man essentially wants to reproduce, nothing can stop him from doing this, not even the intelligence of women, and this will, when it does not produce natural children, gives birth to imaginary children. Philosophy and religion are two of them. ... Schopenhauer says it. Nietzsche asserts it very explicitly: his works are his children."[30]

I have taken this brief foray into the philosophy of will, its sources in a misunderstanding of the role of breath in Eastern traditions and its legacy in Western concepts of consciousness and unconsciousness that span philosophy, biology, and psychology, in order to better answer my initial question: What kind of consciousness is involved with the communicative abilities of the psychomotorial? If biofeedback strategies can train agoraphobics to use body gestures and practices of breathing to consciously intervene in the autonomic processes of the limbic system, do we not have a notion of consciousness that is seeking to remember something about breath and the gestural body that Western traditions of consciousness have "forgotten," as Irigaray says? As we have seen, Western ideas of consciousness and their attendant psychologies of the self are informed by privileging both culturally and biologically masculinist notions of self. But alternative treatments for agoraphobia and their successes for a predominantly female population show us that new remedies focusing on psychmotorial skills, what some call "right-side-to-right-side" brain communication, place the gendered dynamics of agoraphobia in a new light.

The psychomotorial self "remembers" other traditions of embodied consciousness much as philosopher Irigaray "remembers" (via a feminist and cross-cultural perspective) what breathing might yet come to mean for Western philosophy. The psychomotorial self has thus taken us in new directions to think about the relation between the acutely anxious self and its environment. It has challenged Western notions of consciousness and added new complexity to our cultural understanding of gender as it relates to humans' multisensory, proprioceptive modes of knowing their environment. Returning to the agoraphobic's problem of walking in public space, we can now ask anew the questions posed in this book regarding the urban environment and the role of empty space.

### Labyrinth Walking, a Recent (and Ancient) Therapy through Which to Explore the Question: Why Public Space?

To explore the value and significance of proprioceptive knowledge, its embodied and spatially acute sense of consciousness, and the insight it offers to counter misunderstood gendered categories of knowing and being in Western psychology and philosophy, it is useful to explore an alternative therapy that has, like flooding, engaged the anxious patient in public space as an essential component of its cure. Labyrinth walking is an alternative therapy that values psychomotorial skills and kinesthetic knowing in the treatment of anxiety and trauma recovery. Moreover, labyrinth walking is a remedy from older traditions of knowing and being in the world that is enjoying a popular renewal in many U.S. cities. While not yet a clinically studied treatment for agoraphobia, labyrinth walking has become a therapeutic technique used for women recovering from various traumas—in particular, domestic abuse.[31] Easily dismissed by the critical sociologist as a New Age fad, the phenomena of labyrinth walking is instructive when seen in the light of urban development and the history of treatments for agoraphobia I have presented in this book. Notably, it helps answer the question of why public space can be both part of the trigger and the cure of pathologies of modern space.

*Labyrinth Walking: The Therapy*

In the downtown center of Phoenix, where urban flight and suburban sprawl have left 40 percent of the city's terrain pocked by wastelands of emptied space, there is a large inlaid labyrinth mosaic covering the ground of the courtyard outside Trinity Episcopal cathedral. On cooler days in this desert city where I presently live, you can see pedestrians take two steps off the sidewalk that borders the thoroughfare passing in front of this church, turn their backs on the looming cars and buses that give our inner-city air that sickly quality, and amble along the labyrinth's contours. They follow along paths that take them toward the center only to be turned away as the circuitous pattern sends them back once again to the labyrinth's outermost parts. You see them walking back and forth, as if in a trance, apparently trusting that they will eventually be brought to the center. (Unlike its cousin the maze, in the labyrinth's pathways there are no trick turns.) When the labyrinth walkers arrive at the center, they turn around and, like Theseus holding tight to Ariadne's thread, they make their way back out. Neither a linear nor an efficient mode of pedestrian traffic, this is a new phenomenon in our city.

And we are not unique. In San Francisco's Bay Area, where the trend apparently started, there are dozens of such labyrinths. According to Dr.

Lauren Artress, who, in 1995, brought the design back from the floor of the Chartres Cathedral near Paris and helped build the labyrinth outside Grace Cathedral in San Francisco—the first permanent labyrinth to be constructed in the Western Hemisphere in six hundred years, there are some eighteen hundred labyrinths now around the country.[32] Since 1995, the American labyrinths are turning up not only outside churches, those sanctuaries of prime real estate among the built environment of secular modernity, but also outside or in the atriums of hospitals, jails, parks, museums, teen centers, and individual homes (see figure 16).[33] In many ways these premodern pathways appear to be just another New Age trend. But I am convinced that current therapeutic use of this enclosed and abstract space has a place next to the cultural history of psychological and psychiatric treatments for agoraphobia reviewed in this book. It, too, is a treatment that retrains modern urbanites to walk in their cities. Seen next to the history of changes in modern city planning and the social theories that link the metropolis to mental life, therapeutic labyrinth walking can be a heuristic tool to explore the linkages set forth thus far in this book among public space, the self, and the unspeakable, nonsymbolic tactile sensibility so underappreciated in most modern regimes of self-knowledge. Labyrinth walking is a form of psychomotorial consciousness. It is a kind of "bottom-up" therapy that modern urban culture is presently using to retrain the deskilled tactility all urban citizens have been asked to live with in the modern city.

Therapists in Phoenix who use labyrinth walking as a psychological cure recommend it to their patients who are recovering from deep, past trauma. "I use it for my women patients who are recovering from sexual abuse," says Dr. Judy Gifford, a family systems therapist who has studied with Artress. From her downtown Phoenix office she explains to me, "It is a very powerful experience. Walking the labyrinth is a form of kinesthetic knowledge. It allows my patients to feel their experience and to begin thinking about their life metaphorically. They come to understand that the process is the journey, not the goal. In the process they learn to think intuitively, to use metaphor, to feel and inhabit their own body again." With the labyrinth, it is "the physical act of doing something that brings the insight," not the thinking. "You don't always have to know consciously first."[34]

Like the biofeedback treatments previously discussed, labyrinth walking focuses on mind/body connections and makes undervalued surplus sensibility a part of the healing process bringing new insight into an otherwise inexplicable sensation or behavior. Like the behavioral method of flooding, it engages what we have elsewhere seen labeled as a "cathartic" potential of the body: the body's capacity to hold and release nonsymbolized memories as "bioenergetic" body states, elsewhere discussed in terms

**Figure 16** The labyrinth at Mid-Columbia Medical Center in Dalles, Oregon (1999). (Photo courtesy of Robert Ferré of Labyrinth Enterprises.)

of the physiology of "right-side-to-right-side" brain communication. Labyrinth walking as a therapeutic device engages the idea of a body's bioenergetic potential. Kinesthetic knowledge, experiential knowing, feeling and inhabiting one's body again: these are terms offered to the labyrinth walker to engage a mind/body connection. From an individual perspective it makes sense that physical and emotional trauma may settle into patterns that are inaccessible to the conscious self and, in fact, require that self to close down access to an entire range of human sensibility in order to avoid or desensitize an incomprehensible pain. That a wounded person may need to learn new, nonverbal, kinesthetic skills to reopen this dimension of their humanity is also understandable. But this still does not explain why that person would benefit from learning these skills in public space. With labyrinth walking, then, there must be something about the public nature of relearning skills of kinesthetic knowledge and metaphorical thinking.

### *Labyrinth Walking and Public Space*

If labyrinths are turning up in public squares and atriums we need to consider their therapeutic value in broader social terms. Certainly the idea that in modernity, where skills of rational decision making are privileged over intuitive ones, it makes sense that public selves might need to experience the revaluation of the neglected aspects of their sensorium in public space. Just as Georg Simmel had warned us at the beginning of the twentieth century, in his essay "The Metropolis and Mental Life," the metropolitan citizen's need to make rationality the dominant approach to all social encounters in public space could produce its own pathology. Simmel was writing about the European city at a time when its population was multiplying with mass migrations from the rural countryside to urban industrial centers. Compared to the rural village or town square, the streets of the metropolis were chaotic, noisy, unpredictable. Relying on a rational approach to the city, Simmel theorized, the new arrival could live in the illusion that he was in control as if in a closed environment. But rigidity can be the unwelcome side effect of the ultrarational approach. It can bring the urban psyche to neurotic twitches, or so Freud proposed, as the uncontrollable forces of life escape the crusty shell of the rationalist's screen. If today's urban citizens lack trustworthy public skills in metaphorical thinking and kinesthetic knowing, approaches that value openness and flexibility, it would certainly not have surprised Simmel. However, the idea that one day citizens would be relearning how to walk in their cities with full sensibility and awareness by tracing premodern labyrinthine contours—that, I believe, would have thrown even Simmel for a loop.

We can compare the sociopsychological dimensions of labyrinth walking with other theories that propose to explain the relation between kinesthetic knowing and public space. Michel de Certeau, for example, has argued that the rational approach we take to urban space is only one kind of knowing that we engage in the city. In his well-known essay "Walking in the City," Certeau uses the analogy between walking and narration to discuss two kinds of city space, mappable and unmappable.[35] The 1984 essay begins in a now nostalgic mode, with the author viewing New York City from the 110th floor of New York City's World Trade Center. From this height, Certeau writes, the city offers itself as a text of the organized whole, a space that is readable, like a map with fixed coordinates where everyone can share the same spatial meaning by simply recognizing the streets by their official names. We can try to bring that bird's-eye sensibility down to street level, but the experience of the pedestrian, he writes, will in fact create an unmappable city: stubborn, subtle, embodied and resistant meanings are all mobilized when we walk down a lively street. "The ordinary practitioners of the city live 'down below,'" he writes, "below the thresholds at which visibility begins … they are walkers … where bodies follow the thicks and thins of an urban 'text' they write without being able to read it. These practitioners make use of spaces that cannot be seen. …"[36]

From above, there is rational transparency; From below, there is an unreadable city where "walking narrates interests and desires that are neither determined nor captured by the system of signification used to codify them."[37] This is where "spatial practices" develop, writes Certeau. In unmappable space resides "the city's unconscious life."

Where does the social experience of the labyrinth walker fall in Certeau's idea of a mappable and unmappable city? Is labyrinth walking a conscious, rationalized, abstract, mappable practice, or is it an unconscious, daydreamed, unmappable pedestrian one? From above, the abstract contours of the labyrinth's curving pathways are visible, mappable but unnamable, like a puzzle or rebus standing out among angular street grids. From below, the contemplative spatial practice of labyrinth walking opens up Certeau's pedestrian to an experience that, while tactile, is certainly neither unconscious nor unreflected. Certeau's description of walking in the city does not appear to help us understand the function of the increasingly popular labyrinth walking.

Neither is labyrinth walking what that other important philosopher of twentieth century urban life, Walter Benjamin, so famously called "apperception in a mode of distraction." Writing on the modern European city some forty years after Simmel, Benjamin argued that distracted awareness was a mode of being that escaped the rationalization of modern urban life. Modern cities left no time for the contemplative stance of a pedestrian in reflective awe of the monumental architecture and engineering projects that surrounded him.[38] It was in a mode of distraction, Benjamin claimed, that an urbanite came to know his surrounding. Labyrinth walking, on the other hand, is something like a contemplative act. It is a form of awareness whose newfound popularity lies in stark contrast to the mode of distraction. So, neither transparently clear nor darkly inaccessible, nor experienced in distraction, the urban space described by the practice of labyrinth walking falls somewhere in between.

Writing their reflexive descriptions of the city before the mid-twentieth century, neither Simmel nor Benjamin could have foreseen how automobile traffic would so profoundly transform the experience of the pedestrian's urban life. Richard Sennett, as we saw in the preface to this volume, sought to rewrite the history of the public self in urban space transformed by the car. Empty, "dead public space" was, for Sennett, the ubiquitous mark the car made on the modern city. Sennett argued that because the car-centered city street "acquires a peculiar function, to permit motion … [t]oday, we experience an ease of motion unknown to any prior civilization." In these circumstances the public self suffers because "motion has become the most anxiety-laden of daily activities."[39] In the 1970s Sennett thought that a more consciously playful approach to normative social roles would steer modern citizens away from the anxiety and narcissistic, individuated urban life that accompanied the automobile's transformation of public space. Thirty years later in *Flesh and Stone: The Body and the City in Western Civilization*, Sennett was more convinced that the unconscious power of social ritual should not be neglected in any proposed solution to the pathologies triggered and aggravated by modern urban space. Labyrinth walking, with its legitimation of kinesthetic knowing, its expanded notion of embodied consciousness and, importantly, its ritualized use of public space does appear to be a place where U.S. culture is working through the interconnected deficits of Western consciousness, urban space, and the public self. Turning to the practice of labyrinth walking as a heuristic device, then, let us reconsider some of the issues we have elsewhere addressed regarding alternative and normative treatments for agoraphobia and their broader meaning for the spatially embedded public self.

### *Labyrinth Walking as a Heuristic Device to Explore Gender and Public Space*

Labyrinth walking directs us to issues of public space and gender.[40] From a feminist perspective, the therapeutic aims of labyrinth walking might be thought of as initial public steps, as it were, in training women to be visible as subjects (rather than as objects of the public's gaze) and to be attentive to and trustful of their own voice, a voice that has perhaps found little recognition in dominant styles of communciation where reason is the favored authoritative voice. The therapeutic emphasis on both the unspeakable, nonsymbolic tactile sense of embodied sensibility and on metaphor makes it unlike most other modern regimes of self-knowledge, training its users in skills of awareness that go beyond the psychoanalytic dualism of a split conscious/unconscious person.

Above all, the public and spatial dimension of labyrinth walking as a ritualized, therapeutic intervention into the disruptive effects of emotional trauma begs a comparison with flooding that also retrains a traumatized, mostly female population to walk in public space. Like the technique of flooding, which of necessity places the embodied knower in public space to effect its cure ("exposure *in vivo*," as the behaviorist say), labyrinth walking also uses the inseparable link between subjectivity and space discussed in this book. But unlike flooding, the therapeutic aim of labyrinth walking is not to re-create a public self by allowing the person of surplus sensibility a spectacular cathartic release and then desensitizing her to further powers of embodied knowing by leaving her sensibility just as deskilled as it was initially. Rather, labyrinth walking appears to hone the surplus sensibility of the modern public self and, like the bioenergetic biofeedback therapies discussed above, give the self new skills that authorize modes of kinesthetic knowing long unrecognized as useful or insightful for the modern public self.

It appears to me that the labyrinth, a wide open public space whose abstract emptiness is given walkable contours, inhabits public spaces of our cities recently as a therapeutic device because public places are increasingly becoming nonplaces, places of vast homogeneity (even when they are saturated with mass-produced commodities). The labyrinth is like a little training ground, a safe space in which to experiment with recovering the public self. As a therapeutic technique in late-twentieth- and twenty-first-century American cities, themselves recovering from the legacies of modernist public space, labyrinth walking plays with propriocepetive, kinesthetic knowing and revaluates it for a public self. It invokes modes of nonverbal knowing close to what many caretakers of young children recognize: psychomotorial skills that caretakers have often received by transmission from previous generations.[41] As skills of rational apprehension and normative social roles lose their effectiveness to orient and support the public self in spaces of intense urban homogeneity—empty spaces in which urban critics have long noted the reluctance of moderns urbanites to dwell comfortably—labyrinth walking takes its place as a technique to retrain our deskilled surplus sensibility.

Can the skills learned in labyrinth walking create a public self who would finally be comfortable in the kind of empty space that our century's agoraphobics have pointed out? Are labyrinths cropping up in the atriums or parking lots of shopping malls, as they once did in the cathedrals of European Christendom, with the ritual social purpose of viscerally, non-symbolically integrating the pilgrim into a now secular cosmology whose most fundamental ground is homogenous empty space? Does labyrinth walking, in other words—despite its techniques to resensitize the person of surplus sensibility—simply take a place with other therapeutic modalities that have succeeded in reinserting the person of surplus sensibility into the dominant forms of public space? This is one possible interpretation. Certainly we can say that as agoraphobia has become predominantly a women's disease, the dominant treatment modalities have moved from the psychoanalytic therapies that treat the symptomatic value of agoraphobic fear to those that remove the symptom without mediation of psychological analysis—lobotomy in the 1950s and '60s; abreactive behavioral exposure in vivo and pharmacology in the 1980s and '90s. One argument of this book has been that these dominant treatments open a new chapter on the role of desensitization in modern urban space. Their close association with the cathartic, abreactive therapies honed on twentieth-century European battlefields to treat the soldier's war neurosis remain crucial to a social understanding of how women come to be deskilled in kinesthetic knowing, treated as a split mind and body, and reinserted into the public spaces of late modernity. But do these dominant abreactive modalities for agoraphobia share a significant biosocial role with labyrinth walking—in particular, the task of desensitizing the public self to the anxiety-inducing aspects of homogenous, wide open, empty public space?

It seems to me that despite their similarities, the dominant abreactive treatments for agoraphobia are significantly different from either labyrinth walking or the other alternative modalities discussed in this chapter, especially with respect to the revaluation of surplus sensibility into legitimate modes of knowing. Like the biofeedback techniques that use breath control as a means of communicating with an externalized simulation of brain activity, like the "right-side-to-right-side" brain modes of communication such as EMDR that use a retrained awareness of the body's most minute autonomic gestures to interrupt disabling patterns of behavior, labyrinth walking is an alternative modality that uses an undervalued, kinesthetic sensibility and revaluates it into an authoritative mode of knowing. Unlike flooding, cognitive therapies, or psychopharmacology, the alternative treatments discussed here recognize some communicative value beyond the indication of pathology in the agoraphobic's symptoms of rapid breathing, imbalance, and stunted spatial movement. They all recognize in these symptoms a potential capacity of knowing that can be developed by honing proprioceptive skills.

There are many reasons why Western culture appears so lacking when it comes to skills of kinesthetic knowing. While such embodied skills are highly valued in certain domains—in the commercial success of sports, athletic training is a prized arena of kinesthetic skill; musical training is another site where the body's disciplined, intuitive intelligence is well recognized—these skills only appear in their respective and restricted domains. Western culture may recognize these skills in their specific spheres, but how well does it understand that such skill may be transferable into public life? Most often it appears that the skills to better communicate with our embodied, affective social life are reentering Western culture through yoga and other techniques from the meditative traditions of Eastern cultures, as Irigaray has discussed. Neuroscientists also turn to study the brain wave patterns of Tibetan monks in meditative states achieved through well-honed skills in order to better understand a side of consciousness that appears wholly mysterious to Western reason. In Eastern traditions these skills are valued for creating a compassionate citizen; in Western scientific and popular traditions they often appear to be valued for showing us the limitations and misdirections of our own conceptions of consciousness.

There are at least two ways to think about why the full multisensory capacities of kinesthetic skills are so undervalued as to be generally absent (when not medicated into oblivion) from public space in Western culture. Indeed, both of these explanations are related to the sort of large-scale changes in urban space and to the history of treatments for the increasingly female disorder of agoraphobia analyzed in the pages of this book. First, in the West, the skills of kinesthetic knowing we are speaking of have been relegated historically to the undervalued domain of women's work—in particular, to the care of young children. And second, as mixed-use public spaces that accommodate the needs of women and children increasingly shrink in the modern city, so too does the possibility of transferring kinesthetic skills of knowing into public space. What then happens to the proprioceptive self in the kind of "dead public space" described by Sennett, where skills requiring refined kinesthetic sensibility no longer help orient a public self? Agoraphobia tells us that, in modernity, deskilled kinesthetic sensibility can turn to surplus sensibility in the form of acute anxiety and that women, more than men, are left holding surplus sensibility in public space. The history of dominant treatments for agoraphobia suggests that modern psychology increasingly treats the surplus sensibility arising in "dead public space" as it treats the surplus sensibility arising from war zones: with surge suppression or with wild cathartic displays like flooding, both of which approach surplus sensibility as noncommunicative, nonsymbolic material that breaks into consciousness and needs to be evacuated—unlike alternative treatments like biofeedback or labyrinth walking, which treat nonsymbolic, surplus sensibility as unrecognized modes of knowing in need of new communicational skills rather than as incommunicable material with no safe place in the conscious self.

### *Labyrinth Walking, Agoraphobia, and the Psychomotorial Self: Transferring Kinesthetic Skills into Public Space*

While not yet tested in any clinical way, there is evidence to suggest that as the mind/body paradigm shifts toward a nondualist approach in alternative treatments for agoraphobia, the agoraphobic's surplus sensibility will be treated differently. We see this most drastically when comparing the public spectacle of abreactive treatments for agoraphobia—the patient is brought to a shopping center and to a public exhibition of a full-fledged anxiety attack—with the minute bodily sensations that are recognized as therapeutic in biofeedback treatments or in the public practice of labyrinth walking. In an article that calls for an "anthropologist's" attention to how "the body effectively encloses and reveals the psyche," French psychologist François Dagognet notes that a renewed focus on the smaller gestures that make up somatic appearances brings "shelter from the cathartic mania that affects so many theroreticians, including Freud."[42] Instead of the spectacular release of abreacted emotions, Dagognet looks to microfractures, minute muscular contractions that might occur in a patient's speech, gait, facial expressions, or gestures, in order to discover a personal registry of "psychological difficulties, obstructions, genuine blockages … [in order to] better recognize those beleaguered and tense places where the body is besieged than we could with purely psychological or projective investigation (for example, of the Rorschach type)."[43] Dagognet notes that "a key element of [the therapist's] art [is] to externalize buried psychomotility as much as affectivity (which he apprehends during the act of transference). … In effect, the psychomotorial has been obliged to become 'virtual' to such an extent that it has almost disappeared from view. One must learn to represent it, to convert the interior to the exterior."[44]

Bioenergetic body therapies also externalize and represent in biofeedback strategies what Dagognet calls the "psychomotility" of the public self—a psychomotorial self. The reader must initially bristle to see such labored jargon used to speak of the way everyday practices, from breathing to walking, register emotional disturbances. On second thought it appears that, in our own age, the neologism may be necessary to describe what is right under our noses, an almost unrepresentable form of sensibility, just as in Sigmund Freud and Josef Breuer's day *abreaction* was a necessary term coined to depict the sensibility common to the unspeakable experience of the hysteric.

Today, the figure of the agoraphobic is, in this respect, much like the figure of the hysteric a century ago: the agoraphobic's faltering gait is an indication of a sensibility that registers what can only be known to the dominant medical community as a "virtual" reality, a spatial phenomenon with "no there there." Likewise, the problem of empty space in our cities is not yet a "real" enough one. For the emergent domain of mind/body medicine cultural studies scholars can contribute historical background to the newfound appreciation of kinesthetic knowledge in the agoraphobic's complaint, much as feminist historians reappraised the experience of those Victorian women whose complaint was merely hysterical for the founding fathers of psychoanalysis. What does such work add to the tradition of the talking cure? If my gait in the city is also a registry of the pathological relations I accumulate in my life, what will I gain by "translating," as it were, this "psychomotility," this muscle memory into speech? One thing the behaviorists show us with the successes of their abreactive flooding and graded exposure in vivo techniques is that vocal expression alone appears to be an insufficient response to agoraphobia. Agoraphobia is a pathology of modern space whose most successful treatments involve a "psychomotorial" response, a form of embodied knowing whose skills of tangible sensibility can be honed and transferred to public space, where they can engage in nonsymbolic communication. Whether the skills for nonsymbolic communication may be actually forgotten and thus missing from our culture (and only importable through Eastern practices of mindful breathing) or whether they have been mostly relegated and segregated to (predominantly women's) domains of affective labor—especially those domains involving the care of children—is a debatable topic. Nevertheless, labyrinth walking as a premodern and postmodern therapeutic practice offers insight into how skills of kinesthetic knowing would be transferable to public space.

There is one case in the clinical literature on agoraphobia that neatly sums up many of the issues discussed in this chapter and even places labyrinth walking closer than generally thought to being a legitimate treatment for agoraphobia. The study is by Dr. A. Orwin, a British behavioral psychiatrist who claimed success in the *British Journal of Psychiatry* in 1973 with an article titled "The Running Treatment: A Preliminary Communication on a New Use for an Old Therapy (Physical Activity) in the Agoraphobic Syndrome." The author, who had been "involved in the treatment of over a hundred mainly chronic cases" of agoraphobia, writes that he came across the idea of a running treatment while testing a (mostly unsuccessful) respiratory therapy that would induce breathlessness in the overly anxious agoraphobic by having her inhale a mixture of carbon dioxide and oxygen when panicking. (The idea apparently being that one autonomic response, hyperventilation, would interfere with another autonomic experience, panic.) Far from the therapeutic breathing skills one learns from Eastern traditions like yoga, behaviorist respiratory therapy using noxious carbon dioxide counteracts somatic phenomena in a crude and cumbersome way. It is reminiscent of the huffing and puffing breathing exercises many American prenatal classes used in the 1970s to train expectant mothers to counteract the pain of labor and delivery. These exercises were as unsuccessful in birthing as they were in agoraphobic exposure in vivo.[45] When the doctor studying the running therapy ran into "technical difficulties in the transport of carbon dioxide/oxygen cylinders," he was inadvertently lead to use the low-tech skill of simple running as the means to induce breathlessness. Thus, patients were coached to run first in a linear fashion toward and through their "anxiety zone." Eventually, the doctor reports, the linear nature of these flooding in vivo exposures changed as did the pace of the patient's gait until eventually it looks as if the agoraphobic were tracing enormous invisible labyrinths by walking through the city. "[We] assumed," he writes, "that patients extended their distance from the home base in a linear fashion, but generally and for practical reasons this was not the case. Usually patients advanced by running in a linear fashion away from the base until they entered an 'anxiety zone,' and were then made to travel as near as possible *circumferentially*, bearing in mind topographical features, so that they remained a fixed distance (and time) from base … later in therapy walking rapidly might suffice. … Gains were consolidated by normal walking within the newly acquired anxiety-free areas."[46]

The new anxiety-free areas act like the labyrinth in that they become a new form of pedestrian zone where walking is safe. The author of the study successfully treated eight agoraphobic patients with this method (six women and two men). In his report he gives the example of a severe agoraphobic woman whose case neatly recapitulates so much of what is discused in the pages of this book that it is worth quoting at length. Note the urban nature of the anxiety-free zone created by the patient who must learn to walk on "pedestrian crossings in heavy traffic":

> A housebound woman aged 45 with a 13-year history had had previous treatment elsewhere by behavioral methods, including hypnosis, graded performance and a course of methohexitone desensitization … with only moderate effect and with rapid relapse. Therapy was commenced with CO2/O2, and she was soon able to walk in the hospital grounds but she disliked the inhalations. Treatment was then switched to the usual graded performance programs bolstered by

> running or rapid walking (she initially weighed 14 st 5 lb.) at first from the Unit and later, as she improved, from home through the agency of a social worker being trained in behavioral methods.
>
> She had seven weeks in-patient therapy, and then attended two days per week for seven weeks. She was also seen at home four times, at which time *she was free of all symptoms except one which was reality based, i.e. she had minimal anxiety on pedestrian crossings in heavy traffic (fear of crossing a busy main road near her home was her original symptom).* She was made to run about 600 yards to such a crossing (weight was now at 13 st. 61 lbs) and crossed repeatedly with no anxiety. Not only was she completely free from all symptoms but she was very confident because she felt that by her own effort she would have the ability to overcome any tendency to relapse.[47]

The success of the walking sessions suggests that the psychomotility of everyday life can be counterpoised to the spectacle of cathartic release. Labyrinth walking versus abreactive flooding: one treatment comes from simple skills of ambulation in conversation with the mysteries of life; the other comes from the battlefield and the tragic consequences of failed diplomacy. Labyrinth walking may work for agoraphobia on the same principle as biofeedback strategies like mindful breathing worked. In these therapies the body communicates with the self in little understood ways. Whether such communication works disjunctively through intervention and disruption or whether it works in the kind of complex model being studied as right to right brain communication, the successes of these modalities grant new authority to kinesthetic knowing.

Labyrinth walking as a heuristic device and as an actual therapy: our socially conscious consideration of labyrinth walking updates for modernity an old Roman saying, *solvitur ambulando* (it is solved by walking). What is solved by walking? *Horror vacui*, I would say, the modern fear of the emptiness in today's public space. Labyrinth walking as an actual therapy in the above British study was likewise instructive in a broad cultural manner. The heavy canisters for the carbon dioxide/oxygen mixture to induce hyperventilation were themselves a metaphor for the forgetfulness of breathing endemic, as Irigaray has showed, in Western philosophy and psychology. Walking, here as well, is a treatment to counteract breath becoming mere autonomic impulse in Western psychology and to salvage the potential of breathing for the embodied consciousness of the psychomotorial self.

## Conclusion: *Horror Vacui, Solvitur Ambulando* in City Design

If indeed the larger social complex of agoraphobia we have been dealing with in this book could be "solved by walking," the solution might look something like the *woonerf* [literally, "living yard"] that the Dutch have been building for some time now in residential urban areas. Typically, a woonerf creates a new kind of urban commons where trees, planters, and parked cars share the same space as public benches, artwork, and children's play areas (see figure 17). The aim is "to create a street-space so unlike a traditional street that vehicle speeds are significantly reduced by the instinctive, behavioural change in drivers. With vehicles traveling at low speeds, all users are able to establish eye contact and negotiate with one another."[48] In northern Europe the creation of these sites, what the English call "home zones," is subverting the traditional distinction between street and sidewalk.[49] Pedestrians, cyclists, and vehicles share the space on equal terms with children, and cars travel at little more than walking pace. "Home zones embody the design principles of safety through uncertainty, whereby an absence of priority along with short driver sight-lines, social activity and a lack of clarity regarding vehicle routes, significantly reduce vehicle speeds."[50] These are zones of urban life where walking sets the pace for an awareness of surroundings whose most significant orienting device comes not from rational planning

**Figure 17** Woonerf and woonerf street sign showing shared rights to public space held by pedestrians, children, automobile drivers, and local residents. (Photo courtesy of Julia Thomas/Transport 2000.)

that seeks to functionally segregate activity and control space from the top down, nor from commercial directives that overwhelm the senses, but from the individual's participation in an open, yet small-scale, community that can still surprise the self.[51] And, in a most unusual move in the history of the modern city, this urban renewal design allows children to enter public space on an equal footing with the automobile.

Woonerf, living yards, and home zones propose a more radical urban design than many of the new urbanist developments seen in the United States. If Europe appears closer to a cure for the pathologies of modern urban space traced in this book through the agoraphobic's reluctant gait and the dominant treatments to correct it, the new trend of labyrinth walking is a useful trope to consider why. Modernist urban design and, with it, the emptiness of "dead public space" occupies more space in American than in European cities. The labyrinth maintains the empty abstraction so characteristic of public space in modernist cities, but it does so in an artificially enclosed space. Like new urbanist design, these are tentative approaches to relearning to walk in our cities. Like the woonerf, they give new value and authority to tactile modes of knowing. At least the labyrinth offers contours where there once was only empty space. The proliferation of urban labyrinths in public spaces of American cities could suggest that we, as a culture, are searching for the skills of tactile, embodied knowing to treat pathologies of modern urban space.

# Conclusion

At the turn of the twentieth century, sociologist Georg Simmel noted that the explosive rural migration into the modern metropolis demanded a new kind of public self.[1] The metropolitan individual, Simmel argued, experiences city streets teeming with the rush of strangers, trolleys, and market exchanges as so many jolts and shocks. The individual that adapts to this space does so by forming a protective screen to shield the public self from the assaults of city life. Rationality, wrote Simmel, is that screen. The rational man is the successful urban citizen because rationality will filter out the myriad sensate experiences he encounters as an urban pedestrian. Approaching a walk in the city as getting from point A to point B, the rational self can treat the city's multitudes and activities as so much white noise, so much irrational surplus. Money, that most abstract and rational mediator among the enormous diversity of people, things, and relations in metropolitan life will also bolster the rational self as it adapts to the big city. The more social life can be commodified, the more smoothly social exchanges can function. Rationality, Simmel warned, would be the strongest (albeit restrictive) feature in the mental life of the new public self.

One hundred years later in the largest cities of the United States and Europe we have seen what intensified rationality and hyper-commercialization has done to urban life: in the United States, highway rationality lead to highway irrationality as urban sprawl made urban commutes longer and longer; commercial interests as the guiding lights of city planning brought both functional efficiency and greater urban anomie as American and European cities were transformed by large-scale, modernist urban housing projects for the poor, and by shopping centers and strip malls as the new form of public space. And what became of the surplus that the rational city dweller filtered out? She is found in the growing population of agoraphobics. Her deskilled sensibility rendered mere surplus, she is increasingly absent from the public spaces of the modern megalopolis. What does it take to recover her public self? Pharmaceuticals and other techniques of desensitization provided by behavioral and cognitive therapies have been the suggested companions to her reinsertion in public space. But, as we have seen, their effectiveness is unsteady at best.

Simmel also warned that fear and anxiety would be key features of the modern metropolis as explosive population growth and new groups of immigrants made encounters with strangers—so rare in the village square—an inevitable experience of everyday life in the public space of the big city. For Simmel and later sociologists, the stranger is the one who looks different and whose face becomes a screen for the fear, the fantasmatic projection of all that is different from the majority culture's values and norms.[2] The critique of modernist urban planning has much to say about the psychic burden placed on citizens who do not fit the "one-size-fits-all" mentality of modernist public space. City planners have generally solved the fear of otherness through segregation and by making efficient, high-speed traffic flow one of the highest priorities of the supposedly neutral, rational approach to city planning. Countering the hyperrational modernist approach, critical planners have begun to say that "fear in the city is not a problem to be solved, at least not along the lines of the modernist dreams of control, order and transparency. Rather, we face the eternal, impossible question of how 'we', all strangers to each other, can live together in the city."[3] The solutions these critics propose often involve a transformation of the role of the city planner.[4] Instead of managing fear as urban reformers have for the past century and a half, since Georges-Eugène Haussmann, by rendering the city transparent and orderly, creating parks and playgrounds and other "civilizing urban facilities" (as if by controlling space we could control the subjectivities produced in that space), these critics propose a "therapeutic approach" (in the psychoanalytic sense of creating a dialogue) wherein a city planner begins by acquiring a deep understanding of the cultural differences that are behind projections of urban fears. The therapeutic approach asks the urban planner to work as an anthropologist would, hanging out, talking with people, and generally studying the cultural differences that have provoked fear in dominant groups and anger, mistrust, and misunderstanding among minority groups. With the aim of enabling cross-cultural understanding, the city planner then creates safe spaces for antagonistic parties (the "strangers" and the dominant others) to discuss their concerns and negotiate a solution. Different communities will negotiate different solutions and a city planned in these "bottom-up" ways where middle-class, majority values do not silence the differences of the strangers will be a city of great diversity, fostering cross-cultural awareness, tolerance and, more important, new kinds of zoning, new kinds of public spaces.

Important as this is to the problem of urban fear, attention to the stranger as an issue in city planning still does not treat the problems raised by the agoraphobic, for whom anxiety is not so much a result of a projection of negative values onto the stranger as it is an introjection onto the self of a certain kind of spatial complexity that I have identified in this book as empty space. In the preceding chapters I have taken the position that agoraphobia is not just an illness of middle-class, white, suburban women who fear the otherness they encounter on the city streets and thus retreat to the safety of the suburban world. Rather, the research shows that agoraphobia is more properly a problem of living with massive, generally homogeneous forms of public space that do not recognize the difference that the agoraphobic's highly sensitive being presents. For whatever reasons a person experiences her sensibilities in their most heightened forms—because of a traumatic past that stays viscerally present; because a physical frailty creates vulnerability; because a poetic sensibility creates increased openness to the sensory world; or because the demands of gestation and early child care make the adult self vigilantly aware of the needs of those who cannot verbally express themselves—the agoraphobic is the person who has been rendered a person of surplus sensibility by public spaces that have become, to once again quote Marc Augé, "the non-places of supermodernity." These are built spaces of nonrecognition that have powers of their own to train urban citizens to accept the built emptiness of modernity as an aconceptual structure of feeling, a nonsymbolic experience of what Enlightenment thinking proposed as the universal common ground for all the world's citizens. Indeed, it appears that it is not so much the agoraphobic who *introjects* the emptiness of modern public space as it is the space itself that *projects* onto the agoraphobic the sense of a common ground for the public self, a ground where only certain restricted kinds of sensibility can produce authoritative, trustworthy knowledge.

This volume has aimed to show how the changing variety of therapeutic approaches used to make the modern city inhabitable for the agoraphobic are related to treatments that help the modern soldier better handle the trauma of the modern war zone. Behavioral, pharmacological, cognitive, and psychoanalytic therapies are, like the therapeutic approaches used by critical urban planners, also approaches that treat issues of cultural diversity in public space. Unlike the anthropologically inspired approaches of the critical planners, however, psychological approaches to agoraphobia tend to reduce gendered cultural diversity to a set of urban behaviors that reflect culturally masculine skills—specifically, the skills associated with the bourgeois European male whose being in the world is characterized by mastery, control, and making rationality the privileged mode of knowing into which all other modes can be "translated," as it were. But most striking is the fact that the dominant therapies to treat agoraphobia come from the Euro-American battlefields of the twentieth century, suggesting that the normative public self is increasingly best served by strategies of desensitization to the feel of a public space that has become more tolerant of the (virtual and actual) routine violence that accompanies greater speed and mobility. It is as if the soldier's transition back to civilian life had set a norm for transitions from all manner of violence in the western urban world.

In Western states there is no meaningful, collective ritual to process the soldier's reentry to civilian life after the experience of modern warfare. Freud and other psychologists noticed this after World War One when they treated the "shell-shocked" soldier with individualized, cathartic methods. In World War Two the individual soldier suffering from "war neurosis" received a similarly immediate abreactive therapy to treat the unspeakable horrors of his wartime experience. After the Vietnam war, U.S. doctors developed new drugs to treat the anxiety associated with the veteran's chronic "post-traumatic stress disorder." These treatments that defuse the symptomatic complaint of the modern soldier who cannot process or integrate the experience of the battlefield in civilian life can now be used to defuse embodied complaints of all civilians. As we have seen, getting the agoraphobic back on the street is most effectively accomplished in our culture by treatments—behavioral techniques of flooding; pharmacological manipulations of the nervous system; and most recently biofeedback training—which recover a public self not by creating a meaningful relation but by defusing an unbearable reaction to public space. Thus the larger cultural project of collectively creating a process to hear and mediate the complaint, in short the process of ritual, is no longer offered in these treatments to either the traumatized soldier or the phobic civilian. The kind of public empty space that triggers the agoraphobic's reaction may itself be the public space of ritual mythos where those without civic voice publicly act out what is otherwise unrepresentable in civic life. In this respect, such spaces are like what Richard Sennett (see Preface) found in his study of the dark underside of the ancient Greek agora where women once a year acted out the Demeter myth. However, the study of agoraphobia shows us that finding this precarious, spatialized form of political voice for the city's underrecognized only indicates that empty space is itself the mythos behind modern civic life. It tells us that a boundless "universe of nonrecognition," with strong military overtones, is what increasingly holds the modern urban commons together as a culturally shared structure of feeling.

The alternative therapies that use biofeedback strategies and bioenergetic models of embodied consciousness, however, do add another dimension to the picture of desensitizing urbanites to the mythic and real emptiness of public space. In fact, these alternative therapies do not so much desensitize the agoraphobic to the feel of public space as they retool her kinesthetic sensibility to communicate with space that has, for her, become charged with emotion. On a positive note, the alternative therapies project a spatial imaginary that is closer to the mixed-use city design of the *woonerf* (discussed in chapter 7) than to the "dead public space" of international style. In a woonerf, a driver who learns to alter a (modern) right of way does so because a street has suddenly, with little warning, become a protected playground and the temporality of daily life has slowed down to disjunctively accommodate other forms and norms of life. Likewise the agoraphobic who becomes skilled in communicating with urban space through newly acquired, nonconceptual, proprioceptive techniques learns to move with greater ease in the city because he develops a public self that consciously communicates across affective, cognitive and proprioceptive orders of his being. In Western modernity these domains of being have become increasingly disjunctive and unable to communicate with each other. They have been separated, much as the modernist city separated its work space from leisure space, its commercial zones from residential zones, and so forth. Thus the similar spatial imaginary behind both mixed-use public space like the woonerf and a kinesthetically retooled public self that was formerly agoraphobic suggests, from a broader cultural perspective, that repairing community involves changing the larger spatial paradigm of empty space that underpins both cities and modern subjectivity.

The cultural study of the last century of treatments for agoraphobia undertaken in this volume can now be engaged to address a final broadly cultural question posed in the preface and introduction concerning the role played by empty space in the construction of common space in modernity. Many social thinkers have pointed to the way that empty space became the real and imagined background for how universally common space was designed and engineered in the modern era. In early modern political thinkers like John Locke, the so-called New World was wishfully described as *terra nullius*, empty of legitimate community life. This imaginary and legal designation enabled theft, occupation and expulsion of indigenous inhabitants from their lands. Locke's other idea about empty space had both legal and psychological consequences for modern citizens. "Let us suppose, then," wrote Locke in his *Two Treatises of Government*, "the mind to be, as we say, *white paper*, void of all characters, without any Ideas: how comes it to be furnished?"[5] The metaphor of the mind as a *tabula rasa* (empty slate) had persuasive force in arguments to extend the Enlightenment dominium of reason to all non-European minds. The tabula rasa argument (originally in Aristotle) makes Euclidean space—space that is extensive, everywhere the same, static, uniformly subject to the same laws, and abstract in the sense of being empty—the universal foundation of reason. Thus empty, homogeneous space in Locke is an originary fiction of abstract space that serves as a foundation for the seizure of real space by the state or by individuals. Even though these spatial arguments have come to influence domains as diverse as modern law, city design, and psychology, many social critics have pointed out the detrimental consequences for creating community life based on spatial thinking that imputes mythic community-building functions to empty space. Locke's contemporary, the philosopher Gottfried Wilhelm Leibniz was an adamant opponent of the tabula rasa arguments. "[Locke's supporters]" Leibniz argued, "suppose that in the beginning the mind is a blank slate, empty of all characters and ideas. … This tabula rasa that everyone is speaking about is, in my opinion, a fiction that nature finds intolerable."[6]

In our own era, it is the French philosopher Gilles Deleuze who makes Leibniz's philosophical system a starting point for describing a new kind of foundational space, one characterized not by emptiness but by movement.[7] As we saw in chapter 3, Deleuze and co-author Félix Guattari propose the concept of intensive (as opposed to extensive) space to elaborate a new theory of subjectivity. These philosophers also address how many diverse products of the Western philosophical imagination—from sovereignty to mathematics and city design, to name a few—might be thought differently by avoiding the epistemological foundation of static, extensive, empty space. Deleuze's work has inspired my research on the treatments of agoraphobia and made me aware of the broader social importance of how post-1980s treatments for agoraphobia evacuate reference to public space. Thanks to the theoretical work of Deleuze, I more clearly understood that when agoraphobia began to be treated as a "fear of fear" instead of a fear of certain kinds of public space, it was following a path well-established in the modern era to support certain kinds of public selves and delegitimize others. Deleuze's work lays out a conceptual agenda for what is wrong with Western thinking grounded in empty space. But as the present volume shows, understanding empty space as a foundational logic in modern life takes us beyond philosophy. It requires historically astute and culturally sensitive research. That is because emptiness is not so much simply a recurring metaphor for common space in the modern era. It is also a complex figure of modern thought. In other words, empty space is not only a product of the imagination, it is also an orienting device for the public self and a real environment we now inhabit. Empty space is a functionally efficient aspect of the built environment of the modern city. It contributes to the way cities exponentially increase their size and to the way citizens persist in imagining their overgrown cities to cohere. Even when many indicators tell them that their cities no longer function as life-sustaining communities, empty space provides an imaginal framework for citizens—as well as modern architects and advertisers—to continue to insert themselves in city life. Essential to our deeper understanding of this spatial figure of modern thought is the fact that empty space is a structure of modern urban feeling, an unrepresentable phenomenon that is increasingly sensed through anxiety.

Given the many roles played by this dominant spatial imaginary, we should proceed with caution when encountering thematics of empty space in political theories of modern democracy. Poststructuralist social critics may be lured into thinking that making visible the foundational emptiness of modern Western sovereignty and community formation is a sufficient form of critique. They may even ironically propose that the unrepresentable ground of modern democracy is the figure of "an empty place," a figure that must now be represented and embraced as an anti-foundationalist site for our complex, global, multi-cultural society (see introduction).[8] But if we consider, as we have in this volume, the long reach of empty space as a figure of thought in Western modernity, its hold on urban development and its influence in psychological therapies, any further embrace of such metaphors appears an unlikely source of critical thought. The challenge now is to see what new spatial thinking can do for our cities and our public selves.

As I began this study of the relation between empty space and the modern urban self, I often thought of an early child development theory I had once heard where, it was argued, babies needed to be placed out-of-doors, on their backs, facing the wide open sky for a certain amount of time each day in order to develop a sense of comfort and even playfulness with the gaping expansiveness of their natural environment. Reading Le Corbusier's description of the "ineffable" empty space in which the high modernist architect builds his world made me think again about that theory. What kind of city, what kind of child gets its identity from constant contact with boundless space devoid of tactile support? Looking further into the theory I was not surprised to discover that the baby-on-its-back idea was developed by a Hungarian psychologist for use in the orphanages of war-torn Eastern Europe.[9] It was a method of training self-comfort techniques to babies who, because of a shortage of care-givers, would receive very little human touch in their early lives. Under the open sky the babies would begin rocking back and forth and, perhaps engaging a cathartic potential of their animal species, eventually stop crying without being picked up. If the agoraphobic is indeed the miners' canary with regard to the fate of urban sensibilities in modernity, she tells us that modern urbanites, like the wartime orphans, live in public spaces with fewer and fewer tactile supports. They need to develop skills of self comfort and composure in such spaces, skills that defuse the anxiety that can come from built environments of vast homogeneity, regardless of whether the vastness is sterile and empty (like the urban freeway) or saturated with every known consumer commodity (like the modern shopping center). When we add to this picture of twentieth century urban modernity the fact that women are increasingly seeking treatments for agoraphobia, we see that these most common forms of public space have little use for the kind of kinesthetic sensibilities and affective skills learned from labor traditionally associated with women's work—especially the care of children.

In the preceding chapters I have examined the clinical literature on treatments for agoraphobia in the broader context of modernity's large-scale urban renewal projects and the philosophical and literary imagination that brings all these disparate domains into the larger cultural conversation behind the modern public self. My main argument is fundamentally a spatial one concerning the fate of the urban commons. It can perhaps be summarized by imagining the *woonerf* next to the urban bombing range pictured in the Preface to this book. Here is an agoraphobically inspired description of two radical extremes of urban design: one built in the complexities of an already existing material and social world where highly trainable adults learn democratic, kinesthetic skills useful to better communicate with children but transferable to better communicate (albeit disjunctively) with the technologically, biologically, and emotionally diverse forms of life around them; the other built in the empty space of the Sonoran Desert, where a no-man's-land is disguised as a "nightmarish Legoland" and failed diplomacy has made violence the norm. In these two extreme modes is highlighted the potential for the modern urban commons built with and without empty space.

# Notes

## Preface

1. Border guards were already alerting the marines in charge twice a week to halt operations when they spotted "illegals" on the bombing range.
2. See a description of this study in Robin M. Henig, "The Quest to Forget," *New York Times Magazine,* April 4, 2004, 32–37. Dispensation of beta-blocking drugs after any incident that could conceivably bring an urban citizen at some future point to a state of surplus sensibility appears to be the next step in the medicalized treatments of anxiety disorders. In the Boston study propranolol is offered to all patients who present with severe trauma. Offering beta-blockers to all trauma patients is a preemptive move to capture the much smaller 30 percent of trauma patients who actually go on to develop phobias.
3. See Eric Leed, *No Man's Land: Combat and Identity in World War I* (Cambridge: Cambridge University Press, 1979); see also Elaine Showalter, *The Female Malady: Woman, Madness and English Culture, 1830–1980* (New York: Pantheon, 1987).
4. Richard Sennett, *The Fall of Public Man: On the Social Psychology of Capitalism* (New York: Vintage, 1978), 262.
5. Thus, Sennett writes that

   > in sheer physical terms, we deny any limits on physical motion in the city, and then are surprised that the result is a disastrous deadening of the city as an organism. The Victorians struggled with the idea of a boundaryless self; it is the very essence of the discontent produced by the confusion of public and private. We simply deny, in these various ways, limits upon the self. But to deny is not to erase; in fact, the problems become more intractable because they are no longer being confronted. Through contradictions inherited from the past and through the denial of the past, we remain imprisoned in the cultural terms of the 19th Century. Thus the end of a belief in public life is not a break with 19th Century bourgeois culture, but rather an escalation of its terms.
   >
   > The structure of an intimate society is twofold. Narcissism is mobilized in social relations, and the experience of disclosure of one's feelings to others becomes destructive. These structural characteristics also have links to the 19th Century. For narcissism to be mobilized in a society, for people to focus on intangible tones of feeling and motive, a sense of group ego interest must be suspended. This group ego consists in a sense of what people need, want, or demand, no matter what their immediate emotional impressions. The seeds of erasing a sense of group ego were planted in the last century. (Ibid., 262)

6. Butler discusses role-play as an empowerment strategy in terms of parody and subversion; see Judith Butler, *Gender Trouble* (New York: Routledge, 1999), especially section three and the conclusion, 101–90. See also the Mexican political philosopher Maria Pia Lara, *Moral Textures: Feminists Narratives in the Public Sphere* (Berkeley and Los Angeles: University of California Press, 1998), which makes a historical argument for the illocutionary force of women's privatized experience once it finds the proper cultural framework (or genre) that allows it to be recognized in the public sphere. Lara shows how women's privatized social roles are expanded by an aesthetic transformation that functions similarly to Butler's notion of "performance." For Lara, when women's experience was transformed into the proper aesthetic genre—her examples include Hannah Arendt's biographical and philosophical works and the novels of Jane Austen—their circulation in the public sphere led to an expansion of genre conventions as well as an expansion of women's social roles evidenced in changes in public policy and laws that empowered women.
7. Patricia Clough, in "The Affective Turn: Political Economy and the Biomediated Body" (at http://www.le.ac.uk/ulmc/cppe/affective_turn.pdf (2)) critiques Butler's thesis, noting, "Already a move away from a strictly semiotic treatment of the materiality of bodies, Butler's emphasis on the performative aspect of bodily matter, nonetheless, must be brought beyond its emphasis on a discursive construction of bodily matter, as a matter of imaginary surfaces, representation and specular reflection of a morphological normativity." Several recent works seek to readdress the omission of the biological body in social and cultural theories of embodied personhood. These works turn to the persistent role of affect as preindividual, presymbolic materiality, often seeking links with fields like neuroscience that have created new instruments to examine emotions and patterned brain activity. See for example, Elizabeth Wilson, *Psychosomatic: Feminism and the Neurological Body* (Durham, NC: Duke University Press, 2004); and Tim Newton, "Truly Embodied Sociology: Marrying the Social and Biological?" *Sociological Review* 51, no. 1 (2003): 20–42.
8. See Richard Sennett, *Flesh and Stone: The Body and the City in Western Civilization* (New York: W. W. Norton, 1994).
9. For an example of how the Demeter myth and others were used as critical tools for the construction of an empowered feminine self in the second wave of U.S. feminist writing during the 1970s, see Phyllis Chesler, *Women and Madness*, 2nd ed. (New York: Palgrave MacMillan, 2005), which outlines the later feminist criticism of this project.
10. For a critical discussion of the need to temper the social constructivist position in social and cultural geography with a deeper sense of an embodied self that exceeds both symbolic interpretation and biomedical reduction, see Felicity Callard, "The Taming of Psychoanalysis in Geography," *Social and Cultural Geography* 4, no. 3 (2003): 295–312, which notes that cultural and social geographers tend to use only those concepts of psychoanalysis that fit a social constructivists paradigm, thus avoiding the epistemological and ontological commitments that obtain in embracing/examining the fuller spectrum of concepts that follow from Freud's work as well as the work of more recent psychoanalytic thinkers such as Joan Copjec, Jacques Lacan, and Slavoj Žižek. Callard notes that particular aspects of psychoanalysis have been selected and represented as if they were symptomatic of the whole approach, "penis envy" being an example of such gross parody. She writes, "[In] the current field of psychoanalytic geography … figures such as the "abject" and the "ego" [also] have centre stage. The *truly monstrous* (in contrast to the grossly parodic) figures of psychoanalysis—those of the 'repetition compulsion', the 'death drive' the traumatic neuroses, the Freudian unconscious—are kept hiding in the wings. If they enter, the entire stage of psychoanalytic geography might shake, for such figures threaten the models of resistance, agency, and resignification that have, till now, dominated discussions of psychoanalytic geography more broadly. It is time for those figures to make their entrance" (308).

    Also important in this regard is Elizabeth Wilson's critical inquiry into a Freudian legacy that is much more closely attached to the role of the nervous system and its non-symbolic mode of "communicating" with the social, cultural, and political world; see Wilson, *Psychosomatic*.

11. Cultural geographers and anthropologists do not approach emotions as reified labels for concretized psychophysical states or objectivized internal "event-things." In other words, a cultural view of emotions does not study emotions outside of the social and cultural context in which they were experienced, understood, and talked about. Clifford Geertz, the well-known innovator of interpretive anthropology, positioned the study of emotions squarely in the context of cultural analysis. Emotions as well as ideas and beliefs, Geertz argued, are cultural artifacts. See "Bodies of Emotion: Rethinking Culture and Emotion Through Southeast Asia" by Tom Boellstorff and Johan Lindquist, an introduction to the special edition of *Ethnos* 69, no. 4 (2004), 437–444, devoted to recent work in the cross-cultural study of emotions.

## Introduction

1. Agoraphobia, the study shows, is more common in urban than in rural areas. Its incidence is similar across ethnic groups and age groups for those between eighteen and sixty-four years of age. The Catchment Study of 1991 found that the incidence (4 percent) is significantly higher than those found in earlier investigations conducted in England, Germany, Switzerland, and the United States, which reported prevalence rates of agoraphobia ranging from .6 percent to 3.6 percent. The figures on agoraphobia come from the Epidemiological Catchment Area Survey, a comprehensive study of the prevalence of psychiatric disorders in the United States; see Lee Robins and Darrel Regier, eds. *Psychiatric Disorders in America: The American Epidemiological Catchment Area Study* (New York: Free Press, 1991.) The U.S. National Comorbidity Study (1990–1992) that surveyed over 8,000 respondents reported higher rates of agoraphobia: lifetime prevalences for agoraphobia were 6.7/100; for panic disorder they were 3.5/100; for social phobia, 13.3/100. See Kenneth S. Kendler, "Lifetime and 12-month prevalence of DSM-III-R psychiatric disorders in the United States: results from the National Comorbidity Study," *Archives of General Psychiatry* 51 (1994) 8–19. See also Lisa Capps and Elinor Ochs, *Constructing Panic: The Discourse of Agoraphobia* (Cambridge, MA: Harvard University Press, 1995); and Jeffrey E. Hecker and Geoffrey L. Thorpe, *Agoraphobia and Panic: A Guide to Psychological Treatment* (Boston: Allyn and Bacon, 1992), on the difficulty of curing agoraphobia.
2. Indeed, in the clinical literature, agoraphobia is consistently referred to as a "woman's syndrome." Some who study agoraphobia note that the symptoms of the disorder are similar to the behavior of stereotypical female sex roles. Capps and Ochs, in *Constructing Panic* note that "from this [academic] perspective, the socialization of stereotypic feminine behavior—helplessness, dependence, unassertiveness, accommodation—contributes to the development and maintenance of the characteristics of agoraphobia. … One study, for example, found that agoraphobic men portray themselves as shy, submissive, and not fitting into stereotypic male sex roles, and describe entering into relationships with dominant women who may have been more likely to reinforce their unassertive behavior." (2) There are also studies that find no evidence for the link between agoraphobia and dependent, unassertive personality styles, This suggests there may not be one consistent "agoraphobia personality." In the academic research, then, the question remains open. In my review of the clinical literature, I found that the prevalence of agoraphobia in women increased over the last 130 years with the cases reported in the nineteenth century being predominantly males and after the mid twentieth century increasingly females. There are many reasons for this difference in reported cases, and I will address this in subsequent chapters.
3. See American Psychiatric Association, *Diagnostic and Statistical Manual of Mental Disorders*, Third Edition (1980), Third-Revised Edition (1987), and the currently used Fourth Edition (1994) (Washington, D.C.: American Psychiatric Association) to note how agoraphobia goes from being a separate category (DSM-III) to being a subcategory of panic disorder (DSM-III-R).
4. See, for example, Paul Pichot, "Panique: Attaque et trouble historique du mot et des concepts," *L'Encephale* 22, no. 5 (1996): 3–8, for a description of the resistance to the term *panic disorder* in France; see B. Bandelow, Sievert K, Röthemeyer M, Hajak G, and E.

Rüther. "What treatments do patients with panic disorder and agoraphobia get?" *European Archives of Psychiatry and Clinical Neuroscience* 245 (1995):165–171 for a description of the same problem in Germany.

5. See Leonard J. Schmidt and Brooke Warner, "Introduction," in *Panic: Origins, Insight, and Treatment*, ed. Leonard J. Schmidt and Brooke Warner (Berkeley, CA: North Atlantic, 2002), xv, which cites figures from the National Comorbidity Survey.
6. New urbanist design has been praised as one of the most promising antisprawl trends of the past decade. In the United States, where over half the population resides in suburbs, and where large portions of metropolitan cities are composed of low-density, single-use, automobile-oriented development, the emergence of mixed-use, pedestrian-oriented town centers is a promising step. See the *Town Paper*, an online journal that follows debates surrounding new urbanism, at http://www.tndtownpaper.com/ (last visited 5-15-06). For discussions of how sprawl has transformed the American city and the need to rethink trends in urban planning in the United States, see Michael J. Dear, *The Postmodern Urban Condition* (Oxford: Blackwell, 2000); Nan Ellin, *Postmodern Urbanism* (Cambridge: Blackwell, 1996); and Roberta Brandes Gratz and Norman Mintz, *Cities Back from the Edge: New Life for Downtown* (New York: John Wiley, 1998). For a critical look at new urbanism as an insufficient solution to the problems of American city planning, see David Harvey, *Spaces of Hope* (Berkeley and Los Angeles: University of California Press, 2000), who argues that retrofitting suburban malls into town centers and creating more dense housing developments that foster the face-to-face interactions that create community is a solution that has mainly served the suburban needs of upper-middle-class citizens while neglecting the plight of the inner city poor.
7. See Martin Stone, "Shellshock and the Psychologists," in *The Anatomy of Madness: Essays in the History of Psychiatry*, ed. Roy Porter, W. F. Bynum, Michael Shepherd (London: Routledge Kegan and Paul, 1986). See also Elaine Showalter, *The Female Malady: Woman, Madness, and English Culture*, 1830–1980 (New York: Pantheon, 1987).
8. Most new urbanist town centers have put an emphasis on retail and the creation of the "festive marketplace," which Muschamp claims has become by the late 1990s simply a formulaic, overcommercialized response to the alienating effects of the postwar shopping center . However, new urbanist proponents continue to insist that the way back from commercial sprawl must involve confronting each piece of single-use sprawl—residential, office, retail, hotel, civic, and light industry—and reassembling portions of this in the form of traditional neighborhoods, town centers, main streets, and marketplaces. For a review of new urbanist projects in the United States, see Charles C. Bohl, *Placemaking: Town Centers, Main Streets and Transit Villages* (Washington D.C., Urban Land Institute, 2002). For a review of new urbanist design in Europe, see Gabriele Tagliaventi, "New Urbanism in Europe," *Town Paper: Council Report V* (October 2003), online at http://www.tndtownpaper.com/. The original ideas behind America's new urbanism comes from Jane Jacobs, Kevin Lynch, and others in the 1960s who recognized that the modernist vision of the city was flawed. Like the controversial Dutch architect Rem Koolhaas today, they recognized the value of shopping to reanimate the inert public space that was generally agreed to be the failed legacy of modernism, a space resulting from the monumental design plan that had transformed postwar American and European cities into functionally separate zones for commercial, leisure and residential use.
9. Muschamp, "Public Space or Private, A Compulsion to Fill It." *New York Times*, August 27, 2000 (27)
10. Ibid., 27.
11. Ibid., 29.
12. Ibid., 29.
13. For a report on these numbers, see "The State of World Population 2004" report from the United Nations Population Fund at http://www.sahims.net/doclibrary/Sahims_Documents/UNFPA%20State%20of%20World%20Population%20Press%20Summary.pdf.
    On the form of the modernist city and its global expansion see James Holsten, *The Modernist City: An Anthropological Critique of Brasilia* (Chicago: University of Chicago Press, 1989). On the political economy and spatial design of global cities see Saskia Sassen, *The Global City: New York, London, Tokyo* (Princeton, NJ: Princeton University Press, 2001).

14. In any literary tradition, changes in the styles of narration arise in relation to changes in the world described. Other periods of dramatic social change have similarly been reflected in Western culture's modes of narration. The literary form of the novel, for example, arose as the more structured forms of literary narration, the epic, the lyric, and the dramatic failed to adequately capture the loss of regularity, validity, and authority experienced in the collapse of European monarchies.
15. Klaus Scherpe, "Nonstop to Nowhere City? Changes in the Symbolization, Perception, and Semiotics of the City in the Literature of Modernity," trans. by Lisa Roetzel, *Cultural Critique* No. 23 (1992–93): 137.
16. This later observation was made by literary scholar Tom Conley at a presentation at the American Anthropological Association in 1994.
17. See Roland Barthes, *Empire of Signs* trans. Richard Howard. New York: Hill and Wang (1982); Ernst Bloch, *Heritage of our Times*, trans. Neville Plaice and Stephen Plaice (Berkeley and Los Angeles: University of California Press, 1991); Georg Simmel, "The Metropolis and Mental Life," in *On Individuality and Social Forms*, ed. Donald Levine (Chicago: University of Chicago Press, 1971); and Paul Virilio, *Speed and Politics*, trans. Mark Polizzotti. (New York: Semiotext[e], 1991). My own argument in this section of the introduction is based on Scherpe's important essay "Nonstop to Nowhere City? Changes in the Symbolization, Perception, and Semiotics of the City in the Literature of Modernity."
18. Again I am following and agreeing with Scherpe's argument that the literature of modernity picks up on this nonrepresentational figure of empty space but, given the wider culture of empty space in everyday life of urban modernity, cannot use it to help urban citizens better understand how to assert themselves against larger social structures that employ emptiness to orient persons as complacent consumers and subjects of an ever-increasing life of speed and submission to the dictates of abstract space and more restrictive features of abstract thought.
19. Scherpe, "Nonstop to Nowhere City," 140.
20. See the philosophical essays on critical spatial thinking in *Thinking Space*, ed. Mike Crang and Nigel Thrift (London, New York: Routledge, 2000).
21. See David Harvey, *Spaces of Hope* (Berkeley and Los Angeles: University of California Press, 2000), which suggests we resuscitate a utopian imagination and thus produce alternative ideas and spaces of hope to counter the lack of alternatives to the dominant ideologies of neoliberal capitalism and their ill effects on cities, citizens, and environments.
22. For an example of how the study of empty space has been undertaken in premodern societies, see James Weiner, *The Empty Place: Poetry, Space, and Being Among the Foi of Papua New Guinea* (Bloomington: Indiana University Press, 1991).
23. A partial inventory of the exciting work on modern space in various disciplines includes the following authors: Michel de Certeau, Tom Conley, Manuel De Landa, Gilles Deleuze, James Duncan, Nancy Duncan, Derek Gregory, David Harvey, Fredric Jameson, Doreen Massey, Gillian Rose, and Edward Soja.
24. Marc Augé, *Non-Places: Introduction to the Anthropology of Supermodernity*, trans. John Howe (London: Verso, 1995), 5.
25. See George Marcus and Michael M. J. Fischer, *Anthropology as Cultural Critique: An Experimental Moment in the Human Sciences* (Chicago: University of Chicago Press 1986), for a discussion of how anthropological concepts have been rethought as anthropology was repatriated to the study of modern societies.
26. See, generally, Michael M. J. Fischer, "Third Spaces of Anthropology," in *Emergent Forms of Life and the Anthropological Voice* (Durham, NC: Duke University Press, 2003), 1–25; quotation here is from page 3.
27. I read case histories and clinical studies of treatments for agoraphobia from European and American psychiatric journals and books, beginning with the earliest published case in Berlin (1871) to the current issues of the *Journal of Anxiety Disorders*, which began publication in 1990. In addition to archival sources of treatment modalities, I also interviewed a psychologist specializing in agoraphobia and one specializing in the use of space as a therapeutic strategy for urban women.

28. "Empty space only comes into existence on an institutional level once the world has been thoroughly explored and universal degrees of latitude and longitude established," notes sociologist Anthony Giddens; see Giddens, "Preface," In *Now/Here: Time, Space and Modernity*, ed. Roger Friedland and Deidre Boden (Berkeley and Los Angeles: University of California Press, 1994), 3.
29. See Zygmunt Bauman, *Globalization: The Human Consequences* (New York: Columbia University Press, 1998).
30. Two other social theorists are important in pointing out the political dimensions of the epistemic imaginary of empty space in modern political theory. They are Giorgio Agamben in his book *Homo Sacer: Sovereign Power and Bare Life*, trans. Daniel Heller-Roazen (Stanford, CA: Stanford University Press, 1998), who notes how empty space functioned in the Western designation of a space of lawlessness that existed both "outside" of civil society (in the state of nature) and "inside" civil society (as the Jewish ghetto in the history of Europe). Empty space, for Agamben, is the spatial imaginary that supports the creation of political zones where "anything goes." The other political theorist, Bruno Latour, has specifically developed a mode of political thinking against the grain of such empty space in *The Politics of Nature: How to Bring the Sciences into Democracy* (Cambridge, MA: Harvard University Press, 2004). Latour claims that nature, in the Western tradition, has been imagined as a space emptied of due process, with disastrous consequences.
31. See Claude Lefort, *The Political Forms of Modern Society: Bureaucracy, Democracy, Totalitarianism* edited and introduced by John B. Thompson (Cambridge: MIT Press, 1986), 279. Quoted in Roselyn Deutsche, "Agoraphobia." *Evictions: Art and Spatial Politics* (Cambridge, MA; London: MIT Press, 1996), 272.
32. See Claude Lefort, "The Question of Democracy," in *Democracy and Political Theory* (Minneapolis: University of Minnesota Press, 1988), 19, emphasis in original. Quoted in Deutsche, "Agoraphobia" (273). Although Deutsche uses agoraphobia as a trope in her argument, she suggests that the "dissolution of markers of certainty" makes citizens of democratic states like agoraphobics in the sense that both must construct a new sense of self without stable boundaries in social space. I address Lefort's use of the metaphor of empty space further in the Conclusion. It is important to recognize that Lefort's important work on capitalism and democracy cannot be reduced to Deutsche's discussion of the metaphor of empty space. However, more important for the purpose of my argument is the way the metaphor of empty space becomes a useful way for many political theorists to think about the creative (or destructive) potential of self-fashioning in late capitalist democracies. In their own differing ways, then, Lefort, Deutsche, Giddens and Bauman support my claim that empty space is functioning as a founding myth of common space in modernity, whether it operates at the level of individual subjectivity or collective urban life.
33. Similar arguments are made by Michael Hardt and Antonio Negri in their important and controversial book *Empire* (Cambridge, MA: Harvard University Press, 1999), which proposes that there are important positive features to the new identities open to the public citizen/self that has been uprooted from stable forms of sociality due to the radical influence of global capitalism and global media technologies. The new kinds of virtual space in which citizens live create new identity formations which the authors, following the philosophical and psychological writings of Gilles Deleuze and Felix Guattari, call "multiplicities." I will address these ideas in chapter 4. Here it can be said that the spatial dilemmas and treatments for agoraphobia suggest both positive and negative sides to the joyous embrace of the flexible self proposed by these authors. Some of the theoretical optimism of these authors can be tempered by the ethnographic studies of personhood in flexible capitalism by scholars like Emily Martin ("Flexible Survivors," *Anthropology News*, September 1999, pp. 5–7) and Doreen Massey ("Blurring the Binaries? High tech in Cambridge" in *New Frontiers of Space, Bodies and Gender*, Rosa Ainley, ed. (London: Routledge 157–175).
34. In the 1990s agoraphobia was the object of several studies as a psychopathology that not only reacts to but is produced by modern urban space. Under the banner of Jules Henry's famous assertion that psychopathology is the outcome of all that is wrong with a culture, urban geographers, anthropologists, and sociologists have done fine ethnographic studies that give rich detail on agoraphobic experience from the perspective of the agoraphobic

herself. Thus we have a valuable record of how agoraphobic fear encodes the linguistic self-understanding of the agoraphobic (Capps and Ochs, *Constructing Panic*) and of how agoraphobic women develop habits of living with fears of public space that are, in many ways, not all that different from those of nonagoraphobic women. (Carol Brooks Gardner, "Out of Place: Gender, Public Places and Situational Disadvantage," in *Now/Here: Time, Space and Modernity*, edited by Roger Friedland and Deidre Boden (Berkeley: University of California Press, 1994), 335–352; Susan Bordo. "Missing Kitchens," in *Twilight Zone: The Hidden Life of Cultural Images from Plato to O.J.*, (Berkeley, California: University of California Press, 1999) 214–242. Esther da Costa Meyer, "La Donna e Mobile: Agoraphobia, Women and Urban Space," in *The Sex of Architecture*, edited by Diana Agrest, Patricia Conway, and Leslie Kanes Weisman (New York: Harry N. Abrams, 1996); Ruth Bankey, "The Paradox of Panic: A Geographic Analysis of Agoraphobic Experience," M.A. thesis, Carleton University, Ottawa, Ontario, 1999; and Joyce Davidson, "'... The World Was Getting Smaller': Women, Agoraphobia, and Bodily Boundaries," *Area* 32, no. 1 (2000): 31–40. We also have studies by architectural historians noting how agoraphobics somatically register the complaints made by architectural critics who describe the transformation of modern urban space; see, for example, Anthony Vidler, "Spatial Estrangement in Simmel and Kracauer," *New German Critique* 54 (1991): 31–45; and Anthony Vidler, *Warped Space: Art, Architecture, and Anxiety in Modern Culture* (Cambridge, MA: MIT Press, 2000).

35. For the relation between biopolitics and public health, see the essays in *Foucault, Health and Medicine*, ed. Alan Petersen and Robin Bunton (London: Routledge, 1997).
36. See, e.g., Davidson, "'... The World Was Getting Smaller'"; and da Costa Meyer, "La Donna e Mobile."
37. This is Susan Bordo's claim in "Missing Kitchens," *Twilight Zone: The Hidden Life of Cultural Images From Plato to O.J.* (Berkeley: California, University of California Press, 1999) 214–242. See also Bordo, "The Body and the Reproduction of Femininity: A Feminist Appropriation of Foucault," in Alison M. Jaggar and Susan R. Bordo, eds. *Gender/Body/Knowledge* (New Brunswick, NJ: Rutgers University Press, 1989), 13–32.
38. See Kristen Day, "Embassies and Sanctuaries: Women's Experiences of Race and Fear in Public Space," *Environment and Planning D: Society and Space* 17 (1999): 307–28.
39. Here I am summarizing the argument of da Costa Meyer on issues of class and race with respect to agoraphobia. On the history of women's presence in the public realm, da Costa Meyer cites Linda K. Kerber, "Separate Spheres, Female Worlds, Woman's Place: The Rhetoric of Women's History," *Journal of American History* 75 (1988): 9–39.
40. See Steven Friedman and Cheryl Paradis, "African American Patients with Panic Disorder and Agoraphobia," *Journal of Anxiety Disorders* 5 (1991): 35–41.
41. Kimberly Crenshaw, a professor of law, has written of the problems involved in forming legal categories to analyze both race and gender discrimination simultaneously, and we might ask whether the same categorical difficulties arise in psychological studies. In "Whose Story is it Anyway? Feminist and Anti-racist Appropriations of Anita Hill," in *Race-ing Justice, Engendering Power*, ed. Toni Morrison (New York: Pantheon, 1992), 402–440, her study of the Clarence Thomas hearings, Crenshaw notes how Anita Hill's experience of racial and gender discrimination never received a proper hearing because specific forms of domination fall between existing legal categories for recognizing injury. Crenshaw explains that in legal cases of racial discrimination it is the experience of the black man that informs the standard. In cases of gender discrimination, however, law gets its precedent from the experience of white women. This means that black women must mold their experience into either that of black men or that of white women to be legally recognized. Race and gender discrimination form two mutually exclusive domains. In the black community itself, Crenshaw notes, gender domination has long been subordinated to the racial domination of the whole community. That is why Anita Hill was seen by so many in the black community as a traitor, as participating in a public "lynching" of Clarence Thomas. Moreover, the issue of sexual harassment was often glossed over as a cultural problem of whites not understanding that black women are hardier than whites and prefer a "down home style of courting"; white America would never understand how such sexual repartee could be the norm among black men and women. Crenshaw uses the Clarence Thomas case to point to the limits of the current feminist paradigm.

The same problems of doctrinal exclusion that Crenshaw points to in law are operating in the study on agoraphobic African Americans. The researchers themselves in the psychiatric study note that in addition to the absence of race as a factor in previous studies on agoraphobia, "it appears that treatment studies found in the literature are primarily of white middle-class patients"; see Friedman and Paradis, "African American Patients with Panic Disorder," 40. With over 80 percent of the agoraphobic population being female, we see that the issue of gender is also overlooked in a discussion of class. With our categorical approaches to the metropolitan experience of agoraphobia so wanting, it is no wonder that spatial orientation is absent as well.

42. Friedman and Paradis, "African American Patients with Panic Disorder," 40.
43. Ibid. The findings in this study are typical of the bias that pervades medical research generally. Looking at white public space and the construction of white privilege in U.S. health care, one researcher studying racial bias in the nursing profession found that "of the 8,261 clinical studies published in U.S. nursing journals between 1983 and 1991, only 59 included African Americans in the study sample" (and 13 of those were in the *Journal of the Black Nurses' Association*) (See Eileen Jackson, "Whiting-Out Difference: Why U.S. Nursing Research Fails Black Families," *Medical Anthropology Quarterly* 7:4 (1993) 369.) While there is little or no research on the nursing or medical practices that reach African American communities, there is ample research done on the biological incidence of disease among African Americans and other people of color. Sixty-four percent of all the human-subjects research published over the last 70 years in the *American Journal of Epidemiology* referred to the notion of "race," Jackson reported, while 34 percent explicitly included some "nonwhite" population. Medical professionals regularly interpret the behavior of African American subjects in terms that are alien to their experience. They see them as individuals (as opposed to members of complex social networks) who need intervention and behavior modification. No wonder, then, that "noncompliance is a frequent topic in nursing research but not a particular concern among African Americans" (377).
44. Spatial disorders arising with the experience of working-class and ethnic families housed in concrete highrises on the outskirts of postwar European cities present a different issue than what I am addressing here with the large scale inner city housing projects in the United States. I am unaware of any comparative research on this topic and it is beyond the scope of my investigation of treatments for agoraphobia.
45. Joshua M. Perman, "Phobia as a Determinant of Single-Room Occupancy," *The American Journal of Psychiatry* 123, no. 5 (1966): 610.
46. Ibid., 611; emphasis added.
47. Notes Peter Ford, "Deep Roots of Paris Riots," *Christian Science Monitor*, November 4, 2005, "The ugly, often poorly maintained blocks of public housing that have become a nightly battlefield are testament to 40 years of government policy that has concentrated immigrants and their families in well-defined districts away from city centers, as housing there became more expensive. … [In] the 751 zones that the [French] government has designated for special programs, unemployment stands at 19.6 percent—double the national average—and at more than 30 percent among 21 to 20 year-olds, according to official figures. Incomes are 75 percent below the average. … 'Working class suburbs have become ethnic ghettos,' says Marc Cheb Sun, who edits *Respect*, a magazine aimed mostly at young black and North African readers. 'That is the origin of the problem.'" See also Katrin Bennhold, "Suburban Officers Criticized as Insensitive to Racism," *New York Times*, November 8, 2005.
48. When Charles Jencks begins his 1977 book *The Language Of Postmodern Architecture*, he starts with the end of modern architecture. "Modern Architecture," he writes, "died in St. Louis, Missouri on July 15, 1972 when the infamous scheme of the Pruitt-Igoe housing project, or rather several of its slab blocks, were given the final *coup de grâce* by dynamite." That failed housing project was built between 1952 and 1955. See Charles Jencks, *The Language of Post-Modern Architecture* (New York: Rizzoli, 1991 [1977]) 23.
49. The foundational image of undifferentiated expanses that John Locke uses in his well known chapter on property in the *Two Treatises of Government* is of pre-European America. "In the beginning," Locke wrote in 1660, "all the world was America" (II.49.1) This projection of an undifferentiated, homogenous quality onto the diverse, heterogeneous (and unknown) terrain of the New World was the preamble for the justification of the

European "natural rights" theory of property that dispossessed the natives of their land. It functioned logically in the same way as another writing metaphor, the *tabula rasa* (empty slate) did in Locke's arguments to extend the dominium of reason to non-European minds. (Locke's ideas on the *tabula rasa* are further discussed in the conclusion to this volume.)

## Chapter 1

1. See Carl Friedrich Otto Westphal, "Die Agoraphobie: Eine Neuropathische Erscheinung," in *Archiv für Psychiatrie und Nervenkrankheiten* 3 (1871): 138–161. Trans. in *Westphal's "Die Agoraphobie" With Commentary.* (Lanham, MD: University Press of America, 1988) by Terry J. Knapp and Michael T. Schumacher. See in particular Knapp and Schumacher's Introduction.
2. Carl Friedrich Otto Westphal, "Agoraphobia: A Neuropathic Phenomenon," excerpts quoted in Jeffrey H. Boyd and Ted Crump "Westphal's Agoraphobia," *Journal of Anxiety Disorders* 5, no. 1 (1991): 80–81. Westphal translation by Ted Crump; insertion of the original German text and its translation, when necessary, is my own.
3. Søren Kierkegaard, *The Concept of Anxiety,* (ed. and trans. Reider Thomte and Albert Anderson. Princeton: Princeton University Press, 1980). Cited in Assen Jablensky, "Approaches to the Definition and Classification of Anxiety and Related Disorders in European Psychiatry," in *Anxiety and the Anxiety Disorders*, ed. A. Hussein Tuma and Jack D. Maser (Hillsdale, NJ: Lawrence Erlbaum, 1985), 736.
4. Karl Jaspers, 1925. Cited in Jablensky, "Approaches," 736.
5. Boyd and Crump, "Westphal's Agoraphobia," 77, 79.
6. Westphal, "Die Agoraphobie," 138.
7. Crump's translation of "Westphal's Agoraphobia," 80.
8. Camille Sitte, *City Planning According to Artistic Principles*, trans. George Collins and Shristiane Crasemann Collins (New York: Random House, 1965), 45. Cited in Anthony Vidler, "Spatial Estrangement in Simmel and Kracauer." *New German Critique* 54 (1991): 35.
9. See Esther da Costa Meyer, "La Donna e Mobile: Agoraphobia, Women and Urban Space," in *The Sex of Architecture*, ed. Diana Agrest, Patricia Conway, and Leslie Kanes Weisman (New York: Harry N. Abrams, Inc., 1996), 143.
10. See the excellent article by Devon Hinton, "Munch, Agoraphobia, and the Terrors of the Modernizing Urban Landscape," in *Panic: Origins, Insight and Treatment*, ed. Leonard J. Schmidt and Brooke Warner (Berkeley, CA: North Atlantic, 2002) 229–252.
11. Robert Rosenbaum, quoted in Hinton, "Munch," 242–243.
12. See the feminist critique of Benjamin's concept of flaneurie in Janet Wolff, "The Artist and the Flâneur: Rodin, Rilke and Gwen John in Paris," in Keith Tester, ed. *The Flâneur (*New York: Routledge, 1994), 111–137.
13. Vincent, "Confessions of an Agoraphobic Victim," *American Journal of Psychology* 30 (1919): 297–98.
14. Boyd and Crump, "Westphal's Agoraphobia," 78; emphasis added.
15. Jablensky, "Approaches," 745.
16. See Sandy Rovner, "High Anxiety Is a Scary Disorder," *Minneapolis Star Tribune*, May 31, 1990; and Richard I. Shader, "Some Observations on the Problem of Anxiety," in *Anxiety and the Anxiety Disorders,* ed. by A. Hussain Tuma and Jack Maser (Hillsdale, NJ: Lawrence Erlbaum, 1985), 591–594.
17. The zero sign appears as a significant absence where the absence of any explicit signifier functions by itself as a signifier. Silence, for example, can in fact convey information, as in the expression, "a pregnant pause." Roland Barthes has described, the functions of the zero sign in logic; in the structuralist ethnographies of Claude Lévi-Strauss where the zero sign occurs in the notion of mana; in rhetoric, where, carried on to the connotative plane, the absence of rhetorical signifiers constitutes in its turn a stylistic signifier; and in linguistics where the zero sign appears as the unmarked term in the imperative mode, an implied, albeit silent, listener. See *Degre Zero de l'écriture* (Paris: Gonthier, 1964), 77.

18. See Elke Zuercher-White, *Treating Panic Disorder and Agoraphobia: A Step-by-Step Clinical Approach* (Oakland, CA: New Harbinger, 1997), 32, for a discussion of how this collapse of the specificity of fear has been criticized in the psychological literature.
19. Boyd and Crump, "Westphal's Agoraphobia," 85.
20. See Pierre Pichot, "Panique: attaque et trouble. Historique du mot et des concepts," *L'Encephale* 22, no. 5 (1996): 3–8. Pichot traces the recent entry of the term *panique* into French from the English. M Maudsley was the first to use the term in psychiatry, he notes. It entered into American psychiatric usage especially during World War II when it was used to designate acute individual reactions to battle stress. From here it gets picked up by Klein, whose work in the 1960s lead to the revision of the DSM III that brought us the label "panic attack."
21. Jablensky, "Approaches," 743.
22. Ibid., 757; emphasis added.
23. Boyd and Crump, "Westphal's Agoraphobia," 85.
24. Klein's work was foundational in bringing researchers to consider that anxiety attacks—what he called "panic attacks"—came from a different source than the anxious cognitions/thoughts that seem to accompany and follow. Klein argued that the anxiety that occurs just prior to an anxiety attack is significantly different than the anxiety that occurs during the attack. He based his argument on data showing how two classes of drugs, trycyclics and benzodiazepines, produce different results: trycyclics reduce panic attacks but do not appear to affect anticipatory anxiety; benzodiazepines do just the opposite, reducing the anticipatory anxiety but not the attacks. Thus, Klein claimed there were two kinds of anxiety—anticipatory and panic attacks—each of which had different psychobiologies. See the discussions of Klein's work in Roger Baker, editor, *Panic Disorder: Theory, Research and Therapy* (London: Wiley, 1989).
25. See Diane Chambless and Alan Goldstein, "Anxieties: Agoraphobia and Hysteria," in *Women and Psychotherapy*, ed. Annette Brodsky and Rachel Hare-Mustin (Cambridge, MA: Harvard University Press, 1992) 113–134; Nancy Fraser, "Rethinking the Public Sphere: A Contribution to the Critique of Actually Existing Democracy," in *Habermas and the Public Sphere*, ed. Craig Calhoun (Cambridge, MA: MIT Press, 1992) 109–142; and Robert Seidenberg and Karen DeCrow, *Women Who Marry Houses: Panic and Protest in Agoraphobia* (New York: McGraw-Hill, 1983).
26. See Chambless and Goldstein, "Anxieties."
27. Many of the comprehensive guides to the treatment of agoraphobia devote some time to an overview of the contemporary theories of the disorder. The following synopsis is based on Elke Zuercher-White, *Treating Panic Disorder and Agoraphobia*. Zuercher-White is a therapist who worked for the Kaiser health care group in California. Her guide is thorough and well-written, providing examples from her many years of practice. The paragraphs that follow are my summaries of the review of theoretical literature on panic disorder/agoraphobia included in her book.
28. Zuercher-White, *Treating Panic Disorder and Agoraphobia*, 27–31. These neurobiological models of agoraphobia's cause have been challenged by those who note that just because a particular medication works does not mean that the neurotransmitter system impacted by that drug is the cause of the panic disorder. In other words, etiology here is being confused with symptomatology (31). Psychologists are quick to point to the many studies which show that cognitive-behavioral treatments, like pharmacological ones, also affect brain function (37).
29. Ibid., 35.
30. Ibid., 37; emphasis in original. It is useful to read through the full description of agoraphobia here simply to note the complete absence of any reference to space:

    > The perceived unpredictability and uncontrollability of the false alarm, and thus the fear that it will occur again are particularly frightening to the individual. A negative affective state is produced. The person's attention becomes narrowed and results in hypervigilance to somatic events. When the person perceives even slight physiological sensations again, fear activates the autonomic nervous system, which increases the somatic sensations, which increases fear until the point of panic is reached.

It has been hypothesized that the fear of bodily sensations is a conditioned response to internal sensations (called interoceptive conditioning) and this creates an actual phobia of physical cues. The interoceptive conditioning operates outside of the person's awareness, and the panics are perceived as uncued. This conditioning has been further shown to be relatively resistant to extinction. As the person's fear of these unpredictable and uncontrollable attacks continues, a state of anxious expectancy develops, increasing the probability of further panics. The panic attacks become "learned alarms."

Barlow uses the term "anxious apprehension" to denote the heightened fearful state, which results from combined biological, psychological and *environmental events* (37, emphasis added).

31. Ibid., 36.
32. Richard J. McNally, *Panic Disorder: A Critical Analysis* (New York: Guilford Press, 1994), 170.
33. Brian J. Cox, cited in Zeurcher-White, *Treating Panic Disorder and Agoraphobia*, 35.
34. See John Huston's documentary "Let There Be Light" (1946) which shows the use of abreaction treatments for "shell-shocked" American soldiers who sustained neurotic symptoms form their experiences on the battlefields of World War II.
35. Christine Battersby, *The Phenomenal Woman: Feminist Metaphysics and the Patterns of Identity* (London: Polity, 1998), 4.
36. Ibid., 2.
37. In this paragraph I am indebted to Daniel Ussishkin's "Historical Instances of Panic," which summarizes the history of the term *panic* in psychology. Ussishkin argues that this more recent psychological term cannot be separated from the history of the term *anxiety*, and that thus the recent tendency to consider anxiety attacks as panic attacks should be approached with historical understanding and skeptical caution. See Ussishkin, "Historical Instances of Panic," in *Panic: Origins, Insight, and Treatment*, ed. Leonard J. Schmidt and Brooke Warner (Berkeley, CA: North Atlantic, 2002), 5–14.
38. Ibid., 13. I am again following Ussishkin's argument in this paragraph—in particular, his reference to Eve Kosofsky Sedgwick's work on the homosexual panic defense in *Epistemology of the Closet* (Berkeley: University of California Press, 1990).
39. Eve Kosofsky Sedgwick, cited in Ussishkin, "Historical Instances," 13.

## Chapter 2

1. Carl Friedrich Otto Westphal, *Die Agoraphobie,* quoted in Jeffrey Boyd and Ted Crump, "Westphal's Agoraphobia." *Journal of Anxiety Disorders* 5, no. 1 (1991): 81.
2. See Rutherford H. Platt, "From Commons to Commons: Evolving Concepts of Open Space in North American Cities," in *The Ecological City: Preserving and Restoring Urban Biodiversity,* ed. Rutherford H. Platt, Rowan A. Rowntree and Pamela G. Muick (Amherst: University of Massachusetts Press, 1994), 21–39.
3. Ibid., 30.
4. Henri Legrand du Saulle, "De l'agoraphobie," *Le Praticien* viii (1885): 208–9; my translation.
5. See David H. Pinkney, *Napoleon III and the Rebuilding of Paris* (Princeton, NJ: Princeton University Press, 1958), 105, for the following description of Paris during this period.
6. Georges-Eugene Haussmann, quoted in Thomas Hall, *Planning Europe's Capital Cities: Aspects of Nineteenth Century Urban Development* (London: E 7 FN Spon, 1997), 69.
7. Jere Stuart French, *Urban Space: A Brief History of the City Square.* (Dubuque, IA: Kendal-Hunt Publishing, 1978), 54.
8. Louis XV's equestrian statue at the center of the Place de la Concorde was replaced by the guillotine during the revolution, when spectators witnessed 2,625 deaths, including those of the king and queen. In 1836, the broad surfaces of the square provided the expansive background for the obelisk of Luxor, which stands to this day. Eight statues representing French cities were erected in 1854, giving the Place de la Concorde an even greater symbolic role in representing the center of the nation-state.
9. Paul Zucker, *Town and Square: From the Agora to the Village Green* (New York: Columbia University Press, 1959), 179; emphasis added.

10. French, *Urban Space*, 87.
11. Zucker, *Town and Square*, 184.
12. Ibid.
13. Ibid.,186; emphasis added.
14. A. Bernard and Ch. Jung, "Contribution à l"étude de la cremnophobie." *Révue Neurologique* 3 (1929): 438.
15. Ibid., 447; my translation, emphasis added.
16. Henri Lefebvre, in his classic work *Production of Space*, trans. Donald Nicholson-Smith (Oxford: Basil Blackwell, 1991), makes a distinction between monumental space and abstract space that I am only slightly indicating here. For Lefebvre abstract space is where abstractions—homogeneous, rational, statist, bureaucratic, commodified—are the forms of being that hold power. Monumental space, on the other hand, is closest to theatrical space; "such a space," he notes,

    > is determined by what may take place there, and consequently by what may not take place there (prescribed/proscribed, scene/obscene). What appears empty may turn out to be full—as is the case with sanctuaries, or with the "ships" or naves of cathedrals. Alternatively, full space may be inverted over an almost heterotopic void at the same location (for instance, vaults, cupolas). The Taj Mahal, for instance, makes much play with the fullness of swelling curves suspended in a dramatic emptiness. Acoustic, gestural and ritual movements, elements grouped into vast ceremonial unities, breaches opening onto limitless perspectives, chains of meaning—all are organized into a monumental whole. (224)

    The organizational devices of monumental space for Lefebvre are closer to the poetic world expressed dialogically in theater rather than the monological expression of poetry in written texts. The neoclassical squares that appear in the clinical literature on agoraphobia are singled out as squares that have both monumental and abstract functions. The agoraphobic sensibility seems to indicate that giganticism may collapse the communicative function of monumental space into the banality of homogeneous, abstract space.
17. In Kantian terms, the nation is an abstract concept—an idea of reason—much like nature.
18. M. Lannois and C. Tournier, "Les Lésions auriculaires sont une cause déterminante fréquente de l'agoraphobie," *Annales De L'Oreille, Du Larnynx, Du Nez et Du Pharynx* 2:24 (1898): 294; my translation.
19. Dr. G. Mouton, "Un cas d'agoraphobie," *L'Echo medical du nord* 2 (1898) 381–2; my translation, emphasis added. In this case history, no information is given as to what treatment was pursued.
20. Lisa Grenier and Hans Wieser-Benedetti, *Le Siècle de l'éclectisme: Lille 1830–1930* (Paris/Bruxelles: Editions du Moniteur/La Nouvelle Diffusion, 1979), 77. All translations from this book are my own.
21. Ibid., 132; emphasis added.
22. Ibid., 126.
23. See Walter Benjamin, "Paris, Capital of the Nineteenth Century," in *Illuminations*, trans. Harry Zohn (New York: Schocken, 1978), cited in Grenier, *Le Siècle d'éclectisme,* 106.
24. Quoted in Grenier, *Le Siècle d'éclectisme*, 132–33.
25. It is interesting to note that in a more philosophical approach to dynamics of homogenous space, in modernity, Deleuze and Guattari have called homogenous space an unstable dimension of extremely intense striated (state) space. In conditions of such extreme striation/abstraction, spatial homogeneity, the authors argue, more easily reverts to what the authors call "smooth" space, a kind of space given to social formations that, like the military, operate out of a logic that exceeds the directives of reason. See Gilles Deleuze and Félix Guattari, *A Thousand Plateaus: Capitalism and Schizophrenia*, trans. Brian Massumi (Minneapolis: University of Minnesota Press, 1987).
26. M. Lannois and C. Tournier, "Les Lésions auriculaires sont une cause déterminante fréquente de l'agoraphobie," *Annales De L'Oreille, Du Larnynx, Du Nez et Du Pharynx* 2:24 (1898): 294; my translation, emphasis added.
27. Gilbert Gardes, *Lyon l'art et la ville, Urbanisme-Architecture*, tome 1 (Paris: Editions du Centre National de la Recherche Sceintifique, 1988), 50; my translation.

28. Contemporary reports show that the city was struggling to rid itself of waste products from its overflowing population. A report in 1887 by the regional department of health stated that "the innumerable factories vomiting their harmful fumes into the atmosphere and dumping their organic and mineral wastes into our waterways taint two of the most essential elements of life: water and air. But that danger is nothing compared to the one brought on by the concentration in one single place of the refuse and waste products of several million people"; see Gardes, *Lyon l'art et la ville,* 92. Between 1875 and 1900 Lyon was connected to a larger waterway system.
29. Gardes, *Lyon l'art et la ville,* 160.
30. Ibid.
31. In his history of Lyon at this time, Gardes cites an anonymous critic of the new monumental architecture in Place de la Republique, *Lyon l'art et la ville*, 93.
32. Dr. Cherchevsky, "Contribution a l'étude de l'agoraphobie," *Revue de médicine* 5 (1885): 916). This condition continued on until the fall of that year, when after coming close to suicide, the patient arrived at the office of Dr. Cherchevsky.
33. E. A. Gutkind, *International History of City Development. Vol. III: Urban Development in Eastern Europe: Bulgaria, Romania and the U.S.S.R.* (New York: The Free Press, 1972), 383.
34. Walter Benjamin, "Paris, Capital of the Nineteenth-Century," *Reflections*, trans. Edmund Jephcott (New York: Schocken, 1986), 146–62.

## Chapter 3

1. For the middle-class English context during this period, see Lenore Davidoff and Catherine Hall, *Family Fortunes: Men and Women of the English Middle Class 1780–1850* (London: Hutchinson, 1987). More generally, see Elizabeth Wilson, *The Sphinx in the City: Urban Life, the Control of Disorder, and Women* (London: Virago, 1991); Jos Boys, "Women and Public Space," in *Making Space: Women and the Man-made Environment,* ed. Matrix Book Group (London: Pluto, 1985) 37–54; and David F. Noble, *A World without Women: The Christian Clerical Culture of Western Science* (New York: Alfred A. Knopf, 1992).
2. I am grateful to Tom Conley's invocation of Freudian dream analysis as a useful trope to consider puzzling historical phenomena involving modern subjectivity and space; see Conley, *The Self-Made Map* (Minneapolis: University of Minnesota Press, 1996).
3. For example, the complete text of Westphal's case studies has been translated as a short book with commentary that frames Westphal's text within a superficial history of the treatment of agoraphobia in modern psychiatry; see Terry J. Knapp and Michael Schumacher, *Westphal's "Die Agoraphobie" with Commentary: The Beginnings of Agoraphobia* (New York: New York University Press, 1988).
4. Cherchevsky, "Contribution a l'étude de l'agoraphobie," *Revue de médicine* 5 (1885): 912–13; my translation, emphasis added.
5. Henri Legrand du Saulle, "De l'agoraphobie," *Le Praticien* viii (1885): 209; my translation, emphasis added.
6. Ibid., 210.
7. Dr. Gros, "Contribution a l'etude de l'agoraphobie (peur des espaces) et d'autres formes de névroses émotives," *Annales Medico-Psychologiques* 7, no. 1 (1885): 395; my translation.
8. See Melanie Klein, "Some Theoretical Conclusions on the Emotional Life of an Infant." (1952), in Melanie Klein, *Envy and Gratitude and Other Works (1946–1963).* New York: Delta (1977) 61–93; Donald Winnicott, *Playing and Reality,* Harmondsworth, England: Penguin, 1985; Wilfred Bion, *Learning from Experience* (London: William Heinemann, 1962). For the use of these theorists in urban studies, see Paul Hoggett, "A Place for Experience: A Psychoanalytic Perspective on Boundary, Identity, And Culture," *Environment and Planning D: Society and Space* 10, no. 3 (1992): 345–56.
9. According to Klein, there are two subject positions associated with this spatial theory. The first is the paranoid-schizoid subject position, which encounters anomalies in the world as persecutory impingements, poisonous bad objects that require the mobilization of defense mechanisms. Here the subject position is formed in relation to an other where

difference is intolerable. The second position is what Klein calls the "depressive" subject position. Here anomalies are encountered as enriching, novelties, a chance to extend the self's possibilities. The self is thus formulated as a relation to the other that allows for ambiguity and difference. See Hoggett , "A Place for Experience," for a fuller discussion of these ideas with regard to the built environment.

10. Andreas Huyssen, *After the Great Divide: Modernism, Mass Culture, Postmodernism* (Bloomington: Indiana University Press, 1986), 52.
11. Carl Westphal, "Die Agoraphobie: Eine Neuropathische Erscheinung," in *Archiv für Psychiatrie und Nervenkrankheiten* (Berlin: Verlag von August Hirschwald, 1871), 148; my translation, emphasis added. In the German text the word for "moat" is *graben* which is also the word for "grave."
12. Allan Richard Pred and Michael John Watts, *Reworking Modernity: Capitalism and Symbolic Discontent* (New Brunswick, NJ: Rutgers University Press, 1992.)
13. We know that one of Haussmann's underlying goals in the reconstruction of Paris was to prevent an occupation of that city's streets such as occurred in 1848. But such projects are precarious. There are numerous examples of modern urban planning in which architectural design was intended to promote a political aim. In New York city, for example, Robert Moses, the master builder of roads, parks, bridges, and other public works from the 1920s to the 1970s, built some two hundred or so low hanging overpasses on Long Island, notes Langdon Winner, "according to specifications that would discourage the presence of buses on his parkways. According to evidence provided by Moses' biographer, Robert A. Caro, this demonstrated Moses' social class bias and racial prejudice. Automobile-owning whites of 'upper' and 'comfortable middle' classes, as he called them, would be free to use the parkways for recreation and commuting, whereas poor people and blacks, who normally used public transit, were kept off the roads because the twelve foot tall buses could not handle the overpasses." See Winner, *The Whale and the Reactor: A Search for Limits in an Age of High Technology* (Chicago: University of Chicago Press, 1989), 23.
14. See Pred and Watts, *Reworking Modernity.*
15. George L. Mosse, *The Nationalization of the Masses: Political Symbolism and Mass Movements in Germany from the Napoleonic Wars through the Third Reich* (Ithaca, NY: Cornell University Press, 1975).
16. Benedict Anderson, *Imagined Communities: Reflections on the Origin and Spread of Nationalism* (London: Verso, 1983), 6; emphasis added.
17. Georg Simmel, "Raumkonfiguration," in *Soziologie* (Leipzig: Dunker & Humblot, 1908), 703–8.
18. M. Lannois and C. Tournier. "Les Lésions auriculaires sont une cause déterminante fréquente de l'agoraphobie," *Annales De L'Oreille, Du Larnynx, Du Nez et Du Pharynx* 2:24 (1898): 300; my translation.
19. C. W. Suckling, "Agoraphobia and Allied Morbid Fears," *American Journal of the Medical Sciences* 99 (1890): 482; my translation, emphasis added.
20. Ibid.
21. Ibid., 483.
22. Ibid., 478; emphasis added.
23. See Ruth Bankey, "The Paradox of Panic: A Geographic Analysis of Agoraphobic Experience," M.A. thesis, Carleton University, Ottowa, Ontario, 1999; and Carol Brooks Gardner, "Out of Place: Gender, Public Places and Situational Disadvantage," in *Now/Here: Time, Space and Modernity*, ed. Roger Friedland and Diedre Boden (Berkeley: University of California Press, 1994), 335–352.
24. See Robert Seidenberg and Karen DeCrow, *Women Who Marry Houses: Panic and Protest in Agoraphobia* (New York: McGraw-Hill, 1983).
25. Gillian Brown, "The Empire of Agoraphobia," in *Domestic Individualism: Imagining Self in Nineteenth Century America* (Berkeley: University of California Press, 1990), 178.
26. See Dolores Hayden, *The Grand Domestic Revolution: A History of Feminist Designs for American Homes, Neighborhoods, and Cities* (Cambridge, MA: MIT Press, 1981); and Liesbeth Ottes ed., *Gender and the Built Environment: Emancipation in Planning, Housing and Mobility in Europe* (Assen, Netherlands: Van Gorcum, 1995). See, more generally, the essays in Rosa Ainley, ed., *New Frontiers of Space, Bodies and Gender* (London: Routledge, 1998).

27. As we have seen in the introduction to this volume, similar patterns for poor women in American inner-city projects cannot be ignored, even though they have not yet been sufficiently studied.
28. Gilles Deleuze and Félix Guattari, *A Thousand Plateaus: Capitalism and Schizophrenia*, trans. Brian Massumi (Minneapolis: University of Minnesota Press, 1987), 488; emphasis added.
29. Ibid., 500.
30. Ibid., 484; emphasis added.
31. See Deleuze and Guattari, *A Thousand Plateaus*, 26–38.
32. Ibid., 33.
33. Dorothea Olkowski, "Difference and the Ruin of Representation in Gilles Deleuze," in *Sites of Vision: The Discursive Construction of Sight in the History of Philosophy*, ed. David Michael Levin (Cambridge, MA: MIT Press, 1997), 479–480.
34. Deleuze and Guattari, *A Thousand Plateaus*, 479; emphasis added. The agoraphobics need to rely on the "haptic" sense of experience. Several patients mention their fears of being taken for drunk in public because of their staggering gait in the face of the "emptiness" of the crowded street. Staggering steps play a key part in the theory of involuntary memory created in Marcel Proust's novel *A la recherche du temps perdu*. Proust, an agoraphobic by all accounts, wrote from within his famous cork-lined walls a chronicle of Paris at the turn of the century. When his character Marcel staggers in the street, it is a jolt that triggers the flood of involuntary memory, a form of consciousness closely connected to Freud's notion of the unconscious and accessed specifically by the senses of taste (the famous Madeleine), smell, and sound rather than sight. This is the haptic perception that, Deleuze notes, plays a dominant role in the navigation of smooth space. This undertheorized aspect of the sensorium is also what interests Deleuze in the book he wrote on Proust; see Deleuze, *Proust Signes*, trans. Richard Howard (Minneapolis: University of Minnesota Press, 2000).
35. Deleuze and Guattari, *A Thousand Plateaus*, 479, emphasis added. The references to wind and noise come from a previous paragraph in which the authors are discussing local technologies for navigating the smooth space of the sea before maritime space was striated by bearings and the map: "For before longitude lines had been plotted, a very late development, there existed a complex and empirical nomadic system of navigation based on the wind and noise, the colors and sounds of the seas." Likewise, there were ways for traversing the desert and the polar regions that did not employ striated space.
36. The *Oxford English Dictionary* defines *haecceties* as "Hereness and nowness; that quality or mode of being in virtue of which a thing is or becomes a definite individual: individuality."
37. Dr. Perroud, "Agoraphobie," *Lyon Medical* (1873) quoted in M. Lannois and C. Tournier, "Les Lésions auriculaires," 291; my translation, emphasis added.
38. Tom Conley, *The Self-Made Map*, 8; emphasis added.
39. Ibid., 9. The reference is to Guy Rosolato, *La relation d'inconnu* (Paris: Gallimard, 1978).

## Chapter 4

1. Dr. Th. Henusse, "L'Agoraphobie: Etude clinique et pathogénique," *Journal belge de la neurologie et de la psychiatrie* 41 (1941–42): 9.
2. Ibid., 14.
3. See Isaac M. Marks, "Agoraphobic Syndrome," *Archives of General Psychiatry* 23 (1970): 539; and Isaac M. Marks, *Fears, Phobias and Rituals: Panic, Anxiety and Their Disorders* (New York: Oxford University Press, 1987), chap. 10. See also Lisa Capps and Elinor Ochs, *Constructing Panic: The Discourse of Agoraphobia* (Cambridge, MA: Harvard University Press, 1995), 1–2.
4. Isaac M. Marks "Agoraphobic Syndrome (Phobic Anxiety State)," *Archives of General Psychiatry* 23 (1970): 538.
5. See Richard McNally, *Panic Disorder: A Critical Analysis* (New York: Guilford Press, 1994), 209.

6. Thus, researchers have found what they consider culture-bound variants of agoraphobia. "Kayak-angst," for example, is a condition that apparently afflicts "10% of male Eskimos [*sic*] when the hunter is alone at sea hunting seals," notes McNally. "The attacks usually occur on sunny days when the sea is calm, and show the same traits of terror and disorientation that we have seen in European accounts of agoraphobia (with the additional fear of drowning). They subside when the hunter reaches shore or when he is joined by fellow hunters." See NcNally, *Panic Disorder,* 207–8.

   Findings such as these, which discover in various cultures "universal" somatic signs in relation to a notion of space that is itself universal are suspect for several reasons. Both the notion of body as pure biology and the notion of space as Euclidian extension are Western ones. Only the dualist, Western notion of mind is considered as a cultural variant. Body and space are both viewed as nature. Research paradigms that leave the nature/culture divide of Western epistemology intact are insufficient models for cross-cultural inquiry. Space itself is on neither one nor the other side of a nature/culture divide. In this book we are approaching space as a materiality which exists, persists, and insists in various cultural modes.
7. Information on this study comes from the various reports published between 1988 and 1993 by participating clinicians in the American publication *Archives of General Psychiatry* (a journal of the American Medical Association) and in the *British Journal of Psychiatry* (published by the Royal College of Psychiatrists). See also Gerald L. Klerman, "Overview of the Cross-National Collaborative Panic Study," *Archives of General Psychiatry* 45 (1988): 407–12; and Isaac M. Marks (1992, 1993). Klerman was, at the time, chair of an Upjohn scientific team.
8. The arguments for "panic attacks" as a separate category owe much to the work of Donald F. Klein. See his "Anxiety Reconceptualized," in *Anxiety: New Research and Changing Concepts*, ed. Donald F. Klein and Judith G. Rabkin (New York: Raven, 1981). For a discussion of how the Cross National Panic Study took up Klein's thesis see Klerman, "Overview," 408.
9. See Jean-Phillipe Boulenger and Thomas W. Uhde, "Crises aigües d'angoisse et phobies: aspects historiques et manifestations clinques du syndrome d'agoraphobie" *Annales medico-psychologiques* 145; 2 (1987); and Assen Jablensky, "Approaches to the Definition and Classification of Anxiety and Related Disorders in European Psychiatry," in *Anxiety and the Anxiety Disorders*, ed. A. Hussein Tuma and Jack Maser (Hillsdale, NJ: Lawrence Erlbaum, 1985), 755.
10. McNally, *Panic Disorder,* 173.
11. Isaac Marks, John Greist, Metin Basoglu, Homa Noshirvani, and Geraline O'Sullivan, "Comment on the Second Phase of the Cross-National Collaborative Panic Study," *British Journal of Psychiatry* 160 (1992): 202–205.
12. Ibid., 204; emphasis added.
13. Isaac Marks, Richard P. Swinson, Metin Basoglu, Homa Noshirvani, Klaus Kuch, Geraline O'Sullivan, and Paul T. Lelliot, "Reply to Comment on the London/Toronto Study," *British Journal of Psychiatry* 162 (1992): 792–93; emphasis in the original.
14. In Marks' three year study that tested alprazolam against exposure and placebo, exposure also came out as strongly effective. "On most other measures, exposure was superior to alprazolam by the end of the treatment. ... During taper and followup, gains after exposure continued if it had not been given with aprazolam, but gains from aprazolam disappeared." See Isaac Marks, Richard P. Swinson, Metin Basoglu, Klaus Kuch, Homa Noshirvani, Geraline O'Sullivan, Paul T. Lelliot, Marlene Kirby, Gary McNamee, Seda Dengun, and Kim Wickwire, "Alprazolam and Exposure Alone and Combined in Panic Disorder with Agoraphobia: A Controlled Study in London and Toronto," *British Journal of Psychiatry* 162 (1993): 786.
15. See Consumer Reports' critical assessment of the popularity of Xanax at this period. "High Anxiety," *Consumer Reports* January (1993): 21.
16. National space is characterized by the strict territorial borders of the nation-state. Cultural space, on the other hand, is characterized by the fluid networks established in a variety of forms such as language, shared history, and the like.

17. Byron J. Good and Arthur Kleinman, "Culture and Anxiety: Cross-Cultural Evidence for the Patterning of Anxiety Disorders," in *Anxiety and the Anxiety Disorders*, ed. A. Hussain Tuma and Jack Maser (Hillsdale, NJ: Lawrence Erlbaum, 1985) 305; emphasis added.
18. Ivor H. Jones and David J. de L. Horne, "Psychiatric Disorders among Aborigines of the Australian Western Desert," *Social Science and Medicine* 7 (1973): 219–20; emphasis added.
19. Obviously, in such studies we cannot look for descriptive information about the psychic suffering of Aboriginal peoples. This study, for example, describes thousands of Australian Aborigines as being "least affected by Western influences," as if the forced lifeways of missionary settlements brought by colonization were not themselves an enormous psychic factor of Western influence. Reminded of the racist vision behind and within such population studies, our interest here is certainly not whether or not agoraphobia or objectless anxiety occurred among the Aboriginal tribes of the Western Australian Desert. The diagnostic categories themselves are of questionable value for many reasons, not least of which is that they are derived from European ones. "The criteria for diagnosis," write the authors of the Aboriginal study, "were, within the limitations described above, close to the British Glossary of mental disorders. … [and in accordance with] the World Health Organization's Committee on Mental Health." See Jones and Horne, "Aborigines," 221.
20. Ibid., 224.
21. See Martin Heidegger, *Being and Time*, trans. Joan Stambough (Albany: State University of New York Press, 1996).
22. The main theoretical argument behind cognitive therapies is that agoraphobics regularly "misinterpret" bodily signs that, in other circumstances, would be indicators of actual physical harm but in the agoraphobic's case are merely symbolic signs of mental distress. Thus, agoraphobics are said to "falsely" interpret bodily symptoms catastrophically. According to cognitive psychologists, "[c]atastrophic interpretations seem to fall into three general classes of disaster: biological (death), mental (insanity), or behavioral (loss of control)"; see Jeffrey E. Hecker and Geoffrey L. Thorpe, *Agoraphobia and Panic: A Guide to Psychological Treatment* (Boston: Allyn and Bacon, 1992), 54. Since cognitive treatments also involve teaching patients behavioral skills to handle their symptoms, most cognitivists use behaviorist treatments. The main difference between the cognitive and behavioral methods, according to one famous behaviorist who treats agoraphobia, is that whereas behavior therapy "tries to alter avoidance [behavior] in the hope that cognitive and physiological gains will also follow, cognitive methods try first to alter thoughts to pave the way toward change in behavior"; see Marks, *Fears, Phobias and Rituals*, 486. Certainly the literature on agoraphobia shows that cognitive treatments in and of themselves are not as successful for phobic and obsessive compulsive disorders as they are when combined with behaviorist modalities.
23. See Viktor Frankl, *The Doctor and the Soul: From Psychotherapy to Logotherapy* (New York: Bantam, 1986).
24. In the clinical literature, there are several studies that show how techniques of paradoxical intention can enhance behaviorist treatments; see, for example, Matig L. Mavissakalian, Larry Michelson, Deborah Greenwald, Sander Kornblith, Michael Greenwald "Cognitive-Behavioral Treatment of Agoraphobia: Paradoxical Intention vs. Self-Statement Training," *Behaviour Research and Therapy* 21 (1989): 75–86. See also Amr Berrada's book (co-authored with Judith Bemis) *Embracing the Fear: Learning to Manage Anxiety and Panic Attacks*. (Minneapolis: Hazelden, 1994).
25. Amr Barrada, "Metacognition and the Development of Emotional Disorders," Unpublished manuscript, 1987, 3.
26. Ibid., 3–4.
27. Amr Barrada, personal interview with the author, May 6, 1991.
28. See the excellent 1996 essay by Esther da Costa Meyer, "La Donna e Mobile: Agoraphobia, Women, and Urban Space," in *The Sex of Architecture*, ed. Diana Agrest, Patricia Conway and Leslie Kanes Weisman (New York: Harry N. Abrams, 1996). I gratefully acknowledge her treatment of Freud's work on agoraphobia; see pages 144–47.
29. Ibid., 146.
30. Freud, quoted in da Costa Meyer, "La Donna e Mobile," 146.
31. Ibid., 145.

32. In the Belgian cases noted above, Dr. Henusse saw the somatic presentations of agoraphobia—fear, sweating, tremors, and the like—as symbols of orgasm.
33. Edoardo Weiss, "Agoraphobia and Its Relation to Hysterical Attacks and to Traumas," *International Journal of Psychoanalysis* 16 (1935): 68; emphasis added. The viewpoint expressed here—("Probably some inner urge prompts us to put a statue, an obelisk and especially, a fountain in the middle of squares.")—is supported by King Vidor's 1948 film adaptation of Ayn Rand's 1943 novel *The Fountainhead*, which dramatized the resistance to and triumph of International Style in New York City in the 1940s. In the film Gary Cooper plays the modernist architect and Patricia Neal the vagina dentata, destroyer of fountainheads, who eventually learns to live with her repressed love for the tallest skyscraper in New York. Here the link between America's possessive individualism and modern architecture is made most explicit.
34. Weiss, "Agoraphobia," 67.
35. Ibid., 68.
36. Bruce Ruddick, "Agoraphobia," *International Journal of Psycho-Analysis* 42 (1961): 541; emphasis added.
37. See, in particular, Steve Pile's interesting work *The Body and the City: Psychoanalysis, Space and Subjectivity* (London: Routledge, 1996).
38. The "imaginary" has some parallels with Freud's description of the "ego ideal," but Lacan's notion of a mirror stage reduces this part of the ego's development to spatiovisual relations, identifications of the "I" with the "eye." Thus, Freud's resulting notion of intersubjectivity is one that involves a much wider experience of embodiment, whereas Lacan's resulting notion of intersubjectivity will be limited to only one aspect of the body's sensorium, the visual.
39. I am grateful to Steve Pile's excellent summary of Lacan's essay in *The Body and the City.*
40. Ervin Panofsky, *Perspective as Symbolic Form,* trans. C. S. Wood (New York: Zone, 1991), 72.
41. See Terry Cochran's analysis of modernity as the figure of a world picture in *Twilight of the Literary: Figures of the Thought in the Age of Print* (Cambridge, MA: Harvard University Press, 2001), chap. 2.
42. See da Costa Meyer, "La Donna e Mobile"; Carol Brooks Gardener, "Out of Place: Gender, Public Places and Situational Disadvantage," in *Now/Here: Time, Space and Modernity,* Roger Friedland and Diedre Boden, eds., (Berkeley: University of California Press, 1994) 335–352; and Robert Seidenberg and Karen DeCrow, *Women Who Marry Houses: Panic and Protest in Agoraphobia,* (New York: McGraw-Hill, 1983).
43. da Costa Meyer, "La Donna e Mobile," 150, cites Helene Cixous, Catherine Clement, Luce Irigaray, and Michele Montrelay in France, and Elaine Showalter and Carroll Smith-Rosenberg in the United States, among others. da Costa Meyer reads the agoraphobic situation somewhat differently. Her interpretation remains within the psychoanalytic framework without extending to the anthropological dimension that locates the problem in the cultural issue of Western visualization. She offers the following reading:

    > Like other forms of psychopathology, [agoraphobia] is a language with a syntax of its own. Robert Seidenberg and Karen DeCrow, for example, see it as a strategy of opposition to what we might call the ethic of renunciation usually demanded of married women. [The clinical literature does show that agoraphobia most often strikes women shortly after they are married.] It is the somatization of the symptoms that permits the victim to express feelings s/he otherwise finds unacceptable. Conversely, agoraphobics avoid situations that give (unconscious) symbolic expression to their hidden fears or wishes: trains (the wish to flee), elevators and tunnels (fear of being trapped in unhappy marriages), and so on. Space perception depends on mastering institutionalized signs, but agoraphobics tend to read them figuratively. Both the places they avoid and those they designate as shelters have to do with distinct typologies which are metaphors for situations they fear or desire. Their spatial codes are personal and hermetic rather than socialized. (150–51)

    In Da Costa Meyer's account, emptiness, per se, is not of special interest. When we stay with the relation of subjectivity and empty space we can take a route that goes beyond issues of symbolic organization, beyond the epistemological issues of how the world, in this case, the built emptiness of the modern world, is interpreted.

44. See Elizabeth Grosz, *Volatile Bodies: Toward a Corporeal Feminism* (Bloomington: Indiana University Press, 1994).
45. Ibid., 104.
46. Maurice Merleau-Ponty, *The Visible and the Invisible,* trans. Alphonso Lingis (Evanston: Northwestern University Press, 1968), 131, quoted in Grosz, *Volatile Bodies*, 104.
47. Grosz, Ibid., 104.
48. Ibid., 105–6.
49. Luce Irigaray, *Ethique de la difference sexuelle* (Paris: Minuit, 1984), 168, cited in Grosz, *Volatile Bodies*, 107.
50. Monte Meldman, quoted in Seidenberg and DeCrow, *Women Who Marry Houses*, 164.
51. Seidenberg and DeCrow, *Women Who Marry Houses*, 109.
52. Erik Erikson, quoted in Seidenberg and DeCrow, *Women Who Marry Houses*, 45–46; emphasis added.
53. Grosz, paraphrasing Irigaray in *Volatile Bodies*, 107.
54. Seidenberg and DeCrow, *Women Who Marry Houses*, 68.
55. Ibid., 167; emphasis added.
56. Helene Deutsch, "The Genesis of Agoraphobia," *International Journal of Psychonalysis* 10 (1929): 69. da Costa Meyer discusses this as well in "La Donna e Mobile," 151–2.
57. See, for example, Capps and Ochs, *Constructing Panic*, esp. 32–33; and Ruth Bankey, "The Paradox of Panic: A Geographic Analysis of Agoraphobic Experience," M.A. thesis, Carleton University, Ottowa, Ontario, 1999, which offers detailed ethnographic descriptions where informants mention agoraphobic anxiety and their roles as mothers (see esp. 170). None of these authors, however, probe the relation that their informants' agoraphobia may have with the experience of mothering.
58. Given the legal debates over abortion and surrogate pregnancy in the United States, it appears that our individualist society and legal institutions are far from sorting this out. Thus the need for concepts that help us think about how intrauterine experience persists in the everyday experience of the self and how such persistence is reflected in psychological theories of self or Western notions of personhood. The earlier discussion of Deleuze and Guattari's notion of a self as a "multiciplity" aims in this direction (see chapter 3).
59. Although functionalist design was sometimes proposed as a socialist antidote to the appropriation of urban design by capitalist developers, its use was in fact essential to the increasing influence of the marketplace in everyday life. As Nan Ellin, *Postmodern Urbanism* (Cambridge: Blackwell, 1996), 186, notes, "This appropriation of urban design by developers was also signalled by a symposium held at the MoMA in 1947 called 'What Is Happening to Modern Architecture?' where recent regionalist design in the Bay Area was derided and a return to essentialist modernism was championed, with Le Corbusier's Radiant City as the universal model."
60. James Holston, *The Modernist City: An Anthropological Critique of Brasilia* (Chicago: University of Chicago Press, 1989), 40.
61. Michael Dear, *The Postmodern Urban Condition* (Oxford: Blackwell, 2000), 95.
62. Zygmunt Bauman, *Globalization: The Human Consequences* (New York: Columbia University Press, 1998), 40.
63. Ibid., 49.
64. Sigfried Giedion, *Mechanization Takes Command: A Contribution to Anonymous History* (New York: Oxford University Press, 1948) 720, quoted in Vidler, *Warped Space: Art, Architecture, and Anxiety in Modern Culture* (Cambridge, MA: MIT Press, 2000), 51.
65. Vidler, *Warped Space*, 51.
66. Ibid., 53.
67. Ibid.
68. Ibid., 54.
69. Ibid. A French acquaintance once told me that she had worked on a research study of how visitors reacted as they walked through a famous house that Le Corbusier had designed outside of Paris. They didn't walk across the open spaces, she said. "Ils razaient les murs" (They hugged the walls).
70. Ibid., 58.
71. Le Corbusier, quoted in Vidler, *Warped Space*, 60.
72. Ibid., 61.

73. Vidler, *Warped Space*, 61–62.
74. Maurice de Fleury, quoted in Vidler, *Warped Space*, 64; emphasis added.
75. Amr Barrada, interview with the author, November 1999.
76. Isaac M. Marks and Paul Bebbington, also note the case of a fifty-nine-year-old woman "with a seven year history of episodic difficulties in driving if she encountered a wide open road or hollows. … she was occasionally terrified of walking when she felt the ground would move. ("Space Phobia: Syndrome or Agoraphobia Variant?" *British Medical Journal* 2, no. 6031 (1976): 345–347)." "She made a stable marriage," they note, "and had post-partum depression at the age of 31" (346). Marks and Bebbington are unsure of whether she and three other women over fifty with late onset of the spatial phobia were actually agoraphobics or not. They do note, "Our patients might have had some common unknown disturbance of the pathways subserving their visuospatial reflexes. … This might illuminate the mechanisms that mediate anxiety symptoms like dizziness, forms of agoraphobia, and normal fears that are triggered by specific visuospatial and kinaesthetic cues—for example, fears of a visual cliff, of looking up at a skyscraper, and of the total absence of spatial clues" (347). The authors distinguish the cases from the agoraphobics they have also studied because of the "disproportion between the great fear of space and the mild fear of public places in the space syndrome. By contrast, the cardinal feature of agoraphobia is a fear not of open spaces, as is commonly supposed, but of public places, although a mild fear of open spaces sometimes occurs" (346). I would argue that the preponderance of agoraphobics who some twenty-five years later cite the urban freeways as their second most fearful space should give evidence that the two kinds of cases—cases where the object of fear is public places and cases where it is wide, open or empty space ("spaces without visuospatial cues")—are quite similar. Empty space, which is both visible and public in the urban freeways, is simply an instance of the transformation of empty space in modernity.
77. Capps and Ochs, *Constructing Panic*, 1.
78. Henri Lefebvre, *The Production of Space*, trans. Donald Nicholson-Smith (Oxford: Basil Blackwell, 1991), 313–14.
79. See Ellin, *Postmodern Urbanism*.
80. Bernard Huet, quoted in Ellin, *Postmodern Urbanism*, 205.
81. Los Angeles is often singled out as the first American city that, thanks to the automobile, broke entirely with European conceptions of city planning. It thus holds a particular fascination for Europeans. In his history of death in the Western world, French historian Michel Vovelle ends with an image of a drive-in funeral parlor in Los Angeles; see Michel Vovelle, *La Mort et l'Occident, de 1300 à nos jours* (Paris: Gallimard, 1983).
82. See, for example, Jane Jacobs's seminal *The Death and Life of Great American Cities: The Failure of Town Planning* (New York: Vintage, 1961); and Vincent Scully, *American Architecture and Urbanis* (New York: Henry Holt, 1969).
83. Roberta Brandes Gratz and Norman Mintz, *Cities Back from the Edge: New Life for Downtown* (New York: John Wiley, 1998), 33–34.
84. Ibid., 34–35.
85. Ray Banham, *Los Angeles: Architecture of the Four Ecologies* (Harmondsworth: Penguin Books, 1973), 161, 213, quoted in Dear, *Postmodern Urban Condition*, 13; emphasis added.
86. Dear, *Postmodern Urban Condition*, 108. See also the ethnographic documentary *Home Economics*, on Southern California's furthest suburbs, by Jenny Cool, a graduate student of Dear's.
87. Dear, *Postmodern Urban Condition*, 110.
88. Ibid., 111.

## Chapter 5

1. See Nikolas Rose's important work *Governing the Soul: The Shaping of the Private Self* (London: Routledge, 1990), which uses Foucauldian analysis to make this argument in terms of the private self. My understanding of behaviorism in the introduction to this chapter is greatly indebted to Rose's work. As public space is increasingly privatized in

the consumer culture of the postwar era, behavioral techniques assist the invention of a private self fit for the new forms of public space. The discussion of behaviorism and agoraphobia in this chapter adds to Rose's discussion of how this new self was shaped by focusing on the role of space (in particular, public space perceived as empty space) in the creation of a new urban subjectivity.

2. Rose, *Governing the Soul*, 229–30.
3. Ibid., 231–39.
4. The modern shopping center is perhaps the most cited trigger of agoraphobic angst. One study found evidence of a spatial dysfunction in agoraphobics that was specifically manifest in supermarkets. See Barrie Jones, "Do Agoraphobics Interpret the Environment in Large Shops and Supermarkets Differently?" *British Journal of Clinical Psychology* 35 (1996): 635–37.
5. Some of the British journals in which behaviorist research was published during this period include the *British Journal of Psychiatry*, the *British Medical Journal*, the *British Journal of Medical Psychology*, and the *Journal of Behaviour Research and Therapy: An International Multidisciplinary Journal*. I have found many of the British articles on behaviorist treatments of agoraphobia translated in other European journals such as *L'encephale: Journal de Neurologie, de Psychiatrie et de Medecine Psycho-Somatique* during this period. The work is also disseminated in the "international multidisciplinary" *Journal of Behaviour Research and Therapy* and I have found it either translated or cited in various other European psychiatric journals.
6. See Isaac M. Marks, *Living with Fear: Understanding and Coping with Anxiety* (New York: McGraw-Hill, 1978), which provides for a lay audience the results of Marks's clinical work during this period. The book was revised, updated, and supplemented—in short, rewritten—as *Fears, Phobias and Rituals: Panic, Anxiety, and their Disorders* (New York: Oxford University Press, 1978).
7. See Randi Hutter Epstein, "Experts Try Fast-Track Fix for Children with Phobias," *New York Times*, January 20, 2004, D5.
8. Marks, *Fears, Phobias and Rituals*, 473.
9. The general picture of agoraphobia in the British Isles at this time is from J. J. Hawkrigg, "Agoraphobia-1," *Nursing Times*, August 14, 1975, 1280.
10. Quoted in ibid., 1281–82.
11. Ibid., 1282.
12. See William Sargant, *Battle For the Mind: Introduction to Physical Methods of Treatment in Psychiatry* (New York: Doubleday, 1957), 87, and William Sargant "Ten Years Clinical Experience of Modified Leucotomy Operations," *British Medical Journal* 2 (1953) for descriptions of leucotomy/lobotomy treatments in Great Britain at this time. Robert Seidenberg and Karen DeCrow, *Women Who Marry Houses: Panic and Protest in Agoraphobia* (New York: McGraw-Hill, 1983), 129, comments on the use of lobotomy for agoraphobia, accusing the doctors of experimentation on women.
13. Editors, "Agoraphobia," *British Medical Journal* 4, no. 5938 (1974): 177; emphasis added. Subsequent letters to the editors show that there was some disagreement among doctors with the *British Medical Journal*'s prolobotomy editorial statement. These letters, however, do not express any surprise or concern that lobotomy was used for the treatment of agoraphobia. Rather, they show a desire to correct the record about the usefulness of tricyclic or benzodiazepine drugs. In that regard they support my argument that the phasing out of lobotomy in Britain for the treatment of severe agoraphobia goes hand in hand with the rise in pharmacological approaches to the disorder. Thus the following letter—by Dr. Norman Capstick in *British Medical Journal* 4, no. 5946 (1974): 720-721—is typical of the response to the editors' lead article on agoraphobia:

    Sir,--Your leading article on [agoraphobia] (26 October [1974]) dismisses the use of tricyclic compounds in the treatment of this condition somewhat abruptly, yet these compounds are frequently effective in agoraphobic conditions and they are often the first line of therapy in both general practice and psychiatric clinics. ... [B]efore the psychiatrist considers such methods as leucotomy the use of tricyclic compounds in adequate dosages should be considered.

14. Isaac M. Marks, J. L. T. Birley, and M. G. Gelder, "Modified Leucotomy in Severe Agoraphobia: A Controlled Serial Inquiry," *British Journal of Psychiatry* 112 (1966): 768.

15. Ibid., 768; emphasis added.
16. Ibid., emphasis added.
17. Ibid.; emphasis added.
18. Ibid., 766; emphasis added.
19. Ibid., 759.
20. G. W. Brown and Tirril Harris, *Social Origins of Depression* (London: Tavistock, 1978), 235–236.
21. Marks et al., "Modified Leucotomy," 759.
22. Esther da Costa Meyer, "La Donna e Mobile: Agoraphobia, Women and Urban Space," in *The Sex of Architecture*, ed. Diana Agrest, Patricia Conway, and Leslie Kanes Weisman (New York: Harry N. Abrams, 1996), 147; emphasis added.
23. Lauretta Vinciarelli, "Women Internet vs. 'Space of Tyranny': A Reply to Esther da Costa Meyer," *The Sex of Architecture*, eds. Diana Agrest, Patricia Conway, and Leslie Kanes Weisman (New York: Harry N. Abrams, 1996), 158.
24. The term *universe of nonrecognition* was coined by French anthropologist Marc Augé in his study of what he calls the "non-places" of supermodernity; see Augé, *Non-Places: Introduction to the Anthropology of Supermodernity*, trans. John Howe (London: Verso, 1995). I will return in chapter 6 to Augé's formulation of the problem of creating identity in those public spaces of Western modernity characterized by their enormous scale and sterile, homogeneous design.
25. Marks, *Fears, Phobias and Rituals*, 557; emphasis added.
26. In his summary of behavioral treatments of agoraphobia, Richard McNally reminds his readership that "A striking, and largely forgotten, early exception to the emerging dominance of exposure therapy was modified leucotomy. … In contrast to…agoraphobics who had not undergone leucotomy, leucotomized agoraphobics exhibited marked postsurgical reductions in anxiety and (apparently) panic, *and their phobic avoidance became responsive for the first time to exposure therapy*." See McNally, *Panic Disorder: A Critical Analysis (*New York: Guilford Press, 1994), 144–45; emphasis added.
27. Marks et al., "Modified Leucotomy," 768.
28. Jeffrey E. Hecker and Geoffrey L. Thorpe, *Agoraphobia and Panic: A Guide to Psychological Treatment* (Boston; Allyn and Bacon, 1992), 229; emphasis added.
29. Peter R. Breggin, *Brain-Disabling Treatments in Psychiatry: Drugs, Electroshock and the Role of the FDA* (New York: Springer, 1997), 201.
30. Ibid., 204. Breggin also notes that doctors have found that "[w]ithdrawal problems and rebound increases in anxiety and panic were so extreme in key studies used for FDA approval of Xanax [the trade name of a leading benzodiazepine] for panic disorder that many or most patients had more frequent or severe symptoms at the end of the studies than before they took the drug" (205).
31. Ibid., 204.
32. Ibid.
33. Marks, *Fears, Phobias and Rituals*, 506; emphasis added.
34. Abigail Zuger, "Caution: That Dose May Be Too High," *New York Times*, September 17, 2002, F1.
35. Ibid.
36. This observation is supported by manufacturers' recent withdrawal from the market of several drugs routinely prescribed for arthritis pain, weight loss, menopausal symptoms, high cholesterol, and other complaints. The pharmaceutical company Merck, for example, pulled Vioxx from the market worldwide after studies found use of the drug for 18 months doubled one's risk of heart attack and stroke. Pfizer, another large company, pulled their product, Bextra, off the market in April 2005 due to similar cardiovascular risks and the seemingly unique risk of serious skin reactions.
37. Breggin, *Brain-Disabling Treatments*, 232.
38. See Emily Martin's illuminating essay "Flexible Survivors," *Anthropology News*, September 1999, 5–7.
39. Anxiety and depression are predominantly female diagnoses, judging from population studies in Britain and the United States. The rate is generally two to one. See Joan Busfield, *Men, Women and Madness: Understanding Gender and Mental Disorder* (Houndmills, Basingstoke, Hampshire: Macmillan Press, 1996), 16–17. Busfield reports figures

from the *Morbidity Statistics from General Practice* (1981–82) in Britain and the large-scale epidemiological catchment area survey carried out in the United States in the early 1980s.

40. On this topic, I was greatly impressed by Denise Russell, *Women, Madness and Medicine* (Oxford: Blackwell, 1995), an important and clearly argued case against biological psychiatry especially for the treatment of depression and postmenstrual syndrome. I have relied on Russell's arguments for my general statements here.
41. Marks, *Fears, Phobias and Rituals*, 324. Another formulation of Marks's insistence of the fundamental role of public place in the agoraphobic syndrome is as follows:

    In adult psychiatric clinics agoraphobia is the most frequent and handicapping phobic disorder. It is a coherent though protean syndrome. The central feature is a variable combination of characteristic fears and avoidance of public places like streets, shops, public transport, crowds, assemblies, and tunnels. Fear/panic and associated autonomic sensations and thoughts are triggered by entering or thinking about such places, especially when alone. Though multiple, the fears have a pathognomonic [disease causing] pattern and do *not* usually concern non-public situations like cats, darkness, blood, water, glass, dirt, or cancer, though cases may fear being alone at home. Fears with avoidance often restrict ability to work and to leave the home, and can lead to houseboundage. Panic is not pathognomic of agoraphobia, as it is also found in many other conditions. (360; emphasis in the original)
42. Michael G. Gelder and Isaac M. Marks, "Severe Agoraphobia: A Controlled Prospective Trial of Behaviour Therapy," *British Journal of Psychiatry* 112 (1966): 309.
43. Ibid., 309.
44. Ibid.; emphasis added.
45. Ibid., 311.
46. Ibid., 316.
47. Ibid., 318; emphasis added.
48. Richard Stern and Isaac Marks, "Brief and Prolonged Flooding: A Comparison in Agoraphobic Patients," *Archives of General Psychiatry* 28: 2 (1973): 270.
49. Ibid., 271.
50. Ibid., 271; emphasis added.
51. Ibid., 270–71.
52. Ibid., 274.
53. Ibid., 275.
54. Ibid.
55. Ibid.
56. Walter T. A. M. Everaerd, Hanneke M. Rijken, and Paul M. G. Emmelkamp, "A Comparison of 'Flooding' and 'Successive Approximation' in the Treatment of Agoraphobia," *Behaviour Research and Therapy: An International Multi-Disciplinary Journal* 11, no. 1 (1973): 108; emphasis added.
57. Paul M. G. Emmelkamp, "Self Observation versus Flooding in the Treatment of Agoraphobia," *Behaviour Research and Therapy: An International Multi-Disciplinary Journal* 12, no. 3 (1974): 231.
58. Everaerd et al., "A Comparison of 'Flooding,'" 116.
59. See A. Ghosh and Isaac M. Marks, "Self-Treatment of Agoraphobia by Exposure," *Behavior Therapy* 18 (1987): 3–16; and A. Ghosh, Isaac M. Marks, and A. C. Carr, "Therapist Contact and Outcome of Self-Exposure Treatment for Phobias: A Controlled Study," *British Journal of Psychiatry* 152 (1988): 234–38.
60. McNally, *Panic Disorder*, 164.
61. Emmelkamp, "Self Observation versus Flooding," 237; emphasis added.
62. The behavioral notion of *habituation* refers to a decrease in response to a stimulus due to repetition, a common example in the clinical literature being the case when a patient doesn't hear the ticking of a clock after getting used to it.
63. Stern and Marks, "Brief and Prolonged Flooding," 275; emphasis added.
64. Marks, *Fears, Phobias and Rituals*, 494; emphasis added. Marks goes on to note the value of abreactive over cognitive treatments.
65. Ibid., 480; emphasis added.
66. Ibid., 482.

67. Robert L. Moody, "Bodily Changes During Abreaction," *Lancet* 2 (1946):934–935 and "Bodily Changes During Abreaction," *Lancet* 1 (1948): 946, quoted in Marks, *Fears, Phobias and Rituals*, 482; emphasis added.
68. Marks, *Fears, Phobias and Rituals*, 483.
69. Ibid., emphasis added.
70. While I do think that such disregard for meaning is a recipe for misappropriation in the behaviorist context of socializing unwitting patients to public spaces already well known in the larger social world for their asocial environment—the big box structure of the shopping center, for example, is not intended as a social space for shoppers; it is a purely efficient site to bring prices down by buying in bulk (artificially, of course, since someone else's labor is most likely being undervalued in the process)—I am well aware that other cultural systems, such as acupuncture, for example, use techniques of "energy medicine" in ways that are not necessarily attached to symbolic meaning in order to treat a patient. Indeed the popularity of energy medicine at this historical moment in the West should give us pause to reflect on how it might be used in a nonreflective way to simply adapt ourselves to conditions and pathologies of modern life that in fact should be consciously dealt with and in many cases opposed. The situation is, of course, not at all simple. Energy medicine is also entering Western contexts as part of a social movement to address the inadequacies of Western medical knowledge—in particular, to propose alternatives to the market driven pharmacological direction of biomedicine.
71. Sigmund Freud, quoted in Jean Starobinsky, *Action and Reaction: The Life and Adventures of a Couple* (New York: Zone, 2003), 178.
72. Starobinsky (414, n. 40) notes that Freud claims "the term *psychoanalysis* has taken the place formerly occupied by *catharsis*." Ibid., 179.
73. Starobinsky, *Action and Reaction*, 181.
74. Ibid. 182.
75. Eventually Freud formulated a metapsychology that came back to his biological beginnings but used the language of Roman mythology to describe energy in terms of a death drive (Thanatos) and a pleasure principle (Eros).
76. In the 1970s and early 1980s flooding is most often recommended for the agoraphobic patient without drugs. Without drugs it appears to induce abreaction. After the mid-1980s, as was noted previously, in vivo flooding is most often practiced when the patient is under medication. In this state it is not necessarily producing an abreaction.
77. Sargant, *Battle for the Mind*, 65.
78. Ibid., 66.
79. Ibid., 67.
80. Ibid., 67; emphasis added. Marks himself notes, in *Fears, Phobias and Rituals*, that Pavlov's dogs later gradually recovered the reflexes in question. The canine recovery may have invalidated the concept of transmarginal inhibition, but this has not thwarted the use of therapeutic techniques whose effectiveness have been explained by this concept. Electric shock treatment, which is now making a comeback, is one of them.
81. See Russell, *Women, Madness and Medicine.*
82. Marks, *Fears, Phobias and Rituals*, 483.
83. Marks et al., "Modified Leucotomy," 768, emphasis added.
84. Marks, *Fears, Phobias and Rituals*, 360; emphasis added.
85. Ibid., 494; emphasis added.
86. The agoraphobic patient was interviewed by John Wisniewski in the *Syracuse Post-Standard*, November 16, 1978, quoted in Seidenberg and DeCrow, *Women Who Marry Houses*, 117–18.
87. Arthur Handy, cited in Seidenberg and DeCrow, *Women Who Marry Houses*, 162–63. The book's publisher was part of the national organization that sponsored Hardy's particular treatment plan.

## Chapter 6

1. For an excellent description of the political economy of neoliberalism, see David Harvey *A Brief History of Neoliberalism* (Oxford: Oxford University Press, 2005).

2. The following history of the shopping center in Britain comes from Rachel Bowlby's excellent research in *Carried Away: The Invention of Modern Shopping* (New York: Columbia University Press, 2001).
3. Bowlby, *Carried Away*, 154.
4. Ibid., 171; emphasis added.
5. Ibid., 172; emphasis added.
6. Ibid., 170.
7. Ibid., 158.
8. Ibid., 165; emphasis added.
9. Ibid., 175–86.
10. British Market Research Bureau Limited, *Shopping in Suburbia: A Report on Housewives Reactions to Surpermarket Shopping* (London: J. Walter Thompson Company Limited, 1963) 15, 47. Quoted in Bowlby, *Carried Away*, 226, 227.
11. Bowlby, *Carried Away*, 231.
12. British Market Research Bureau Limited, *Shopping in Suburbia*, 18, 30. Quoted in Bowlby, *Carried Away*, 229, 230.
13. Bowlby, 230; emphasis added.
14. British Market Research, 17. Quoted in Bowlby, 230.
15. Bowlby, 233; emphasis added.
16. See Michael Sorkin, ed., *Variations on a Theme Park: The New American City and the End of Public Space* (New York: Hill and Wang, 1992).
17. Facts from the Mall of America press kit, reported by David Guterson in his essay "Enclosed. Encyclopedic. Endured: One Week at the Mall of America," *Harpers*, August 1993, 49.
18. Guterson, "Enclosed. Encyclopedic. Endured," 49.
19. Ibid.
20. According to Amr Barrada, director of a clinic that treats agoraphobic patients in Minneapolis. Interview with the author, November 1999.
21. Britt Griffin, "The Mega-Mall," *North Country Anvil* 55 (1987): 24. The West Edmonton Mall has continued to add to its square footage in competition with the Mall of America and more recent challenges emerging from upstate New York. It still claims to be "the world's biggest mall," boasting a European boulevard "fashioned after various European city streets," its own version of Chinatown, "replicas of the crown jewels of the British Empire from William I to George VI," and "a premier piece of Hellenistic sculpture," to name a few of its attractions. See its website, http://www.westedmall.com.
22. See William S. Kowinski, *The Malling of America: An Inside Look at the Great Consumer Paradise* (New York: William Morrow, 1985).
23. See Mike Davis, *City of Quartz: Excavating the Future in Los Angeles* (New York: Vintage, 1992), 223–63).
24. "A More Perfect Union" radio broadcast, quoted in *Harper's* August (1993) 22.
25. See Marc Augé, *Non-Places: Introduction to the Anthropology of Supermodernity*, trans. John Howe (London: Verso, 1995), in which shopping centers, the freeway, airports, high-speed commuter trains and other sites are described as "non-places."
26. The most influential proponents of new urbanism in the U.S. are Peter Calthorpe, James Howard Kuntsler, Anton Nelessen, and especially Andres Duany and Elizabeth Plater-Zyberk. See Andres Duany, Elizabeth Plater-Zyberk, and Jeff Speck, *Suburban Nation* (New York: North Point Press, 2000).
27. Susan Fainstein, "New Directions in Planning Theory," *Urban Affairs Review* 35, no. 4 (2000): 61, notes, "Within the United Kingdom Charles, the Prince of Wales, has been associated with the neo-traditional movement and has sponsored development in accordance with principles of the new urbanism. In Britain and other parts of Europe, however, many of the tenets of the new urbanism have always formed the basis of planning regulation and thus do not represent as much of a reorientation as in the United States." New urbanist planners' ideas on urban life closely resemble those of the early twentieth century planning theorists—Patrick Geddes, Ebenezer Howard, and Frederic Law Olmsted.
28. James Howard Kunstler, quoted in Fainstein, "New Directions," 61.

29. Fainstein's "New Directions" compares new urbanism with two other current trends in planning theory—the Habermasian theory of communicative rationality and what the author calls "the just city," a political economy approach. I fully agree with the author's assessment of new urbanism as an ideally important but ultimately flawed approach to the problems of sprawl in American cities. In the United States, the model communities built according to new urbanist principles have been both praised for their innovative attempt to break with the alienation effects and ecological damage of postwar suburban sprawl (James Howard Kunstler) and critiqued for being a partial solution that continues the economic drain on the inner city that the original suburbs began in the 1950s (David Harvey). It is true that new urbanist community design has been most influential in creating new suburban developments that are more densely organized rather than in creating denser existent suburbs or creating new housing in the inner city. New urbanist designers need to follow the money to realize their designs, and developers build where land is cheaper, farther out from city centers. Thus, the integrationist view of new urbanism has been rightly criticized as often being simply another form of suburbia rather than a plan to curb the segregation of American cities. The new urbanist communities may provide a better spatial design for suburban developments but they end up being no more diverse in their social composition. See David Harvey's critical study of the new urbanist development in Kentlands, Maryland, designed by Andres Duany and Elizabeth Plater-Zyberk (in Harvey, *Spaces of Hope*, Berkeley: University of California Press, 2000). See also Peter Katz's *The New Urbanism: Toward an Architecture of Community*, (New York: McGraw-Hill, 1994), which contains pictures of and plans for a number of these endeavors within the United States.
30. Barbara Flanagan, "A Massachusetts Mall is Just Disappeared." *New York Times*, March 3, 1991.
31. One social group had warned of the inevitable collapse of the New Seabury Mall long before it became the Mashpee Commons. Residents of this region may remember from the late 1970s the land-claim case brought by the Mashpee Indians against the Seabury Corporation for its development plans. The case is now famous because it turned on an attempt on the part of the Mashpee Tribe to establish in a court of law that they were legally Native Americans. Because the Mashpees were unsuccessful, they were unable to file a suit against the Seabury Corporation. Before this case was transformed into a legal contest involving Indian identity, however, it had been an attempt to file legal charges against Seabury for the planned overdevelopment of the area. The Mashpee Tribe and several other local groups said the area could not physically support the increased population and land-use scheme proposed by the Seabury corporation. When the Mashpee lost the legal standing to register their complaint, Seabury went ahead with their privatized mall project, only to be forced—nearly two decades later, when the shopping center failed—to turn it over to the developers who built the Mashpee Commons. It would be interesting to know whether the Mashpee Indians, whose tribe is still active in the area, gained any rights over the governance of Mashpee Commons, or if they were offered monetary compensation for the use of their name, just as Indian tribes who brought huge land-claims cases to U.S. courts in the 1970s were only compensated with money and not land a century after losing these lands to the federal government. Over a century ago, Native American presence appeared across America in the names of cities, lakes, and rivers while the tribes themselves were being killed and cornered into reservation lands. See Gerald Torres and Kathryn Milun, "Translating Yonondio by Precedent and Evidence," *Duke University Law Journal* 625 (1990): 401–435.
32. See the volume of *The Town Paper* devoted to new urbanism in Europe (*Council Report V*, September 2003, online at http://www.tndtownpaper.com/council/ShopAwe.htm).
33. Jacqueline Leavitt, "Where's the Gender in Community Development?" *Signs: Journal of Women in Culture and Society* 29 (2003): 207.
34. See Sherry Ahrentzen, "The Space Between the Studs: Feminism and Architecture," *Signs: Journal of Women in Culture and Society*, 29/1 (2003): 179–206. Ahrentzen notes how the ratio of women in architecture compare to other male-dominated professions:

    In dentistry, 19.8 percent of the professionals are women, 26.6 percent of physicians are women, and 28.6 percent of professionals in the law and the judiciary are women. Women account for more than 43 percent of executives, managers, and administrators nationwide. But women's presence in architecture looks favorable when compared with the clergy, where only 12 percent are women—because there are more clergy than architects in the United States, however, you are more likely to encounter a clergy-woman than a woman architect (U.S. Bureau of Labor Statistics 1999). Other depictions of the status and influence of women in the architectural profession are virtually impossible to assemble since the professional organization, the AIA, does not compile statistics on job types and employee gender within its member firms. (21)

35. For full statistics consult the online publication of librarian historian Matthew White, entitled *Source List and Detailed Death Tolls for the Man-made Megadeaths of the Twentieth Century*, http://users.erols.com/mwhite28/warstats.htm, (accessed 16 May 2006). For a sense of how the experience of changing warfare has affected the soldier, see Lorrie Goldensohn, ed., *American War Poetry: An Anthology* (New York: Columbia University Press, 2006).
36. See Joan Busfield, *Men, Women and Madness: Understanding Gender and Mental Disorder* (Houndmills, Basingstoke, Hampshire: Macmillan Press, 1996) in which she discusses how the traumatic experiences of the battlefields came to be designated "shell shock" and "war neurosis" during World War I, noting, "The key symptoms were loss of memory and disturbances of vision, smell and taste. … As with cases of hysteria" (213). Her principal findings are that in the cases of shell shock, social class made a noticeable difference (officers were diagnosed with shell-shock twice as often as privates). Addressing the difficulty the English military had in accepting this diagnosis, Busfield notes,

    > Officers could not be expected to face the stigma of the asylum as cases of insanity, and as a group they could not be assumed to be weaklings, lacking in masculine qualities of courage and endurance. Yet it was precisely the officers rather than privates who displayed, in the symptoms of shell-shock, more fearfulness and anxiety (neurasthenia rather than hysteria), emotions more commonly associated with women and children than men. Such behavior had to be explained, and explained in a way that did not threaten existing conceptions of masculinity and the standing courage of officers. …
    >
    > The case of shell-shock shows how a male mental disorder was constructed in circumstances in which alternative designations of the phenomenon in question posed considerable problems, threatening as they were both to conceptions of masculinity and to conceptions of class. (213–14)

    In World War Two, the symptoms were called "war neurosis" and "battle fatigue." Later, after the Vietnam War, the term "post-traumatic stress disorder" was employed.
37. Richard McNally, *Panic Disorder: A Critical Analysis*. (New York: Guilford Press, 1994) 170.
38. See Paul Pichot, "Panique: attaque et trouble. Historique du mot et des concepts." *L'Encephale* 22, no. 5 (1996): 3–8, on the history of the word *panique* in France and its recent use, since the 1980s, in describing agoraphobia.
39. Jacques Galibert, "Subnarcose amphétaminée et psychothérapie des états d'angoisse." *L'Encéphale*: [Journal de Neurologie, de Psychiatrie et de Medicine Psycho-somatique] 4 (1960) 333.
40. R. J. Kerry, "Phobia of Outer Space," *Journal of Mental Science* 106 (1960): 1384.
41. Ibid.
42. Ibid., 1383; emphasis added.
43. Ibid., 1386; emphasis added.
44. It is not uncommon, for example, to see a female agoraphobic patient introduced in the clinical literature of this century in the following way: "Consider 38-yr-old Mrs. CLF, who was house-bound by anxiety soon after the birth of her first child 16 years previously." See Arnold Lazarus, "Broad-Spectrum Behaviour Therapy and the Treatment of Agoraphobia," *Behavioral Research and Therapy* 4 (1966):95.
45. *The Economist's* "Mum's the Word," December 5, 1998, 20. Quoted in Helen Penn, "How should we care for babies and toddlers? An analysis of practice in out-of-home care for children under three," Occasional Paper 10, Centre for Urban & Community Studies: University of Toronto (June 1999) 15. For more general discussions of women's fears in public space see Gil Valentine, "The Geography of Women's Fear " *Area* 21.4 (1989) 385–390; Nan Ellin, Ed. *Architecture of Fear.* (Princeton: Princeton Architectural Press, 1997);

Katheen M. Kirby *Indifferent Boundaries: Spatial Concepts of Human Subjectivity* (New York: Guilford, 1996); Robyn Longhurst, "(Re)presenting Shopping Centers and Bodies: Questions of Pregnancy," in *New Frontiers of Space, Bodies and Gender*, ed. Rosa Ainley, (London: Routledge, 1998), 20–34.

46. Nathan C. Goldman, *American Space Law: International and Domestic* (San Diego, CA: Univelt, 1996), 14.
47. See Colum Kenny, *Fearing Sellafield: What It Is and Why the Irish Want It Shut* (Dublin: Gill & Macmillan, 2003).
48. William B. Terhune, "Fear and Phobias," *Connecticut Medicine* 23, no. 12 (1959): 766; emphasis added.
49. See Steven L. Simon and Andre Bouville, "Radiation Doses to Local Populations Near Nuclear Weapons Test Sites Worldwide" *Health Physics*. 82:5 (2002):706–725, and Valerie Kuletz, *Tainted Desert: Environmental Ruin in the American West*. (New York: Routledge, 1998).
50. See Camilla Griggers, *Becoming Woman* (Minneapolis: University of Minnesota Press 1997); and Michael Taussig, *The Nervous System* (New York: Routledge, 1992). Griggers uses a Deleuzian conceptual framework in her analysis of the socialization of women in late modernity. Taussig, who has training as a medical doctor, also uses concepts from Deleuze and Guattari's work to show that modernity under capitalism has vast, systematic means that deterritorialize and reterritorialize the human sensorium.
51. See Nancy N. Chen, "Urban Spaces and Experiences of QiGong," in *Urban Spaces in Contemporary China: The Potential for Autonomy and Community in Post-Mao China*, eds. Deborah S. Davis, Richard Kraus, Barry Naughton, Elizabeth J. Perry (Cambridge: Cambridge University Press, 1995) 347–361; and Nancy N. Chen *Breathing Spaces: Qigong, Psychiatry, and Healing in China* (Columbia University Press, 2003).
52. G. Liotti and V. Guidano, "Behavioural Analysis of Marital Interaction in Agoraphobic Male Patients," *Behaviour Research and Therapy: An International Multidisciplinary Journal* 14, no. 2 (1976): 161; emphasis added.
53. Jeffrey E. Hecker and Geoffrey L. Thorpe, *Agoraphobia and Panic: A Guide to Psychological Treatment* (Boston; Allyn and Bacon, 1992), 241–42; emphasis added.
54. Ernst Bloch, *Erbschaft dieser Zeit* (Frankfurt: Suhrkamp, 1973) cited in Klaus Scherpe, "Nonstop to Nowhere City? Changes in the Symbolization, Perception and Semiotics of the City in Literature of Modernity" trans. Lisa Roetzel in *Cultural Critique* No. 23 (1992–93) 137–164.
55. Marc Augé, *Non-Places: Introduction to the Anthropology of Supermodernity*. Translated by John Howe. London: Verso, (1995) 78.
56. See Paul Rabinow, "Artificiality and Enlightenment: From Sociobiology to Biosociality," in *Incorporations*, ed. Jonathan Crary and Sanford Kwinter (New York: Zone, 1992).
57. Literary scholar Wlad Godzich once told me that his young son who worked as a financial analyst in Geneva spent his days fantasizing in front of a stream of stock market figures whose fluctuations could in no way be grasped by any known cognitive skills. Only in a mode of distraction, he suggested, could a perception of a systematic trend be grasped and translated into a decision to buy or sell. Godzich described how his students analyzed something of this world by discovering that the city's banking institutions were sponsors of the rave parties that were popular among young professionals of this period of "dot-com" economic boom. The relation between the speed of semicognitive financial judgments and the speed of a body moving to rave music with its electronically generated, complex, and counteracting rhythms was an anthropological find that Augé would have appreciated, as it told of new skills forming in a universe of nonrecognition.

## Chapter 7

1. See Candida Graham, Abigail Franses, Mark Kenwright, and Isaac Marks, "Problem Severity in People Using Alternative Therapies for Anxiety Difficulties" in *British Journal of Psychiatry* 25 (2001): 12–14; The authors studied agoraphobia and obsessive-compulsive patients and found that, since similar studies in 1970, use of alternative remedies had increased from 15 percent to 55 percent. See also David M. Eisenberg, Roger B.

Davis, Susan L. Ettner, Scott Appel, Sonja Wilkey, Maria Van Rompay, Ronald C. Kessler, "Trends in Alternative Medicine use in the United States, 1990–1997: Results of a Follow-up Survey," *Journal of the American Medical Association* 208 (1998): 1569–1575; and Peter Fisher and Adam Ward, "Complementary Medicine in Europe," *British Medical Journal* 309 (1994): 107–111.

2. Remedies for agoraphobia that treat the body/mind holistically include: homeopathy, based on principles of the body's subtle energy fields, where pathology is said to be related to vibrational frequencies that are out of tune; acupuncture, based on a Chinese medical system where pathology is related to blocked flows of chi energy through an embodied network of meridians; and finally, a range of modalities under the umbrella term *bioenergetics*, somatically based analytic psychotherapies (also known as body psychotherapy) where pathology manifesting as observable physical behavior engaging the body's autonomic system is treated as precognitive—that is, nonsymbolized—behavior. For a discussion of how concepts from Chinese healing practices are becoming psychological concepts in Western contexts see Linda L. Barnes, "The Psychologizing of Chinese Healing Practices in the United States," *Culture, Medicine and Psychiatry* 22 (1998): 413–443.
3. Bioenergetic treatment is generally traced to the work of Alexander Lowen (see his *The Language of the Body* [New York: Collier, 1958]) and to Peter Levine's work on trauma (see his *Walking the Tiger: Healing Trauma* [Berkeley: North Atlantic Books, 1997]). Wilhelm Reich's psychoanalytic work is also seen as a seminal influence on much of body psychotherapy. See Ron Robbins, "Body Approaches to the Treatment of Panic," in *Panic: Origins, Insight, and Treatment*, ed. Leonard J. Schmidt and Brooke Warner (Berkeley, CA: North Atlantic, 2002), 332, n. 2. For a treatment modality especially suited to women, see Helen Resneck-Sannes, "A Feeling in Search of Memory," *Women and Therapy* 16, no. 4 (1995): 97–105.
4. There is a growing body of social theory dedicated to a new look at the Western self, focusing on kinesthetic knowing, proprioceptive capacities, and the transmission of affect. See, for example, Teresa Brennan, *The Transmission of Affect* (Ithaca, NY: Cornell University Press, 2004); and Brian Massumi, *Parables for the Virtual: Movement, Affect, Sensation*, (Durham, NC: Duke University Press, 2002). Massumi's work extends the work of Deleuze and Guattari on subjectivity and addresses issues raised in this volume concerning concepts of the self based in movement and anti-oedipal forms of becoming.
5. The studies on agoraphobia use EEG technologies, but the same biofeedback therapy is currently being researched with MRI equipment, which is the technology being developed to market these treatments for commercial use.
6. Siegfried Othmer, Susan F. Othmer, and David A. Kaiser, "EEG Biofeedback: A Generalized Approach to Neuroregulation," available online at http://www.eegresearch.com/articles/general_5.htm. (Last viewed April 5, 2006) 10. The reports of the authors compare favorably with the scant peer-reviewed studies done on EEG biofeedback and agoraphobia. Most of these studies were conducted in the 1970s and '80s. It could be that after this time, much of the research for anxiety orders like agoraphobia is funded by pharmaceutical companies who are not interested in testing their products against biofeedback therapies. One typical study from this period carried out at the Institute of Psychiatry at the University of Rome demonstrates many of the same features discussed by the authors of the report mentioned above. In this study (Gabriele Chiari and Roberto Mosticoni, "The Treatment of Agoraphobia with Biofeedback and Systematic Desensitization," *Journal of Behavioral Therapy and Experimental Psychiatry* 10 (1979): 109–113), four patients, three women and one man, were treated with some success by EEG biofeedback for their agoraphobia.

   > Susanna, 39 and unmarried, had a law degree and worked in the civil service. Suffering for four years from agoraphobia (avoiding wide streets, crowds, closed places and public transport), her cultural and recreational activities were severely limited. She had to be escorted everywhere. … At the conclusion of the treatment Susanna, while able to make the home-office and home-laboratory journeys alone … reported that the only improvement was a moderate reduction in the intensity, frequency and length of the tachycardia attacks. (111–112)

> Another patient, at the end of her treatment "felt completely independent and said that the problem for which she had come to the Institute was resolved. ... from the beginning of the treatment the patient did not think it opportune to take drugs. ... At final follow-up, [she] reported a continuing fear of marriage and inability to engage in stable affective relationships. Following acceptance of a marriage proposal, she had experienced several anxiety attacks, causing her to break off the relationship, but no relapse occurred regarding the initial problem." (111)

For more recent work on the effectiveness of neurofeedback therapies, see Marco Congedo, Joel F. Lubar, and David Joffe, "Low-resolution Electromagnetic Tomography Neurofeedback," *IEEE Transactions on Neural Systems and Rehabilitation Engineering* (a publication of the IEEE Engineering in Medicine and Biology Society) 4 (2004): 387–97; and Verner Knott, David Bakish, Stacey Lusk, and John Barkely, "Relaxation-Induced EEG Alterations in Panic Disorder Patients," *Journal of Anxiety Disorders* 4 (1997): 365–76.

7. Othmer et al., "EEG Biofeedback," 4.
8. Ibid.
9. See, in particular, Elizabeth Wilson's treatment of affect, including her review of neurological and psychological treatments of affect in *Psychosomatic: Feminism and the Neurological Body* (Durham, NC: Duke University Press, 2004). See also Elizabeth Grosz, *The Nick of Time: Politics, Evolution, and the Untimely* (Durham, NC: Duke University Press, 2004), which discusses Henri Bergson's theory of instinct and intuition as concepts that demonstrate a link between human and nonhuman biology so as to offer Western philosophy and psychology conceptual tools to go beyond the mind/body dualism.
10. Wilson, *Psychosomatic: Feminism and the Neurological Body*, 9.
11. See Richard McNally, "EMDR and Mesmerism: A Comparative Historical Analysis," *Journal of Anxiety Disorders* 13, nos. 1–2 (1999): 225–36, which offers a sociocultural comparison of the controversies and popularity of EMDR and the late-eighteenth-century practice of mesmerism, whose claims of harnessing electromagnetic force to cure various afflictions were eventually associated with the charisma of the therapist. The author notes that one EMDR technique—using the common "body starter" of to-and-fro eye movement—is similar to Mesmer's technique of having patients follow a pendulum-like shiny object with their eyes back and forth until they are "mesmerized," or brought into an altered state of consciousness.
12. This is based on the work of Francine Shapiro, who later discovered that the bilateral mechanism that intervened in the central nervous system with back-and-forth eye movement was also at work in other bilateral body gestures and could likewise be used therapeutically to release the hold of intensely charged emotions on behavior. See Shapiro, "Eye Movement Desensitization and Reprocessing (EMDR) and the Anxiety Disorders: Clinical and Research Implications of an Integrated Psychotherapy Treatment," *Journal of Anxiety Disorders* 13, nos. 1–2 (1999): 35–67. There are now many popular accounts of the effectiveness of EMDR therapy; see, for example, Maggie Scarf, *Secrets, Lies, Betrayals: The Body/Mind Connection, How the Body Holds The Secrets of a Life, and How to Unlock Them* (New York: Random House, 2004). Some clinicians have championed its success; see, for example, Francine Shapiro and Margot Silk Forrest, *EMDR: The Breakthrough Therapy for Overcoming Anxiety, Stress, and Trauma* (New York: Basic, 1997). There have likewise been many studies and critiques of the method; see, for example, Camille DeBell and R. Deniece Jones, "As Good as It Seems? A Review of EMDR Experimental Research," *Professional Psychology: Research and Practice* 28 (1997): 153–63.
13. Ron Robbins, "Body Approaches to the Treatment of Panic," in *Panic: Origins, Insight, and Treatment*, ed. Leonard J. Schmidt, and Brooke Warner (Berkeley, CA: North Atlantic, 2002), 327.
14. See Scarf, *Secrets, Lies, Betrayals*, on the relation to REM sleep; see also Robbins, "Body Approaches," 328, on the speed (and surprise) with which patients relinquish their anxiety symptoms once they have located their "body starter" and have begun to use it as a strategic intervention with this therapy.

15. Shapiro, "Eye Movement Desensitization and Reprocessing (EMDR) and the Anxiety Disorders," 44. Shapiro cites the following study by Dutch researchers: A. De Jongh and E. Ten Broeke, "Eye Movement Desensitization and Reprocessing (EMDR): een procedure voor de behandeling van aan trauma gerelateerde angst," *Tijdschrift voor Psychotherapie* 22 (1996): 93–114.
16. See Robbins, "Body Approaches"; see also Alan J. Goldstein, Edwin de Beurs, Dianne L. Chambless, and Kimberly A. Wilson, "EMDR for Panic Disorder with Agoraphobia: Comparison with Waiting List and Credible Attention-Placebo Control Conditions," *Journal of Consulting and Clinical Psychology*. 68, 6 (2000) 947–956.
17. See Goldstein et al., "EMDR for Panic Disorder."
18. The following discussion is taken from the review article by Alain Berthoz and Isabelle Viaud-Delmon, "Multisensory Integration in Spatial Orientation," *Current Opinion in Neurobiology* 9 (1999): 708–12.
19. Maria Paganini discusses the memory patterns that are repeated throughout Proust's *A Remembrance of Things Past* after the main character trips and momentarily loses his sense of equilibrium while walking. See Paganini, *Reading Proust: In Search of the Wolf-Fish*, trans. Carole Litherland and Kathryn Milun (Minneapolis: University of Minnesota Press, 1994).
20. Berthoz and Viaud-Delmon, "Multisensory Integration," 32–35.
21. Ibid., 36–37.
22. By pursuing this line of questioning I am following in the direction of Elizabeth Grosz, *The Nick of Time: Politics, Evolution, and the Untimely* (Durham, NC: Duke University Press, 2004), which seeks to bring the biological sciences back into the philosophical and political discussion of what life is about. As Grosz notes,

    > We need to return to, or perhaps to invent anew, the concepts of nature, matter, and life, the most elementary concerns of the cosmological and the ontological, if we want to develop alternative models to those inscriptive and constructivist discourses that currently dominate the humanities and social sciences, in which the transformation of representation is the only serious discourse, its constitution in representation, or its mediation by images. We need an account of what the social and the political, the individual and the sexual must use in the "construction" of identity, the body, or culture, its natural resources—if construction and inscription still remain relevant metaphors, that is, if this image of subject-constitution or -construction is to have any complexity or explanatory power. If the body is to be placed at the center of political theory and struggle, then we need to rethink the terms in which the body is understood. We need to understand its open-ended connections with space and time, its place in dynamic natural and cultural systems, and its mutating, self-changing relations within natural and social networks. In short, we need to understand the body, not as an organism or entity in itself, but as a system or series of open-ended systems, functioning within other huge systems it cannot control, through which it can access and acquire its abilities and capacities. (3)

23. Resneck-Sannes, "A Feeling in Search of Memory," 308.
24. Luce Irigaray, *Between East and West: From Singularity to Community*, trans. Stephen Pluháček (New York: Columbia University Press, 2002), 6.
25. Ibid., 6–7.
26. Ibid., 24.
27. Ibid., 25.
28. Ibid., 26.
29. Ibid., 24.
30. Ibid., 27.
31. I contacted 10 professional therapists (among them, Lauren Artress, Creator and Founder of the Veriditas-Voice of the Labyrinth Movement, www.Veriditas.net) who have used labyrinth walking in their practice. None of them reported using it specifically for agoraphobics but all noted that it was an intriguing idea. Thus Donald Altman, former Buddhist monk and psychotherapist, author of *Art of the Inner Meal: The Art of Mindful Practice to Heal our Food Cravings* (Oregon City, OR: Moon Lake Media, 2002) and *Living Kindness: The Buddha's Ten Guiding Principles for a Blessed Life* (Maui, HI: Inner Ocean Publishing, 2003), noted

I have not specifically used a labyrinth walk for patients suffereing from agoraphobia. However, I have used mindful walking for patients who are dealing with high levels of anxiety and panic—as a transitional tool to help them move from one location and/or activity to another. Some of these patients have difficulty leaving the house because of anxiety, so it seems that mindful walking could likewise assist agoraphobics to redirect their mind away from negative thoughts and emotions, and to do this within a cityscape with the safety of a labyrinth seems a natural extension. Labryinths promote mindfulness, and I have led groups in labyrinth walking during mindfulness retreats. (communication with author 12/9/2005)

Similarly Robert McLellarn, Ph.D. reported,

I am a psychologist in Portland Oregon and I specialize in treating anxiety disorders. … I haven't heard of anyone using labyrinth walking as a treatment for agoraphobia, but what an interesting idea. Exposure is the ultimate key to treating agoraphobia and if labyrinth walking facilitated clients doing more exposure then it would probably help. Perhaps there would be a calming/soothing/safe, even hypnotic, aspect to the labyrinth walking that would make the walking not feel so scary and dangerous. (communication with author 12/15/2005)

32. Lauren Artress tracks labyrinths on the website for her nonprofit organization, Veriditas: The World-Wide Labyrinth Project (www.Veriditas.net). Labyrinths appear in many historical periods and diverse cultures. In the European Middle Ages, labyrinths were inscribed on floors in virtually every church and abbey of Christiandom. Indeed, medieval pilgrims would kneel their way along the labyrinth's paths, making a metaphorical journey of the longer journey they had just made to ask for a miracle or fulfill a vow. For a historical and social analysis of the phenomena of labyrinth walking in France, see Jacques Attali, *The Labyrinth in Culture and Society: Pathways to Wisdom,* trans. Joseph Rowe (Berkeley, CA: North Atlantic Books, (1999). For a discussion of the therapeutic uses, see Lauren Artress, *The Sacred Path Companion: A Guide to Walking the Labyrinth to Heal and Transform* (New York: Riverhead Trade/Penguin, 2006).
33. Heather Knight, "The Peaceful Path: In Troubled Times, More People Turn to Labyrinths to Walk their Worries Away," *San Francisco Chronicle,* Feb. 28, 2003. Robert Ferré, whose construction firm builds labyrinths for hospitals and medical centers in the United States, believes that "[w]ithin the next decade or two, labyrinths will become standard and valued features of healing environments. Indeed, the process is well underway, with labyrinths at more than sixty health-care facilities across the country, led in 1997 by California Pacific Medical Center in San Francisco. The day will be soon be upon us in which no progressive architect will design a healthcare facility without including a meditation labyrinth. The day is not far off when patients, staff members, and doctors will insist that their existing facility install a labyrinth." See Robert Ferré, "Labyrinths: Spiritual Technology for Inner Healing," available online at www.labyrinth-enterprises.com/healing.html.
34. Judy Gifford, interview with the author, May 5, 2003.
35. See also Steve Pile's commentary on Certeau's essay in *The Body and the City: Psychoanalysis, Space and Subjectivity* (London: Routledge, 1996), 224–29.
36. Michel de Certeau, "Walking in the City," in *The Practice of Everyday Life,* trans. Steven F. Rendall (Berkeley and Los Angeles: University of California Press, 1984), 93.
37. Pile, *The Body and the City,* 225.
38. Walter Benjamin refers to this man-about-town in several writings. On the general category of the "man in the crowd" and Benjamin's "flaneur," see the essays in Keith Tester, ed., *The Flâneur* (New York: Routledge, 1994). On the flaneur as a gendered category of social analysis, see Janet Wolff, "The Artist and the Flâneur: Rodin, Rilke and Gwen John in Paris," in Tester's *Flâneur,* 111–137.
39. Richard Sennett, *The Fall of Public Man: On the Social Psychology of Capitalism* (New York: Vintage, 1978), 262.
40. In my search of the popular literature and interviews, it appears that more women than men are involved with the therapeutic activity of labyrinth walking.
41. I am using the term *transmission* in the sense described by Teresa Brennan in *The Transmission of Affect,* (Ithaca, NY: Cornell University Press, 2004).
42. François Dagognet, "Toward a Biopsychiatry," in *Incorporations,* ed. Jonathan Crary and Sanford Kwinter (New York: Zone, 1992), 517– 535.

43. Ibid., 535.
44. Ibid., 517.
45. While no longer used in birthing classes, these puffing gestures remain alive at the level of collective fantasy as they are still the ones we see in American television and popular film scenes when a woman is shown giving birth in a hospital delivery room. For my part, I can attest to the power of breath training learned in yoga for childbirth. I managed my labor pain delivering twins without anesthetic medication by achieving a trancelike meditative state in my hospital room through focused breathing. I felt almost no pain during contractions. It worked so well that even through the most painful period called transition, the doctor claimed she could not tell from my face when I was experiencing a contraction and when I wasn't. The technique worked well until the doctor decided it was time for me to start pushing and thus moved me to a delivery room, breaking my concentration and sending me into paroxysms of pain. It is interesting to note that Western medicine is now asking itself whether the practice of having mothers push during contractions while delivering is at all useful; see Eric Nagourney "Rethinking the Big Push during Contractions," *New York Times*, January 3, 2006. Reporting that a recent study in the *American Journal of Obstetrics and Gynecology* shows that "there is no evidence that bearing down during contractions helps either the mother or the child." The researchers also report that women who are encouraged to push may be at higher risk for urinary problems after delivery. In the study women in childbirth were divided into two groups, one told to "do what feels natural to do" and the other instructed to "take deep breaths, hold them and bear down for 10 seconds at the peak of a contraction." Researchers in the study were unclear as to how the practice of encouraging women to push came about, "the researchers say it was not in the medical literature before 1950." In the United States, the 1950s mark the period when birthing was moved to hospitals and many mothering practices that "felt natural" were discouraged by modern medicine, breastfeeding included, to the point of their being kept alive for future generations in alternative movements like the LaLeche League. Placing this historic "forgetfulness" in the same tradition of what Irigaray discusses regarding Schopenhauer's forgetfulness of breathing and its consequences for Western psychology and biology, it is essential to note that when women in childbirth did "what feels natural" they were not necessarily abandoning all culturally transmitted practices in order to be directed by mere biological sensations. Many skills—of breathing, body postures, and focused concentration—would have been passed down through generations of women's culture. But certainly having a woman deliver with no historically transmitted practical knowledge of the process would be a setup for sheer anxiety in the face of the unknown and the attendant pain of an anxious mind working against the body. When the researchers in the study pondered why the practice of pushing came about, they offered that it "might have been to decrease the amount of time women were in discomfort." Given the current tendency in the United States to schedule cesarean births well in advance for convenience and comfort, it seems that instrumental reason and efficiency dictate a norm that has been key in erasing generational skills of kinesthetic knowing. In suggesting this, however, I am not denigrating the important advances in biomedicine that have saved many women from the dire consequences of difficult deliveries.
46. A. Orwin, "The Running Treatment: A Preliminary Communication on a New Use for an Old Therapy (Physical Activity) in the Agoraphobic Syndrome," *British Journal of Psychiatry* 122 (1973): 176; emphasis added.
47. Ibid., 177; emphasis added. This patient had fifteen running sessions and seventy-five walking sessions. I want to emphasize the under-recognized role in this therapy of learning to walk *in public urban places*. The few recent studies that cite and reproduce the success of Orwin's findings focus on exercise itself as the effective physiological component in the cure of agoraphobia. Thus a 1989 study in Germany that trained agoraphobic patients to run in local "parks and forests" also found the running therapy to be more effective than placebo, but not quite as effective as the well-proven tricyclic clomipramine. (Andreas Broocks, Borwin Bandelow, Gunda Pekrun, Annette George, Tim Meyer, Uwe Bartmann, Ursula Hillmer-Vogel, and Eckart Rüther, "Comparison of Aerobic Exercise, Clomipramine, and Placebo in the Treatment of Panic Disorder," *American Journal of Psychiatry* 155 (1998) 603–609. The patients chosen for the study had "a diagnosis of panic

disorder and agoraphobia." (3)) The picture I am drawing in this book, on the other hand, argues that urban space itself be recognized as an inseparable feature of both the pathology and the treatments.

48. Ben Hamilton-Baillie, *Home Zones—Reconciling People, Places and Transport: Report of a Study Tour of Denmark, Germany, Sweden and The Netherlands* (Cambridge, MA: Harvard Design School Publication, 2002) 1–2.
49. In the United Kingdom, home zones are primarily promoted as "traffic management" projects; still, the emphasis is on community involvement.
50. Hamilton-Baillie, *Home Zones*, 2.
51. When I once described woonerfs at a public presentation, a member of the audience informed me that she had heard the engineer who originally designed the woonerf plan speak about why the woonerf traffic signs that showed a car, a house, and children at play were so counterproductive to the project that they were eventually taken down and the woonerf left to be encountered by cars with no official, visual warning. Apparently a driver would see the sign, understand a woonerf was coming up, look to see if children were around, and if not, proceed to drive through the area at the same speed he would have driven through a residential street. In other words, the signs did not slow the traffic down to any significant extent. Only when a driver unexpectedly came upon an area of what he thought should be a street but what looked more like a playground did he actually slow down to the speed of walking; that is, only through being completely confused would a driver interfere with his normative, internalized driving habits and slow down. As in much speculation about the communicatve mechanisms of biofeedback, it appears that interference between systems plays as much a role as skill building when changing habits through nonsymbolic communication.

## Conclusion

1. See Georg Simmel, "The Metropolis and Mental Life," in *On Individuality and Social Forms*, ed. Donald Levine (Chicago: University of Chicago Press, 1971).
2. See Georg Simmel's classic work, "The Stranger," in Kurt Wolff (Trans.) *The Sociology of Georg Simmel* (New York: Free Press, 1950) 402–408.
3. Leonie Sandercock, "When Strangers Become Neighbors: Managing Cities of Difference," *Planning Theory and Practice* 1, 1: (2000): 13–30.
4. Sandercock, "When Strangers Become Neighbors"; see also the essays in *Urban Planning in a Multicultural Society*, ed. Michael Burayidi (Westport, CT: Praeger, 2000).
5. John Locke, *Two Treatises of Government*, ed. P. Laslett (Cambridge: Cambridge University Press, 1988), II: 49: 1.
6. Gottfried Wilhelm Leibniz, *Nouveaux essais sur l'entendement humain* (Paris: Presses universitaires de France, 1961). Préface, §3, and §4, quoted in André Lalande, *Vocabulaire technique et Critque de la Philosophie* (Paris: Presses Universitaire de France, 1983), 1099. Lalande notes that the expression "*table rase*" (blank slate) probably came into French philosophical discourse thanks to Leibniz. (Translation mine.)
7. See Gilles Deleuze, *The Fold: Leibniz and the Baroque*, trans. Tom Conley (Minneapolis: University of Minnesota Press, 1993).
8. The reference, mentioned in the introduction, is to political theorist Claude Lefort whose important work on radical democracy proposes that democracy is not only a form of government but a new form of society characterized by the disappearance of certainty about the meaning of "the people" in whom democratic power is said to reside. For Lefort, the disappearance of certainty leads to an ongoing, open dialogue about who constitutes "the people." I am not taking issue with Lefort's argument here but only with the spatial image he uses to represent the productive uncertainty of democratic societies: Lefort speaks of the site of democratic uncertainty as "an empty place." See Claude Lefort, "The Question of Democracy," in *Democracy and Political Theory*, David Macey, trans. (Cambridge, U.K.: Polity Press/Basil, Blackwell, 1988), 19.
9. Better known in Europe, the baby-on-its-back theory was first described to me by a French child-development specialist. The theory is associated with the work that Hungarian pediatrician Dr. Emmi Pikler carried out with orphans in Budapest at the Loczy

Institute. The Loczy method emphasizes the individuality and autonomy of infants. It trains caregivers to provide sustained tactile support when needed, but encourages them to allow the baby to develop what it sees as an innate sense of individualized learning. The method has been especially influential in France, Belgium, and Italy which have strong traditions of state-run daycare for infants. (See Emanuela Cocever, *Bambini attivi e autonomi. A cosa serve l'adulto? L'esperienza di Loczy* (Florence: La Nueva Italia, 1990). The Sensory Awareness Foundation, a non-profit organization based in California, is set up to promote the ideas of Loczy in the USA (online at http://www.sensoryawareness.org). For an excellent review of how culture and market context influence theories of early childhood development, including the Loczy method, see Helen Penn, "How should we care for babies and toddlers? An analysis of practice in out-of-home care for children under three," Occasional Paper 10, Centre for Urban & Community Studies: University of Toronto June 1999 *iv*, 66 pp. (online at http://www.childcarecanada.org/pubs/op10/index.html. Last viewed May 2006). Penn, Senior Research Fellow at the University of London, notes that "the work of the Loczy Institute has now been partly discredited in Hungary itself because many of the children who attended were the children of imprisoned dissidents, and in retrospect it has been argued that the very particular circumstances of the children's referral should have been acknowledged; the children's background was not an accidental one and could not be discounted." (footnote 56).

# Bibliography


Agamben, Giorgio. *Homo Sacer: Sovereign Power and Bare Life*. Trans. by Daniel Heller-Roazen. Stanford, CA: Stanford University Press, 1998.

______. *State of Exception*. Chicago: University of Chicago Press. 2005.

Ahmed, Sara. "Collective Feelings." *Theory, Culture and Society* 21, no. 2 (2004): 25–41.

Ahrentzen, Sherry. "The Space Between the Studs: Feminism and Architecture." *Signs: Journal of Women in Culture and Society*, Autumn 2003, 29/1, 179–206.

Ainley, Rosa, ed. *New Frontiers of Space, Bodies and Gender*. London: Routledge, 1998.

Altman, Donald. *Living Kindness: The Buddha's Ten Guiding Principles for a Blessed Life*. Inner Ocean Pub, 2003.

______. *Art of the Inner Meal: The Art of Mindful Practice to Heal our Food Cravings* USA; Moon Lake Media (2002).

American Psychiatric Association. *Diagnostic and Statistical Manual of Mental Disorders*. 4th ed. Washington D.C.: American Psychiatric Association, 1994.

Anderson, Benedict. *Imagined Communities: Reflections on the Origin and Spread of Nationalism*. London: Verso, 1983.

Artress, Lauren. *Veriditas: The World-Wide Labyrinth Project*, 2005. Available online at http://www.gracecathedral.org/labyrinth/locator/index.shtml.

______. *The Sacred Path Companion: A Guide to Walking the Labyrinth to Heal and Transform*. New York: Riverhead Trade/Penguin, 2006.

Attali, Jacques. *The Labyrinth in Culture and Society: Pathways to Wisdom*. Trans. Joseph Rowe. Berkeley, CA: North Atlantic Books, 1999.

Augé, Marc. *An Anthropology for Contemporaneous Worlds*. Trans. by Amy Jacobs. Stanford, CA: Stanford University Press, 1999.

______. *Non-Places: Introduction to the Anthropology of Supermodernity*. Translated by John Howe. London: Verso, 1995.

Baker, Roger, ed. *Panic Disorder: Theory, Research, and Therapy*. New York: Wiley, 1989.

Bandelow, B.K., Sievert M., Röthemeyer G., Hajak and E. Rüther. "What Treatments Do Patients with Panic Disorder and Agoraphobia Get?" *European Archives of Psychiatry and Clinical Neuroscience* 245 (1995): 165–171.

Banham, Ray. *Los Angeles: Architecture of the Four Ecologies*. Harmondsworth: Penguin Books, 1973.

Bankey, Ruth. "The Paradox of Panic: A Geographic Analysis of Agoraphobic Experience." M.A. thesis, Carleton University, Ottowa, Ontario, 1999.

Barlow, David H. "In Defense of Panic Disorder with Agoraphobia and the Behavioral Treatment of Panic: A Comment of Kleiner." *Behavior Therapist* 5 (1973): 99–100.

Barlow, David H., and Michelle G. Craske. "The Phenomenology of Panic." In *Panic: Psychological Perspectives*. Ed. by Stanley Rachman and Jack D. Maser. Hillsdale, NJ: Lawrence Erlbaum, 1988.

Barnes, Linda L. "The Psychologizing of Chinese Healing Practices in the United States." *Culture, Medicine and Psychiatry*. 22 (1998) 413–443.

Barrada, Amr. Interview with the author, May 6, 1991.

______. Interview with the author, November 1999.

______. "Metacognition and the Development of Emotional Disorders." Unpublished manuscript, 1987.

______. *Empire of Signs*. Trans. Richard Howard. New York: Hill and Wang, 1982.

Barnes, Linda L. "The Psychologizing of Chinese Healing Practices in the United States." *Culture, Medicine and Psychiatry* 22 (1998): 413–443.

Barthes, Roland. *Degre Zero de l'écriture*. Paris: Gonthier, 1964.

Battersby, Christine. *The Phenomenal Woman: Feminist Metaphysics and the Patterns of Identity*. London: Polity, 1998.

Baudelaire, Charles. *Les Fleurs du Mal*. Trans. Richard Howard. London: Pan Books (Picador) 1987.

Bauman, Zygmunt. *Globalization: The Human Consequences*. New York: Columbia University Press, 1998.

Beard, George Miller. *A Practical Treatise on Nervous Exhaution (Neurasthenia): Its Nature, Sequences and Treatment*. New York: Wood, 1880.

Bemis, Judith and Amr Barrada. *Embracing the Fear: Learning to Manage Anxiety and Panic Attacks*. Minneapolis: Hazelden, 1994.

Benedikt, M. "Über Platzschwindel." *Allgemeine Weiner Medizinische Zeitung*. 15 (1870) 488–489.

Benjamin, Walter. "On Some Motifs in Baudelaire." *Illuminations*. Trans. by Harry Zohn. New York: Harcourt Brace & World, 1968.

______. "Paris, Capital of the Nineteenth-Century." *Reflections*. Trans. Edmund Jephcott. New York: Schocken, 1986.

Bennhold, Katrin. "Suburban Officers Criticised as Insensitive to Racism." *New York Times*, Nov. 8, 2005.

Berman, Marshall. *All That is Solid Melts into Air: The Experience of Modernity*. New York: Penguin, 1982.

Bernard, A., and Ch. Jung. "Contribution à l"étude de la cremnophobie." *Révue Neurologique* 3 (1929): 437–450.

Berthoz, Alain, and Isabelle Viaud-Delmon. "Multisensory Integration in Spatial Orientation." *Current Opinion in Neurobiology* 9 (1999): 708–712.

Bion, Wilfred. *Learning from Experience*. London: William Heinemann, 1962.

Birch, Eugenie Ladner. "From Civic Worker to City Planner: Women and Planning, 1890–1980," In *The American Planner: Biographies and Recollections*. Ed. Donald Krueckeberg, (New Brunswick, NJ: Center for Urban Policy Research, 2nd ed., 1994).

Bloch, Ernst. *Heritage of Our Times*. Trans. by Neville Plaice and Stephen Plaice. Berkeley and Los Angeles: University of California Press, 1991.

Boden, Diedre and Roger Friedland, eds. *Now/Here: Time, Space and Modernity*. Berkeley and Los Angeles: University of California Press, 1994.

Boellstorff, Tom and Johan Lindquist. "Bodies of Emotion: Rethinking Culture and Emotion Through Southeast Asia." *Ethnos* 69; 4 (2004) 437–444.

Bohl, Charles "Shop and Awe: The Peril of American-Style Commercial Development for Europe" *The Town Paper: Council Report V* (2003) at http://www.tndtownpaper.com/council/ShopAwe.htm.

Bohl, Charles. Placemaking: Town Centers, Main Streets and Transit Villages. Washington D.C., Urban Land Institute, 2002.

Bordo, Susan. "Missing Kitchens," In *Twilight Zone: The Hidden Life of Cultural Images From Plato to O.J.* Berkeley, CA: University of California Press, 1999.

______. "Anorexia nervosa: Psychopathology as the Crystalization of Culture," in Irene Diamond and Lee Quinby, eds. *Feminism and Foucault: Reflections on Resistance*. Boston: Northeastern University Press, 1988.

______. "The Body and the Reproduction of Femininity: A Feminist Appropriation of Foucault." In Alison M. Jaggar and Susan R. Bordo, eds. *Gender/Body/Knowledge* New Brunswick, NJ: Rutgers University Press, 1989.

Borsi, Franco

Bowlby, Rachel. *Carried Away: The Invention of Modern Shopping.* New York: Columbia University Press, 2001.

Boyd, Jeffrey H. and Ted Crump. "Westphal's Agoraphobia." *Journal of Anxiety Disorders* 5, no. 1 (1991): 77–86.

Boys, Jos. "Women and Public Space." In *Making Space: Women and the Man-made Environment.* Ed. by Matrix Book group. London: Pluto, (1985) 37–54.

Breggin, Peter R., M.D. *Brain-Disabling Treatments in Psychiatry: Drugs, Electroshock and the Role of the FDA.* New York: Springer, 1997.

Brennan, Teresa. *Transmission of Affect.* Ithaca, NY: Cornell University Press, 2004.

Breuer, Joseph and Sigmund Freud. *Studies in Hysteria (1895).* Boston: Beacon Hill Press, 1950.

British Market Research Bureau Limited, *Shopping in Suburbia: A Report on Housewives Reactions to Supermarket Shopping.* London: J. Walter Thompson Company Limited, 1963.

*British Medical Journal* Editors. "Agoraphobia." *British Medical Journal*, no. 5938 (1974): 177–178.

Broocks, Andreas, Borwin Bandelow, Gunda Dekrun, Annette George, Tim Meyer, Uwe Bartmann, Ursula Hillmer-Vogel, and Eckardt Rüther. "Comparison of Aerobic Exercise, Clomipramine, and Placebo in the Treatment of Panic Disorder." *American Journal of Psychiatry* 155 (1998) 603–609.

Brown, G. W., and Tirril Harris. *Social Origins of Depression.* London: Tavistock, 1978.

Brown, Gilian. "The Empire of Agoraphobia." In *Domestic Individualism: Imagining Self in Nineteenth Century America.* Berkeley: University of California Press, 1990, 170–195.

Burayidi, Michael, Ed. Planning in A Multicultural Society, Westport, CT: Praeger, 2000.

Busfield, Joan. *Men, Women and Madness: Understanding Gender and Mental Disorder.* Houndmills, Basingstoke, Hampshire: Macmillan Press, 1996.

Busscher, J. de. "Tabes et agoraphobie: Réflexions sur les psychothérapies médicales et paramédicales." *Journal belge de la neurologie et de la psychiatrie* 34 (1934): 111–125.

Butler, Judith. *Gender Trouble*, New York: Routledge 1999.

Callard, Felicity. "The Taming of Psychoanalysis in Geography." *Social and Cultural Geography* 4, no. 3 (2003): 295–312.

Capps, Lisa, and Elinor Ochs. *Constructing Panic: the Discourse of Agoraphobia.* Cambridge, MA: Harvard University Press, 1995.

Capstick, Norman. "Letter to the Editors on Agoraphobia Article." *British Medical Journal* 4, no. 5946 (1974): 720–721.

Certeau, Michel de. *The Practice of Everyday Life.* Trans. by Steven Rendall. Berkeley and Los Angeles: University of California Press, 1984.

Chambless, Diane, and Alan Goldstein. "Anxieties: Agoraphobia and Hysteria." In *Women and Psychotherapy.* Ed. Annette Brodsky and Rachel Hare-Mustin. Cambridge, MA: Harvard University Press (1992) 113–134.

Charcot, Jean-Martin. *Leçons du mardi á la Salpêtriére*, Notes de cours de MM. Blin, *Charcot et Colin.* Paris: Centre d'étude et de promotion de la lecture, Les classiques de la psychologie, 1974.

Chen, Nancy N. *Breathing Spaces: Qigong, Psychiatry, and Healing in China.* Columbia University Press.

______. "Urban Spaces and Experiences of QiGong," *Urban Spaces in Contemporary China: The Potential for Autonomy and Community in Post-Mao China.* Eds. Deborah S. Davis, Richard Kraus, Barry Naughton, and Elizabeth J. Perry. Cambridge: Cambridge University Press, 1995.

Cherchevsky, Le Dr. "Contribution a l'étude de l'agoraphobie." *Revue de médicine* 5 (1885): 909–934.

Chesler, Phyllis. *Women and Madness.* 2d ed. New York: Palgrave MacMillan, 2005.

Chiari, Gabriele, and Roberto Mosticoni. "The Treatment of Agoraphobia with Biofeedback and Systematic Desensitization." *Journal of Behavioral Therapy and Experimental Psychiatry*, 10 (1979): 109–113.

Clifford, James. "On Collecting Art and Culture." In *The Predicament of Culture: Twentieth Century Ethnography, Literature and Art.* Cambridge, MA: Harvard University Press, 1988.
Clifford, James, and George E. Marcus, eds. *Writing Culture: The Poetics and Politics of Ethnography.* Berkeley and Los Angeles: University of California Press, 1986.
Clough, Patricia. "The Affective Turn: Political Economy and the Biomediated Body" http://www.le.ac.uk/ulmc/cppe/affective_turn.pdf, accessed April 5, 2006.
Cocever, Emanuela. *Bambini attivi e autonomi. A cosa serve l'adulto? L'esperienza di Loczy.* Florence: La Nueva Italia, 1990.
Cochran, Terry. *Twilight of the Literary: Figures of the Thought in the Age of Print.* Cambridge, MA: Harvard University Press, 2001.
Colum, Kenny. *Fearing Sellafield: What It Is and Why the Irish Want It Shut.* Dublin: Gill & MacMillan, 2003.
Congedo, Marco, Joel F. Lubar, and David Joffe. "Low-resolution Electromagnetic Tomography Neurofeedback." *IEEE Transactions on Neural Systems and Rehabilitation Engineering* (a publication of the IEEE Engineering in Medicine and Biology Society) 4 (2004): 387.
Conley, Tom. *The Self-Made Map.* Minneapolis: University of Minnesota Press, 1996.
Consumer Reports. "High Anxiety." *Consumer Reports,* January (1993), 19–24.
Cordes, Emil. "Die Platsangst (Agoraphobie): Symptom einer Erschöpfungsparese," *Archiv für Psychiatrie und Nervenkrankheiten.* 3:3 (1872): 521–574.
Crang, Mike and Nigel Thrift, eds. *Thinking Space.* London; New York: Routledge, 2000.
Crenshaw, Kimberly. "Whose Story is it Anyway? Feminist and Anti-racist Appropriations of Anita Hill." In *Race-ing Justice, Engendering Power.* Ed. Toni Morrison. New York: Pantheon, (1992.) 402–440.
da Costa Meyer, Esther. "La Donna e Mobile: Agoraphobia, Women and Urban Space." In *The Sex of Architecture.* Eds. Diana Agrest, Patricia Conway, and Leslie Kanes Weisman. New York: Harry N. Abrams, 1996.
Dagognet, François. "Toward a Biopsychiatry." Trans. Donald M. Leslie. Incorporations ed. Jonathan Crary and Sanford Kwinter. New York: Zone (1992) 517–541.
Davidoff, Leonore, and Catherine Hall. *Family Fortunes: Men and Women of the English Middle Class 1780–1850.* London: Hutchinson, 1987.
Davidson, Joyce. "'... The World Was Getting Smaller': Women, Agoraphobia, and Bodily Boundaries." *Area* 32, no. 1 (2000): 31–40.
Davis, Mike. *City of Quartz: Excavating the Future in Los Angeles.* New York: Vintage, 1992.
Day, Kristen. "Embassies and Sanctuaries: Women's Experiences of Race and Fear in Public Space." *Environment and Planning D: Society and Space* 17 (1999): 307–328.
Dear, Michael J. *The Postmodern Urban Condition.* Oxford: Blackwell, 2000.
DeBell, Camille, and R. Deniece Jones. "As Good as It Seems? A Review of EMDR Experimental Research." *Professional Psychology: Research and Practice* 28 (1997): 153–63.
de Certeau, Michel. "Walking in the City." In *The Practice of Everyday Life.* Trans. Steven F. Rendall. Berkeley and Los Angeles: University of California Press, (1984) 91–110.
De Jongh, A. and E. Ten Broeke. "Eye Movement Desensitization and Reprocessing (EMDR): een procedure voor de behandeling van aan trauma gerelateerde angst." *Tijdschrift voor Psychotherapie* 22 (1996): 93–114.
DeLanda, Manuel. *A Thousand Years of Nonlinear History.* New York: Zone, 1997.
Deleuze, Gilles. *The Fold: Leibniz and the Baroque.* Trans. Tom Conley. Minneapolis: University of Minnesota Press, 1993.
______. *Proust Signs.* Trans. Richard Howard. Minneapolis: University of Minnesota Press, 2000.
Deleuze, Gilles, and Félix Guattari. *A Thousand Plateaus: Capitalism and Schizophrenia.* Trans. Brian Massumi. Minneapolis: University of Minnesota Press, 1987.
Deutsch, Helene. "The Genesis of Agoraphobia." *International Journal of Psychoanalysis* 10 (1929): 51–69.
Deutsche, Roselyn. "Agoraphobia." *Evictions: Art and Spatial Politics.* Cambridge, MA: London: MIT Press, 1996.
Dostoyevsky, Fyodor. *Notes from Underground.* Trans. Richard Pevear and Larissa Volokhonsky. New York: Alfred A. Knopf, 1993.
Duany, Andres, Elizabeth Plater-Zyberk, and Jeff Speck. *Suburban Nation.* New York: North Point Press, 2000.

Duncan, James S., and Nancy C. Duncan. *Landscapes of Privilege: The Politics of the Aesthetic in an American Suburb.* New York: Routledge, 2004.

Duncan, Nancy, ed. *Bodyspace: Destabilizing Geographies of Gender and Sexuality.* London: Routledge, 1996.

Eisenberg, David M., Roger B. Davis, Susan L. Ettner, Scott Appel, Sonja Wilkey, Maria Von Rompay, Ronald C. Kessler. "Trends in Alternative Medicine Use in the United States, 1990–1997: Results of a Follow-up Survey," *Journal of the American Medical Association* 280 (1998): 1569–1575.

Ellin, Nan. *Postmodern Urbanism.* Cambridge: Blackwell, 1996.

______. Ed. *Architecture of Fear.* Princeton: Princeton Architectural Press, 1997.

Emmelkamp, Paul M. G. "Self Observation versus Flooding in the Treatment of Agoraphobia." *Behaviour Research and Therapy: An International Multi-Disciplinary Journal* 12, no. 3 (1974): 229–237.

Epstein, Randi Hutter. "Experts Try Fast-Track Fix for Children with Phobias." *New York Times,* January 20, 2004, D5.

Everaerd, Walter T. A. M., Hanneke M. Rijken, and Paul M. G. Emmelkamp. "A Comparison of 'Flooding' and 'Successive Approximation' in the Treatment of Agoraphobia." *Behaviour Research and Therapy: An International Multi-Disciplinary Journal* 11, no. 1 (1973): 105–117.

Fainstein, Susan. "New Directions in Planning Theory." *Urban Affairs Review* 35, no. 4 (2000): 451–478.

Fischer, Michael M. J. *Emergent Forms of Life and the Anthropological Voice.* Durham, NC: Duke University Press, 2003.

Fisher, Peter and Adam Ward, "Complementary Medicine in Europe." *British Medical Journal* 309 (1994): 107–111.

Flanagan, Barbara. "A Massachusettes Mall is Just Disappeared." *New York Times,* March 3, 1991.

Ford, Peter. "Deep Roots of Paris Riots." *Christian Science Monitor,* November 4, 2005.

Foucault, Michel. *Technologies of the Self: A Siminar with Michel Foucault.* Edited by Luther H. Martin, Huck Eatman, and Patrick H. Hutton. Amherst, MA: University of Massachusettes Press, 1988.

Frankl, Viktor. " Paradoxical Intention: A Logotherapeutic Technique." *American Journal of Psychotherapy* 14 (1960): 520–535.

______. *The Doctor and the Soul: From Psychotherapy to Logotherapy.* New York: Bantam, 1986.

Fraser, Nancy. "Rethinking the Public Sphere: A Contribution to the Critique of Actually Existing Democracy." In *Habermas and the Public Sphere.* Ed. Craig Calhoun. Cambridge, MA: MIT Press, (1992) 109–142.

French, Jere Stuart. *Urban Space: A Brief History of the City Square.* Dubuque, Iowa; Kendal/ Hunt Publishing, 1978.

Freud, Sigmund. *The Interpretation of Dreams.* Trans. James Strachey. New York: Basic Books, 1955.

______. *Group Psychology and the Analysis of the Ego.* New York: Norton, 1959.

______. "On the Grounds for Detaching a Particular Syndrome from Neurasthenia under the Description 'Anxiety Neurosis' (1895)" in the *Standard Edition of the Complete Works of Sigmund Freud.* Translated and edited by James Strachey, Vol. 3 London: Hogarth Press (1953–1974) 90–115.

Friedman, Steven, and Cheryl Paradis. "African American Patients with Panic Disorder and Agoraphobia." *Journal of Anxiety Disorders* 5 (1991): 35–41.

Galibert, Jacques. "Subnarcose amphétaminée et psychothérapie des états d'angoisse." *L'Encéphale* 4 (1960) 332–366.

Gardes, Gilbert. *Lyon l'art et la ville, Urbanisme-Architecture Tome I.* Paris: Editions du Centre National de la Recherche Scientifique, 1988.

Gardner, Carol Brooks. "Out of Place: Gender, Public Places and Situational Disadvantage." In *Now/Here: Time, Space and Modernity.* Ed. Roger Friedland and Diedre Boden. Berkeley: University of California Press, 1994.

Gelder, Michael G., and Isaac M. Marks. "Severe Agoraphobia: A Controlled Prospective Trial of Behaviour Therapy." *British Journal of Psychiatry* 112 (1966): 309–19.

Giddens, Anthony. "Preface." In *Now/Here: Time, Space and Modernity.* Ed. Roger Friedland and Diedre Boden. Berkeley and Los Angeles: University of California Press, 1994.

Giedion, Sigfried. *Mechanization Takes Command: A Contribution to Anonymous History.* New York: Oxford University Press, 1948.

Goldensohn, Lorrie, ed. *American War Poetry: An Anthology.* New York: Columbia University Press, 2006.

Goldman, Nathan C. *American Space Law: International and Domestic.* San Diego, CA: Univelt, 1996.

Goldstein, Alan J., Edwin de Beurs, Dianne L. Chambless, and Kimberly A. Wilson. "EMDR for Panic Disorder with Agoraphobia: Comparison with Waiting List and Credible Attention-Placebo Control Conditions." *Journal of Consulting and Clinical Psychology.* 68, 6 (2000) 947–956.

Ghosh, A., and I. M. Marks. "Self-Treatment of Agoraphobia by Exposure." *Behavior Therapy* 18 (1987): 3–16.

Ghosh, A., I. M Marks, and A. C. Carr. "Therapist Contact and Outcome of Self-Exposure Treatment for Phobias: A Controlled Study." *British Journal of Psychiatry* 152 (1988): 234–38.

Good, Byron J. and Arthur Kleinman. "Culture and Anxiety: Cross-Cultural Evidence for the Patterning of Anxiety Disorders," In *Anxiety and the Anxiety Disorders.* Ed. A. Hussain Tuma and Jack Maser. Hillsdale, NJ: Lawrence Erlbaum, 1985.

Graham, Candida, Abigail Franses, Mark Kenwright, and Isaac Marks. "Problem Severity in People Using Alternative Therapies for Anxiety Difficulties." *British Journal of Psychiatry* 25 (2001): 12–14.

Gratz, Roberta Brandes, and Norman Mintz. *Cities Back from the Edge: New Life For Downtown.* New York: John Wiley, 1998.

Greed, Clara H. "Public Toilet Provisions for Women in Britain: An Investigation of Discrimination Against Urination." *Women's Studies International Forum* 18, nos. 5/6 (1995): 573–584.

Gregory, Derek. *Geographical Imaginations.* Cambridge, MA: Blackwell, 1994.

Grenier, Lise and Hans Wieder-Benedetti. *Le Siècle de l'éclectisme: Lille 1830–1930.* Paris/Bruxelles: Editions du Moniteur/La Nouvelle Diffusion, 1979.

Griffin, Britt. "The Mega-Mall." *North Country Anvil* 55 (1987): 23–24.

Griggers, Camilla. *Becoming Woman.* Minneapolis: University of Minnesota Press, 1997.

Gros, Dr. "Contribution a l'etude de l'agoraphobie (peur des espaces) et d'autres formes de névroses émotives." *Annales Medico-Psychologiques* Vol. 7 No.1 (1885): 394–407.

Grosz, Elizabeth. *The Nick of Time: Politics, Evolution, and the Untimely.* Durham, NC: Duke University Press, 2004.

______. *Volatile Bodies: Toward a Corporeal Feminism.* Bloomington: Indiana University Press, 1994.

Guterson, David. "Enclosed. Encyclopedic. Endured: One Week at the Mall of America." *Harpers,* August 1993.

Gutkind, E. A. *International History of City Development. Vol. III: Urban Development in Eastern Europe: Bulgaria, Romania and the U.S.S.R.* New York: The Free Press, 1972.

Hall, Thomas. *Planning Europe's Captial Cities: Aspects of Nineteenth Centry Urban Development.* London: E 7 FN Spon, 1997.

Hamilton-Baillie, Ben. *Home Zones—Reconciling People, Places and Transport: Report of a Study Tour of Denmark, Germany, Sweden and The Netherlands.* Cambridge, MA: Harvard Design School Publication, 2002.

______. "No Sign of the Times." *Surveyor* 4/7 (2002): 13.

Hand, Iver, Yves Lamontagne, and Isaac M. Marks. "Group Therapy for Agoraphobics; Real-life Retraining by Floodings in Vivo." *Psychotherapy and Psychosomatics* 25; 1–6 (1975) 76–82.

Hardin, Garet. "The Tragedy of the Commons." In *Managing the Commons.* Ed. G. Hardin and J. Baden. San Francisco: W. H. Freeman, 1977.

Hardt, Michael, and Antonio Negri. *Empire.* Cambridge. MA: Harvard University Press, 1999.

Harvey, David. *A Brief History of Neoliberalism.* Oxford: Oxford University Press, 2005.

______. *Spaces of Hope.* Berkeley and Los Angeles: University of California Press, 2000.

Hawkrigg, J. J. "Agoraphobia-1." *Nursing Times,* August 14, 1975, 1280–82.

______. "Agoraphobia-2." *Nursing Times,* August 21, 1975, 1337–38.

Hayden, Dolores. *The Grand Domestic Revolution: A History of Feminist Designs for American Homes, Neighbothoods, and Cities.* Cambridge, MA: MIT Press, 1981.

Hecker, Jeffrey E., and Geoffrey L. Thorpe. *Agoraphobia and Panic: A Guide to Psychological Treatment.* Boston: Allyn and Bacon, 1992.

Heidegger, Martin. "The Age of the World Picture" in *The Question Concerning Technology and Other Essays.* New York: Harper Row. (1977) 113–154.

______. *Being and Time.* Trans. John Macquarrie and Edward Robinson. New York: Harper Row, 1962.

Henig, Robin M. "The Quest to Forget." *New York Times Magazine,* April 4, 2004, 32–37.

Henusse, Th. "L'Agoraphobie: Etude clinique et pathogénique." *Journal belge de la neurologie et de la psychiatrie* 41 (1941–42): 1–28.

Hinton, Devon. "Munch, Agoraphobia, and the Terrors of the Modernizing Urban Landscape." In *Panic: Origins, Insight and Treatment.* Ed. Leonard J. Schmidt and Brooke Warner. Berkeley, CA: North Atlantic, (2002) 229–252.

Hoggett, Paul. "A Place for experience: a psychoanalytic perspective on boundary, identity, and culture." *Environment and Planning D: Society and Space* 10; 3 (1992): 345–356.

Holston, James. *The Modernist City: An Anthropological Critique of Brasilia.* Chicago: University of Chicago Press, 1989.

Huet, Bernard. "The City as Dwelling Space: Alternatives to the Charter of Athens." *Lotus* 41 (1984) 6–17.

Huston, John, dir. "*Let There Be Light ... !*" Documentary produced by the U.S. Army Signal Corp Pictorial Service, 1946.

Huyssen, Andreas. *After the Great Divide: Modernism, Mass Culture, Postmodernism.* Bloomington: Indiana University Press, 1986.

Irigaray, Luce. *Between East and West: From Singularity to Community.* Trans. Stephen Pluháček New York: Columbia University Press, 2002.

______. *Ethique de la difference sexuelle.* Paris: Minuit, 1984.

Jablensky, Assen. "Approaches to the Definition and Classification of Anxiety and Related Disorders in European Psychiatry." In *Anxiety and the Anxiety Disorders.* Ed. A. Hussain Tuma and Jack Maser. Hillsdale, NJ: Lawrence Erlbaum, 1985.

Jackson, Eileen. "Whiting-out Difference: Why U.S. Nursing Research Fails Black Families." *Medical Anthropology Quarterly* 7, 4. (1993) 363–385.

Jacobs, Jane. *The Death and Life of Great American Cities: The Failure of Town Planning.* New York: Vintage, 1961.

Jameson, Fredric. *Postmodernism, Or, the Cultural Logic of Late Capitalism.* Durham, NC: Duke University Press, 1991.

Jaspers, Karl. *Psychologie der Weltanschaaugen.* 3d ed. Berlin: Springer, 1925.

Jencks, Charles. *The Language of Postmodern Architecture* New York: Rizzoli, 1991 (1977).

Jones, Ivor H., and David J. de L. Horne. "Psychiatric Disorders among Aborigines of the Australian Western Desert." *Social Science and Medicine* 7 (1973): 219–228.

Jones, R. B., G. Humphris, and T. Lewis. "Do Agoraphobics Interpret the Environment in Large Shops and Supermarkets Differently?" *British Journal of Clinical Psychology* 35 (1996): 635–37.

Kant, Immanuel. *The Critique of Practical Reason and Other Writings in Moral Philosophy.* Trans. Lewis W. Beck. Chicago: University of Chicago Press, 1949.

______. *The Critique of Pure Reason.* Trans. Werner Pluhar, Indianapolis: Hackett, 1996.

Katz, Peter. *The New Urbanism: Toward an Architecture of Community.* New York: McGraw-Hill, 1994.

Kendler, Kenneth S. "Life time and 12-month prevalence of DSM-III-R psychiatric disorders in the United States: results from the National Commorbidity Study." *Archives of General Psychiatry* 51 (1994) 8–19.

Kerber, Linda K. "Separate Spheres, Female Worlds, Woman's Place: The Rhetoric of Women's History," *Journal of American History* 75 (1988): 9–39.

Kerry, R. J. "Phobia of Outer Space." *Journal of Mental Science* 106 (1960): 1383–1387.

Kierkegaard, Søren. *The Concept of Anxiety.* Edited and translated by Reidar Thomte and Albert Anderson. Princeton: Princeton University Press, 1980.

Kirby, Kathleen M. *Indifferent Boundaries: Spatial Concepts of Human Subjectivity.* New York: Guilford, 1996.

Klein, Donald. F. "Anxiety Reconceptualized." In *Anxiety: New Research and Changing Concepts*. Ed. Donald. F. Klein and Judith G. Rabkin. New York: Raven, (1981) 235–263.
Klein, Melanie. "Some Theoretical Conclusions on the Emotional Life of an Infant (1952)." In Melanie Klein, *Envy and Gratitude and Other Works 1946–1963*. New York: Delta (1977) 61–93.
Klerman, Gerald L. "Overview of the Cross-National Collaborative Panic Study." *Archives of General Psychiatry* 45 (1988): 407–12.
Knapp, Terry J., and Michael Schumacher. *Westphal's "Die Agoraphobie" with Commentary: The Beginnings of Agoraphobia*. New York: University Press, 1988.
Knight, Heather. "The Peaceful Path: In Troubled Times, More People Turn to Labyrinths to Walk their Worries Away." *San Francisco Chronicle*, February 28, 2003.
Knott, Verner, David Bakish, Stacey Lusk, and John Barkely. "Relaxation-Induced EEG Alterations in Panic Disorder Patients." *Journal of Anxiety Disorders* 4 (1997): 365–76.
Koolhaas, Rem, dir., and Jeffrey Inaba, coordinator. *Harvard Design School Guide to Shopping*. Köln: Taschen/Cambridge, MA: Harvard Design School, 2001.
Kowinski, William S. *The Malling of America: An Inside Look at the Great Consumer Paradise*. New York: William Morrow, 1985.
Kuletz, Valerie *Tainted Desert: Environmental Ruin in the American West*. New York: Routledge, 1998.
Lacan, Jacques. "The Mirror Stage as Formative of the Function of the I." In *Ecrits: A Selection*. Transl. Alan Sheridan. London: Tavistock, 1977.
Lalande, André. *Vocabulaire technique et Critque de la Philosophie*. Paris: Presses Universitaire de France, 1983.
Lannois, M., and C. Tournier. "Les Lésions auriculaires sont une cause déterminante fréquente de l'agoraphobie." *Annales De L'Oreille, Du Larnynx, Du Nez et Du Pharynx* 2:24 (1898)s: 286–301.
Lara, Maria Pia. *Moral Textures: Feminists Narratives in the Public Sphere*. Berkeley and Los Angeles: University of California Press, 1998.
Latour, Bruno. *Politics of Nature: How to Bring the Sciences into Democracy*. Cambridge, MA: Harvard University Press, 2004.
Lazarus, Arnold. "Broad-Spectrum Behaviour Therapy and the Treatment of Agoraphobia." *Behavioral Research and Therapy* 4 (1966): 95–97.
Leavitt, Jacqueline. "Where's the Gender in Community Development?" *Signs: Journal of Women in Culture and Society*, 29 (2003), 207–231.
Le Clezio, Jean-Marie Gustave. *Les Géants*. Paris: Gallimard 1973.
Leed, Eric. *No Man's Land: Combat and Identity in World War I*. Cambridge: Cambridge University Press, 1979.
Lefebvre, Henri. *Eléments de rythmanalyse: Introduction à la connaissance des rythmes*. Paris: Éditions Syllepse, 1992.
______. *The Production of Space*. Trans. Donald Nicholson-Smith. Oxford: Basil Blackwell, 1991.
Lefort, Claude. *Democracy and Political Theory*. Trans. David Macey. Cambridge, UK: Polity Press/ Basil Blackwell, 1988.
______. *The Political Forms of Modern Society: Bureaucracy, Democracy and Totalitarianism*. Edited and introduced by John B. Thompson. Cambridge: MIT Press, 1986.
Legrand du Saulle, Henri. "De l'agoraphobie." *Le Praticien*. viii (1885): 208–10.
______. *Etude clinique sur la peur des espaces (agoraphobie des allemands), névrose émotive*. Paris: V. Adrien Dalahaye, 1878.
Leibniz, Gottfried Wilhelm. *Nouveaux essais sur l'entendement humain*. Paris: Presses universitaires de France (1961).
Levine, Peter. *Walking the Tiger: Healing Trauma*. Berkeley, CA: North Atlantic, 1997.
Lévy, Paul Emil. "Die Agoraphobie und ihre Behandlung durch Erziehung ohne Isolierung." *Allgemeine wiener medizinische Zeitung* lvi (1911): 403–4.
Liotti, G., and V. Guidano. "Behavioural Analysis of Marital Interaction in Agoraphobic Male Patients." *Behaviour Research and Therapy: An International Multidisciplinary Journal* 14, no. 2 (1976): 161–62.
Locke, John. *Two Treatises of Government*. Ed. Peter Laslett. Cambridge: Cambridge University Press, 1988.

Longhurst, Robyn. "(Re)presenting Shopping Centers and Bodies: Questions of Pregnancy." In *New Frontiers of Space, Bodies and Gender.* Ed. Rosa Ainley. London: Routledge, (1998) 20–34.

Lowen, Alexander. *The Language of the Body.* New York: Collier, 1958.

Lyotard, Jean-François. *The Differend: Phrases in Dispute.* Trans. Georges van den Abbeele. Minneapolis: University of Minnesota Press, 1988.

Massey, Doreen. "Blurring the Binaries? High tech in Cambridge." In *New Frontiers of Space, Bodies and Gender,* ed. Rosa Ainley. London: Routledge, 1998.

Marcus, George, and Michael M. J. Fischer. *Anthropology as Cultural Critique: An Experimental Moment in the Human Sciences.* Chicago: University of Chicago Press, 1986.

Marks, Isaac M. "Agoraphobia, Panic Disorder and Related Conditions in the DSM III and ICD-10." *Journal of Psychopharmacology* 1 (1987): 6–12.

______. "Agoraphobic Syndrome (Phobic Anxiety State)." *Archives of General Psychiatry* 23 (1970): 538–553.

______. *Fears, Phobias and Rituals: Panic, Anxiety and Their Disorders.* New York: Oxford University Press, 1987.

______. *Living With Fear: Understanding and Coping With Anxiety.* New York: McGraw-Hill, 1978.

Marks, Isaac M., Richard P. Swinson, Metin Basoglu, Klaus Kuch, Homa Noshirvani, Geraline O'Sullivan, Paul T. Lelliot, Marlene Kirby, Gary McNamee, Seda Dengun, and Kim Wickwire. "Alprazolam and Exposure Alone and Combined in Panic Disorder with Agoraphobia: A Controlled Study in London and Toronto." *British Journal of Psychiatry* 162 (1993): 776–787.

Marks, Isaac M., Richard P. Swinson, Metin Basoglu, Homa Noshirvani, Klaus Kuch, Geraline O'Sullivan, and Paul T. Lelliot. "Reply to Comment on the London/Toronto Study." *British Journal of Psychiatry* 162 (1992): 790–94.

Marks, Isaac M., John Greist, Metin Basoglu, Homa Noshirvani, and Geraline O'Sullivan "Comment on the Second Phase of the Cross-National Collaborative Panic Study" *British Journal of Psychiatry* 160 (1992): 202–205.

Marks, Isaac M., and Paul Bebbington. "Space Phobia: Syndrome or Agoraphobia Variant?" *British Medical Journal* 2, no. 6031 (1976): 345–47.

Marks, Isaac M., J. L. T. Birley and M. G. Gelder. "Modified Leuctomy in Severe Agoraphobia: A Controlled Serial Inquiry." *British Journal of Psychiatry* 112 (1966): 757–69.

Martin, Emily. "Flexible Survivors." *Anthropology News,* September 1999, 5–7.

Massumi, Brian. "The Autonomy of Affect." In *Deleuze: A Critical Reader.* Ed. P. Patton. Cambridge, MA: Blackwell, 1996.

______. *Parables for the Virtual: Movement, Affect, Sensation.* Durham, NC: Duke University Press, 2002.

Mathiot, Madeleine, ed. *Ethnolinguistics: Boas, Sapir and Whorf revisited.* New York: Mouton, 1979.

Maudsley, Henry. *The Pathology of Mind.* London: MacMillan, 1879.

Mauss, Marcel. "A Category of the Human Mind: The Notion of the Person; the Notion of Self" in *The Category of the Person.* Edited by Michael Carrithers, Steven Collins and Steven Lukes. Cambridge: Cambridge University Press (1985) 1–25.

Mavissakalian, Matig, Larry Michelson, Deborah Greenwald, Sander Kornblith and Michael Greenwald. "Cognitive-Behavioral Treatment of Agoraphobia: Paradoxical Intention vs. Self-Statement Training." *Behaviour Research and Therapy* 21 (1989): 75–86.

McNally, Richard. "EMDR and Mesmerism: A Comparative Historical Analysis." *Journal of Anxiety Disorders* 13, nos. 1–2 (1999): 225–36.

______. *Panic Disorder: A Critical Analysis.* New York: Guilford Press 1994.

Merleau-Ponty, Maurice. *The Visible and the Invisible.* Trans. Alphonso Lingis. Evanston, IL: Northwestern University Press, 1968.

Milun, Kathryn, with Gerald Torres. "Translating Yonondio by Precedent and Evidence." *Duke Law Journal* (1990)4: 625.

Mitchell, Silas Weir. *Fat and Blood: an essay on the treatment of certain forms of neurasthenia and hysteria.* London: Lippincot, 1884.

Moody, R.L. "Bodily Changes During Abreaction." *Lancet* 2 (1946): 934–935.

Mosse, George L. *The Nationalization of the Masses: Political Symbolism and Mass Movements in Germany from the Napoleonic Wars through the Third Reich*. Ithaca, NY: Cornell University Press, 1975.

Mouton, G. "Un cas d'agoraphobie" *L'Echo medical du nord* 2 (1898). 381–382.

Muschamp, Herbert. "Public Space or Private, A Compulsion to Fill It." *New York Times*, August 27, 2000, AR27, 29.

Nagourney, Eric. "Rethinking the Big Push during Contractions." *New York Times*, January 3, 2006.

Newton, Tim. "Truly Embodied Sociology: Marrying the Social and Biological?" *Sociological Review* 51, no. 1 (2003): 20–42.

Noble, David F. *A World without Women: The Christian Clerical Culture of Western Science*. New York: Alfred A. Knopf, 1992.

Olkowski, Dorothea. "Difference and the Ruin of Representaion in Gilles Deleuze." In *Sites of Vision: The Discursive Construction of Sight in the History of Philosophy*. Ed. David Michael Levin. Cambridge, MA: MIT Press, (1997) 467–492.

Orwin, A. "The Running Treatment: A Preliminary Communication on a New Use for an Old Therapy (Physical Activity) in the Agoraphobic Syndrome." *British Journal of Psychiatry* 122 (1973): 175–9.

Othmer, Siegfried, Susan F. Othmer, and David A. Kaiser. "EEG Biofeedback: A Generalized Approach to Neuroregulation." at "http://www.eegresearch.com/articles/general_5.htm". (Last viewed April 5, 2006) 1–13.

Othmer, Siegfried, Susan F. Othmer and David A. Kaiser. "EEG Biofeedback: Training for AD/HD and Related Disruptive Behavior Disorders." In *Understanding Diagnosing and Treating AD/HD in Children and Adolescents: An Integrative Approach*. James Incorvaia, Bonnie Mark-Goldstein and Donald Tessmer (Eds.). New York: Aronson. (1999) 235–297.

Ottes, Liesbeth, ed. *Gender and the Built Environment: Emancipation in Planning, Housing and Mobility in Europe*. Assen, Netherlands: Van Gorcum, 1995.

Packard, Vance. *The Hidden Persuaders*. New York: D. McKay Co., 1957.

Paganini, Maria. *Reading Proust: In Search of the Wolf-Fish*. Trans. Caren Litherland with Kathryn Milun. Minneapolis: University of Minnesota Press, 1994.

Panofsky, Ervin. *Perspective as Symbolic Form*. Trans. Christopher S. Wood. New York: Zone Books, 1991.

Penn, Helen. "How should we care for babies and toddlers? An analysis of practice in out-of-home care for children under three." Occasional Paper 10, Centre for Urban & Community Studies: University of Toronto June 1999 *iv*, 66 pp. (Online at http://www.childcarecanada.org/pubs/op10/index.html. Last viewed May 2006.)

Perman, Joshua M. "Phobia as a Determinant of Single-Room Occupancy." *The American Journal of Psychiatry* 123, no. 5 (1966): 609–613.

Perroud, Dr. "Agoraphobie." *Lyon Medical* (1873): 291. In M. Lannois and C. Tournier. "Les Lésions auriculaires sont une cause déterminante fréquente de l'agoraphobie." *Annales De L'Oreille, Du Larnynx, Du Nez et Du Pharynx* 2:24 (1898): 286–301.

Petersen, Alan, and Robin Bunton, eds. *Foucault, Health and Medicine*. London: Routledge 1997.

Pichot, Pierre. "Panique: attaque et trouble. Historique du mot et des concepts." *L'Encephale* 22, no. 5 (1996): 3–8.

Pile, Steve. *The Body and the City: Psychoanalysis, Space and Subjectivity*. London: Routledge, 1996.

Pinkney, David H. *Napoleon III and the Rebuilding of Paris*. Princeton, NJ: Princeton University Press, 1958.

Platt, Rutherford H., Rowan A. Rowntree and Pamela C. Muick. *The Ecological City: Preserving and Restoring Urban Biodiversity*. Amherst: University of Massachusetts Press, (1994).

Pred, Allan Richard, and Michael John Watts. *Reworking Modernity: Capitalism and Symbolic Discontent*. New Brunswick, NJ: Rutgers University Press, 1992.

Proust, Marcel. *A La Redrerche du temps perdu*. Paris: Gallimard, 2002.

Rabinow, Paul. "Artificiality and Enlightenment: From Sociobiology to Biosociality." In *Incorporations*. Ed. Jonathan Crary and Sanford Kwinter. New York: Zone, 1992.

Resneck-Sannes, Helen. "A Feeling in Search of Memory." *Women and Therapy* 16, no. 4 (1995): 97–105.

______. "There Really is Something to Be Afraid of: Body-Oriented Psychotherapy for the Treatment of Panic Disorder." In *Panic: Origins, Insight, and Treatment.* Ed. Leonard J. Schmidt and Brooke Warner. Berkeley, CA: North Atlantic, 2002.

Robbins, Ron. "Body Approaches to the Treatment of Panic." in *Panic: Origins, Insight, and Treatment.* Ed. Leonard J. Schmidt and Brooke Warner. Berkeley, CA: North Atlantic, 2002.

Robins, Lee and Darrel Regier, eds. *Psychiatric Disorders in America: The American Epidemiological Catchment Area Study.* New York: Free Press. 1991.

Rose, Gillian. *Feminism and Geography: The Limits of Geographical Knowledge.* Cambridge: Polity, 1993.

Rose, Nikolas. *The Psychological Complex: Psychology, politics and society in England 1869–1939.* London: Routledge, 1985.

______. *Governing the Soul: The Shaping of the Private Self.* London: Routledge, 1990.

Rosolato, Guy. *La relation d'inconnu.* Paris: Gallimard, 1978.

Rosenbaum, Robert. "Edvard Munch: Some Changing Contexts." In *Edvard Munch: Symbols and Images.* Ed. A. Eggum, R. Heller, T. Nergaard, R. Strang et al. Washington, D.C.: National Gallery of Art, 1978.

Rovner, Sandy. "High Anxiety is a Scary Disorder." *Minneapolis Star Tribune,* May 31, 1990.

Ruddick, Bruce. "Agoraphobia." *International Journal of Psycho-Analysis* 42 (1961): 537–543.

Russell, Denise. *Women, Madness and Medicine.* Oxford: Blackwell, 1995.

Sandercock, Leonie. "When Strangers Become Neighbors: Managing Cities of Difference." *Planning Theory and Practice* 1,1 (2000): 13–30.

Sargant, William. *Battle for the Mind: Introduction to Physical Methods of Treatment in Psychiatry.* New York: Doubleday, 1957.

______. "Ten Years Clinical Experience of Modified Leucotomy Operations." *British Medical Journal* 2 (1953): 800.

Sartre, Jean Paul. *Being and Nothingness.* Translated by Hazel E. Barnes. New York: Philosophical Library, 1943.

Sassen, Saskia. *The Global City: New York, London, Tokyo.* Princeton, NJ: Princeton University Press, 2001.

Scarf, Maggie. *Secrets, Lies, Betrayals: The Body/Mind Connection, How the Body Holds The Secrets of a Life, and How to Unlock Them.* New York: Random House, 2004.

Shapiro, Francine. "Eye Movement Desensitization and Reprocessing (EMDR) and the Anxiety Disorders: Clinical and Research Implications of an Integrated Psychotherapy Treatment." *Journal of Anxiety Disorders* 13, nos. 1–2 (1999): 35–67.

Shapiro, Francine, and Margot Silk Forrest, *EMDR: The Breakthrough Therapy for Overcoming Anxiety, Stress, and Trauma* New York: Basic, 1997.

Scherpe, Klaus. "Nonstop to Nowhere City? Changes in the Symbolization, Perception, and Semiotics of the City in the Literature of Modernity." Trans. Lisa Roetzel. *Cultural Critique* No. 23 (1992–93): 137–164.

Schmidt, Leonard J., and Brooke Warner, eds. *Panic: Origins, Insight, and Treatment.* Berkeley CA: North Atlantic, 2002.

Schopenhauer, Arthur. *The World as Will and Representation.* Vol. 2. Trans. E. F. Payne. New York: Dover, 1966.

Schwartz, V. *Leningrad: Art and Architecture.* Moscow: Progress, 1959.

Scully, Vincent. *American Architecture and Urbanism.* New York: Henry Holt, 1969.

Sedgwick, Eve Kosofsky. *Epistemology of the Closet.* Berkeley and Los Angeles: University of California Press, 1990.

Seidenberg, Robert, and Karen DeCrow. *Women Who Marry Houses: Panic and Protest in Agoraphobia.* New York: McGraw-Hill, 1983.

Sennett, Richard. *The Fall of Public Man: On the Social Psychology of Capitalism.* New York: Vintage, 1978.

______. *Flesh and Stone: The Body and the City in Western Civilization.* New York: W. W. Norton, 1994.

Shader, Richard I. "Some Observations on the Problem of Anxiety." In *Anxiety and the Anxiety Disorders.* Ed. A. Hussain Tuma and Jack Maser. Hillsdale, NJ: Lawrence Erlbaum, (1985) 591–594.

Shapiro, Francine. "Eye Movement Desensitization and Reprocessing (EMDR) and the Anxiety Disorders: Clinical and Research Applications of an Integrated Psychotherapy Treatment." *Journal of Anxiety Disorders* 13, nos. 1–2 (1999): 35–67.

Showalter, Elaine. *The Female Malady: Woman, Madness, and English Culture, 1830–1980*. New York: Pantheon, 1987.

Simmel, Georg. "The Metropolis and Mental Life." In *On Individuality and Social Forms*. Ed. Donald Levine. Chicago: University of Chicago Press, 1971.

______. "The Stranger." In *The Sociology of Georg Simmel*. Trans. Kurt Wolff. New York: Free Press (1950) 402–408.

______. *Soziologie*. Leipzig: Dunker & Humblot (1908).

*Simon, Steven L. Bouville and Andre "Radiation Doses to Local Populations Near Nuclear Weapons Test Sites Worldwide." Health Physics*. 82:5 (2002): 706–725.

Sitte, Camille. *City Planning According to Artistic Principles*. Trans. G. Collins and C. Crasemann Collins. New York: Random House, 1965.

Soja, Edward W. *Postmodern Geographies: The Reassertion of Space in Critical Social Theory*. London: Verso, 1989.

Sorkin, Michael, ed. *Variations on a Theme Park: The New American City and the End of Public Space*. New York: Hill and Wang, 1992.

Starobinsky, Jean. *Action and Reaction: The Life and Adventures of a Couple*. New York: Zone, 2003.

Stern, Richard, and Isaac Marks. "Brief and Prolonged Flooding: A Comparison in Agoraphobic Patients." *Archives of General Psychiatry* 28: 2 (1973): 270–276.

Stone, Martin. "Shellshock and the Psychologists." In *The Anatomy of Madness: Essays in the History of Psychiatry*. Ed. Roy Porter, W.F. Bynum, Michael Shepherd. London: Routledge and Kegan Paul, 1986.

Suckling, C. W. "Agoraphobia and Allied Morbid Fears." *American Journal of the Medical Sciences* 99 (1890): 476–83.

Sutherland, Henry. "Agoraphobia." *The Lancet*, Jan. 17 (1885): 131.

Taussig, Michael. *The Nervous System*. New York: Routledge, 1992.

Terhune, William B. "Fear and Phobias." *Connecticut Medicine* 23, no. 12 (1959): 765–71.

Tester, Keith, ed.*The Flâneur*. New York: Routledge, 1994.

Torres, Gerald, and Kathryn Milun. "Translating Yonondio by Precedent and Evidence." *Duke Unversity Law Journal* 625 (1990): 401–435.

Tuma, A. Hussain, and Jack Maser, eds. *Anxiety and the Anxiety Disorders*. Hillsdale, NJ: Lawrence Erlbaum, 1985.

United Nations Population Fund. "The State of World Population 2004." Online at http://www.sahims.net/doclibrary/Sahims_Documents/UNFPA%20State%20of%20World%20Population%20Press%20Summary.pdf.

Ussishkin, Daniel. "Historical Instances of Panic." In *Panic: Origins, Insight, and Treatment*. Ed. Leonard J. Schmidt and Brooke Warner, Berkeley, CA: North Atlantic, 2002.

Valentine, Gil. "The Geography of Women's Fear." *Area* 21.4 (1989): 385–390.

Vidler, Anthony. "Spatial Estrangement in Simmel and Kracauer." *New German Critique* 54 (1991): 31–45.

______. *Warped Space: Art, Architecture, and Anxiety in Modern Culture*. Cambridge, MA: MIT Press, 2000.

Vincent. "Confessions of an Agoraphobic Victim." *American Journal of Psychology* 30 (1919): 297–98.

Vinciarelli, Lauretta. "Women Internet vs. 'Space of Tyrany': A Reply to Esther da Costa Meyer." *The Sex of Architecture*. Eds. Diana Agrest, Patricia Conway, and Leslie Kanes Weisman, New York: Harry N. Abrams, Inc., 1996.

Virilio, Paul. *Speed and Politics*. Trans. M. Polizzotti. New York: Semiotext(e), 1991.

Vovelle, Michel. *La Mort et l'Occident, de 1300 à nos jours*. Paris: Gallimard, 1983.

Weiner, James F. *The Empty Place: Poetry, Space, and Being Among the Foi of Papua New Guinea*. Bloomington: Indiana University Press, 1991.

Weiss, Edoardo. "Agoraphobia and Its Relation to Hysterical Attacks and to Traumas." *International Journal of Psychoanalysis* 16 (1935): 67–68.

Westphal, Carl Friedrich Otto. "Die Agoraphobie: Eine Neuropathische Erscheinung." *Archiv für Psychiatrie und Nervenkrankheiten* 3 (1871): 138–61.

Westphal, Carl Friedrich Otto. *Die Agoraphobie.* Trans. Michael T. Schumacher and Commentary by Terry J. Knapp. Lanham, MD: Univerrsity Press of America, 1988.

White, Matthew. *Source List and Detailed Death Tolls for the Man-made Megadeaths of the Twentieth Century.* http://users.erols.com/mwhite28/warstats.htm, accessed 16 May 2006.

Wilson, Elizabeth. *The Sphinx in the City: Urban Life, the Control of Disorder, and Women.* London: Virago, 1991.

Wilson, Elizabeth A. *Psychosomatic: Feminism and the Neurological Body.* Durham, NC: Duke University Press, 2004.

Winner, Langdon. *The Whale and the Reactor: A Search for Limits in an Age of High Technology* Chicago: University of Chicago Press, 1989.

Winnicott, Donald. W. *Playing and Reality.* Harmondsworth, England: Penguin, 1985.

Wirka, Susan. "The City Social Movement: Progressive Women Reformers and Early Social Planning." In *Planning the Twentieth-Century American City*, Ed. Mary Corbin Sies and Christopher Silver. Baltimore: The Johns Hopkins University Press, 1996.

Wolff, Janet. "The Artist and the Flâneur: Rodin, Rilke and Gwen John in Paris." In *The Flâneur.* Keith Tester, ed. New York: Routledge. 1994, 111–137.

Wolpe, Joseph, and Arnold A. Lazarus. *Behavior Therapy Techniques: A Guide to the Treatment of Neuroses.* New York: Pergamon, 1966.

Zucker, Paul. *Town and Square: From the Agora to the Village Green.* New York: Columbia University Press, 1959.

Zuercher-White, Elke. *Treating Panic Disorder and Agoraphobia: A Step-by-Step Clinical Approach.* Oakland, CA: New Harbinger, 1997.

Zuger, Abigail. "Caution: That Dose May Be Too High." *New York Times*, September 17, 2002. F1.

# Index

## A

## B

## C

## D

## V



## W

## X



## Y



## Z